D0146854

Restructuring Schooling for Individual Students

Restructuring Schooling for Individual Students

WILLIAM M. BECHTOL
Southwest Texas State University

JUANITA S. SORENSON
University of Wisconsin—Eau Claire

ALLYN AND BACON
Boston   London   Toronto   Sydney   Tokyo   Singapore

Copyright © 1993 by Allyn and Bacon
A Division of Simon & Schuster, Inc.
160 Gould Street
Needham Heights, Massachusetts 02194

All rights reserved. No part of the material protected by this copyright
notice may be reproduced or utilized in any form or by any means, electronic
or mechanical, including photocopying, recording, or by any information
storage and retrieval system, without written permission from the
copyright owner.

Library of Congress Cataloging-in-Publication Data

Bechtol, William M.
    Restructuring schooling for individual students / William M.
Bechtol, Juanita S. Sorenson.
        p.   cm.
    Includes bibliographical references and index.
    ISBN 0-205-13929-9
    1. School management and organization—United States—Case
studies.   2. Educational change—United States—Case studies.
3. Teaching—Case studies.   I. Sorenson, Juanita S.   II. Title.
LB2805.B345   1992
371.2′00973—dc20   92-15401
                                                                    CIP

Printed in the United States of America

10 9 8 7 6 5 4 3 2   96 95 94 93

*We dedicate this book
to our spouses
Mildred Bechtol
and
Douglas Sorenson*

*who helped and encouraged us
while we wrote this textbook.*

Contents

Appendix   377

Introduction

One would never know that children and youth were involved in all that is reported about restructuring schools in the United States.

Newspaper articles and televised reports focus on racial politics; low test scores; high dropout rates; budget slashing of nonessentials such as art, music, and classroom supplies; the hiring and firing of administrators or coaches; and the shaky fiscal support for the new school year.

Politicians and educational leaders point fingers at one another. Politicians complain, "It's incompetent teachers who cause the problems." Educators respond, "It's your fault. Our per-pupil spending is too low to provide quality schooling." Each one has a special plan to raise academic achievement and to lower dropout rates: "We need vouchers." "Year-round schools are the answer." "The career ladder is what will change our teachers." "Outcome-based education is the way."

You'd never know that children and youth were involved.

If children and youth really mattered, schools would be different. Instructional decisions would be based on educational research findings about teaching and learning. These decisions would be made close to the problem by teachers, administrators, parents, and community members—not by political or educational leaders in a state or national capital. All youngsters would be placed in classrooms where they are appropriately challenged and can succeed.

This book is written from the point of view that schools are primarily about children and youth. The purpose of the book is to help teachers and administrators develop the skills they need to restructure schools to provide for individual students. It's a source book for changing classrooms and schools from traditional programs to systems that take into account the differences of today's students. A variety of restructuring strategies are presented so that school staffs are empowered to make appropriate choices for their students.

The multicultural, diverse student population presents a challenge to teachers, principals, and district instructional leaders. Today's schools must be structured in such a way that all students feel secure and valued. These students must be given an opportunity to develop a positive picture of their future inside their heads. The two stories that follow illustrate these points.

A principal was showing an important visitor through an elementary school just as the tardy bell rang. A small boy named Dwight ran up to the principal and said, "Mr. Spencer, I can't find my room."

"Who's your teacher?" asked Principal Spencer.

"Mrs. Butler. I looked in the room. It was all different."

"I'll take you to your room, Dwight."

"O.K."

When Dwight, Mr. Spencer, and the visitor entered the room, they found that Mrs. Butler was wearing a wig. Dwight recognized his teacher and said, "I didn't know you."

Mrs. Butler hugged him and said, "I'm wearing a wig."

"Oh!"

She patted Dwight and said, "I'm glad you're here. Now go to your seat and get started on your journal."

Later, as the visitor described the event to a friend, he said, "Dwight is lucky. He's got a teacher who values little boys. Mrs. Butler gave him a hug and a positive greeting. If she had valued school rules, she would have sent him to the office for a tardy slip. If she had wanted to impress visitors and principals, she would have ignored Dwight and said, 'Mr. Spencer, I'd like you to and your visitor to see our new learning centers.' But Dwight was lucky. Mrs. Butler likes and values students."

The second story is about a black high school student in Louisiana. L.S. explained, "In the spring of my junior year my dad died. After the funeral my mother said that we'd have to move to Monroe and live with grandmother. I argued with her.

"I said, 'Mom, I'm going to be co-captain of the football team. I don't want to move. I want to spend my senior year here.'

"My mother said, 'We can stay here until June. But without your dad's paycheck, we can't pay the rent. We have to move.'

"'I'm going to talk to Coach about it.'"

L.S. said, "I talked with the coach and he said that I could live with his family during my senior year. What an experience! That house was full of books and magazines. I didn't know that *Sports Illustrated* came every week and that there were magazines for coaches. It was great. There were two elementary girls in that home. These little girls were always talking about when they went to college. In January I decided to talk about college with coach.

"'Coach, do you think I could go to college?'

"'L.S., you don't play football well enough to get a scholarship. I'll see what I can do.'"

L.S. continued: "The coach helped me get a small scholarship and some work study so that I could go to a community college. Then I got financial assistance to get into an athletic trainer program at a four-year college. Now I've finished my master's degree and I'm an athletic director. It all started when those little girls talked about going to college and put that picture inside my head."

These are thoughtful stories. The first one illustrates how a school can be structured so that a student feels secure and valued. The second story describes how a caring teacher helped a student develop a positive picture of a future inside his head and how the student then became the person he pictured.

This book is designed to help school staffs build schools where students learn and are valued. Chapter 1 answers the question, "Why restructure schools to provide for individual students?" In Chapters 2 and 3 the instructional and organizational components of restructured schools are described. Chapter 4 is exciting: The programs of eight model restructured schools are described. In Chapter 5 effective teaching strategies such as mastery learning, cooperative grouping, and early intervention programs are explained. In Chapter 6 the content, processes, and products of the "Learning How to Learn" curriculum is presented. In Chapter 7 the research on learning and teaching styles is related to restructuring schools to meet students' needs. Restructuring cannot take place until an effective classroom management program has been established. In Chapter 8 management and motivation strategies are presented. The next chapter focuses on a key concept in restructuring: parent–school–community partnerships. In Chapter 10 staff development strategies for restructuring are described. Finally, the appendixes contain sample lessons, management strategies, administrative forms, and other instructional materials.

The need for school restructuring cannot be overemphasized. Schools must be restructured to provide for individual students. We hope that this book will help teachers, administrators, parents, and community leaders build effective instructional programs and that it will be useful for graduate and undergraduate students who are studying the concepts of restructuring.

Acknowledgments

The task of writing this book would have never been completed without the help and encouragement of many, many people. We would like to acknowledge and thank Linda Avila, associate professor, Southwest Texas State University; Bill Bechtol, Jr., elementary principal, Northside Independent Schools in San Antonio, Texas; Beverly Hardcastle, chair, department of Education, Azusa Pacific University; and Kay Shaw, staff development coordinator, Aurora Schools, Aurora, Colorado, for their suggestions on the manuscript. We would also like to thank the teachers, administrators, and staff of the model schools for sharing their classrooms and their ideas with us; H. Y. Price, Jr., of the San Marcos Civic Foundation for his encouragement and support; Mylan Jaixen of Allyn and Bacon for believing that these restructuring concepts should be shared; and Delia V. Hernandez, Maribel Garcia, and Sonia Gonzalez for typing and organizing the manuscript.

Most thanks must be expressed to our spouses for their help and support. They helped us with research, proofread each draft, and encouraged us each day. This book is dedicated to Millie Bechtol and Doug Sorenson.

CHAPTER ONE

Why Restructure Schools to Provide for Individual Students?

Children, like fingerprints, are all different.

At the end of a two-hour television special about successful restructured schools, three fifth-graders were being interviewed in front of their elementary school building. All three were Hispanic students whose parents had not finished high school.

The reporter asked, "What's your favorite place to be?"

Raul answered, "School is my favorite place to be because the teachers are nice and make you feel special."

Laura explained, "They're not just nice to us. They treat all children like they're special persons."

The reporter said, "Robert, I understand that you went to another school a few years ago. How is this school different?"

Robert replied, "In that school they only teach you once. They wouldn't reteach you until you learn it like they do here. At this school I became a good student."

The reporter asked the students, "What kind of grades do you get?"

Robert answered, "All A's."

Laura replied, "All A's."

Raul said, "All A's."

Then the reporter asked, "Think of yourself in the future, ten or fifteen years from now. What will you be doing?"

Laura said, "I'll be going to college, studying to be a lawyer."

Robert said, "I'll be going to college, also. I want to be a petroleum engineer."

The reporter turned to Raul and asked, "What about you?"

Raul smiled and replied, "I'll be in college and I'll be in politics." He smiled again. "I may be running for an office. Someday I want to be the president." (*Learning in America,* 1990).

These are not the responses one would expect to receive from three elementary students who are ready to enter middle school. These are students who qualify for free lunches, students whose parents did not finish high school. How did these children get such ambitious pictures of their future inside their heads? How did they as eleven-year-olds become so competent and confident? What kind of school program helped these students become so positive about themselves and their futures?

For many schools in the United States, it's the worst of times. Daily newspaper stories describe the lowest Scholastic Aptitude Test (SAT) scores ever, dropouts, drugs, youth crime and violence, child abuse, and the decline of the family structure; all are indicators of the worst of times. But for some students like Laura, Raul, and Robert, it's the best of times.

The worst of times gives school leaders opportunities to try different things. In every state there are schools that have restructured their instructional programs so that their students have greater opportunities to be successful. The good news for students, parents, teachers, administrators, and community leaders is there are many choices of effective strategies and curriculum sequences. Schools can be restructured to provide for individual students. There is an abundance of research-supported programs that school staffs can choose to use. For many more students like Laura, Raul, and Robert, school can be their favorite place.

The purpose of this book is to help teachers and administrators develop the skills needed to restructure schools to provide for individual students. It's a sourcebook for changing classrooms and schools from traditional programs to systems that take into account the differences of learning aptitudes of their students. A variety of restructuring strategies are presented so that school staffs are empowered to make choices to "put their children first."

This chapter addresses the question, "Why restructure schools to provide for individual students?" There are three reasons for restructuring.

1. Each child is unique. Schools must be organized to provide for the individual differences of their students.
2. The present school system needs improvement. We are producing fewer quality high school graduates than the countries with whom we compete for international trade.
3. There are many choices of organizational and instructional strategies for restructuring schools. A variety of research-tested programs are available so that school staffs can tailor a program for their students.

Each Child Is Different

"My teacher has an interesting theory," explained Jimmy, an 8-year-old. "She says that teaching is like bowling. All you can do is roll the ball down the middle and hope that you touch most of the students."
"What do you think of her theory?" asked John, his older brother.
"She's a terrible bowler."

One might suspect that these two boys had read this research on individual differences of students and schooling practices in the United States. For more years than one cares to remember, we educators have been giving lip service to the concept of taking youngsters where they are and letting them develop to their optimums. All this time, we've been kidding ourselves. Jimmy and John are right. In actual practice, very little has been done in taking students where they are. Too often we herd youngsters into the same classroom because they are all ten years old, for instance, and have been in school for five years. Then we expect all the students to master the work assigned to them in this classroom.

Few schools are organized to permit students to develop to their optimums. We hear a middle school teacher say, "I can keep all four of my social studies sections on the same page. Or a principal state, "All our first grades started the third primer today." Or a worried teacher ask, "But, Mrs. Miller, if you teach some of your second-graders from the third-grade mathematics book, what will I do with them next year?" How can Mrs. Miller help her children develop to their optimums with the practices that are evident in our schools today?

Veteran teachers and principals are aware that students have changed over the past ten years. There is much more student diversity in today's classroom—and many more students with problems that require special attention. For example, the "crack babies" are now in the elementary schools. Yet the sad truth is that teaching in the United States is now and has been essentially for groups, not individuals.

The movement to restructure schooling provides an appropriate time to relook at the concepts of individualized instruction. Rolling the bowling ball down the middle is an inappropriate way of teaching the students who will become our leaders in the twenty-first century.

Why do we want to individualize? Why have there been movements across the United States to individualize instruction? The answer is simple, but the solution is difficult. *Children, like fingerprints, are all different.* They just do not fit in the lockstep structure that is currently used in most elementary and middle schools today. Schools need to be restructured to provide for the diversity of their students.

Children really are different. We know that if a teacher deals with 150 students each year for forty years — and that is a long teaching career — that educator will never encounter any two children who are precisely alike. if this teacher were able to teach six million or six billion human beings instead of six thousand, the same would be true (Tyler, 1969).

Children differ anatomically, physiologically, and biochemically from one another. Organs of the body differ markedly in size and shape. The chemical composition of body fluids shows considerable variation. Heart rate, respiration rate, and other processes show the same variabilities. In short, if we consider these characteristics, there is no "normal" person who might serve as a medical standard or model (Tyler, 1969).

What does it mean when we relate these differences to teaching? Within a given fifth-grade class, students may differ in ability, motivation, achievement, attitude, personality, learning style, ethnicity, and socioeconomic status. The face of youth is changing. Classrooms appear to be more diverse than they were fifteen years ago. The mainstreaming of special education students since the passage of Public Law 94-142, the increased attention to students with limited English-speaking ability, and the federal and state emphases on ensuring equal treatment of students have resulted in classrooms filled with students with a wide range of characteristics (Peterson, 1982). Fetal alcohol and crack babies add to this diversity. One-parent homes and "grandparent" homes make teaching more challenging. But nothing has been as dramatic as the increase in poor children. Nearly 25 percent of all school-age children live below the poverty level; for black and Hispanic students the percentage is much higher (Johnson, 1988). These individual differences won't go away. Society seems to be more and more diverse.

This multicultural, diverse population presents a challenge to classroom teachers, principals, and other instructional leaders. It's the reason that restructured schools to provide individualized instruction are once again a timely alternative. The unifying theme of *Megatrends 2000* is the triumph of the individual. Technology is empowering the individual. Global television, videocassettes, computers, cellular phones, and fax machines empower individuals (Naisbitt & Aburdence, 1990). This same technology is now available to let us instruct students as individuals. Instead of moving students in lockstep through the grade-level system, they can go through on a knowledge-level ladder (*Ohio's Classroom of the Future*, 1988) at their own speed.

In an individualized teaching program, it is recognized that there is no standard student. Each student is a unique individual who learns in his or her own way. In beginning individualized instruction, one school system examined student achievement. The differences in achievement of students of the same age and the differences in individual students' scores on achievement subtests were used as a rationale for individualizing instruction (Bechtol, 1973).

The first finding was that every class is nongraded. Look at the reading scores in Figure 1-1. The students have tested at many different grade levels. The norm of this group should be according to graded standards, sixth grade, fifth month. In the suburban community studied, the norm was seventh grade, sixth month. Only 25 of the 160 students tested, or 16 percent, actually scored within the sixth grade. The rest scored either higher or lower.

Teachers and principals have known for a long time that an achievement range exists in any class, but they act as if it were not true. Many teachers treat all students as if they were the same. They say, "You're not acting like a fifth-grader," or, "That's not sixth-grade work" (whatever that means).

In most schools, teachers look upon the class, grade, or group as an entity. All students are presumed to have relatively equal learning needs, abilities, and responses. The school is teacher-centered and the curriculum is group-paced. All students are generally given the same assignment, regardless of their individual capabilities or progress.

The danger of rolling the bowling ball down the middle is that students who test much higher or lower are often treated incorrectly. Elementary students whose test scores indicate that they are capable of reading high school materials are rewarded with A's for work that is probably much too easy for them. Then they hear teachers, principals, and parents say, "Good work! You made the honor roll." In reality, the youngsters may not have been working much at all.

FIGURE 1-1 • *Reading Achievement Range of Sixth-Graders in Tipp City, Ohio*

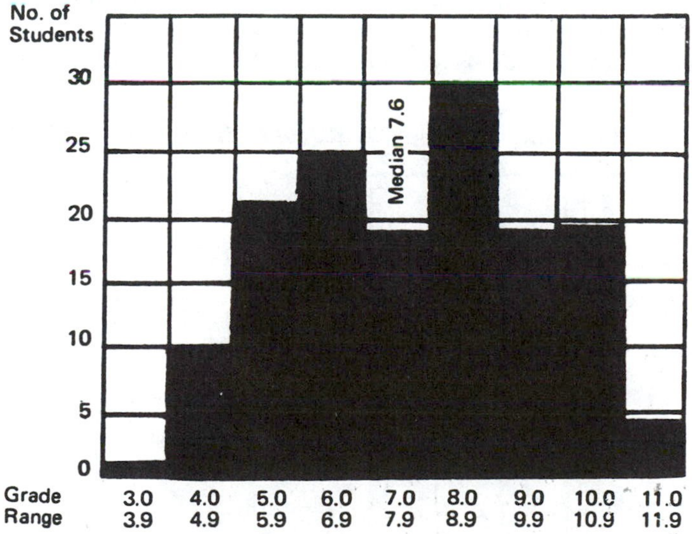

Source: Tipp City Exempted Village Schools, Tipp City, Ohio.

How about the other students? How do we treat the student whose performance is well below his or her grade level?

With the student who is functioning well below grade norm, we do even more wrong. A track coach would not require every child to run a six-minute mile simply because the child was eleven years old, for example. The coach would know that while some eleven-year-olds could perform the task, and a few might even surpass it, still others would be unable to achieve it. Coaches would know that the skill and stamina involved are not factors of chronological age alone. In the same way, to insist that every student master a sixth-grade reader by June of the sixth year in school is unrealistic and unfair. Programs like this are unrealistic and unfair.

To expect more than is reasonable is bad enough, but to see parents and teachers react to a student's failure as if the student and not the system is wrong is even worse. For example, the Georgia kindergarten testing program has drawn fire from early childhood specialists because it requires many children to be retained or placed in other curricular programs (O'Neil, 1988). Fortunately, effective programs are available to help young children start school successfully. Strategies like Reading Recovery and Success for All are described in Chapter 5.

One reason that schools restructure to implement individualized programs is that students the same age and in the same class function in many, many grades. Restructured schools with individualized instructional programs are designed to provide for these differences.

The second reason for moving toward individualized instruction is that an individual student tests in different grades for different subjects. In Figure 1-2, individual test scores for three sixth-graders (from the group in Figure 1-1) are compared. All three students tested in at least three different grades.

FIGURE 1-2 · *Grade Levels of Three Tipp City (Ohio) Sixth-Graders by Subject*

Subject	Pupil		
	A	B	C
Reading vocabulary	5.7	7.7	10.0
Reading comprehension	3.6	7.2	10.1
Arithmetic reasoning	6.3	7.5	6.8
Arithmetic fundamentals	5.3	5.4	7.2
English	4.8	6.8	6.2
Spelling	4.8	6.5	7.0

Source: Tipp City Exempted Village Schools, Tipp City, Ohio.

For Joe, a sixth-grade student, to test at seventh-grade level in spelling, tenth-grade level in reading, and fifth-grade level in arithmetic is not unusual. The problem is that none of his sixth-grade materials happen to fit him. The reason, then, is that a child within himself is nongraded.

These two differences in student achievement are only two indicators of the individual differences of children. Students differ in multiple ways. No matter how carefully students are selected for a homogeneous group, each student will learn, think, and react in a unique way. There are differences in talents and aptitudes, in interests and motives, and in habits and learning styles.

Our Present System of Education Needs Improvement

Perhaps no one has made a stronger case for school restructuring than Chrysler Corporation Chief Executive Officer Lee Iacocca (1991) when he spoke at the annual conference of the Association for Supervision and Curriculum Development. He had a blunt message for American educators: "Your product is faulty! Graduating a student who can't read is like selling a car without an engine under the hood. It's a massive consumer fraud! Right now, American education has a lot of dissatisfied customers.

"Your product needs a lot of work, and it's your job to fix it. I know that you face considerable hurdles like scarce resources and an increasing number of children living in poverty. But in the end, your customers don't want to hear about your raw materials problem. They want results. That's your problem and you can't duck it."

Iacocca is correct. Our present system of education is not working well. We are producing fewer quality graduates than the countries we compete with for international trade. Consumers are "shopping around" and employing graduates from other countries while our graduates are jobless.

Historically, education in the United States is for all children. The promise of education in the United States is that *all*, regardless of race or class or economic status, are entitled to a fair chance to learn and to develop the skills to secure gainful employment and to manage their own lives. And it has worked well. For years each generation of Americans has outstripped its parents in education, in literacy, and in economic attainment. Student achievement was at its highest in the decade after the Sputnik challenge. But in the 1970s student achievement began to decline. For the first time in the history of our country, the educational skills of one generation did not surpass, did not equal, did not even approach those of its parents (*The Excellence Report,* 1983).

What are the indicators that our education system needs to be improved?

The following are some that were identified in the report, *A Nation at Risk* (National Commission on Excellence in Education, 1983).

- International comparisons of student achievement reveal that on nineteen academic tests U.S. students were never first or second, and, compared with other industrialized nations, were last seven times.
- About 13 percent of all 17-year-olds can be considered functionally illiterate. Functional illiteracy among minority youth may run as high as 40 percent.
- Average achievement of high school students on most standardized tests is now lower than the scores when Sputnik was launched. On the SATs average verbal scores fell over fifty points and average mathematics scores dropped nearly forty points.
- Both the number and the proportion of students demonstrating superior achievement on the SATs (i.e., those with scores of 650 or higher) have also dramatically declined.
- Average tested achievement of students graduating from college is lower.
- Business and military leaders complain that they are required to spend millions of dollars on costly remedial programs in such basic skills as reading, writing, spelling, and computation.

Current international comparisons are even more sobering than those identified in *A Nation at Risk*. In 1969, the United States ranked first in basic literacy of the 148 nations in the United Nations. Ten years later, in 1979, we ranked twenty-first. In 1989, we were forty-ninth (Daggett, 1989).

Shanker (1990) reports that we are producing fewer quality high school graduates. Less than 6 percent of the U.S. high school graduates can do quality college work. This compares poorly with countries with whom we compete for international trade. For example, in Germany, 28 percent of the high school graduates can do quality work; in Canada, 23 percent; in Australia, 22 percent; in France, 21 percent; and in Great Britain, 16 percent.

In 1991, 13-year-olds in the United States ranked last in overall mathematics achievement when compared with a six-nation study of countries that are international competitors. The same students are near the bottom in geographical knowledge. Heavy television watching and small amounts of homework contributed heavily to the poor showing of U.S. youth (Vita, 1991).

The criticisms identified in *A Nation at Risk* prompted state leaders to initiate a series of reforms across the United States. The proposals for reform made by legislative committees and commissions have reflected the ideas of the members and suggestions of special-interest groups. Little consideration has been given to evidence that a reform was practical and will accomplish what is claimed for it. Because members of the committees and commissions had varied backgrounds, far more reforms were proposed than any school could do (Tyler, 1987).

Though the reforms have been inconsistent across state lines, most included changes in curriculum, in testing, and in promotion standards. The results have been disappointing. Dropout rates have increased. Retentions have increased. Remedial programs have increased. The high hopes for increased student achievement have not been accomplished. In 1991, the verbal scores on the SAT declined to an all-time low and mathematics scores fell for the first time since 1980 (DeWitt, 1991).

Few of the reforms have helped teachers and principals provide more effectively for the individual differences of students. In fact, the reforms seem to assume there are no individual differences in children of the same age.

The curriculum programs that were implanted were data based. All yielded measurable outcomes based on test scores. This has been both a strength and a weakness. At the state, district, and school levels, more data about students is available. Consequently, data can be used for better diagnosis and instructional planning. The weakness is the emphasis on accountability has resulted in instructional programs that are group- and grade-level-oriented. Welsh (1986) states that teaching has been defined in terms of rigid, mechanistic guidelines for meeting grade-level standards. Teachers in many schools complain about the increased bookkeeping necessary to document that requirements for each student have been met.

The emphasis on testing has affected instruction in most elementary and middle schools. Technology exists so that all teachers, schools, or districts can be compared grade by grade, school by school, or district by district. Teachers can be identified by their effectiveness with different pupils (ethnic minority, bilingual, etc.). This emphasis has caused teachers to teach directly to the test. It has led to the direct teaching of the minimal requirements of each grade level. Thus, schools are producing fewer excellent students. More students have minimal skills and knowledge. In studying the direct teaching to minimal test standards, Stallings (1987) asks, "Are we evaluating what we value?" Are tests of minimal grade standards appropriate for students who will live and work in a complex society?

Since the reforms were implemented, there has been an increase in retentions, in dropouts, and in the number of students entering universities who need remediation in basic skills.

If any trend could be said to grow as we watch it, it is retention. Data collected before the reform movement shows an overall retention rate of 15 to 19 percent. At this rate, retention practices in the United States most closely resemble those in such countries as Haiti and Sierra Leone. The Japanese system, like the educational systems in most European countries, has a retention rate of less than 1 percent (Office of UNESCO Statistics, 1984). Since the reform movement there has been an increase in retentions and in transitional rooms; social promotion has dramatically decreased in most school districts. The instructional programs with strict, rigid grade requirements tended to retain at higher rates or to assign children to transitional rooms or special education. We visited one school district in south Texas that retained 15 percent of the students in each grade (K–8) during one academic year.

Smith and Shepard (1987) say that there is no justification for retentions or for programs that add a year to a student's career in school. They state, "The evidence is quite clear and unequivocal that the achievements of retained children are no better — and in most instances are worse — than those of comparable children who are promoted. Retention is one part of the current reform program that does not work." They believe that these retention practices are discriminatory to boys, poor children, the relatively young, and the relatively small (Smith & Shepard, 1987). Yamamoto (1979) states that children rate academic retention as the third most stressful life event. Only the death of a parent and going blind were rated as more stressful.

Failing a grade in school has multiple effects. Students who have been held back are up to four times more likely to drop out than those who have never been held back (Hahn, 1987).

A second sign that the reform movement is not working is an increase in the dropout rate. Bondi and Wiles (1986) reported that since Florida has implemented rigid curriculum programs and standardized testing programs, the state has the highest dropout rate (38 percent) in the nation. Rosales (1988) states that since the testing reforms the Texas dropout rate has increased to 34 percent. He also reports that in Texas, 40 percent of all black students and 50 percent of all Hispanic students drop out. Large cities report even higher dropout rates; in Chicago 38 percent of whites, 56 percent of blacks, and 57 percent of Hispanics dropped out (Hahn, 1987). The societal effects of dropping out are expensive. Seventy percent of people on welfare did not graduate from high school. Ninety-one percent of Texas prisoners did not graduate from high school. In 1989, it cost the state $38,000 a year to keep someone in a state prison (Barrientos, 1989).

The third indicator that the reform movement is not working is the high percentage of university freshmen who need remedial instruction in writing, reading, or mathematics. A fifteen-state survey conducted by the Southern Regional Education Board found that approximately 36 percent of the entering university students needed remedial instruction (Jones, 1988). Of the states surveyed, Oklahoma and Virginia were the best with 25 percent of their entering freshmen requiring remedial courses; Louisiana was the worst with 56 percent requiring remediation. At Southwest Texas State University thirty-nine sections of remedial mathematics were offered Spring semester (Schedule of Classes, 1992).

The present system of education must be improved. The emphasis of the reforms on a more standard curriculum and testing for minimal grade requirements has resulted in more retention, more dropouts, and more entering university students who need remediation. Overall student achievement levels have declined or stayed the same. Rolling the bowling ball down the middle does not touch the students at either end of the achievement range. When teachers teach to the minimal grade requirements, the ball isn't even rolled down the middle; it's on the low side of the alley. More attention to students as individuals is required. School restructuring is needed.

Choices: Ways Schools Can Be Restructured

The reform movement assumed that the school structure was acceptable. With a few changes — better prepared teachers, a more standard curriculum, accountability — schooling could be improved. This was a false assumption. Things weren't going that well. Compare schooling results with that of industry. What would a manufacturer do if it were found that one of the factories got these results? Each time the factory made one hundred machines six were excellent; twenty-five were OK; thirty-five needed immediate repair before they could be sold; and thirty-four were never finished. Those are the results in our high schools (Shanker, 1990).

Here is another example. What happens if a doctor gives a patient a medicine that doesn't work — one that even causes the patient to break out in a rash. Does the doctor say, "How dare you not take my medicine right?" Does the doctor suggest that the patient take it longer or take stronger doses? No, the doctor would say, "I'm sorry the medicine didn't work. Let's try something else."

Our schools need to be restructured. There is a concern about our educational system turning out a class of permanent social dependents who are squeezed out of any meaningful economic role by the better schooling and work ethics prevailing abroad (Morris, 1989). Our results must change. We must produce more graduates who can compete on an international level. We believe that the restructuring movement has the potential to make a positive impact on U.S. education. Many choices of effective strategies are available so that school staffs, parents, and community leaders can design a school that graduates students who are able and well prepared.

While preparing this book, we had the opportunity to visit many outstanding schools (eight of these schools are described in detail in Chapter 4). The school staffs had restructured their instructional programs to meet the needs of their students. All schools were effective. Their results are impressive. Each school was different. Our visits convinced us that there is no standard model for all U.S. students. We believe that there are many choices for restructuring schools to provide for individual students.

Two stories illustrate these choices. The first story describes an enriched instructional program that demanded heavy parent involvement. Paul, a university colleague of ours, spent a year in Malaysia. When Paul and Pat enrolled their son in the first grade, the classroom looked similar to those in the United States. The biggest difference was that the room was filled with books.

The teacher smiled at them and said, "I see that you've noticed the books. I challenge you to help your son become a super reader this year."

"What's the challenge?" asked Paul.

"See those boxes of library books? I've gathered thirty-six levels of books for this room. Your son will probably start reading at level four or five. I challenge you two to listen to your son read or to read to him thirty minutes every day this school year. If he reads 200 books, he'll receive a blue ribbon for excellence in reading."

Paul looked at Pat; they're both competitive people. Pat nodded. Paul said, "We accept your challenge."

Later Paul explained to us. "Josh brought home a book every night. Usually the book was about thirty pages long. We'd take turns spending time with him listening to him read, helping him read, or, once in a while, reading to him. The funny thing was that Josh enjoyed it. Pat and I got so that it was a special time for us, not a chore. But the teacher was tough. On the weekend, Josh would bring home two or three books or a longer book. During Christmas vacation he read a 270-page book. It was a book that a teacher had started to read to our older son when he was in first grade. But it was too long. She'd never had time to finish it. Josh read it at Christmas. Wow!"

"Oh yes," Paul answered proudly. "He read 225 books."

He continued, "He did a research problem. He studied crocodiles in the library and ended up writing a research report about crocodiles. The teacher helped him Xerox pictures and bind it like a book. It's the best report I've ever seen a first-grader do. I had worried that Josh might not be as good a reader as our other kids. I'm not worried about that anymore."

We asked, "What happened when you came back to the United States?"

"A sad story," he answered. "His teacher said, 'I challenge you to help your son earn a blue ribbon in reading. I challenge him to read six books in the second grade.'"

This story illustrates how a school reading program can be structured to help students become good readers. It also shows how the structure of this program affected the home in a positive way.

One of the problems that stands in the way of restructuring is our tunnel vision; our preconceived idea of how an elementary and a middle school classroom should look. With our tunnel vision we see a teacher in front of a class of twenty to thirty students. We see the teacher lecturing. We see all the students the same age using the same book and on the same page. The next story illustrates how schools can be different.

While we were visiting an elementary school, the assistant principal pointed to the office. "You might get a kick out of watching that for a couple of minutes."

A father was enrolling a five-year-old in kindergarten on November 14.

"Don't they all have to enroll together," I asked, "in September?"

"No. It's her birthday today. The big deal is on your fifth birthday you get to go to school. It's like getting your driving license at 16."

"Won't she be behind her class?"

"She's an individual. There's diagnostic information about her on the computer. We can concentrate on what she knows and what she's ready to learn." (*Ohio's Classroom of the Future*, 1988).

"Won't the classes get too large as five-year-olds enroll all year?"

"No. When teachers know that children are ready for the third reader they can be placed in the next unit. Kids can move when they're ready. Schools don't have to be run by calendars."

Who decided that algebra was a nine-month, ninth-grade, once-in-a-lifetime event? There is a world of difference between viewing algebra as a body of knowledge that students will learn and viewing algebra as a course students take their freshman year.

Schools exist *for children*. All that is done to establish and maintain schools must be measured in terms of what is best for each child. Systems that attempt to restructure instructional programs do so to provide appropriate learning experiences for each learner in the school. The first thing that many adjust is the calendar.

The calendar-defined teaching model promotes teaching that emphasizes curriculum coverage over student mastery (Spady, 1988). Graded curriculum requirements cause teachers to hurry through materials to have their classes ready for the state test in February. We have observed a teacher who "covered" the countries of Europe in a three-week unit. We have visited a teacher in Texas in April who had twenty science "essential elements" to cover before the school term was over. What happens in programs like this is that teachers document that they taught the required content. There is much evidence that students have not learned these materials.

Outcome-based education is one choice for restructuring schools. What is done in the classrooms is based on the outcomes the school wants to achieve. The practitioners start by determining the knowledge, competencies (skills), and qualities they want students to demonstrate (Spady, 1988) when they exit elementary school or enter high school. The curriculum is outcome based rather than time based. Focusing on outcomes creates an inevitable need for educators to accommodate the differences in learning rates inherent in any group of students. Schools are challenged to design a curriculum that focuses students to achieve future outcomes, to vary the length and sequencing of instructional opportunities, or to use a variety of grouping strategies (Spady, 1991).

In the chapters that follow we have emphasized that there are many choices available for school staffs to select from to restructure their instructional program. A first step in restructuring is the development of a set of goals to guide the school improvement efforts. Each school staff develops its own set of goals. These goals provide a philosophical base for their instruction and school organization. Our philosophical base in this book includes four generic goals for restructuring schooling to provide for individual students that can be adapted by school staffs to fit their school mission:

1. *Competence:* Students should master the skills and content of the curriculum. Students must master those skills that are essential for success at the next level of schooling.

2. *Confidence:* Restructuring should improve the self-concept of each student. The main change is a structure that facilitates teachers to know their students well. By establishing student–teacher relationships over much longer time periods than a calendar year, students can be matched more efficiently with appropriate learning materials and placed in learning groups that fit their individual differences. In this way students can experience daily success in learning and in peer relationships—they develop confidence.

3. *Independence:* Restructuring should help students develop the skills to be lifelong independent learners. Students learn the process skills of how to learn. Study skills, inquiry skills, and thinking skills are emphasized. Giving students choices from portions of the curriculum is a good strategy for permitting students to practice independent learning skills. It also gives students power to select relevant learning activities. Students who have had these experiences will become independent learners who are able to live more effectively in a technological society.

4. *Responsibility:* Restructuring should help students become positive school and community citizens. The oldest students in a good individualized program should be the best role models for younger students because they have had the most time to learn and to practice these skills. The program is organized so that students learn the rights and responsibilities of concerned citizens, develop a sense of social consciousness, and have a well-grounded framework for dealing with what is right and what is wrong. Experiences in helping others succeed and in modeling appropriate citizenship behaviors will prepare students who can live more efficiently in a changing, diverse society.

These are the generic goals of a restructured school program, a program in which the individual differences of students are accepted. Such a program provides a structure so that youngsters can develop to their optimums.

Summary

"Nobody would quarrel with giving students instruction suited to their needs. Wasn't that tried in the 1960s and 1970s?"

"Yes, remember that time in our history? The American College Testing Program (ACT) and Scholastic Aptitude Test (SAT) scores were at the highest in the magic decade (1963–1973). Many nongraded schools and Individually Guided Education (IGE) schools were achieving outstanding results. However, the results in some schools were disastrous. Teachers made individualized materials and had youngsters work on them all by themselves. Students could not do these independent activities on their own. The individualized concept was correct; the way in which it was implemented was foolish. While they were accomplishing one goal—adapting instruction to individual needs—they were interfering with other goals, such as providing students with explanations by qualified teachers and motivating students to learn (Brandt, 1988). Research in teaching, instructional materials, and technology are now available to implement effective individualized instructional programs."

"Changes through restructuring can be quite different from past reforms. Education research provides guidelines, practices, and programs for effective change. Faculty and administrators can select research-based programs that will result in positive student outcomes."

Why restructure anyway?

1. Each child is different. The graded, calendar-driven instructional program does not provide for these individual differences.
2. The present school system needs improvement. Achievement scores are too low. More students are being retained. Dropout rates are increasing in many states. The number of freshmen entering college who need remediation has increased.
3. There are many choices of organizational and instructional strategies for restructuring schools. Research-tested programs are available so that schools can be structured to provide for individual students.

References

Barrientos, P. (1989). Presentation to San Marcos Rotary Club, San Marcos, Texas.

Bechtol, W. (1973). *Individualizing instruction and keeping your sanity.* Chicago: Follett.

Bondi, J., & Wiles, J. (1986). School reform in Florida—Implications for the middle school. *Educational Leadership,* 44(1): 44–46.

Brandt, R. (1988). On research and school organization: A conversation with Bob Slavin. *Educational Leadership,* 46(2): 22–29.

Daggett, W. (1989). *The challenging nature of work: A challenge to education.* Presentation to Kansas legislative and educational leaders.

DeWitt, K. (1991). Verbal scores hit new low in Scholastic Aptitude Test. *New Times,* 140(48), 705: 1–14.

The excellence report. (1983). Arlington, VA: American Association of School Administrators.

Hahn, A. (1987). Reaching out to America's dropouts: What to do? *Phi Delta Kappan,* 29(4): 256–263.

Iacocca, L. (1991). *Business challenge to education.* San Francisco: Annual Conference of the Association for Supervision and Curriculum Development.

Johnson, C. (1988). *Demographic changes: Challenges for educational administration.* Cocking Lecture, National Council of Professors of Educational Administration, Indianapolis, IN.

Jones, M. (1988). College survey shows need for remedial aid. *Austin American-Statesman,* 118(156): 1–13.

Learning in America: Schools That Work. (1990). Public Broadcasting System.

Morris, C. (1989). The coming global boom. *The Atlantic,* 264(4): 51–64.

Naisbitt, J., & Aburdence, P. (1990). *Megatrends 2000.* New York: William Morrow.

National Commission on Excellence in Education. (1983). *A nation at risk,* Washington, DC: U.S. Government Printing Office.

Ohio's Classroom of the Future. (1988). Columbus, Ohio Department of Education.

Office of UNESCO Statistics. (1984). Wastage in primary education from 1970–1980. *Prospects,* 14: 347–368.

O'Neil, J. (1988). Failure at age five? *ASCD Update,* 30(5): 1–3.

Peterson, P. (1982). Individual differences. In *Encyclopedia of educational research,* 5th ed. (pp. 844–851). New York: Collier Macmillan.

Rosales, J. (1988). Texas can pay now or it will pay later. *San Antonio Light,* 107(258): 1–6.

Schedule of classes. (1992). San Marcos: Southwest Texas State University.

Shanker, A. (1990). *A case for restructuring our schools.* Paper presented to the Annual Conference of the Association for Supervision and Curriculum Development, San Antonio, Texas.

Smith, M., & Shepard, L. (1987). What doesn't work: Explaining policies of retention in the early grades. *Phi Delta Kappan,* 69(2): 129–134.

Spady, W. (1988). Organizing for results: The basis of authentic restructuring and reform. *Educational Leadership,* 46(2): 4–8.

Spady, W. (1991). *The transformational paradigm of OBE.* San Marcos, TX: OBE Fiesta.

Stallings, J. (1987). Symposium hosted by the College of Education of Memphis State University and the Barbara K. Lipman Early Childhood Research Institute.

Tyler, L. (1969). Individual differences. *Encyclopedia of Education Research* (pp. 639–641). Macmillan.

Tyler, R. (1987). Educational reforms. *Phi Delta Kappan,* 69(4): 277–280.

Vita, M. (1991). Is there something America can learn? *Austin American-Statesman,* 121(66): 10–11.

Welsh, P. (1986). What reform? *Educational Leadership,* 44(1): 56–63.

Yamamoto, K. (1979). Children's ratings of the stressfulness of experiences. *Developmental Psychology,* 15(5): 581–558.

CHAPTER TWO

The Components of a Restructured School

The restructured school accepts nongrading/continuous progress, diagnostic prescriptive teaching, multiage grouping, and the "learning how to learn" curriculum not as innovations, but as the way schools ought to be organized.

"I can't get individualized instruction to work with my kids," complained the teacher. "Only a few of my students can handle independent work. I don't have time to tutor each of them."

The teacher has identified the most common misconception about instructional programs that have been restructured to provide for individual students. Meeting the individual needs of students does not mean teaching each student separately. It's not just tutoring or independent study. It *does* mean appropriate placement. Students are using correct materials, in appropriate groups, at the right time.

A school in which the learning needs of students are placed first is quite different from a typical elementary or middle school. Schools that provide developmentally appropriate learning for students must be organized in a much more flexible structure. Spady (1988) describes the outcome-based school as one that is organized to accommodate the different learning rates of students. Shanker (1990) describes a school that is structured so that students spend more time with the same teachers. Glasser (1990) focuses on quality education by adapting a curriculum that is appropriate for student needs. All three seem to support a more personalized instruction program.

The restructured school accepts nongraded–continuous-progress programs, diagnostic-prescriptive teaching, multiaged grouping, and differentiated curriculum not as innovations but as the way schools ought to be organized.

The purpose of this chapter is to describe the components of a school program that is restructured to provide for individual students. It also describes strategies that teachers, principals, district administrators, parents, and community leaders can consider as they restructure their school programs.

Nongrading–Continuous Progress

There is a story about a boy who ran to his fourth-grade teacher with a bug he had found on the playground. "Teacher!" the boy cried, "Look at this bug!"

The teacher, who wasn't too enthusiastic about bugs, replied, "That's nice, Johnny."

The boy asked, "Can we study it?"

"Oh, no," the teacher replied. "That's a fifth-grade bug."

This is a ridiculous story — one that probably isn't true — but it reflects the absurdity of the graded school organization.

The nongraded school or continuous-progress model began to emerge when educators started questioning the graded system. An alarming number of students were failed (not promoted) each year. At the same time, educators were apprehensive because bright students were being restricted to unchallenging situations. Plans to alter the organization of the graded school system began to appear in the early 1900s. The Winnetka Plan and the Dalton Plan are the best known of the early developments. The modern concept of the nongraded school began in 1934. Milwaukee adopted a nongraded program in 1942.

The work of Drs. John Goodlad and Robert Anderson and the publication of their classic book, *The Nongraded Elementary School* (1963) did more to disseminate the nongraded concept than any other single act. Nongraded schools emerged all over the United States. In the 1960s and 1970s schools in Garden Springs, Kentucky; Melbourne, Florida; Newton, Rhode Island; Plainview–Old Bethpage, New York; and Tipp City, Ohio, were among those that received national publicity for nongraded programs. Current school descriptions by Spady (1988), Shanker (1990), and Glasser (1990) include nongraded–continuous-progress concepts. Lake George Elementary School in Lake George, New York, is a model of nongraded–continuous-progress organization. This program is described in Chapter 4.

Nongrading is a vertical pattern of school organization. In the traditional graded school, students of the same age move together at a regular pace from kindergarten through grade 12, one grade a year. In a nongraded school, students progress at their own individual rates according to their abilities. Students master as much of an appropriate curriculum as they can during the year. At the beginning of the next year, each student starts where he or she left off and works at his or her own speed. Grade labels are not attached to the nongraded curriculum. There are no promotions or retentions. Academically talented students may master the curriculum quicker than they would in a graded school, but they do not skip material or mark time waiting for less able students to catch up. Immature students and slower learning students may take longer to master work, but they are not "held back a year" or "pushed to keep up with the class." Ideally, the curricula are adapted to individual students so that there is no question of going faster or slower, only of using each student's abilities to best advantage (Bechtol, 1973).

In a graded school, teachers, parents, and administrators have certain expectations for fifth-grade students, for example. The students are matched with a label on textbooks. They are expected to learn fractions and to study the United States — even though students of the same chronological age range in attainment over many school grades. It is as if the school handed the teacher only size 10 clothes. How many children would the clothes fit? For some they would be too small; for others, too large. But in the graded school we say: "Wear the clothes. It's okay if they sag or if the shoes are too tight. A little discomfort is good for children."

Just the opposite happens in the nongraded school. Teachers are asked to measure their students to find out what sizes of clothes they need. A size

FIGURE 2-1 • *In a graded school, it's as if the school handed the children twenty-two size eight suits. How many students would the clothes fit?*

Source: Used with permission of Nannette W. Wilson.

12 suit with long legs. Shoes with narrow widths. Fine! No discomfort for children in the nongraded school.

For example, in the nongraded "birthday school" described in Chapter 1, the school superintendent could send a child a card on the day before the child's fifth birthday. The card would read, "Happy Birthday! We'll see you in school tomorrow." This change would permit children to enter kindergarten all the time. Then, when the kindergarten teacher thought that the student was ready to begin reading, the child would be assigned to a primary classroom. The yearly progression system of the graded system would be broken.

This flexibility of the nongraded school closely fits the developmentally appropriate structure advocated by the National Association for the Education of Young Children (Bredekamp, 1987). It is opposite of the academic hothouse approach found in many preschools and kindergartens. In these programs children are hurt because they're treated like first-graders and placed in instructional activities that they're not ready to learn (Drew, 1991). Nongraded programs are tied to children's development. Students are not hurried or held back.

The implications of nongraded schools become apparent when students enter high school. There it becomes evident that in a continuous-progress subject such as mathematics, able students enter high school ready for Algebra II.

While visiting a Florida school that had a continuous-progress program from nursery school through junior college, we were guided through the campus by the captain of the high school football team. We asked, "Larry, what grade are you in?"

He laughed and said, "Well I haven't taken government yet because if I complete that course I'll graduate. And if I graduate, I won't be eligible for spring sports, and my coach says that I may have a chance for a baseball scholarship."

We visited with him more and discovered that almost all his work was at the junior college level. He was in a school that gave a student the right to be both a high school senior and a college freshman.

A friend's son had the same opportunity in mathematics. He was in a nongraded school. By the time he left the primary building, he was a year ahead in math. He finished Algebra I in middle school and took Algebra II his first year in high school. The Algebra II section made up of the nongraded students significantly outscored the Algebra II section of juniors. The high scores of the nongraded students helped the high school mathematics teachers become strong supporters of the nongraded program. During his senior year this young man and many other students completed two semesters of Calculus on a university campus. He also served that year as student council president. The next year he entered a major state university with eight semester hours of university credit. The option to be both a high school senior and a college freshman is a sound one for many students.

The research supporting nongrading–continuous progress has been generally positive (Slavin, 1987). Studies in a classroom where the nongraded program was used conscientiously found positive effects on student achievement (Bechtol, 1970; Bowman, 1971; Machiele, 1965). The effects of nongraded–continuous-progress programs in reading and mathematics have been quite positive overall (Slavin, 1988). In the nongraded schools in which we have worked and visited, student achievement was consistently high. The model schools at McFarland and Lake George had been recognized for their high achievement and their success with students.

Acceleration

What about acceleration? That's the key to increasing student achievement. Acceleration programs that permit students to take Algebra I early produce much better achievement outcomes than enrichment (Slavin, 1988). In Tipp City, fifth-graders in a nongraded–continuous-progress mathematics program achieved significantly higher than those in a graded program (Bechtol, 1970). When compared to similar students who did not take Advanced Placement courses, middle school and high school students who received advanced high school and college-level courses had much better academic records in college, graduated from college with more honors, engaged in more leadership activities, and took more advanced courses (Feldhusen, 1989). Brody and Benbow (1987) found no harmful effects as a result of acceleration; on the contrary, they reported that accelerated students earned more state and national awards than nonaccelerated students and a greater number attended highly selective colleges.

In many nongraded schools acceleration permits some students to graduate and to enter college early. Compared to unaccelerated peers matched for ability, accelerated students earned higher grade point averages (GPAs), earned more honors, associated with older and more intellectual students, and were equal in psychological adjustment to unaccelerated peers (Feldhusen, 1989).

Acceleration works. There is evidence of superior achievement in school and superior performance in college. There is an absence of evidence suggesting social or emotional problems due to acceleration. Feldhusen (1989) recommends that to provide for gifted students we must upgrade the level and pace of instruction. It's a good recommendation for many students.

One of the surprising finds is that continuous-progress programs that accelerate student learning work well with students who are at risk (Slavin & Madden, 1989). In elementary schools in Aurora, Colorado, we observed this strategy working effectively with students who were poor, who had only one parent, and who came from minority groups. Accelerated learning is described in Chapters 4 and 5.

Nongrading for At-Risk Students

What about the students who are behind the pace of the graded school curriculum? How does the nongraded–continuous-progress school help these at-risk students?

Let's look at what doesn't work first. One of the most frequently used strategies with low-achieving students is also the least effective: flunking them. Failing students does have a misleading positive short-term effect on standardized test scores; but, the long-term effect on students' achievements is negative (Slavin & Madden, 1989). In many states, once students have been retained they are then labeled at risk of dropping out (see Figure 2-2).

Another widely used program is the pull-out program used under Chapter 1 and in special education. At best, these programs may keep students from falling further behind their age-mates, but even this effect is limited to the early grades and is more apparent in mathematics than in reading (Slavin & Madden, 1989; Carter, 1984).

A third strategy that doesn't work for low-achieving students is tracking. The mathematics curriculum sequence is a good example of this concept. Willoughby (1990) reports that a study of best-selling mathematics series reflected "dumbing down" the curriculum. Students in grades 6, 7, and 8 learned little new content. For example, only 30 percent of the grade 8 curriculum contained new material. Willoughby (1990) asked how we could hope that students in grade 9 would be successful with a textbook that contained

---

FIGURE 2-2 • *What Works With Students at Risk: Research Findings*

- Commonly used strategies such as retention and pull-out programs are ineffective at producing lasting achievement gains.

- Preventive programs that provide intensive tutoring of young children to correct their reading problems very early so that they are not placed in special education or the remedial cycle are effective.

- Instructional methods that accelerate student learning like continuous-progress programs and nongrading produce better achievement than enrichment programs.

Source: Adapted from R.E. Slavin and N.A. Madden, "What Works for Students at Risk: A Research Synthesis," *Educational Leadership,* 46 (February 1989), pp. 4–13.

90 percent new material. By tracking students along some imagined ability lines in middle school and allowing good students to pursue a reasonably challenging curriculum while relegating low-achieving and other students to minimal textbooks, we've locked low-achieving students out of regular high school classes.

French and Bing (1990) reported that Boston's tracking program holds back students. Only 60 percent were at grade level in mathematics by middle school; only 25 percent at grade 9. Only one Hispanic student in Boston's schools has taken calculus while in high school. Tracking doesn't work. As one low-achieving student reported, "In sixth grade the teachers complained that no one does the homework. Now that we're in eighth grade they don't give us any" (French & Bing, 1990).

Concerned high school teachers are frustrated by students who were incorrectly labeled special education or remedial education in elementary or middle school. One teacher explained, "Even though they don't belong in my remedial class, by the time I get them they have few skills and are quite comfortable sitting in class not working hard. Some graduate from high school without many marketable skills. It's frustrating!"

Retention, pull-out programs, and tracking are not effective at producing lasting achievement results with students who perform below graded standards.

What works with low-achieving students who are at risk? High-impact first-year prevention programs that apply intensive resources, including tutoring and small-group instruction, are extremely successful in increasing a student's reading achievement (Slavin & Madden, 1989). Schools must do a better job in serving the students who have the most difficulty in learning. It's important to correct reading problems early so that students don't get placed into special education or the remedial cycle (Brandt, 1988).

High-impact first-year prevention programs are based on the argument that success in reading is the essential basis for success in school. Therefore, the key moment for intensive intervention is when a student begins to read. Instead of incorrectly placing a student in special education or a remedial class, students are given intensive instruction. Two early intervention programs, Reading Recovery and Success for All, are described in Chapter 5.

Diagnostic-Prescriptive Teaching

An accepted component of a restructured school program is diagnostic-prescriptive teaching. A primary goal is that students should master the skills and content of the curriculum. This mastery curriculum (Glatthorn, 1987) meets two criteria: it is essential for all students and it requires careful structuring. Disciplines such as mathematics and reading might be organized into levels instead of grades. For example, one school system's mathematics program is made up of continuous-progress levels, ranging from number readiness to algebra. Students can move through this linear sequence at their individualized paces. Teachers diagnose the students' present levels of achievement, prescribe appropriate placement, and monitor the students' progress through a series of formative and summative tests.

Diagnosis is a critical component of the teaching of non-graded–continuous-progress curriculum programs. Students must be assigned the correct materials and placed in an appropriate instructional setting. The Instructional Management Model, shown in Figure 2-3, illustrates the steps that teachers must follow in diagnosis and prescription. This model has been used to identify the competencies a teacher needs in a system that uses diagnostic-prescriptive teaching.

1. A teacher must know what educational outcomes or goals are required. Mastery curricula are organized with a sequence of instructional objectives. The teacher begins by studying objectives that students have mastered and then identifying the material they will study next.

FIGURE 2-3 · *Instructional Management Model*

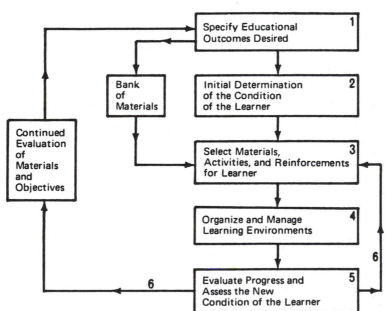

Source: Adapted from Competency-Based Teaching Materials, Division of Education, Southwest Minnesota State College.

2. The teacher needs skills in preassessment. The teacher must determine the initial condition of the learners; that is, which objectives the students have achieved. Then the assessment information is used to determine the students' next learning objectives.

Preassessment is necessary for two reasons: (1) Students should not study something they already know. Preassessment may reveal that students already possess the behaviors that the teacher has as objectives. In this case, the original objectives can be revised upward or new objectives can be selected, saving many hours of unnecessary instructional time. (2) Students should not study objectives they are not ready to learn. Preassessment may reveal that students do not have the prerequisite skills to achieve the objectives.

Preassessment takes time. In the long run, it also gives time by guaranteeing worthwhile instruction and appropriate content for each student.

3. Once it has been determined that students do not have certain skills but have the necessary skills to learn them, the teacher must be able to select materials, activities, and reinforcements for the learners. This selection takes into consideration the students' test scores and their learning styles.

4. The teacher must have the skills to organize and manage the learning environments so that all students in a unit or a class can efficiently achieve their objectives.

5. The teacher must be able to evaluate the progress of students. The teacher must determine if students have mastered the objectives. If students have not mastered their objectives, the teacher must have the skills to recycle them to corrective learning activities.

6. If the students have achieved mastery, the teacher must have the skills to assess their new conditions and start the cycle again.

In the model schools described in Chapter 4, good diagnostic practices were observed. Systems to assess new students quickly were used. Test data and other assessment materials were used to make appropriate instructional decisions.

Multiaged Grouping

In our classes in teacher education, the age range of the students is almost always twenty years or more. Each class is made up of students who are 20 to 40 years old or older. This diversity allows students to learn from each other. This age range makes the class more interesting for the students to attend and for us to teach. Multiaged classes are normal in the university setting and in high schools. Yet nothing has been resisted more at elementary and middle schools than multiaged grouping.

The research conducted by the Wisconsin Research and Development

Center for Cognitive Learning and the Institute for the Development of Educational Activities (IDEA) that led to the IGE model included a multiaged component. In the 1970s thousands of schools implemented IGE concepts. The one component that was implemented poorly or not at all was multi-aged grouping. Nothing has been harder to change than same-age grouping patterns of the graded school.

Yet when one studies recent research, grouping across grade lines and continuous-progress programs are the most effective grouping strategies. As one curriculum leader explained, "I chose to use multiaged grouping to camouflage that students were above or below grade level." It may have been a poor reason, but the achievement results in that school district were outstanding.

A form of regrouping that works extremely well for elementary students is an updated version of the Joplin Plan (Slavin, 1988; Floyd, 1954). In this plan students are regrouped for reading and for mathematics without regard for grade levels. For example, at a specific time in the day, all teachers teach reading. Mrs. Giddings teaches the students who are at fourth-grade first-semester level (4-1). Her class might contain some third-, some fourth-, and some fifth-graders. One important advantage of this plan is that it reduces or eliminates the need for within-class grouping for reading and mathematics since students in each regrouped class are on the same level. Teachers have more time for direct instruction of students in reading and mathematics. The time that students spend doing follow-up seatwork is reduced (Slavin, 1988).

The grouping strategies are as follows: First, students remain in a heterogeneous setting most of the day. This strategy permits students to identify with their homeroom group and teacher. It allows students to be appropriately placed in reading and mathematics but not totally tracked. The labeling effect of all-day grouping is reduced.

Second, at specific times each day students are regrouped by their performance levels in reading and mathematics. Students are regrouped according to their diagnosed learning level in a particular subject. Students may be at one level for reading and another level for mathematics. This regrouping, even though it results in multiaged classes, reduces the heterogeneity in the skill being taught. Teachers can adapt their level and pace of instruction in regrouped classes to accommodate students' levels of readiness and learning rates.

Third, group assignments in reading and mathematics are flexible and are frequently reassessed. Changing students between reading or mathematics classes is less disruptive than changing basic class assignments. Any errors in initial assignments can be easily remedied. Changes in student performance can also be accommodated with a change in grouping (Slavin, 1988). Frequent reassessment is a true strength of the plan; children are allowed to change and to grow.

Since many students are accelerated and use materials above their grade level, the effects of the Joplin Plan and closely related forms of nongrading have been quite positive overall. Slavin (1987) estimated the median effect size at + .44 for reading achievement. Similar achievement results were found in mathematics.

Whether a school initiates multiaged grouping in the students' heterogeneous homeroom is a school-level decision. Implementing cross-grade multiaged classes in reading and mathematics is an initial step in restructuring. Important changes in student achievement will result from Joplin-like nongraded–continuous-progress programs.

Other positive changes can occur in the multiaged homeroom. The multiaged homeroom or unit is based on two *if's*.

1. If children learn more from other children than they do from teachers, and
2. If children learn more by teaching a subject than from taking a subject, then students have the right to be the youngest in a room so that they can learn from older children, and they have the right to be the oldest in the room so that they can teach younger children.

For example, we visited schools in England and Scotland and were impressed with the family group structure in the British Infant School. Older students are concerned and care for the "little ones." Pairing, in which the older student serves as a model or tutor for a younger one, helps the students' learning and their feelings about their personal worth. Parkay and Hardcastle (1990) report that cross-age tutoring works well with at-risk students.

Take the case of Joey and Tommy. Joey, a nine-year-old, was having difficulty learning his multiplication facts. Tommy was just starting his multiplication. So the teacher asked Joey if he would help Tommy. Tommy began to learn his facts. Joey began to master his facts and to feel good about himself. His statement sums up this concept: "Teacher chose me to help Tommy with multiplication. Me! Wow! I don't multiply too well myself, but I can teach Tommy a few things. And Tommy—he's getting better at multiplication." There are many possibilities for pairing students in an individualized school program.

Won't parents and teachers resist multiaged grouping because it's such a change? Without careful explanation of results, resistance does occur. One of the best examples of multiaged grouping is the school band. What are the criteria for being in the school band? Are all 16-year-olds automatically in the band? No. To be in the band a student must be able to read music, play an instrument, and march. In band, meeting the criteria, not age, is what matters. Multiaged reading and mathematics classes work in the same manner.

There's a story about a principal at a Parent–Teacher Association (PTA) meeting who asked all the parents who were 32 years old to come to the front of the group. When they got to the front of the room, he said that he was going to teach them a song that they could sing at the annual PTA revue. The parents began complaining all at once.

"I can't sing."

"I can't carry a tune."

Only the soloist in the church choir seemed pleased to be up front.

"Why us?" asked one father.

"You're 32 years old," explained the principal. "You ought to be able to sing a song to the group."

"Why did you choose 32-year-olds?" asked the father. "You must choose based on other factors, not just age."

"Exactly," the principal answered, "and that's what we're going to talk about tonight: why our school is planning to use multiaged groups in reading and mathematics." (IGE Multiaged Grouping, 1971).

One Colorado school district uses multiaged grouping frequently for the following reasons: (1) multiaging facilitates students' social and academic growth, (2) multiaging allows freer movement within the curriculum, (3) multiaging allows for more economy and efficiency in using facilities and time, and (4) multiaging allows a teacher or a teaching team more time and opportunities to get to know the students (Shaw, 1990).

Multiaged grouping is a key component of an individualized school for three reasons. The first is obvious: The use of multiaged grouping in reading and mathematics in a nongraded–continuous-progress program causes higher student achievement. The second reason is more subtle: In a multiaged setting all school personnel tend to treat students more as individuals than as second-graders. The third reason makes sense for today's students who are at risk: There is much stability for a student who spends two years or more in the same homeroom with the same teacher. Multiaged grouping provides a structure that enables teachers to make instruction developmentally appropriate for students. Three multiaged schools are described in Chapter 4.

A "Learning How to Learn" Curriculum

A "learning how to learn" curriculum allows for students' individual differences in the study of subject matter in terms of content, process, learning environment, and end products expected of them. *Content* consists of ideas and concepts, facts, principles, and theories that make up knowledge. It can vary in abstractness, complexity, and organization according to the subject matter being studied (Sorenson, Engelsgjerd, Francis, Miller, & Schuster, 1988; Maker, 1982).

Process emphasizes strategies to learn how to learn. It includes how information is gathered, how it is presented, what kinds of activities students carry out to learn, and what questions are asked about a subject. Thinking skills and problem solving are elements of process. Thinking skills include Bloom's cognitive levels of thinking, inquiry processes, creative processes, critical thinking skills, and single-step problem-solving techniques. Multistep problem solving includes a set of sequential steps with a divergent and convergent stage at each step:

1. Generate several problem statements and select the best statement.
2. Generate several ways to solve the problem and pick the best one.
3. Generate optional designs to test the solution, then select the best design and implement it.
4. Organize and interpret the results, then evaluate them and decide whether or not the stated problem was solved.

Models and a more detailed discussion of thinking skills and problem solving are the major emphasis of Chapter 6.

Product refers to kinds of outcomes students are expected to produce as end products of learning. They can be tangible or intangible, but they should be related to real problems and real audiences. Students should transform information from primary and secondary sources — that is, interpret it in their own words and apply it in new situations — not copy or summarize from sources. And products should be subject to real evaluations by real audiences. In a language arts classroom, products can vary from an assignment to write a paragraph or a limerick to developing a series of poems or short stories or a book around a theme or storyline.

Environment is the setting in which learning takes place. This includes both the physical setting, such as the classroom, school, or community, and the psychological climate or atmosphere of human resources, teaching and learning styles, uses of technology, and personal characteristics of learners. All kinds of environments need to be considered in a learning how to learn curriculum that is individualized and personalized.

Summary

"You're right. An individualized program in the restructured school is much more than tutoring or independent study. I'm impressed with the way the curriculum is organized. Some subjects are designed so that students can go at their own pace; other subjects are planned so that students can study at different levels." "Yes, there's a wide range of possibilities for restructuring schools, rather than one particular model." "I like your phrase — developmentally appropriate. It's a neat concept."

"Yes, it's a neat concept and a good description of what an instruction program in a restructured school is organized to do."

The components of a restructured school are (1) nongraded–continuous-progress programs, (2) diagnostic-prescriptive teaching, (3) multiaged grouping, and (4) a learning how to learn curriculum. All components provide a structure that is developmentally appropriate for students. More able students can accelerate. Immature students are not hurried through the curriculum.

References

Bechtol, W. (1970). An analysis of educational leadership in developing a nongraded school system: A case study. Ed.D. dissertation, Miami University.

Bechtol, W. (1973). *Individualizing instruction and keeping your sanity.* Chicago: Follett.

Bowman, B. (1971). A comparison of pupil achievement and attitude in a graded school with pupil achievement and attitude in a nongraded school 1968-69 1969-70 school years. *Dissertation Abstracts,* 32, 86-A. University Microfilms, 71-20: 958.

Brandt, R. (1988). On research and school organization: A conversation with Bob Slavin. *Educational Leadership,* 46(2): 22-29.

Bredekamp, S., ed. (1987). *Developmentally appropriate practice in early childhood programs serving children from birth through age 8.* Washington, DC: National Association for the Education of Young Children.

Brody, L., & Benbow, C. (1987). Accelerative strategies: How effective are they for the gifted? *Gifted Children Quarterly,* 31: 105-109.

Carter, L. (1984). The sustaining effects study of compensatory and elementary education. *Educational Research,* 13(7): 4-13.

Drew, M. (1991). From garden to hothouse. *Teacher,* March: 58-59.

Feldhusen, J. (1989). Synthesis of research on gifted youth. *Educational Leadership,* 46(6): 6-11.

Floyd, C. (1954). "Meeting children's reading needs in elementary school: A preliminary report." *Elementary School Journal,* 55: 99-103.

French, D., & Bing, S. (1990). Tracking practices in Boston public schools. International Conference of the Association of Individually Guided Education, Cambridge, Massachusetts.

Glaser, W. (1990). The quality school. *Phi Delta Kappan,* 71(6): 424-435.

Glatthorn, A. (1987). *Curriculum leadership.* Glenview, IL: Scott, Foresman.

Goodlad, J., & Anderson, R. (1963). The nongraded elementary school. New York: Harcourt, Brace, and World.

IGE multiaged grouping. (1971). Dayton: Institute for Development of Educational Activities.

Machiele, R. (1965). A preliminary evaluation of the non-graded primary at Leal School, Urbana. *Illinois School Review,* 1: 20-24.

Maker, C. (1982). *Teaching models in education of the gifted.* Rockville, MD: Aspen.

Parkay, F., & Hardcastle, B. (1990). *Becoming a teacher: Accepting the challenge of a profession.* Boston: Allyn and Bacon.

Shanker, A. (1990). The case for restructuring our schools. Paper presented to the

Annual Conference of the Association for Supervision and Curriculum Develop
    ment, San Antonio, Texas.
Shaw, K. (1990). Multiaging. Inservice presentation Aurora Public Schools, Aurora,
    Colorado.
Slavin, R. (1987). Ability grouping and student achievement in elementary schools:
    A best evidence synthesis. *Review of Educational Research,* 57: 213-336.
Slavin, R. (1988). Synthesis of research on grouping in elementary and secondary
    schools. *Educational Leadership,* 46(1): 67-77.
Slavin, R., & Madden, N. (1989). What works for students at risk: A research syn-
    thesis. *Educational Leadership,* 46(5): 4-13.
Sorenson, J., Engelsgjerd, J., Francis, M., Miller, M., & Schuster, N. (1988). *The
    gifted program handbook.* Palo Alto, CA: Dale Seymour Publications.
Sorenson, J., Poole, M., & Joyal, L. (1976). *The unit leader and individually guided
    education.* Reading, MA: Addison-Wesley.
Spady, W. (1988). Organized for results: The basis of authentic restructuring and
    reform. *Educational Leadership,* 46(2): 4-8.
Willoughby, S. (1990). *Mathematics education for a changing world.* Alexandria,
    VA: Association for Supervision and Curriculum Development.

CHAPTER THREE

How a Restructured School Is Organized

Schools exist for students. All that is done to establish and maintain schools must be measured in terms of what is best for each child.

Two teachers were driving home from school after a team planning meeting. The passenger spoke: "For a teacher like me who's been used to being told what to do, having the freedom to decide is scary."

The driver replied, "It's exciting, too."

"Do you think the multiaged classroom is the right decision?"

"Yes. I believe that it will provide stability for our kids and they'll learn more. What do you think?"

"I agree. It's just that I've been so comfortable being a second-grade teacher."

"You always taught children, not second-graders. You're a super teacher now. You'll be a super teacher in a multiaged classroom."

The teacher settled back in the passenger seat and said, "I guess so. I think that we can teach as well as those teachers we visited in Colorado."

The driver smiled, "Then people who want to restructure their programs will come and visit us."

These teachers have identified one of the difficult tasks innovative educators must face: the organization of an instruction program that provides for individual students requires that the professional staff change. Traditionally, elementary schools and middle schools have been organized in a mass-production structure similar to the industrial plant across the river. In other words, we have adjusted the students to the curriculum instead of the curriculum to the students. These inflexible organizations sustained grouping through grades and evaluation by standardized norms.

Experience in the traditional schools has made it difficult for us to envision an organization that could facilitate the teacher's role in providing appropriate instruction for each student. We speak about restructuring using words like "teacher empowerment" and "site-based management." Few of us can picture how an empowered teacher behaves or how a school that is site-based managed works.

This chapter and Chapter 4 describe how restructured schools are organized. The problem in describing restructured schools is that there are many choices for organization. In this chapter, one generic model, the multiunit school, is presented. This model illustrates clearly the organizational issues—communication, decision making, and student placement—that school staffs must address while restructuring. In the next chapter, eight model schools are described so that the reader can picture restructured schools in action.

Findings from the Effective Schools Studies

The research from the effective schools movement has helped set a standard for organizing today's schools. It is appropriate to study these findings before discussing the multiunit school. Lewis (1986) has summarized this research and identified the common features of effective elementary and middle schools. She identified the following:

1. *There is strong community collaboration.* Not only are parent organizations strong, but the schools define community very broadly, involving businesses, senior citizens, neighbors, and civic organizations. The involvement is real, not token, with community members participating in instruction and decision making.

2. *All the school's strategies and work are geared toward providing students with maximum opportunities.* The schools offer maximum opportunities by creating warm environments in which kids feel welcome and by offering assistance beyond what they are contracted to give. The teachers' openness and caring shows students that the school cares not only about their academic achievement but also about them as human beings.

3. *The curricula teach important content and skills.* The emphasis is on hands-on experience, but in the context of the school's fundamental mission: to develop competence in reading, writing, and computing; to develop reasoning and analytical skills; to provide a foundation in the core disciplines of language, mathematics, science, and social studies; and to expose students to their cultural heritage.

4. *The principal provides the vision and energy to create success.* Styles of leadership vary from school to school. All principals fit with their school community. Principals are devoted to their schools, their staff members, and their students.

5. *The excellent schools have specific educational goals.* Management and instructional policies and practices focus on attaining these goals; student assessments are integrated with these goals. The written goals of these exemplary schools are no different from those of most schools. What is different is that these specific goals are taken seriously and are translated into action in day-to-day activities.

6. *Teachers not only share the goals and values of their schools, they also have the opportunity to influence them.* Teachers adhere to high standards of professionalism and accept responsibility for meeting the needs of students. In return, they are treated with respect and given an environment in which they feel secure and empowered.

7. *Standards for expectations of students are high.* Standards are seldom lowered to fit the students. Instead, students are prepared to meet the standards. Behavioral standards for students are consistent and applied fairly.

8. *Schools provide teachers with adequate resources.* These include adequate time for instruction, organizational structures that are flexible and encourage collegiality, supplemental materials, opportunities for professional growth, both human support and moral support for teachers, and sufficient space.

9. *The schools accept no excuses.* Excellent schools are not immune to problems. Poor socioeconomic conditions, lack of parent support, and a mobile student population exist. Rather than view these problems as impossible constraints, personnel in excellent schools see them as opportunities to marshall help. The schools do not stand still; they continually implement programs and policies that reduce or eliminate obstacles to educational success.

These common features (Lewis, 1986) related directly to the practices we observed in the model schools that we visited (see Chapter 4). The principal and teachers in each model school had clear goals and high expectations for student achievement. They had selected appropriate strategies, curricula, and materials to give their students maximum opportunities to learn. In each model school there was strong parent and community collaboration. The principal and teachers were empowered to accomplish the school mission. They worked hard and achieved positive results.

School-Based Management

All the restructured schools that we visited were organized so that teachers could make more decisions about instructional practices. This empowerment of teachers in the model schools relates to school-based management.

Current interest in school-based management is a response to evidence that our education system is not working and, in particular, that strong central control actually diminishes teachers' morale and, correspondingly, their level of effort (Meier, 1987). Under school-based management, professional responsibility replaces bureaucratic regulation; districts increase school autonomy in exchange for the staff's assuming responsibility for results (Cohen, 1988). Because of federal and state laws, court decisions, and district policies, today's teachers and principals do not have the autonomy that educators had in the 1960s when U.S. test results were at their highest. School-based management is an attempt to restore that autonomy. We were taken aback by the views of Sam, a teaching colleague:

> *"One more year of teaching. I'm going to try a different grade level. If that doesn't go well, I'm going to retire."*
>
> *"Sam, you're one of the best teachers we've ever worked with. Why are you so negative about teaching?"*
>
> *"Changes that don't make sense for kids. I've been teaching for 25 years. I can't remember all the changes I've been through. In recent years, all of them are from the top down. It's not like it was when we worked together. Then children came first — not some superintendent's or governor's new idea. I'm always teaching someone else's dumb plan."*
>
> *Sam continued, "Why is it so hard for people outside the classroom to understand that we teachers know much more about our students, teaching, and ways to improve than they do? To be blunt, they don't treat me like a professional. I'm being forced to teach in ways that I know are not in the best interest of my students."*

We are sorry to report that Sam's views reflect the sentiments of scores of other respected teachers across the country. Surveys show that teachers are frustrated with the amount of paperwork, lesson alignment, teaching to test objectives, and being appraised and evaluated according to how closely they follow a lockstep sequence of instruction (Boyer, 1988). Sam retired at the end of the school year.

What motivates teachers to work harder and smarter is not money but a work environment that lets professional teachers make decisions and that nurtures a free exchange of ideas and information (Glickman, 1989). School-based management in the restructured school means bringing the responsibility for decisions as close as possible to the problem. It means creating ownership for those responsible for carrying out decisions by involving them directly in the decision-making process — and by trusting their abilities and judgments (Harrison, Killion, & Mitchell, 1989). Perhaps for teachers like Sam, the time to make decisions to improve school has come.

Cawelti (1989) has identified the following key elements of school-based management:

1. Various degrees of site-based budgeting affording alternative uses of resources
2. A team operation affording groups the opportunity to expand the basis for decision making
3. School-site advisory committees with key roles for parents, community representatives, and older students
4. Increased authority for selecting personnel who are assigned to the school
5. Ability to modify the school's curriculum to better serve the students
6. Clear processes for seeking waivers from local or state regulations that restrict the flexibility of local staffs
7. An expectation for an annual report on progress and school improvement

What is the role of the school district in school-based management? This is a key question because the school principal's and teachers' motivation and interest in restructuring is influenced by the motivation of district leaders. Of course, the unit for change in school-based management is the school itself. However, district support from the outset is essential. Neither top-down nor grass-roots efforts are sufficient. Collaboration between district leaders and the school staff make restructuring to provide for individual students the most successful (Roy, 1989).

Does research support school-based management? The answer is a clear "Yes." In her synthesis of research, David (1989) found that school-based management is an efficient strategy to transform schools into effective learning environments. She reports that school faculties make more student-based decisions about staffing, schedules, and curriculum when they are given actual control over their budget and relief from restrictions. She also found that teachers had increased job satisfaction and feelings of professionalism when the extra time and energy demanded by on-site management are balanced by real authority (David, 1989).

Empowered teachers are different. We found the teachers in the model schools that we visited to be more competent, confident, and enthusiastic than those in a traditional setting. Restructuring seemed to increase their professional performance. This same type of professionalism was observed in schools that were in the Mastery of Education network, the Association for Individually Guided Education, and the Outcome-Based Education network. Restructuring seems to empower teachers and make them more effective.

How does school-based management relate directly to the organization of restructured schools? The key to excellence in the restructured school is the involvement of a knowledgeable faculty that is empowered to make teaching and learning meaningful to the students. School-based management empowers school staffs to make appropriate instructional decisions. Decisions to accelerate the pace for one student and expand learning opportunities for another must be made by faculty members close to the problem. School-based management strategies allow school staffs to make such decisions.

A model of school organization that has proven to be effective is the multiunit school. This organizational structure is flexible enough to permit school staffs to accommodate the differences in learning rates, aptitudes, and ability that they find in their students. In the next section the multiunit school is described as one organizational structure that empowers teachers and principals to meet their students' instructional needs.

The Multiunit School

The multiunit school is an organizational administrative structure designed to provide for educational and instructional decision making at appropriate levels. This structure was developed by Herbert J. Klausmeier and his staff at the Wisconsin Research and Development Center for Cognitive Learning and was the organizational model for IGE (Klausmeier, Quilling, Sorenson, Way, & Glasrud,d 1971). When adapted by IDEA, the unit was called the Learning Community (*Working Together,* 1974). In New England states the unit or learning community was also called the house. In current restructuring programs this organizational plan is called nesting. Regardless of the term used, this structure is designed so that teachers have time to get to know their students much better than do teachers in a traditional class or homeroom. In this book the generic term *unit* will be used. The multiunit organization provides a structure for open communication among students, teachers, and administrators. When decisions are shared and when more people are involved in making decisions, the decisions tend to be better and more readily carried out. The multiunit school is an effective structure for school-based management because all teachers are fairly represented and share in the decision making.

Figure 3-1 shows the formal organizational plan of a multiunit program for 500 students. This organizational hierarchy consists of two distinct levels of operation: the unit and the Instructional Improvement Committee (IIC). The multiunit school receives support from the school district, parent and community organizations, regional education agencies, universities, and the state department of education.

Decisions at the unit level are made by all the people in the unit — adults and students. Each unit has a unit leader or chair; two or more teachers;

FIGURE 3–1 · *Multiunit Organization of a School of 400–600 Students*

	Principal	
• Parent Representatives		• Special Teachers & Coordinators

Unit Leader A	Unit Leader B	Unit Leader C	Unit Leader D
3-6 Teachers	3-6 Teachers	3-6 Teachers	3-6 Teachers
• Bilingual or Chapter 1 or Special Education Teacher	• Bilingual or Chapter 1 or Special Education Teacher	• Chapter 1 or SpecialEducation Teacher	•Chapter 1 or Special Education Teacher
• Student Teacher or Intern	• Student Teacher or Intern	• Student Teacher or Intern	• Student Teacher or Intern
• Aide	• Aide	• Aide	• Aide
75-150 Students Age: 5-7	75-150 Students Age: 6-9	75-150 Students Age: 8-11	75-150 Students Age: 10-12

————— Instructional Improvement Committee
————— Unit
Inclusion of these persons will vary according to school setting.

Source: Adapted from H. Klausmeier, R. Morrow, and J. Walter, *Individually Guided Education in the Multiunit Elementary School* (Madison: Wisconsin Research and Development Center for Cognitive Learning, 1968).

an instructional aide; in some cases, pre-service teachers or interns; and from 75 to 125 students.

The unit staff is charged with the total educational experience and the instructional process of the students assigned to the unit. The assessment of each student, the assignment of objectives, the selection of instructional materials and activities, the placement of each student, and the means of evaluation are decided jointly. This process permits each student to benefit from the combined talents of all the teachers in the unit.

Decisions at the building level are made by the IIC, which is composed of the principal, the unit leaders (or chairs), and, in some schools, parents. The IIC is not only a decision-making body, it is the communication lifeblood of the individualized school. Its primary function is to move the decision-making process to the appropriate level so that decisions are made as close to the problem as possible and by those most capable of making them. This shared decision making changes the role of the principal from that of an authoritarian administrator to one of an instructional leader.

What kinds of decisions are made by the IIC? A principal in a large city reports that unit assignments of both teachers and students, school rules, and selection of fund-raising projects were shared decisions (Camealy, 1988). The IIC in a small Wisconsin city planned in-service programs, scheduled computer usage, and prioritized budget spending (McDermott, 1989).

"Why do we use the IIC concept? Because it works!" explained Elementary Principal Bob Ross (1990). "Better decisions are made and there is a stronger commitment to the decisions because we all own them. The IIC has increased the accountability of all the teachers. The structure provides a more productive way to share the skills and talents of teachers. We can creatively solve problems and implement needed changes.

"The teachers believe that the IIC works because Lake George Elementary School has an able professional staff, strong leadership, clear goals and objectives, and an effective structure for feedback and monitoring" (Ross, 1990). Two multiunit schools are described in detail in Chapter 4.

The multiunit organization is effective because all people in the restructured school are involved in choosing goals and in deciding how to achieve them. This process causes teachers and administrators not only to understand the school goals but also to internalize them. As we found in the effective schools research, the students, unit teachers, and IIC members take the school goals seriously and plan their day-to-day activities to achieve them.

While restructuring school programs, school staffs must answer a set of broad questions about school organization. Following is a sampling of the types of questions school staffs must address as they restructure their instructional programs to provide for their students:

- *How are students assigned to teachers?* By age or grade level? Multi-aged? Parent requests? Siblings together or apart? Friends together or apart? There are many choices.
- *How do students progress through the curriculum?* By grade standards? Nongraded–continuous progress? Integrated whole language approach?
- *How will teachers work together to help students achieve?* Same as always — grade meetings? Unit planning teams? Team teaching? Departmentalized schedule?
- *What are the roles of teachers and principals in the restructured progrm?* No changes? Many changes? Teacher leaders? Unit chairs? Coaches? Empowered teachers?

The structure of the multiunit school is one model that can be used so that all teachers are included in answering key questions about students. Let's look at how these questions have been answered in multiunit schools so that we can better understand the organizational issues of restructuring.

Assigning Students to Units

In the multiunit school the staff develops its own plan for assigning students to units. There are, however, some general guidelines that all schools should consider.

Size of the unit is important. How many students can a unit staff "know" so that an individualized learning program based on diagnosed needs and learning styles can be developed for each student? Individualized school staffs have found that a teaching team can manage an individualized program for 75 to 150 students. When a unit becomes larger than 150, management becomes more difficult.

Multiaged grouping is an important element. How many age levels should be included in each unit? The curriculum must be organized so that students are assigned appropriate materials in reading and mathematics. Multiaged grouping facilitates acceleration and camouflages placement of students who are behind in achievement. Students of at least two age/grade levels should be placed in each unit. Some units have age spans of three or four years. It is much more desirable to take seventy-five 9-year-olds, seventy-five 10-year-olds, and seventy-five 11-year-olds and make two multiaged units than to put all the students of one age together. Multiaged grouping helps place the individual student as the important factor in instructional decision making instead of grade norms or a textbook. When students stay with the same teachers for two years or longer, positive things happen. This structure provides bonding and security for the students. It allows teachers to know students better and to provide for their individualities more effectively. In the model schools (see Chapter 4), three have used multiaged grouping strategies.

Each unit should have a full range of achievement. The research in grouping supports heterogeneity (Slavin, 1988). There is no advantage, and there are many disadvantages, in developing a "smart" unit and a "dumb" unit. Children learn very quickly how they are viewed by teachers. Both labeling children and labeling units have negative consequences. (Many school staffs examine the achievement range of a particular age group using standardized reading scores and then divide students of the same achievement between two or more units.)

Gifted and talented students and special education students are placed in the units. Staffs of individualized schools have found that a single unit can accommodate students who perform at the extreme ends of the achievement range. Some schools have found it more efficient to put a number of students who qualify for special education in the same unit. In this way, a special education teacher can be a regular member of the unit team. This strategy is especially effective for high-impact reading programs. When this arrangement was first used in one school, a student who had previously been assigned to a resource room told the principal, "I don't think they (the unit team and the other students) know anything is wrong with me."

It is important to achieve balance in the units. In assigning students to units, the staff must consider the personal characteristics of the students.

- Each unit should have some "sparklers" (students who have a positive attitude toward learning and who serve as leaders or role models for other students). The staff should identify the sparklers and see that each unit has a share of them.
- Each unit should have some problem (hard to teach) students. These are children who have some learning disability (emotional, physical, or intellectual) that requires excessive one-to-one teacher time. If all of these students are put in the same unit, it becomes a difficult situation.
- Peer relationships should be considered in placing students in a unit. Students who work well together can be kept together. Students who do not work well together or who are too dependent on each other can be separated.
- Student-teacher relationships must also be considered. Students who need a special kind of teacher can be placed in a unit with that kind of teacher. Whether a student works well or does not work well with a particular teacher should be considered in placement.
- Sibling position is another factor to be considered. The unit is a family. Is it better that a student be the youngest in the "family," in the middle, or the oldest?
- A balance of boys and girls and ethnic groups should be achieved.

The delightful thing about the multiunit school is that students and parents can have a voice in the assignment process. In a traditional school, parents try to get their children into Mrs. X's class or to keep them out of Mr. Y's class. Students are assigned classrooms by the principal, and sometimes the wishes of vocal parents are honored. But usually student assignments are based on administrative efficiency—not the personal characteristics of the students and teachers. In the multiunit school the individual learning differences in students can be considered. Is it better that Joey be the youngest student in the unit since he is the oldest child in his family? Will Judy and Pam learn better together or apart? At a year-end parent conference, if either the parent or teacher believes that Albert will perform better with a male teacher, he can be placed in Mr. E's homeroom. There are many possibilities in the multiunit school. Involvement in the assignment process makes parents more supportive and committed to the school program. This strategy also works well in building balanced advisory groups in middle schools and high schools.

Assigning Teachers to Units

In multiunit schools teachers are assigned to units in many ways. Ideally, instructional units should be formed by looking first at the learners and then assigning teachers to the units to meet the learners' needs (Bechtol, 1976).

The goal of unit staff selection is to build an instructional team that has the greatest potential for implementing and planning an individualized program. This team is charged with the total educational experience and the instructional process of the students assigned to the unit. The unit leader must lead this small problem-solving, decision-making society.

The first decision when a school restructures to provide for individual students is to determine who on the staff will stay and who will leave. It is best if a school can adopt the multiunit structure with total staff consensus. But teachers who are unwilling to participate in a unit should be allowed to transfer to other schools.

The second decision is the selection of the unit leaders, which is the responsibility of the principal. The unit leader should (1) be a master teacher with excellent skills; (2) have leadership capabilities and be willing to accept extra responsibilities; (3) command the respect of students, parents, and other staff members; (4) believe in individualized instruction; and (5) want the job. It is suggested that the principal develop a job description for unit leaders and that formal applications be requested. Even though a teacher fits the formal criteria for the job, the principal should consider the informal criteria. Is the teacher acceptable to the staff, skilled enough in group dynamics to keep the unit on target, and able to follow through on tasks? (Bechtol, 1976).

Once unit leaders are selected, the IIC should meet to make preliminary assignments to units. These assignments are preliminary because all teachers should be consulted to see if the assignments are suitable. If not, some shifting may be necessary.

Since the students in each unit range in age, achievements, and styles of learning, teachers assigned to each unit should have diverse talents, interests, and skills.

Unit teams should be deliberately organized to provide learning alternatives for students. One possibility is to ensure that each team has teachers who have the qualities necessary to (1) provide a very structured learning environment to serve those students who function best in directed activities, (2) provide a flexible environment in which students can make many choices, and (3) provide a warm environment in which each student feels needed and appreciated. This structure provides better instruction for the different learning styles of students in the unit.

Teachers are selected for unit teams because of their particular strengths. Perhaps the least desirable way to organize a unit team is to put a grade or two grades together and select the teachers of those grades to become the unit staff.

Team Teaching

If restructured schooling is truly going to affect the lives of boys and girls, it cannot be a one-teacher, self-contained program. Successful instructional programs require cooperation among teachers within the unit and among the units in the school. Team teaching is an accepted organizational structure in the multiunit school.

Teaming is not new. In good schools, good teachers have always worked together. Good teachers want their students to succeed so it's natural to seek help from colleagues. It's also natural for teachers to help their colleagues succeed. Team teaching is a logical plan for instructional organization. It gives teachers a structure within which to share ideas, to learn from others, and to plan together.

Team teaching is a formal type of cooperative staff organization in which a team of teachers accepts the responsibility for planning, carrying out, and evaluating an educational program, or some major portion of a program, for a group of students.

Perhaps that definition is too formal. Somehow successful teaching occurs when "my" students become "our" students. Mr. Leigh said he used to teach "Mrs. Miller's students" social studies while she taught "his" students language arts. That's not teaming; it's trading. Mrs. Miller and Mr. Leigh were not checking what each other taught. There was no shared planning or evaluating.

Here is another example of a school program where teaming does not exist. A visitor was standing in the hall of an elementary school. A small boy was yelling and running down the hall; he zoomed past the teacher and the visitor. The teacher smiled and said, "He's not one of my students." The visitor knew that he was not in a team-teaching school.

In a good team-teaching school, teachers see all students as "their" students. The student who was yelling and running down the hall would be corrected. Appropriate student behavior would be praised. For example, Coppock Elementary School a teacher might explain, "You're darned right he's a good kid. He's a Coppock kid!"

There are many advantages to team teaching. These include (1) increased opportunities to individualize instruction; (2) better preparation and better instruction; (3) greater flexibility in grouping, scheduling, and use of space; (4) broader acceptance of student diversity; and (5) greater opportunity for staff development (Bechtol, 1973). Good team planning can provide for student diversities; team teachers are able to solve tough instructional problems.

The biggest advantage of team teaching is the way teachers teach in a team setting. A thoughtful quotation describes what happens to teachers as they team. The saying is "Family synergism produces serendipity." *Family* means that the team members become a family that support each other as they work together. *Synergism* means that one teacher plus one teacher plus one teacher equals more than three teachers. Working together has a synergistic effect, which results in professional accomplishments that are greater than any of them could achieve alone. *Serendipity* means that the team will discover creative exciting ways to achieve team goals. In the model schools we observed functional teams that supported each other as they selected creative strategies to help at-risk students achieve. Their family synergism produces desirable results in unexpected ways.

If there are all these advantages, why are schools primarily organized into self-contained classrooms or departmental programs? Teaming is time consuming, teaming is not easy; it is difficult to establish effective teaching teams. Team teaching has been compared to an arranged marriage. Keeping a marriage going in our society has been difficult even when there has been a long courtship period and when one selects one's own partner. Consider the problem that occurs when someone else selects your partner (or partners). That is how much of teaming happens—a new teacher is guided by the principal to three other teachers who are seated together at a table. The principal says, "Mrs. Jones, I'd like you to meet the other members of the unit team." It's an arranged marriage! But as our friends from India explain, "Our arranged marriages work quite well."

All of the model schools described in Chapter 4 used team-teaching strategies. At Diamond Middle School four teachers from different disciplines—language arts, social studies, mathematics, and science—have worked hard to make their interdisciplinary teams work. There is a strategy for developing team-teaching skills. This strategy and the activities to achieve it are presented in Chapter 10.

Teaming is a key concept. Restructuring cannot occur unless teachers and administrators work together.

Roles in the Multiunit School

The Principal's Role

As the principal goes, so goes the school. Good individualized schools have good principals. Principals are never neutral; they either make a school program better or they make it worse.

If principals assume that their role is that of a benevolent dictator, the organization of the restructured school may not be for them. The multiunit school organization assumes shared decision making; it assumes a democratic administration. Making the change from authoritarian to democratic leadership is not easy for many principals. But in good schools this change has occurred.

The principal of a multiunit school is a highly involved educational leader. The principal (1) facilitates the staff members' roles in implementing, maintaining, and refining individualized instructional programs; (2) serves as a catalyst for change; (3) is a resource to each unit, to the students, and to the community; and (4) observes and evaluates the staff, the instructional program, and the students.

There is no standard individualized school principal. Each principal must follow his or her unique leadership style. For example, Mrs. M. is a supporter of students and teachers. This principal spends her lunch hour hugging students. Each noon students stand in line to hug Mrs. M. and to share with her how their day is going. During school and before and after school, Mrs. M. works with teachers individually and with unit teams. She supports, encourages, and facilitates the teachers as they work to meet the diverse needs of the students in the building.

Mr. N. is a principal in a school whose students live mainly in a low-cost housing development. He supports his teachers by giving them extra time for planning and by being very visible to the students and to the community. Mr. N. takes most of the bus, playground, and lunchroom duties so that teachers have extra time for preparation and for working with individual students. He makes frequent home visits to make certain that students attend regularly and do their assignments. He visits parents to encourage them to participate in the school program. Visitors to this school are surprised at the high achievement scores and the fact that this school has the highest percentage of parent participation in a large school district.

Mr. C. and Mrs. R. are principals who encourage student learning by emphasizing a skill area. Mr. C. emphasizes reading. he has a small rocking chair placed on a red carpet in his office. Students are given the "red carpet" treatment. They select a reading passage and read it to Mr. C. He rewards them with juice, a cookie, or a sticker. When visitors are in the building, the rocking chair and red carpet are moved to the hall so that the visitors can join the group.

Mrs. R. emphasizes writing. She evaluates and marks the writing sample of every student in the building each semester. Improved papers are posted. Creative students are recognized. Skill areas such as spelling, sentence structure, or use of adjectives can be emphasized by posting outstanding papers. One can understand why reading and writing achievement are high in these schools.

There are no standard principal styles. All the principals in the multiunit schools we visited were effective. Each used different strategies to accomplish school goals and to support teachers and staff. While the means to achieve goals and to provide support are different, there are responsibilities that principals in individualized schools must accomplish.

The principal in the multiunit school organizes and chairs the IIC, arranges for its meetings, and develops the agenda. The principal is responsible for seeing that decisions of the IIC are communicated clearly and are carried out.

Team teaching affects the principal's role. The principal should attend unit meetings on a regular basis. The principal's attendance should be frequent enough so that problems can be caught in the early stages, but not so frequent that a dependency relationship develops. The principal must support the unit teachers as decision makers. All of the teachers are developing new roles for themselves, and in this time of change they depend on the principal for moral, emotional, administrative, and intellectual support.

The most effective way principals in the restructured schools communicate and support their values is by attention. DuFour (1990) states that attention is all there is. What principals pay attention to—and what they don't—is probably the single most powerful communication of what they value. Effective principals must answer five questions about their leadership behavior.

1. What do I plan for? Is this planning concentrating on the factors that are most critical in advancing the school toward its vision?
2. What do I monitor? Principals who devote considerable time and attention to the continual assessment of a particular condition within the school send a message that the condition is important.
3. What do I model? Is there congruency between my stated values and my behavior?
4. What do I reinforce by recognition and celebration? A powerful way to communicate values is to celebrate success.
5. What behaviors am I willing to confront? Principals who are not willing to confront behavior that is contrary to the values they espouse will quickly lose credibility.

Effective principals are willing to place upholding the values of the school before the desire for popularity. One multiunit principal explained, "I use these five questions to evaluate myself and my leadership. Answering these questions makes me aware of what I'm giving attention and if it fits with my vision for the school."

The vast responsibilities cited only emphasize that the principal, more than anyone else in the school, has the responsibility for seeing that a successful restructured instructional program is achieved.

The Unit Leader's Role

The unit leader in the multiunit school is a fairly new role in education. The role has many names. In this book, we have labeled it unit leader from the IGE concept (Klausmeier et al., 1971). In some individualized programs the unit leader is called learning community coordinator, team leader, department chair, house leader, and so on. Regardless of the title, the unit leader has a key role in the success of a restructured instructional program.

Unit leaders have three major responsibilities: they are the leaders of the unit staffs of students and adults, members of the IIC, and teachers of children. Within the unit, the unit leaders provide leadership for developing, executing, and evaluating the restructured instruction program; they coordinate the assessment program and the placement of students in appropriate learning activities; and they assume leadership in initiating, establishing, and maintaining good home–school–community relations. The unit leader organizes the unit staff, arranges for and chairs its meetings, and develops the agenda for the meeting with input from the unit staff.

As a member of the IIC, the unit leader contributes to the planning and development of the instructional program at the building level and serves as a liaison among the unit staff, the principal, and the other units.

In most schools, unit leaders teach approximately three-fourths of the time. In this role, they are master teachers who are willing to demonstrate new techniques for their unit staff and execute high-quality lessons with children. The unit leader is a model for unit staff who is capable of learning to build bridges between theory and practice and of explaining how research results in curriculum, psychology, and philosophy can be adapted to improve children's learning in the classroom.

One unit leader with ten years of teaching experience summed it up like this: "After eight years of teaching third grade in the same room with the same four walls, I was becoming bored and burned out. Then I was offered the unit leader position. This gave me the chance to break out of my mold to lead adults to plan and carry out a creative and meaningful instructional program for kids ages 6 to 9. I also represent the unit staff at the IIC and helped develop a more effective home–school–community program. I've had all of these new opportunities and still taught children — my first love — about 70 percent of the time. And I received a small amount of extra money for the position, too. Being a unit leader gave me new challenges and I stayed in teaching at the same time. This position is a great professional opportunity for classroom teachers."

Another unit leader explained, "What has proven to me to be most interesting is my change in perception. For the first time in my career I can see the Big Picture of the school. I can see the goals we need to reach and the actions we teachers must take to achieve these goals. I also realize that teachers working in isolation in their classrooms are too busy to see this Big Picture. My goal as a leader is to help my fellow teachers look outside their classrooms and develop a more global picture of schooling."

Personal qualities necessary for the unit leader include commitment, positive perception of self, positive perception of others, openness, facilitator of change, self-renewal, charisma, and flexibility (Sorenson, Pooler, & Joyal, 1976).

Professionally, unit leaders must be teachers who are master teachers, have leadership skills, and are willing to spend increased time and energy on professional activities. Specifically, qualifications include certification as a teacher; three or more years of successful teaching experience; master's degree or progress toward one; graduate education in human learning and development, curriculum, and instruction; commitment to a career in teaching; positive attitudes toward curriculum improvement, development, and teacher education; flexibility and inventiveness in the adaptation of methods, materials, and procedures; ability to recognize and utilize capabilities of the unit personnel; and ability to maintain effective interaction with all personnel in the unit — children and parents, principal, central office personnel, special teachers and coordinators, regional education agency, and university representatives (Sorenson et al., 1976; Klausmeier et al., 1971).

In opposition to the competitive career ladder plans, the role of the unit leader is a much more natural position for the mature teacher. Once teachers have acquired instructional expertise, they are ready to accept the challenges of out-of-class roles. The unit leader position allows mature teachers to contribute to the growth of their colleagues. It empowers them to participate in a broad range of decisions at the school level (Leithwood, 1990). Helping others and contributing to school-level decisions more appropriately reflect the promotion and advancement vision of professional teachers. The career ladder does not.

The Unit Teacher's Role

The unit teacher's role is different from that of the self-contained teacher or the teacher in a departmentalized program. Unit teachers are members of the unit team, which cooperatively plans for and teaches a larger number of students than in a self-contained setting and more subject disciplines than in a departmentalized setting. This broader involvement tends to result in more professional levels of teaching.

Because unit teachers are involved with all the relevant functions of the school program, unit teachers usually find their new roles rewarding and stimulating. One teacher, who chose to work on a unit team her last two years before retiring, said, "I wanted to make my last two years my best ones.

Now I don't want to quit. I wish that individualizing had been available earlier in my career."

For beginning teachers, the unit concept provides an appropriate structure for entering the teaching profession. One teacher describes his first year of teaching in a multiunit school as follows: "I was twenty-two and a bit scared about moving to a new city to teach. My introduction to my teaching colleagues came at a summer barbecue in the unit leader's backyard. I met the teachers that I'd be working with and their spouses. It occurred to me that I was surrounded by a bunch of positive people who wanted me to succeed. My first year was hard work learning the kids and the curriculum. But there was always someone there to help me if I had trouble. I never had the sink-or-swim hell that my university friends described during their first year."

The multiunit school provides an organization that helps teachers to enter the profession, to develop professional expertise, and to become teacher leaders.

A Restructured School Program

What would a school look like if we rethought all the givens about how schools should be organized and run? What if students were treated as individuals and taught by a unit team?

Holweide Comprehensive School in Cologne, Germany, is an example of such a place. It is a model program, which started as an experiment and has been operating for over fifteen years (Shanker, 1990; Ratski, 1988).

Holweide's student body (the equivalent of U.S. grades 5 through 11) has a diversity that is rare in Europe. The students include children of Turks, Moroccans, and other foreign workers as well as many native German children from poor or single-parent families. Unlike most German schools in which children are tracked according to perceived ability, Holweide has a mixture of students with few identified as college material (Shanker, 1990).

What makes Holweide different is its structure. Teachers work in teams of six or eight. Each team is assigned the same number of students they would ordinarily teach—about 120. This arrangement does not last for just one year but for the full six years that the students are in school (Shanker, 1990).

The team of teachers decides how to group the students; how the school day will be organized; which teachers will teach science, math, history, and so forth; how much time will be allotted to each subject; and what materials will be used. No one is locked into a schedule for the whole year because the system allows for readjustments according to the needs of the students and the teachers (Shanker, 1990).

This structure provides for genuine accountability. Since each teaching team has the same students for six years, no one can blame a student's deficiencies in reading or math on last year's teacher. No one can pass time with a problem student until that student is moved on to the next grade. On the one hand, teachers have to confront difficulties and live with the consequences of their decisions. On the other hand, because they are part of the unit team, they never have to face these challenges alone (Shanker, 1990).

The system has the practical effect of vastly increasing instructional time without adding hours or days to the school year. In many schools much time is lost in beginning- and end-of-the-school-year rituals. In the fall it takes many teachers weeks to know the names of their students. Much time and student learning is lost with the job of ending the school year because record keeping, promotions, retentions, and articulation are very time consuming. In Holweide, teachers have the same students from year to year; therefore, they don't have to finish with this batch in June and get ready to start a new group in the fall. These teachers know their students' individual differences; they know their strengths, weaknesses, interests, and learning styles. Instructional time is not wasted.

The structure allows students to actively engage in their own education. Pupils of mixed ability sit at tables in cooperative groups of five or six. They work together on problems, helping and taking responsibility for one another. This peer influence promotes learning. The terrible discipline problems that plague urban schools disappear. The students' affinity for peer groups becomes an asset, not a liability (Shanker, 1990).

The results at Holweide are impressive. Most students enter the school already diagnosed as lacking academic potential. Despite this, a disproportionately large number end up going to universities, which, in Germany, means passing a national examination that requires a high level of scholastic achievement (Shanker, 1990).

Is the Holweide model one that can be considered for the diverse student populations currently found in U.S. schools? We believe it is. The results are impressive. Holweide illustrates what can happen when the multiunit model is implemented. The teachers in the unit team were empowered to make instructional decisions for students over a much longer period of time. These teachers collaborated and designed strategies that provided students with maximum learning opportunities. The unit team had a clear vision of what they wanted to achieve. Their expectations were high and their students lived up to these expectations.

The student population at Holweide is similar to what is found in the multicultural classrooms in California, in Texas, and throughout the United States. Their positive results illustrate what can happen when the assumptions behind the graded, calendar-driven model are overturned and an individualized program is implemented. U.S. schools can be restructured to provide for students' individual differences.

Summary

In this chapter the multiunit school was described as a generic model for school organization. This model was selected because it uses some of the important findings from the research from effective schools studies and from school-based management. It was also selected because organizational components are flexible. School staffs can use these strategies as they restructure their school programs to accommodate the differences in learning styles, aptitudes, and abilities that they find in their students. It is a structure that empowers teachers and provides opportunities for career advancement.

The components of the multiunit school were described. These included the IIC and the Instructional Unit. The options and choices for assigning students to units were explained. The importance of team teaching in the restructured school was described. Finally, the professional roles in the multiunit school were illustrated.

The organizational components for restructuring a school that provides for students' individual differences include the following:

1. Clear educational goals and a vision to achieve them
2. An open communication system
3. Shared decision making (teacher empowerment)
4. Flexibility
   a. To match students with appropriate materials
   b. To permit students to work together
   c. To allow teachers to work together
5. Teacher leadership positions
6. A principal who is an instructional leader and also a coordinator of teachers who are instructional leaders

In the next chapter, eight model schools are described. The schools are different. However, they have some commonalities: All restructured their instructional programs to provide for their individual student needs and all implemented the organizational components listed above.

A caveat: Each of the model schools was small (fewer than 600 students) so that the principal and teacher leaders could know all the students and their parents. Each school had three or more age/grade levels so that student leadership could be developed. We believe that this size and age range are also organizational components to be considered during restructuring.

References

Bechtol, W. (1976). Guiding the I & R unit. In J. Sorenson, M. Poole, & L. Joyal (Eds.), *The unit leader and individually guided education* (pp. 91–123). Reading, MA: Addison-Wesley.

Bechtol, W. (1973). *Individualizing instruction and keeping your sanity.* Chicago: Follett.

Boyer, E. (1988). *Report on school reform: The teachers speak.* New York: Carnegie Foundation for the Advancement of Teaching.

Camealy, L. (1988). Interview. Association for Individually Guided Education National Conference, Columbus, Ohio.

Cawelti, G. (1989). Key elements of site-based management. *Educational Leadership,* 46(8): 46.

Cohen, M. (1988). *Restructuring the education system: Agenda for the 1990s.* Washington, DC: National Governors' Association.

David, J. (1989). Synthesis of research on school-based management. *Educational Leadership,* 46(8): 45–53.

DuFour, R. (1990). *How effective instructional leaders get results.* Preconference Institute, Annual Conference of the Association for Supervision and Curriculum Development, San Antonio, Texas.

Glickman, C. (1989). Has Sam and Samantha's time come at last? *Educational Leadership,* 46(8): 4–9.

Harrison, C., Killion, J., & Mitchell, J. (1989). Site-based management: The realities of implementation. *Educational Leadership,* 46(8): 55–58.

Klausmeier, H., Quilling, M., Sorenson, J., Way, R., & Glasrud, G. (1971). *Individually guided education and the multiunit elementary school.* Madison: Wisconsin Research and Development Center for Cognitive Learning.

Klausmeier, H., Morrow, R., & Walter, J. (1968). *Individually guided education in the multiunit elementary school.* Madison: Wisconsin Research and Development Center for Cognitive Learning.

Leithwood, K. (1990). The principal's role in teacher development. In B. Joyce (Ed.). *Changing school culture through staff development.* (pp. 71–90). Alexandria, VA: Association for Supervision and Curriculum Development.

Lewis, A. (1986). The search continues for effective schools. *Phi Delta Kappan,* 68(3): 187–188.

McDermott, G. (1989). Interview. Association for Individually Guided Education National Conference, Madison, Wisconsin.

Meier, D. (1987). Success in East Harlem: How one group of teachers built a school that works. *American Education,* Fall: 36–39.

Ratski, A. (1988). The remarkable impact of creating a school community: One model of how it can be done, an interview. *American Education,* Spring: 10–17, 38–43.

Ross, R. (1990). School cabinet: Shared decision making plus. International Conference of the Association of Individually Guided Education, Cambridge, Massachusetts.

Roy, P. (1989). The journey toward becoming a staff developer. *Journal of Staff Development,* 10(3): 28–32.

Shanker, A. (1990). The end of the traditional model of schooling—and a proposal for using incentives to restructure our public schools. *Phi Delta Kappan,* 71(5): 344–357.

Slavin, R. (1988). Synthesis of research on grouping in elementary and secondary schools. *Educational Leadership,* 46(1): 67–77.

Sorenson, J., Poole, M., & Joyal, L. (1976). *The unit leader and individually guided education.* Reading, MA: Addison-Wesley.

Working together. (1974). A sound filmstrip. Dayton, OH: Institute for the Development of Educational Activities.

CHAPTER FOUR

Model Schools in Action

For many of our kids, school is the best part of their day. We feed them breakfast and lunch and treat them with respect.

The beauty and the promise of restructuring is that teachers, principals, parents, and community leaders have an opportunity to create school programs that have never existed before. Effective strategies are available to restructure schooling so that students can exit as competent, confident, and responsible citizens. There are many choices of organizational and instructional strategies for restructuring schools. What impressed us was the vast potential of teachers and principals to design schools that work.

In this chapter, eight model schools are described. In a Public Broadcasting System (PBS) special about schools that worked, the five qualities that made these schools successful were described (*Learning in America,* 1990). These qualities of good schools are as follows:

First, at each school was an embedded commitment to the cause of public education and its worth in a democracy.

Second, there was a collegiality among teachers. In most schools across the country teachers tend to teach in isolation. This was not the case of the schools featured on the broadcast.

Third, the schools were relatively independent from their local school districts, and the principals shared with the teachers much of their own authority and responsibility.

Fourth, the principals regarded mothers and fathers as crucial to the success of their schools.

Fifth, there was a commitment to children—to their importance, to their self-esteem, and to their capacity for learning.

We could not have said it better. The schools we visited (one was featured in *Learning in America*) valued and demonstrated these five qualities. There was a camaraderie among the teachers, a caring sharing principal, a commitment to quality education, some independence from the bureaucracy, an involvement of parents, and a belief in children.

There was not a standard pattern for restructuring in the schools. Yes, we found some nongraded–continuous-progress programs, we found multi-aged grouping, and we found team teaching. But we also found a number of surprises. Successful schools don't work because they follow a prescriptive program; they work because they follow the professional judgment of their teachers and principals (Glickman, 1991). These professional decisions have resulted in quality programs for their students. We chose to visit these eight restructured schools because they got results and had received state and national recognition. Our visits were exciting, positive, and fun.

The schools that we visited represent the diversity that exists in U.S. schooling today. We visited schools in wealthy suburbs, in small towns, in inner-city settings, and in transient neighborhoods. We visited schools in safe neighborhoods and in urban neighborhoods laced with crime, drugs, and gangs. The students were wealthy, middle class, poor, gifted, at risk, white, black, Hispanic, Native American, Asian, happy, hungry, abused, motivated, and listless.

For each school we have described the organization, its instructional programs, and its concerns for students. In each description we tried to provide a personal glimpse of the school in action. What struck us as we visited these schools and talked with principals, teachers, students, and parents are the many varied possibilities for restructuring to provide quality educational programs for students.

Nongrading–Continuous-Progress Schooling
Lake George Elementary School, Lake George, New York

Lake George Elementary is located in a resort community in the eastern Adirondack Mountains. About halfway between Montreal and New York City, the Lake George community combines the quiet beauty of mountains and lakes with easy accessibility to metropolitan centers. Lake George Elementary School is an example of a nongraded–continuous-progress instructional program. The school was a recipient of the Excellence in Education Award in 1986.

The goal of the Lake George Elementary School is to provide an environment that will allow students to become successful learners, to enjoy learning, and to develop abilities in making responsible decisions. The school is organized in family clusters of students aged 6 to 13. This structure is based on the premise that students learn most successfully by working at their own levels of ability. Students move through the curriculum without regard to age or grade-level barriers. Students do not compete and are not compared with other students. They do compete and are compared with their own measured abilities and achievements.

Assessment is an important part of the instructional process. Instruction is based on a carefully sequenced curriculum in the basic skills of reading, mathematics, and spelling. Students progress through these curriculum sequences by mastering skills and concepts. Students do not receive letter grades. Written reports to parents state the reading, mathematics, and spelling levels at which the student is working.

Principal Bob Ross (1990) explained that when parents ask how their child is doing he almost always says, "Terrific! For the level he is working on."

"We've eliminated the pecking order in the school by eliminating grades and other student competition," he continued (Ross, 1990).

The 600 students in Lake George Elementary are organized into four major teams. The Orange Cluster includes the Kindergarten students and five teachers. The Green, Yellow, and Red clusters include students who are ages 6 to 13. Each cluster has seven teachers. A diagram of the building shows this organization (Figure 4-1). The structure facilitates teachers teaching in a child-centered way). Team teaching and multiaged grouping are natural outcomes of this nongraded–continuous-progress structure.

"In reality, our concept of family grouping has divided the school into small schools. It makes learning more personal and positive," explained Principal Ross (1990).

Decisions at Lake George are shared by teachers and administrators. Teachers are empowered to make decisions and to set priorities by the Educational Cabinet. This decision-making organization consists of a representative (the team coordinator) from each cluster and two individuals representing the specialists. The elementary principal chairs the Cabinet. Decisions by the Cabinet are made in relation to how they affect the students. Decisions may be made by consensus or by voting. The principal will make any decision the Cabinet wants him to make or share any decision they want him to share. Everyone is accountable for Cabinet decisions (Ross, 1990).

Ross (1990) reports that better decisions are made and that there is stronger commitment and ownership in the decisions. He believes that this decision-making process is a more productive and creative way to share skills and talents of teachers, to solve problems, and to create change.

Does it work? Test scores and parent reactions are positive. Ninety-nine percent of the parents think the school is great, and 99 percent participated in parent conferences (Ross, 1990).

FIGURE 4-1 · *Lake George Elementary School, 1991–1992*

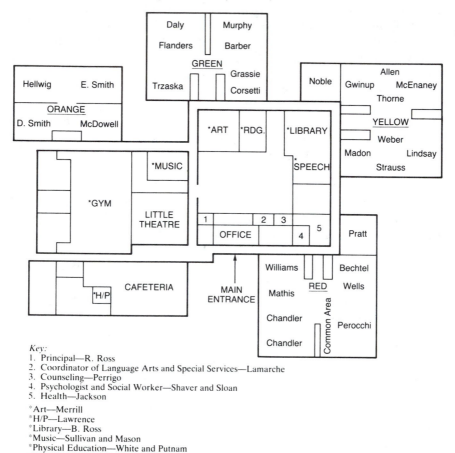

Key:
1. Principal—R. Ross
2. Coordinator of Language Arts and Special Services—Lamarche
3. Counseling—Perrigo
4. Psychologist and Social Worker—Shaver and Sloan
5. Health—Jackson

*Art—Merrill
*H/P—Lawrence
*Library—B. Ross
*Music—Sullivan and Mason
*Physical Education—White and Putnam
*Reading—Simms, Hussa, and Kearns
*Speech—McPhillips and Sandy
*Resource Room—Farrell and Sager

Source: Used with permission of Robert J. Ross.

One parent stated, "I like the fact that children progress at their own pace. Each year I feel stronger and more comfortable with the school system. I have a kindergartner starting in the fall and I'm excited and optimistic that her experience will be as good as my son's" (*Lake George Elementary School Newsletter,* 1989).

Posted on a bulletin board in the Yellow Cluster was this composition that was written by two students.

We are reading and writing about friendship. We like studying about friends because friends are important and special to us. Friends make you feel better when you are sad. Friends are what you need when you are lonely. Friends are to have fun and to help each other.
— *Arikida and Jessica, both age 7*

What we saw at Lake George was a school that had been restructured into family clusters so that friendships like Arikida's and Jessica's developed naturally. The concepts of nongraded–continuous-progress schooling have been refined in a positive way at Lake George Elementary School.

Using Gifted Strategies for All Students
Meredith Elementary School, Temple, Texas

Meridith Elementary School provides a content-rich and an experience-rich instructional program for its third-, fourth-, and fifth-graders. When fifth-graders were ready to read Robert Louis Stevenson's *Treasure Island,* a classroom was transformed into the deck of a pirate ship, complete with broken barrels, skull and crossbones, and gold nuggets (Bennett, 1988). Whether the book is *Charlotte's Web, Robin Hood,* or *The Secret Garden,* the teachers at the school bring an enthusiasm to their classrooms that make children savor the experience of reading good literature. "They teach children to love good books," explains Principal Bonnie Martin.

But much more than reading good books happens at Meridith. A child's school year is filled with exciting, meaningful learning activities such as Super Science Spree, operettas and schoolwide musicals, a mathematics teacher dressed as a Chinese character to introduce tangrams, a mentoring program for at-risk students, and a Fit-a-Rama physical education activity. It's not an accident that Meridith was featured as one of the top seven schools in the United States in the thoughtful book, *James Madison Elementary School: A Curriculum for American Students* (Bennett, 1988) and that Principal Martin was the recipient of the Distinguished Leadership in Science Education Elementary Principals Award for Texas.

Columnist Jeff Whitmill (1988) wrote, "I lived in Temple, Texas, for five years. My daughter attended Meridith, and, yes, it is an outstanding school, enormously worthy of emulation: There is indeed a strong emphasis on fundamentals and the success of all students at Meridith. But there is much more. My daughter had music every day, drama and computers twice a week. She was in a choir that rehearsed after school and she took part in full-fledged productions of *Peter Pan* and *Hansel and Gretel.*"

What caused Temple's old black high school, which is bordered on three sides by housing projects and on the fourth by a pasture where cattle often stray, to become an elementary school known for its invigorating curriculum? Meridith has a super principal and an extraordinary faculty: there's fire in their eyes (Whitmill, 1988). "We try to bring education alive for children. We make children excited about learning. This is a go-getter school," explained Principal Martin (Dixon, 1988).

As we entered the school we were greeted by art caricatures of three life-sized smiling students holding a sign that said, "Welcome to Meridith." We visited in October. Children's Halloween artwork, pumpkins, and orange balloons were displayed in the foyer. A paper-mâché giraffe almost ten feet tall greeted us at the entrance to the library. A "Quest for Excellence" banner was displayed over the hallway. The artwork set a positive tone for the building; it seemed to reflect the energy and the enthusiasm of the students and the faculty.

The student population of Meridith includes an interesting group of third-, fourth-, and fifth-graders. Two hundred twenty-five neighborhood children are combined with 150 gifted and talented students and 165 transfer students who attend the school on a voluntary basis. The ethnicity of the students is approximately 50 percent white, 40 percent black, and 10 percent Hispanic. Almost 40 percent qualify for free or reduced-cost lunch.

What makes Meridith special is that the staff uses the strategies designed for gifted and talented students with all kids. All students receive content-rich instruction. Principal Martin explained: "Our strength is the diversity of our kids. They learn from each other and enter middle school much more able to succeed."

The philosophy of Meridith School is the commitment to excellence through the development of lifelong learners who will contribute to society as a result of a quality educational experience. It is the mission of the Meridith professional staff to assist students to acquire knowledge, to develop skills to the maximum of their capacities, and to learn patterns that will make them responsible members of society. Because Meridith is a magnet school, the staff members believe that they have a unique opportunity to help children to understand and to appreciate all ethnic origins (*Meridith Magnet National Exemplary School,* 1990).

The school has twenty-five homeroom classrooms, a gymnasium, an auditorium with a theater stage, and special classes and areas for activities. Each homeroom is heterogeneously grouped and racially balanced. Students remain in their homeroom groups for social studies and for activities; the activities include daily classes in music and physical education and rotating classes in art, computer lab, reading lab, and theater arts. Students are grouped homogeneously for a daily two-hour language arts block and for one-hour blocks in mathematics or science. Homogeneous grouping is derived from a nationally normed test given each spring, district gifted and talented identification guidelines, and teacher recommendations. A copy of the master schedule is shown in Figure 4-2.

Perhaps the best way to envision the Meridith program is to describe a dialogue with Debbie Dannelly, a fifth-grade language arts teacher. A few years ago her students had read *The Secret Garden* and had decided to make a garden in an alcove of the building. Children drew landscape plans and voted on which plan would be best. Now there's a stone marker identifying the student and explaining that the landscape plan was designed by a fifth-grader.

This year Ms. Dannelly's theme for literature was "conflict and adaptation." The students were learning that the hero or heroine in the story would have a conflict and would then adapt to solve the problem. This year a project for handicapped students resulted from reading the core book *Follow the Leader*. This reading led to the discovery of an excerpt from a Television program about a boy who had a debilitating illness. The boy had a good mind, but he was bedridden. An organization supplied the boy a dog who was trained to pull him around. In due time the boy became mobile and was even able to attend school with the dog. The fifth-graders decided to meet after school to collect money for the organization.

"How will you raise the money?" we asked.

"That is up to the kids. I'm just the facilitator," Ms. Dannelly explained.

"Who are the children who will meet tonight?"

"My language arts classes. They're going to decide which committee they will serve on this year."

"How many will be there?" we asked.

"Probably all of them — it's optional. Yes. I believe that all forty-five of them will be there." (And they were.)

The class research projects related directly to the Conflict and Adaptation theme. Ms. Dannelly explained: "The purpose of the research project is to give students an opportunity to apply what they learned to solve conflicts that are happening in the world right now and that we have to face everyday. The students will use what they are learning about adaptation and apply it to their research problems. Children are hypersensitive to problems anyway. My job is to teach them not to be undone by the problem but to help to solve or improve at least parts of the problem. We have a responsibility to help children become problem solvers. I try to teach them that if they are not part of the solution they are part of the problem."

FIGURE 4-2 • Master Schedule, Meridith Elementary School, Temple, Texas

File: MASTER SCHEDULE
Report: MERIDITH ELEMENTARY

GRADE	PERIOD 1	PERIOD 2	PERIOD 3	PERIOD 4	PERIOD 5	PERIOD 6	PERIOD 7	PERIOD 8	PERIOD 9
THIRD	ACTIVITY 1 8:15–8:45	BLOCK 1 8:50–9:50	BLOCK 2 9:50–10:50	LUNCH 11:00–11:30	SOC.STUDIES 11:30–12:05	BLOCK 3 12:05–1:00	BLOCK 4 1:00–2:00	ACTIVITY 2 2:05–2:35	ACTIVITY 3 2:40–3:10
FOURTH	SOCIAL STUDIES 8:00–8:45	ACTIVITY 1 8:50–9:20	BLOCK 1 9:25–10:25	BLOCK 2 10:25–11:25	LUNCH 11:30–12:00	ACTIVITY 2 12:00–12:30	ACTIVITY 3 12:35–1:05	BLOCK 3 1:10–2:10	BLOCK 4 2:10–3:10
FIFTH	SOCIAL STUDIES 8:00–8:45	BLOCK 1 8:45–9:45	ACTIVITY 1 9:45–10:15	ACTIVITY 2 10:20–10:50	BLOCK 2 10:55–11:55	LUNCH 12:00–12:30	BLOCK 3 12:30–1:30	ACTIVITY 3 1:35–2:05	BLOCK 4 2:10–3:10

ACTIVITIES SCHEDULE

3-1 8:15–8:45	5-1 9:45–10:15	5-2 10:20–10:50	PLANNING/ LUNCH 10:50–12:00	4-2 12:00–12:30	4-3 12:35–1:05	5-3 1:35–2:05	3-2 2:05–2:35	3-3 2:40–3:10
4-1 8:50–9:20 *PLANNING								*PLANNING

Source: Used with permission of Bonnie Martin.

Meridith has been recognized for its exceptional science program. During our visit we saw a fifth-grade science classroom set up with twenty-five microscopes with similar slides. Children learn by doing, by being actively involved in hands-on activities. In another science classroom, each student team was placing fruit in a pan of water. They were trying to find out why some fruit floated. The excitement of these children for science was obvious. One mother of a third-grader said "My son has learned more science here in two months than he learned in the first three years of school."

The science year culminates with the annual Super Science Spree. The Super Science Spree replaces the traditional science fair with a week-long celebration of the various disciplines of science. The entire Meridith staff pitches in to make the Super Science Spree succeed. Activities include Adopt-A-Scientist Day, Special Science Assemblies, Can Car Rally (every student makes a car and competes), Mr. Wizard, and a hands-on open house in which every room is decoratred with the favorite science experiments of that class (the children teach the parents). This effort builds a camaraderie between teachers of all disciplines.

A child's year at Meridith is filled with excitement. A schedule of activities follows. Most of these activities will be described in detail in later chapters.

Yearly Events

September	Cookie/T-Shirt Sale
October	Fourth-Grade Operetta—*H.M.S. Pinafore* (Each grade presents an operetta with three casts during the school day; the emphasis is on performance—not on a program for parents.) FIR (Fun in Reading Week)
November	Santa's Secret Shop (Students receive coupons in Physical Education for participation, dress, and sportsmanship; they can use these coupons to buy gifts for others. It's a great strategy for poor kids)
December	Fifth-Grade Operetta—*Amahl and the Night Visitors*
January	FIR (Fun in Reading Reading Olympics (This is a week filled with both schoolwide and classroom activities to promote excellence in reading.)
February	Barbecue Supper
March	Texas Public School Week Schoolwide Spring Musical—*Annie* (All students are eligible to audition for parts in the musical. In the

	past, students have presented such shows as *Peter Pan, Oliver, The Wizard of Oz,* and *Tom Sawyer.*)
April	Super Science Spree FIR (Fun in Reading)
May	Choir Concert Third-Grade Operetta—*Hansel and Gretel*

The faculty members at Meridith display what an active learning community should be like. The assistant principal proclaimed: "We energize each other. We all feel a part of what is going on here. We support each other. We get high on each other." Everyone in the school has two jobs: teaching and extracurricular activities. Both roles provide opportunities for teachers to help children succeed. It certainly was working during our visits. Both students and teachers were excited about what was going on at Meridith.

The achievement of the students at Meridith is impressive. The school first received recognition because the students scored consistently in the top 5 percent of the state in the Texas tests in reading, writing, and mathematics. In this criterion-referenced test 98 percent of the fifth-graders mastered mathematics, 96 percent mastered reading, and 93 percent mastered writing.

On the Metropolitan Achievement Test the students scored consistently above the students in other Temple schools and in the United States. Table 4-1 shows Meridith grade equivalent and percentile scores. The Meridith fifth-graders scored one grade higher than the other fifth-graders in the district. For example, the reading scores were 6.4 for the district and 7.3 for Meridith; the mathematics scores were 6.9 for the district and 8.7 for Meridith.

The student achievement increased each year at Meridith. Consequently, fewer students qualified for required special services in middle school. More qualified for Gifted and Talented programs. These results were opposite the

TABLE 4-1 · *Grade Equivalent (G.E.) and Percentile (Per) Scores of Grade Means, 1990 Metropolitan Achievement Test Results, Meridith Elementary School, Temple, Texas*

	Grade 3		Grade 4		Grade 5	
Mean Scores	*G.E.*	*Per*	*G.E.*	*Per*	*G.E.*	*Per*
Reading	5.1	69	6.6	74	7.3	72
Mathematics	4.9	75	7.4	87	8.7	84
Language	5.6	75	7.0	79	8.4	81
Science	5.0	75	6.8	79	8.5	80
Social studies	5.1	75	6.9	80	8.0	77
Total battery	5.1	75	7.2	83	8.2	81

findings in many Texas schools in which fifth-grade achievement scores declined. It demonstrated how a school that is structured to provide a content-rich, experience-rich program can make a difference in student achievement.

Family-like Classrooms
Montview Elementary School, Aurora, Colorado

Tiffany and Sandra Gash recited the same story: "Today we read about a dragon and a knight who didn't want to fight; it was a neat story." So did Charles and Willie Plentywolf, Chris and Derrius Mack, and Stephanie and Jonathan Barrett. These siblings did not share this reading at home the way many brothers and sisters would. They instead read it in Ms. Cheryl Lico's classroom of Montview Elementary School where children from the same families in kindergarten through second grade attend class together (Hernandez, 1990).

"It's worked," said Ms. Lico. "This year for the first time in my eight years of teaching there was 100 percent turnout for parent–teacher conferences. I've never had this happen before" (Schluter, 1990).

The aim of the program was to improve the bonds between families and teachers, and to decrease the mobility of a transient population. The results have been productive. Students are allowed to learn at their own pace. Elycia Schinsky said that her kindergarten daughter, Heather, is writing and using punctuation and her second-grade son said, "Mom, some of the second-graders are reading better than I am. I'd better get on the ball" (Hernandez, 1990).

Another mother, Donna Trowbridge, who has three children in the class, said that she has seen improvements in reading, math, and overall confidence. She explained: "You know how you hear kids say they did nothing in school when you ask them. From my kids I never hear 'nothing'" (Hernandez, 1990).

Montview Elementary School has 538 kindergarten through fifth-grade students. The ethnic make-up is 50 percent black, 40 percent white, and 10 percent other (mainly Cambodians). It's a highly transient population – 120 percent mobility. Principal Debbie Backus explained: "Many of our students are at risk. These students need a strong base – one teacher to communicate with. So do their parents. That's why we restructured to make family-like classrooms. We wanted to make our school so good that families wouldn't want to move."

Montview's classrooms are organized in many multiaged combinations: K–2, 2–3, 3–4, 3–5, and 4–5.

The goals of this multiaged organization are

1. To provide a wider range of curriculum and more accurate placement for children, which will ensure increased academic success
2. To provide a natural social setting for positive student interaction
3. To increase parents' knowledge of how children learn so they may more actively participate in their children's schooling
4. To create a school atmosphere that decreases a family's feeling of isolation and encourages bonding between parent, teacher, and child
5. To support the community by decreasing the mobility of the school population

Montview School is in a changing neighborhood. It is a neighborhood in which families are transient, often moving at the first of the month when the rent is due. It is a neighborhood that has caused school personnel to be concerned with the safety of children. The doors to the building are kept locked and the playground is carefully supervised. The faculty at Montview has worked carefully to design an instructional program to help these neighborhood children succeed and to keep their families from moving so frequently.

"What we have done," explained Principal Backus, "is to envision what would work with our kids and then put this program in place. The multiaged classroom provides a kind of stability for both children and parents. Our diagnostic-prescriptive curriculum sequences allow these children to be successful on grade level."

At-risk students have strengths that need to be identified as well as gaps in their education. When a student enrolls at Montview, the faculty quickly diagnoses what this student knows in language arts and mathematics and the student's learning potential. "Street kids are smart with money," explained Lana Enlow, an Instructional Resource Teacher (IRT) for grades 3 through 5, "but they need special help to succeed with fractions and reading comprehension. That's what our school is designed to do."

At the K–2 level, Helen Pugel, a PAS (Program for Assessment and Support) teacher, works in the classroom tutoring the new student, coaching the classroom teacher, or teaching the class to free the classroom teacher to provide special help for individual students. The 1st teacher has the same role with third-, fourth-, and fifth-grade students.

This team helps students to achieve at grade level or to be accelerated. "We want these kids to be successful, so we provide extra help for them," explained Kay Shaw, a District Staff Development Director. "What we do not want to do is label the student Chapter One or Special Education just because he has moved a lot. We found that once they are labeled, they are labeled for life. If possible, we try to accelerate the students. Acceleration keeps them motivated and interested in school."

The idea of an Accelerated School is to bring disadvantaged students to grade-level performance by the end of elementary school (Barton, 1988). At Montview it is working. At the end of the 1989–90 school year 85 percent of the fifth-graders were on or above grade level. "One of the exciting things is that fewer fourth- or fifth-graders qualify for Chapter 1. They are testing too high to remain in that program," said Principal Backus.

The classrooms at Montview are "dripping with print." In a K–2 room, children's work was displayed: experience stories, songs, processes, and sentences such as "This is a table," and "This is the north wall." The daily schedule was written on the chalkboard. It read:

Opening
Poem of the Day
Old Favorite
Print Walk
Book of the Day
Activities
Sharing
Writing
Lunch
DEAR
PE
Math
Daily News
Recess
Home

As we entered, the children were seated on the floor and Ms. Lico was reading them a story about a knight and a dragon who did not want to fight. (The theme for the day was dealing with conflict.) We could pick out two pairs of Cambodian brothers and sisters. The children were attentively listening to Ms. Lico read. She read a page and then asked the children questions.

"What was the dragon doing?"

"Practicing making mean faces in the mirror."

"Is he fierce?"

"No."

"How do you know?"

"You're not mean if you have to practice making mean faces."

"Good thinking."

Ms. Lico continued reading the story; at the end of the book she asked, "Who won the fight?"

The class answered in chorus, "No one!"

"What happened?"

"They made the K–D barbecue stand."

"What does K–D stand for?"

"Knight and Dragon."

"Good work. How many of you liked this book?"

Almost all the students raised their hands.

"Great. Now if everyone is sitting up, we will make a story map." On a large piece of yellow paper Ms. Lico had drawn a circle with four lines extending from it. The circle was labeled Title and Author. The lines were labeled Main Characters, Setting, Problem, and Solution. The students began by writing the Title and the Author. Each took turns writing until the story map was completed. Older children spelled words for younger children.

"Now we have some choices to complete our map. I need someone to make a dragon." The children raised their hands. Two were selected. "A knight." "The castle." Children were selected in pairs, usually an older child with a younger child. One pair was assigned to "read the room." The children immediately went to work. They seemed to be very self-directed.

Ms. Lico explained the students' journals to us. We looked at one that had begun with kindergarten scribbles, progressed to pictures, and now contained a list of "Books I Have Authored."

We stayed in the room until the children posted their artwork on the story map. When the map was completed, the children were reassembled. They explained their drawings, and the story was retold.

Later we visited a 2–3 classroom. The students were making a main-idea map of a nonfiction book titled *Animal Homes*. The teacher was carefully integrating language arts and science. We saw a 3–5 room working on a social studies unit on government. The students in both classrooms were active and enthusiastic.

The yearly calendar is designed to bring excitement and meaning to Montview students. Activities include

Book It! A Reading Read-On
Black Modern Dance Company
Colorado Children Chorale
Cherry Creek Dance Group (an after-school instructional program)
Music and Art Show
A Taste of Montview (an after-school picnic and ice cream social with performances by all classes)
Talent Show

The results of multiaged grouping of siblings and an instructional program designed to accelerate disadvantaged students have been impressive. By the end of the third quarter more than 90 percent of the third-, fourth-,

TABLE 4-2 • *Percentage of Students Scoring below, on, or above Grade Level in Reading, Montview Elementary School, Aurora Public Schools, March 1990*

Grade	Below	On	Above	On or Above
1	25	37	38	75
2	17	37	46	83
3	10	30	60	90
4	0	78	22	100
5	10	61	29	90

and fifth-graders were reading on or above grade level (see Table 4-2). Scores for the multiaged classrooms are surpassing the expectations set for them.

Because of these positive results, Montview has received four grants to expand their programs for at-risk students. One teacher described the family-like classrooms like this: "Multiaged grouping just seems natural. Kids automatically level themselves and achieve at their level. This is the best year of teaching that I have ever had" (Hernandez, 1990).

Year-Round Education
Crawford Elementary School, Aurora, Colorado

No change helps a school staff restructure to provide for individual students quicker than the year-round school concept. Crawford, a K–5 school of 600, is the first school in Colorado to adopt a year-round schedule for academic, and not budget, reasons (George, 1990). Patsy Conley, a Crawford teacher who works with at-risk kids in grades 2 through 5, says that there is a difference, "My time now is used in moving forward, not so much in moving back to review. Because of the year-round calendar there is no big time gap where the kids can forget things" (George, 1990).

Year-round education at Crawford was designed to have all children learning at their fastest rate. The staff gambled on the change, figuring it would help kids retain their lessons and keep them off the streets of this urban neighborhood, which is laced with poverty, crime, and gangs (George, 1990). Once branded as a problem school, Crawford now gets high marks for both student achievement and citizenship (Hernandez, 1989).

Crawford's year-round calendar has the same number of instructional days as the traditional calendar. Students and teachers are divided into four groups called "tracks." Each color track has a kindergarten, first, second

third, fourth, and fifth grade. Students and teachers attend school approximately 45 weekdays (9 weeks) and then they are on vacation for 15 weekdays
(3 weeks). This is repeated four times a year. Three tracks are always in school
or "on track," while one track is on vacation or "off track." Students have
the same classroom teacher for the entire academic year. Children in the same
family are assigned to the same track (*Year-Round Education at Crawford,*
1989).

The school year begins in July and ends in June. For example, in the
1991–1992 school year the Orange track began school July 9. The first vacation for these students and teachers was September 10–30. Their second
quarter began October 1. Because of Christmas week, these students had a
four-week vacation in December. Quarter 3 began January 2. The students
had a three-week vacation in March. Their last quarter began April 1 and
ended June 7. A three-week June vacation ended the school year for the
Orange track (see Figure 4-3).

Survey findings indicate that parents, students, and faculty are positive
about the year-round calendar. Eighty-four percent of the parents were highly
supportive of the year-round program. Eighty-seven percent of the students
liked the year-round calendar. Eighty-nine percent of the teachers favored
the year-round program (*We're on Track,* 1990).

Parents' comments were as follows: "We enjoy it and so do our
children." "My children like it." "My child seems to have learned more and
learned quicker."

Classroom teachers' comments included the following: "I have less burn
out." "I see the benefits for the kids. They have retained what they have
learned. I look forward to returning and three weeks is certainly enough time
to re-energize." "It gives me a chance to do things with my daughter's class
when I'm off track" (*We're on Track,* 1990).

These survey findings and comments are heartwarming when we are
aware that five years ago Crawford was considered an ineffective school.
One administrator thought the school at that time should be branded with
a skull and crossbones and the warning "Beware" (Hernandez, 1989).

Crawford is located in a neighborhood of primarily apartment buildings
and rental houses. Most of the crime in the neighborhood is considered
serious—burglary, larceny, rape, and homicide. Ninety percent of the students
receive free or reduced-price lunches. The student population is approximately
half black and a third white, with Hispanic, Asian, and Native American
comprising the rest. Rapid student turnover is demonstrated by the fact that
from fifteen to thirty-five students check in and out each week—a mobility
rate of 140 percent. Five years ago playground fights, hall scuffles, and power
struggles in class took away from teaching. Students lined up outside the
principal's office to get suspended. "It was like a game," explained one teacher.

FIGURE 4-3 • *1990–1991 Crawford Year-Round Elementary School Calendar, Crawford Elementary School, Aurora, Colorado*

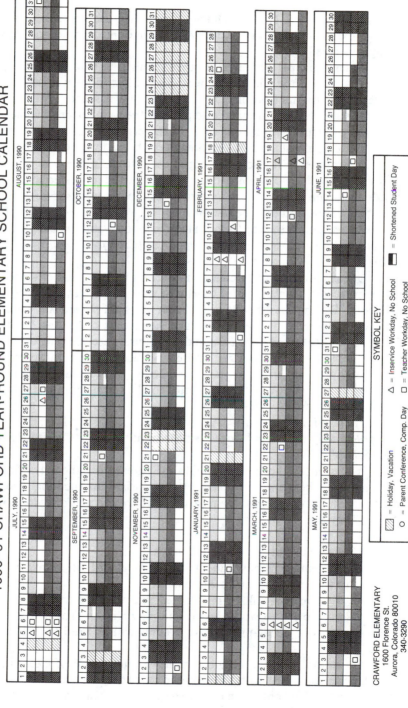

1990–91 CRAWFORD YEAR-ROUND ELEMENTARY SCHOOL CALENDAR

SYMBOL KEY

▨ = Holiday, Vacation   △ = Inservice Workday, No School   ■ = Shortened Student Day

○ = Parent Conference, Comp. Day   □ = Teacher Workday, No School

CRAWFORD ELEMENTARY
1600 Florence St.
Aurora, Colorado 80010
340-3290

Source: Used with permission of Vern Martin.   71

"Let's get suspended. Nobody's home. We can hop the bus to the mall." Test scores were the lowest of any of the twenty-eight elementary schools in Aurora (Bingham, 1988).

When Principal Vern Martin arrived, his first task was to determine the staff's view of the school's main problems. Discipline was ranked as the single most important problem. Parent apathy was second. Martin agreed with the staff. He, too, ranked discipline as the number one problem. The staff and principal felt that one cause of the problem was a lack of security and stability in the students' lives. Steps were taken to provide a more structured environment. The school stopped the internal movement of students and established self-contained classrooms. Martin requested and received funds from the board for an Assertive Discipline workshop for all staff members of the school. The outcome of the workshop was a set of rules, consequences, and rewards for both the classrooms and the building, which all staff members have consistently supported (*Crawford Elementary School,* 1987).

One key strategy was a change in Martin's role. Instead of sending kids to the principal, teachers called Martin to the class to deal with the disruptive child. During the 1985–86 school year the staff slogan was "We refuse to allow 10 percent of the kids to take 90 percent of the teacher's time." Students who followed these rules and procedures received tangible rewards: stickers, notes, special privileges, praise, and recognition from the principal. The result was an improvement of students' self-esteem; there was less challenging of authority. Students started to like adults more and that helped teaching (Hernandez, 1989).

The mission statement is "All students at Crawford will achieve to their full potential." The school slogan is "Alive with Pride" (*Crawford Elementary School,* 1987).

A school task force was established to examine the ways Crawford students learn best and to implement appropriate instructional programs. Five precepts have emerged from this study (*Crawford Elementary School,* 1987). They are

1. All students can learn and will learn.
2. All students will have no upper limits placed on expectations for behavior and academic achievement.
3. An environment will be maintained that values learning.
4. A secure place to work, learn, and play will be provided.
5. A rapid diagnostic-prescriptive process will be used for evaluation.

The school program began to improve after a year of clear rules and high expectations. Test scores were raised by 10 to 20 percentiles at all grade levels. Crawford School began to receive special recognition. The state education commission came to visit; the governor and the city manager sent letters of praise (Bingham, 1986).

Process Education

Perhaps the biggest change in teaching at Crawford has been the emphasis on the processes of learning. During our visits to the school we were impressed by the number of process charts that were displayed in each classroom. Some sample process charts follow:

Sequencing Process

1. What happened first?
2. What happened second?
3. What happened next?
4. What happened last?

Cause > Effect

1. Identify what happened first. This is the *cause*.
2. Label the cause in blue.
3. Identify what happened as a result of the cause. This is the *effect*.
4. Label the effect in red.
5. Stop and think! Does your answer make sense? Does your cause → effect?

The Writing Process

1. Pre-writing—thinking of ideas
2. Draft—writing your ideas
   a. Skip a line while writing.
   b. Do not focus on spelling.
3. Editing—making your story sound good
   a. Read your story to a friend for suggestions.
   b. Read it to yourself.
4. Revision—making your story look good
5. Publishing—making your story into a book

Successful Problem Solving

1. Read the problem.
2. Find the question and circle it in *red*.
3. Say the question in your own words.
4. Find the data and underline it in *blue*.
5. Plan what to do.

Some teachers at Crawford began experimenting with process learning. Their results encouraged more experimentation and study. The process approach fits the current research regarding the teaching of reading and writing as the teaching of thinking. The emphasis on thinking processes seemed appropriate for Crawford students. A committee of teachers and Principal Martin identified a set of critical skills that students should achieve in language arts and be able to use in other content areas such as science and social studies. This committee published the booklet, *Critical Skills* (1989). Twenty-two vocabulary, comprehension, and study skills were identified. Each skill is defined and the processes teachers can use to teach them are described in the booklet.

"What we wanted to happen was for our kids to be able to use these critical skills effectively," explained Principal Martin. "They should be able to transfer them to different subjects whenever the process is appropriate. For example, the process for using cause and effect in literature is the same process a student would use for cause and effect in social studies and science. That's why we keep the charts posted in the room to remind kids to use the process.

"Our most effective staff development program was conducted by teachers who were on the committee," said Principal Martin. "We set up a classroom that modeled what an integrated language arts program would look like. We posted process charts and built a reading center, a library corner, a listening center, and a writing center. We set up a thematic unit table and made vocabulary cards. We built portfolio boxes and sample portfolios. Then our teachers modeled how to use each area. Finally, we taught a model lesson using a film. We had pre-viewing, during viewing (no sound was used), and after viewing activities."

He smiled and said, "It was effective. I have seen carry-over of all the activities in some of the classrooms. I monitor to see if students understand the processes. Most of them do."

As an example of process teaching, the beginning of a fifth-grade science lesson is described.

Teacher: Is our classroom a community?

Girl: Yes, it is our home away from home.

Teacher: Are we interdependent? [Wrote word on the board.]

Boy: Yes.

Teacher: In what way?

Boy: Students depend on the teacher for learning and for schedules.

Girl: The teacher depends on students to teach her about things.

Boy: We can talk about things here we cannot talk about at home.

Teacher: It is a safe place then. Let me give you a situation. What happens when we add or remove a member from the classroom community?

Boy: When Glen was here, lots of people were his friends. At recess there were lots of people on the basketball court. Now that he is gone, you do not see anyone playing basketball.

The boy made a long stammering speech that did not make much sense.

Teacher: I hear your words. Is what you are trying to say that you miss him?

Boy, nodding and smiling: Yes.

Teacher: What else happened?

Girl: People changed.

Teacher: Tell me more.

Girl: Class was not as cheerful.

Teacher wrote "Less cheerful" on the board.

Boy: There was less excitement.

Girl: Glen was the class clown. When he left, everyone tried to take his place, but they could not. Even you changed.

Teacher: I changed?

Girl: Yes, when there was a problem, you would say 'Mr. Glen! Help me with this!' You do not say that now.

Teacher: So you are saying that our classroom changed when Glen left. This discussion leads right into our science lesson. Let's see what happens when a group decides to kill all the predators in this community. Relate your reading to our discussion of Glen's leaving.

Class members began reading the science lesson.

When we visit many schools with similar student populations to those at Crawford, we find tense classroom settings. Teachers are working hard to keep fifth-graders on task and to keep them behaving properly. We were impressed with this thoughtful dialogue.

The work of Principal Martin and the faculty led to state and national recognition for Crawford Elementary School. During the fall of the first year of the year-round calendar, Martin won the National Distinguished Principal's Award for being the best elementary school principal in the state of Colorado. He received the award at the White House (O'Connor, 1989).

One can see that moving to a year-round calendar was but another step in the restructuring that was already taking place at Crawford.

Results of Year-Round Education

Prior to the implementation of year-round education, the staff and parents identified four reasons for the new calendar.

1. There would be less loss of learning because of three-week rather than three-month vacations.
2. More instructional time would be available for new materials because less review time would be needed.
3. Street activity would be minimized because only one-fourth of the students would be on vacation at a time.
4. More space would be available in the Crawford building for other programs.

The first two reasons have been found to be true. Kids do not forget during short vacations, so less time is needed for review. Consequently, there is more time available for instruction in new materials. One teacher compared the year-round instructional program to the operation of a tape recorder. She said, "Our instruction stays in a forward mode. I do not have to use the Rewind button. If I try to review, kids complain that they have had that before. Since we do not have to reteach so much in reading kids are farther along in the basal and they read more trade books."

Student achievement has improved much more than anticipated. The staff goal was to have 60 percent of the students on or above grade level. Actually over 70 percent are functioning on or above grade level in reading, writing, and mathematics.

Chapter 1 teachers report that there is a decrease each year in the number of students who qualify for additional assistance. Students in the program are learning more. With the old calendar there was a five- or six-week lag before Chapter 1 instruction started. Now it is in place by the second week of the term and it remains in place for the entire school year.

The third reason for the change was to minimize the opportunity for street activity. This has occurred. The traditional street corner problems one observes in low-income neighborhoods still exist, but Crawford kids do not seem to be included in the gangs. Why? It may be because their vacations are different—shorter and at times different from other students. It may be that school has more meaning to students who are learning and being successful. But it is working. Crawford students achieve, fit in well, and behave much better at middle school.

The fourth reason was obviously true. Changing to a year-round program in which one-fourth of the students were out of the building made classroom space available for a preschool program for three- and four-year-olds. This program has been implemented and is functioning smoothly.

More has been achieved than the four reasons that had been identified by the staff. A number of unexpected but positive outcomes have occurred: The staff seems to be rejuvenated, there is greater communication between grades, and more individualized instruction is occurring.

The enthusiasm of the staff for the year-round calendar has been a delightful surprise. Each three weeks a team of teachers returns to Crawford rejuvenated. Since the structure regularly changes, the staff members perform at a high energy level. Each three weeks one team is off track; this team leaves for vacation. One team is returning energized. The returning students also return ready to start. The students' eagerness motivates the energized teachers even more. Their enthusiasm seems to motivate the other two teams who are also on track. It's neat!

The staff feels more in control and more empowered by the year-round calendar. If a teacher wants to make more money, that teacher can substitute during the time that he or she is off track. This is good for both the teacher and the other Crawford students. A regular teacher who knows the curriculum and the school can substitute much more efficiently. Teachers can change their calendars. For example, if a teacher wants to return to her hometown in another state for a school or family reunion, that teacher can switch days or weeks with a teacher who is off track. Teachers feel good about their professional lives because they can control them more.

The track family of teachers plans together and works together. There is much more communication between grades than ever before. The year-round calendar allows teachers to deal with individual students much more efficiently. Promotion technically occurs in July, but kids can be moved to more difficult materials whenever they are ready. Since the kids are achieving more, the teachers do not have to push to finish grade materials. Enrichment and acceleration are easier to implement. Students can be treated more and more as individuals. Nongraded–continuous-progress concepts are being achieved. Students are moving through curriculum sequences at their own rates.

As we entered Crawford, two slogans were prominently displayed. They were "School—a place of hope, laughter, and learning for people who are experiencing life and its wonder" and "Crawford: A School for All Seasons." The fifth-grade dialogue was a natural outcome for a school that values both children and learning.

The positive effects of Year-Round Schooling was a pleasant surprise. Staffs who are restructuring schooling to minimize gang problems and summer forgetting should consider this strategy.

Every Student CAN Learn
Lozano Special Emphasis School, Corpus Christi, Texas

Each time that we visit Lozano School, we are impressed with the students' enthusiasm, behavior, and achievement. And we are shocked by the neighborhood where these children live. We are quickly aware that these are poor, Hispanic kids. The directors of the PBS special *Learning in America* (1990) were affected the same way. They took many shots of the small homes—many that are just one- or two-room shacks. But the accomplishments of these students cannot be denied. In 1983, Principal Maggie Ramirez received special recognition by the Texas Elementary Principals and Supervisors Association. In 1986, Lozano received the Excellence in Education Award from the U.S. Department of Education. In 1990, it was selected as one of four outstanding elementary schools for *Learning in America.*

The recognition is well deserved. Lozano's students scored at the eighty-seventh percentile on the California Achievement Test. These scores ranked second in the district; only the Gifted/Talented Elementary School scored higher. In 1988, 100 percent of the third-graders mastered the criterion of the Texas state test in reading, writing, and mathematics. Students' attendance is over 98 percent.

How has this been accomplished? By setting high expectations for both students and parents, the faculty and staff believe and live the school philosophy, "Every student CAN learn." They have set high expectations for the students and parents regarding attendance, homework, school performance, and discipline. They have structured an instructional program so that these high expectations can be achieved. Now the school families also believe that all of their children can learn.

"It was not easy in the beginning," explained Mary Munguia, Lozano school attendance and parent coordinator. "At first, Mrs. Ramirez and I had to go to the homes and get the children out of bed to come to school. Now parents call me to tell me that one of their children is sick. They come to school to pick up homework assignments.

"And homework was a problem at first." Munguia reported. "We are known as the school that gives lots of homework. At first parents resented it. Now they question their children if they do not have homework."

Mrs. Munguia coordinates the parent volunteer program. Lozano has a parents' work room and parents are on campus working all the time. Last year volunteer parents worked over 6,000 hours. Munguia says that she really works to get parents to volunteer. Each year a questionnaire is sent to each family. Parents volunteer to laminate, duplicate, cut out letters, make charts, make bulletin board materials, run stores, and do other jobs to keep the school program functioning.

We asked Mrs. Munguia to share a success story. She smiled and said, "One parent did not want to come. She said that she did not speak English and could not read or write. I asked her, 'Can you cut? Can you color?' She came. Now that mother has learned to speak English. She's gotten her GED. She learned to drive and has gotten a driver's license. She has a good job now. I am proud of her."

Success stories like this are a natural outcome of the Lozano program. The school mission statement is "We strive to instill in our students important values such as courtesy, cooperation, and punctuality. At Lozano, our students acquire a genuine love for learning, an ability to think critically, a positive self-image, and the foresight to see difficulties in life as merely challenges."

One can see evidence of the school philosophy, "Every student CAN learn," displayed throughout the building. Signs are posted at the doorway to each classroom.

Shhh! Literary masterpieces are being written here!
Mrs. Torres' Class Where . . . Every Child CAN Learn.

This room contains
    Motivators,
    Believers,
      and
    Achievers.

Mrs. Purcell's 3rd grade
    When you
Enter this
    Little room
    Consider yourself
    One of the special
    Members of a group
    Enjoying working and learning.

Inside the rooms, students' work is displayed on bulletin boards labeled

Power Readers
Super Spellers
Writers' Corner
Homework Hot Spot
Spelling Stars
"You do a whale of a job!" (drawing of a whale above a set of good students' papers)
Shining Math Stars

Something to Crow About
Perfect Attendance Second 6 Weeks

The following chart was typical of motivational room displays.

The Keys to Success:
    Try your best at everything you do!
    Quitters never win!
    If at first you don't succeed, try, try again!
    Honesty is the best policy.
    Never say, "I can't."
    Aim for the stars—The sky is the limit.

The Lozano instructional program is very structured. There is a carefully constructed campus improvement plan to monitor and assess students' progress. There are strategies to help students achieve the objectives of the Texas Assessment of Academic Skills Test and the California Achievement Test. Teachers from each grade meet daily for planning and for assessing student achievement. Grade section leaders meet weekly with the principal for planning and evaluation. Each six weeks teachers graph their homeroom's percentage passing rate for reading, mathematics, science, and social studies. Students who are not achieving are retaught and given help or encouragement. Each six weeks students are recognized for academic achievement and for academic improvement (Duran, 1990).

Instruction in reading and language arts has been carefully organized. The *Open Court Headway Program* is a highly structured program with a synthetic phonics approach. Reading and language arts are totally integrated. Students are taught reading, spelling, and composition skills as a total entity. The composition cycle enables students to learn and apply grammar skills through composition tasks (Ramirez & Rosales, 1983).

The phonics strand of the program has provided the students with a decoding and encoding system. Students are regularly drilled in phonics skills so that by the end of third grade most students have mastered these skills and can read independently.

The school is structured so that there is deliberate reteaching of the skills and content in language arts and mathematics. Two media centers (K–2 and 3–5) have been organized to serve the 500 Lozano students. Each center is staffed with a media teacher and an aide. One half of a homeroom is sent to the media center for instruction. The other half stays with the classroom teacher. This structure allows deliberate reteaching, review, and enrichment for the students. Both the media teachers and the classroom teachers believe that the small group is the key. It provides a different atmosphere and a better opportunity for students to master skills.

We also found the media center to be a place where children's learning could be enriched. On the day we visited, it was not the primary media center; it was "Whoville." "Feel the Whoville Warmth" was a welcoming sign. Children were using the Dr. Seuss book *How the Grinch Stole Christmas* to relate to Christmas giving. They were being taught that children do not have to give material gifts to parents. They can give hugs and kisses or do chores. The structure of daily use of the media center helps Lozano children to master skills and also to enjoy good literature.

A strength of the Lozano School is the counseling program. A full-time counselor has developed a guidance program that is compatible and suportive of the highly structured environment of the Special Emphasis School. The counselor meets with every homeroom each week for twenty to thirty minutes. The goal of this program is to help each student have a positive self-concept. Counselors in Corpus Christi Independent School District (ISD) have found that the highest indicator of school performance is self-esteem. The developmental guidance program, the weekly meetings with parents, and the counseling sessions with individuals are designed to help students feel self-worth as they make decisions, handle peer pressure, and develop self-discipline. The counseling component is an integral part of the total education effort at Lozano. The cooperative efforts of the counselor, administrators, and teachers have helped Lozano students to excel. The motto, "Your school counselor: someone you can count on when you need a friend to talk to" is true at Lozano School.

Probably more than any school that we have visited, Lozano has developed activities and programs to build a positive climate for students, staff, and parents. Some of these activities are as follows (*Lozano Special Emphasis School*, 1990):

Homework Pyramid Treats
Attendance Incentives
Student of the Day Awards
"Good For You" Tokens
Artist of the Week
Super Kid Awards
Sports Person of the Month
Honor Roll Awards
Student/Parent/Teacher On-Campus Picnics
Teacher Appreciation Treats and Luncheons (hosted by parents)
Parent Appreciation Luncheons (hosted by staff)
Treasure Chest Rewards
Treats for students
Letters to students from Principal
Birthday cards for all staff members (from administrators)

Paraprofessional Appreciation Week
Nurse's Appreciation Week
Counselor's Day
Teachers' "Good for You" Aprons

The care in teaching both writing and self-concept is illustrated by the following fifth-grade lesson:

"Class, now it is time for us to hear some stories and to give the authors feedback. Jennifer, read your story to the class. Remember, class, our job is to be good listeners."

Jennifer read her story to the class. It was about a girl who had come to school with a frog in her pocket. The frog got loose in the classroom. It got into a lot of trouble.

After Jennifer finished reading, the teacher said, "Class, it's your turn to say something nice about the composition. What did you like about the story?"

Four children raised their hands immediately.

"Jennifer, you may call on people."

"Gracie."

"I liked the part about the frog eating the apple."

George said, "I liked the part about the frog getting in people's desks and eating their candy."

The teacher asied, "Can a frog do that or did Jennifer use fantasy?"

Class responded chorally, "Fantasy."

"Do you think it's easier for a frog to eat flies than aples?" the teacher asked.

"Yes."

A boy raised his hand and said, "Frogs do not have teeth. It has to be fantasy."

The teacher nodded in agreement. Then she said, "Are there any questions you want to ask Jennifer about her composition?"

A girl asked, "Why didn't the frog jump away?"

Jennifer answered, "It was scared of the children."

"Why did he eat people's candies?"

Jennifer hesitated and then said, "I wanted to make the story funny."

The class laughed and then applauded for Jennifer's composition, "A Frog in Our Room."

The teacher shared with us that compositions are marked "excellent," "good," or "fair." Usually students edit and rewrite until they receive "excellent" or "good." Then they read them to the class.

When we visited Lozano, the school was getting ready for Christmas.

Volunteer parents were setting up Kid's Korner, a store where children can buy gifts for their families for $0.25 to $5.00. Before the store, few children could buy gifts.

Mrs. Munguia, the parent coordinator, enthusiastically explained the Christmas lottery to us. She said that the teachers give her a list of the needy students in their rooms. Lozano School staff members ask them who needs shoes, sweaters, toys, and so on. Then the parent volunteers and the administrators collect, buy, and beg gifts for the children. On the last day of school before Christmas vacation the lottery is held at an assembly for all kids. Children write their names on paper and then wish and wish. The lottery is won by both chance and prior arrangement. She said, "We have designed gifts that we can draw or pretend to draw. Kids are excited when they win. And we save their pride and their dignity. At times, it is emotional. I remember when a black girl opened her doll gift and began crying. We all cried."

Our eyes teared as we reflected the care the Lozano staff uses to structure a school program where every child learns and where children's self-concepts are valued.

Staffs with school populations similar to Lozano's should consider the positive effects of high expectations, structured reteaching, and daily homework on student achievement as they plan and reconstruct their school's instructional program.

Empowered Students
William Diamond Middle School, Lexington, Massachusetts

We are aware that William Diamond Middle School serves a different group of students from those that we visited in Colorado and Texas. These are bright middle school students who are enrolled in advanced mathematics and science programs and who may study foreign languages in France and Mexico each summer. Lexington schools have had a long tradition for excellence in education. For years professors from Harvard and the Massachusetts Institute of Technology have chosen to live in Lexington so that their children could attend these quality schools. What happens when an outstanding school district decides to restructure its school program and to implement an integrated, student-centered, developmental curriculum? This restructuring led to a new organizational structure for Diamond. The school changed from a junior high school for seventh and eighth-graders to a middle school for 472 sixth-, seventh-, and eighth-graders.

The idea of developing a vision that guides decisions as a school program changes is a key concept. The research from effective schools emphasizes this. As restructuring occurred, the Diamond faculty developed such a vision.

"Fortunately we had two years to study before we actually changed the organization," explained Suzanne Lipsky, chair of the English Department. "We had time to develop a vision of what a middle school is. Now that vision is internalized. I can say to my team, this idea is part of the philosophy, isn't it? And they will all nod. Without the vision, we could not have moved to a new program."

Ron Godfrey agrees, "Teachers must accept the middle school philosophy. It's not elementary or junior high. It's much more affective than content centered. We must allow kids to grow socially and affectively. We must pay attention to their learning styles."

One thing that facilitated the faculty was the Mastery in Learning Project. This is a school-based education reform that is designed to help school faculties take an active role in directing school restructuring efforts (Livingston & Castle, 1989). Sharing a vision of what the school should become and the processes needed to achieve this vision are key first steps in the Mastery in Learning Project. Participation as a project school has helped the teachers, students, and administrators learn to work together more effectively.

The philosophy of Diamond School—its vision for middle school education—is reflected in "A Message to Parents" from the *Program of Studies* (1990).

> *The world of the middle school learner is one beset by rapid and profound physical change, by an increased interest in relationships with other people, especially one's peers, and by a desire to understand both personal values and those of adults, while simultaneously dealing with the developmental task of separation. Moreover, middle school learners as a group demonstrate a broad range of intellectual capabilities and potential, requiring programs which address the individual cognitive needs of these children during a period of rapid personal change.*
>
> *The middle school learner needs and seeks to wrestle actively with problems and solutions, yet wants the reassurance that incorrect attempts are permitted. The middle school learner wants to question, wants knowledge, wants to experiment, wants to experience success and approval; he or she looks for clearly defined boundaries with freedom within those limits to develop decision-making skills; he or she responds to goal-setting and some measure of routine as he or she seeks to achieve independence. Clearly, the complexity of the young adolescent challenges our professional skill and vision as we work to configure a school organization and develop a curriculum plan that responds to the variation in each individual student.*

We believe that a successful middle school is one in which the individual learner is the critical factor in both the organizational and curricular planning. With this concept in mind, our middle school stresses mastery of basic skills and essential concepts, equipping the middle school learner for subsequent academic experiences; formulates a system of goals, structures, and routines which foster school-wide consistency, yet encourages the exercise of student self-determination when appropriate; and responds to individual differences by developing and supporting richly diverse and adaptable instructional programs which provide essential information, opportunities for aesthetic appreciation and expression, experiences of competence and achievement, and occasions for personal discovery.

In addition to these instructional opportunities, our middle schools offer students innovative programs for physical activity consistent with the developmental needs of this group and sensitive to the significance of competitive events for the less athletic. They also provide opportunities for students to participate in the activities of their community and school to cultivate a sense of responsibility, of belonging, of personal security, and of self-esteem. Finally, our schools support opportunities for the student to examine his or her "humanness" and to test and compare value systems as he or she works, with our help, toward a clearer self-definition and understanding of his or her own beliefs and role in the world beyond the school.*

Diamond Middle School is organized in interdisciplinary teams of four teachers. A teacher from English, mathematics, science, and social studies was assigned to each team of eighty students. Each teacher also serves as a teacher advisor for approximately fifteen students. These new roles as an interdisciplinary team member and as a teacher advisor were hard for the teachers to implement.

Suzanne Lipsky said, "It was difficult for teachers from four different subject groups to come out of isolation and to work with each other."

Team leader Ron Godfrey explained: "The Mastery in Learning Project came at just the right time for the school. It was a terrific vehicle to propel us to change. We did an assessment and made a profile of the school. We answered the question, 'What is Diamond like now?' It was difficult at first. We spent a year opening closets and looking for problems. We should open windows and let in fresh air. We started looking out to see what we could bring in to improve Diamond. This idea helped us get involved immediately with cooperative learning and learning styles."

*Used with permission of Joanne M. Hennesey.

"The problem approach did not work," explained Principal Joanne Hennesay. "We had bright kids. We did not have low reading, writing, or math scores. It was hard to identify five problem areas (as Mastery in Education suggested) and improve them. What changed the faculty most was the Myers Briggs Personality Inventory. After we took this test we learned what our learning styles were like."

"I knew before the Myers Briggs that we had an able, well-educated, hard-working staff. I also knew that we had little professional collegiality. We talked about outside events. We did not talk about teaching and kids. The Myers Briggs helped us discover that most of our teachers were introverts. They enjoyed closing their classroom doors and teaching. Planning together was difficult. Discovering why has made a difference. Now the teachers make a conscious effort to work together. There's been a major change in the teachers' behavior with students. Teachers and students work together and talk together in a reasonable manner."

Let's look at some of the changes that have been implemented at Diamond. Cooperative Learning, the advisor-advisee program, and student empowerment are three things we will study.

Cooperative Learning has changed the way teachers at Diamond teach. As an English teacher said, "I stopped being a talking head. I've given my power to the kids. Instead of telling them to look for a particular idea as they read a story, I ask them to respond to a story. I've learned that the important thing is their response to the literature—not their response to what I think. They've come up with questions or thoughts that I hadn't even thought about. It's made literature come alive."

The structure for this cooperative group is as follows:

1. Pre-reading vocabulary: New words or new meanings that the students will encounter in the story are introduced and discussed.
2. Focus: The teacher tells students what to focus on during their reading of the story; for example, character development could be the focus.
3. Read and write in Response Journal: The students need to ask five questions and respond to them (or answer them) in their journals.
4. Exchange journals: In cooperative groups of four or five, students exchange journals and pass journals around the group until all students have read all the journals.
5. Select questions: The teacher instructs the cooperative groups to select one or two questions that they really want someone in their group to answer.
6. Discussion: Cooperative groups discuss questions; the teacher monitors the groups.
7. Sharing with the whole class: Cooperative groups discuss the questions and share their conclusions.

This is only one example of Cooperative Learning from Diamond. However, early successes with this strategy convinced teachers that their vision of a middle school was a possibility, not just a dream.

The *Advisor-Advisee* program was implemented so there was a time to address numerous developmental and adjustment issues that are important in the world of the pre-adolescent. Advisor-advisee groups (AA is what the kids call it) meet twice each week during regularly scheduled periods. These advising periods form an integral part of the middle school program. They supply a framework that allows teachers and students to build supportive and trusting relationships around nonacademic, more personal concerns. As advisory groups develop a sense of community, students are more comfortable in asking questions that are of special, more personal importance to them (*Program of Studies,* 1990).

The advisor leads the group through a series of activities designed to help students develop trust, to have open communication, and to build a helping relationship. After this team-building sequence, advisors encourage students to ask the kinds of questions that might go unconsidered at other middle schools. These could be practical questions (Who do I see about locker problems? What if I have to call home?), questions about class and studying (How do I budget my time so I can get all my homework done? How do I ask for extra help?), and questions about getting along with others (Should I let someone copy my homework? How can I be sure that other kids will like me?). The strength of the program is located in the combination of structured activities with the latitude to accommodate immediate concerns (*Program of Studies,* 1990).

"Each team keeps AA groups small because special teachers agree to be advisors," explained a team leader. "We have twelve students in each AA group. After the team-building activities, motivation for what happens in a group can come from either the kids or the teacher. We can talk about the election, go for a walk, have a party, watch a film on AIDS, talk about a recent report card, play a game, or discuss cafeteria behavior."

We asked him about results. The team leader responded quickly, "Kids are much happier. They've got a place to go with their concerns. A mother rarely said anything positive to her daughter. She was quick to criticize the daughter's performance in a school play. My advisee talked to me about this. We discussed the matter in a general way in advisee group. Then I talked with the mother. The situation has improved."

He smiled, "It's hard. We are training middle school kids to be independent (to speak for themselves) and we are teaching parents to be supportive, but to let go. I can see growth. There's a tremendous difference between our sixth-graders and our eighth-graders."

The principal said, "At first, faculty members were furious about their new roles and responsibilities as teacher advisors. Now they'd fight to keep the AA program."

The teachers' initial negative reactions to the Advisor-Advisee program are normal. It's natural for teachers not to want extra responsibilities or to feel that they've not been trained as a counselor or a social worker. Once teachers have had some in-service training and have worked with students, they see the many advantages of getting to know students as individuals. That's what happened at Diamond Middle School.

The *Student Empowerment* program at Diamond Middle School is an outstanding model for teaching the principles of democracy. The faculty and administration believe that the notion of teacher empowerment has positively contributed to teacher self-esteem and school climate. They believe that the same rationale can be used for the encouragement of student empowerment.

Diamond Middle School uses student government as a vehicle to empower students. Each grade has its own student council and its own faculty advisor. In the sixth and seventh grades each AA group has one representative and one alternate. The eighth-grade council has elected officers, but representation is open to any eighth-grader who wants to attend student council meetings. Advisor Richard Kollen states, "This eliminates a popularity contest. Thirty to forty kids attend regularly" (Kollen, Olive, Attanuccia, Neumann, & O'Conner, 1990).

Students are empowered to make recommendations at the school level at the Principal's Advisory Committee. The process for this committee is as follows:

1. Student representatives from each grade meet with class advisors to create an agenda for subsequent meetings with administrators. The agenda is a list of questions, suggestions, or grievances that students want to discuss with the principal.
2. The agenda is submitted to the administrators prior to the meeting.
3. The principal and assistant principal meet with students and advisors to respond to the items on the agenda.

Some accomplishments identified by the past eighth-grade officers and their advisor were the use of a juice machine, rearranging of cafeteria tables, permission for students to read morning announcements, a three-period lunch format, a class mural, and the codification of school dance rules (Kollen et al., 1990).

Student empowerment can result in students becoming more responsible. The principal told the Advisory Committee that she had a complaint about student behavior at school dances. She said students were wrestling, chasing each other, running, and tearing down decorations. She asked the student council to set some dance rules. The students discussed it in AA groups and at council meetings. They developed a set of rules and a system to monitor them. "Dance behavior was great!" exclaimed an officer. "We rate each dance by behavior now. Our behavior has been so good that we have one dance a month" (Kollen et al., 1990).

The juice machine was an example of student empowerment. A student request was implemented, but it took over two years of discussion and voting. The school dance behavior is a good example of how student empowerment leads students to become more responsible for their actions.

"It's risky empowering students," explained Assistant Principal Vickie Kollen. "I was scared when we gave the students the opportunity to vote to have two or three lunch periods. I knew three lunch periods would administratively work better, but I also believe in the democratic process. Kids campaigned for both choices. Three periods won!"

These three glimpses of life at William Diamond Middle School provide a picture of how this school has been restructured to implement a middle school philosophy and to permit students to take more responsibility for their own behavior.

"Our test scores are still very good (eighty-third percentile in reading; eighty-fifth in mathematics). But people are less concerned about grades. We are more concerned about how students learn and whether students learn," said Principal Hennesay.

We observed that the Diamond School faculty does understand its mission. The school is organized to help middle school students make that transition from elementary to high school in as positive way as possible.

Individually Guided Education
Conrad Elvehjem School, McFarland, Wisconsin

When we entered the Conrad Elvehjem School, we immediately felt at home as educators. The emphasis "Think Kids" is evident everywhere. The banners overhead proclaim the subjects they're studying — environment, computers, space research. The posters and bulletin boards focus on student development: self-esteem, positive attitudes, concern for others, and responsibility of the individual child. And the work of the students is shown everywhere — not all of the work is perfect — but all of it represents the best effort of an individual student.

In this school, which has instructional areas clustered around a central Instructional Materials Center, one can see individualized instruction in action. A teacher has her arm around a student while she talks to her; students are working in small groups, pairs, alone, and in class-sized groups according to their needs and learning styles and the subject matter to be learned. There are boxes of hands-on materials for students to use to help them better learn math, science, and other subjects in every available corner. Sometimes you see an instructional area empty or occupied by only two or three students. Are the students on a field trip, working outdoors, studying in another part of this school, working in another building, or in a resource room? All of these are options in this school.

In addition to the open and flexible instructional space, there are adjacent closed rooms for music, art, and special education, as well as a computer lab. And there are a large gym and lunchroom, locker rooms, teacher and aide workrooms, along with pupil services and nurse rooms, the principal's and school office, an audiovisual room, a storage room, and a teacher's lounge—all on the same level.

Conrad Elvehjem School, which houses third- and fourth-graders, is one of four buildings in the district of 1,739 students. Others are the McFarland Elementary School for grades (kindergarten through 2, the Indian Mounds Middle School for grades 5 through 8, and the McFarland High School for grades 9 through 12. McFarland, once a small, rural farm town, is now considered a suburb of Madison, the capital of Wisconsin. Students in this district come from a wide range of socioeconomic levels, but only a few of them are from minority groups.

The principal, Dr. Don Barnes, has guided education in this school since 1969. He received the Wisconsin Principal of the Year award in 1988 and the McFarland Citizen of the Year and Distinguished Alumnus of the Year (University of Wisconsin–Eau Claire) awards in 1989 for his leadership efforts in education. He is often not in his office when you walk into the building. He's in an instructional area observing staff, attending a student special production or event, or observing interns and student teachers. Or he's at a meeting—one where the goal is to improve the education of students in his school and district. He might be meeting in the local district, at the University of Wisconsin, at the State Department of Public Instruction in nearby Madison, or in Washington, DC. He might also be in another district sharing his know-how as administrator, instructional leader, and manager of personnel and finances. Wherever he is, he's in constant contact with his staff and students in person or via modern communications.

How did this school develop its unique personality? How has it sustained its excellence in education reputation for twenty years—excellence that was recognized in 1985–86 when it received a national excellence in education award. In a pamphlet describing education in the elementary schools, the staff suggested they received the award through constant work and for the following reasons: teaming—individuals working together, community involvement and support, dedicated staff with group decision making, students having first priority—individualized instruction, and administrative leadership and school board support.

The underlying philosophy of this school comes from IGE. "Our instructional program is organized so we can individualize instruction to the best of our ability and resources. We believe students can successfully learn, taking into account motivation, ability, and rate of learning. It is our goal to recognize and respect individual differences in learning. Therefore, we are committed to providing a variety of instructional experiences for learners." The instructional organization system includes units with team leaders and an IIC as described in Chapter 3.

The "We Agree . . . Goals" developed by the staff over several years guide the education of students at Conrad Elvehjem School. They address three basic areas: the basic functions of a school, the philosophy of the school, and specific elements of major lifetime goals of education for grades kindergarten through 4. Each of these is presented below:

Purpose of Conrad Elvehjem School

A school is responsible for nine basic functions. These functions cannot change as long as school is perceived by the majority of parents and citizens as a school. Some day education may be significantly different. Until such a time, however, school is defined as follows:

1. *A place to prepare students for the future*
2. *A place that identifies knowledge, skills, and attitudes*
3. *A place that defines intelligence, intellectual ability, and good behavior*
4. *A place that evaluates behavior*
5. *A place that defines the role of the "student" and "teacher"*
6. *A place that structures time and activities*
7. *A place that provides supervision*
8. *A place that provides a system of accountability*
9. *A place that prepares students for economic and social realities*

People may debate and adjust curriculum, materials, schedules, time, space, and methods of management all reflecting the majority opinion, but no one can change the nine functions. The result would be to abolish the institution known as school.

Philosophy and Lifetime Goals

We agree with and actively support the focus on the individuality and uniqueness of the child. We reconfirm our commitment to major lifetime goals of education.

A. Getting Along with Others
  1. *Appreciate self*
  2. *Contribute to society*
  3. *Develop satisfactory relationships with others*

   4. *Manage conflict*
   5. *Recognize strengths and limitations*
B. Choosing (Skills in Decision Making)
   1. *Develop problem-solving techniques*
   2. *Cope with decision making*
   3. *Cope with diversity*
   4. *Acknowledge decisions*
   5. *Cope with novelty*
   6. *Deal with decision and conflict*
C. Learning, Unlearning, and Relearning
   1. *Deal — new situation*
   2. *Independent — self-fulfilling*
   3. *Search, analyze, and evaluate*
   4. *Changing environment awareness*
   5. *Desire for continued self-development*

The Conrad Elvehjem staff recognizes the need for daily awareness of these three goals. On a regular basis, time will be spent identifying strengths and weaknesses and addressing ourselves to the development of activities to strengthen weaker aspects of these goals.

What are the ingredients that have caused the staff to develop and sustain what appears to be a complex and all encompassing system of schooling? The principal suggests that shared decision making is the most important element. Teachers and students are divided into two groups or units — the "discovery" and "explorer" units. Each unit has some 145 to 150 elementary students, six regular teachers, an aide, and two interns (student teachers who are paid a portion of a beginning teacher's salary), and varying numbers of student teachers. Students in each unit are multiaged and multigraded and are assigned to homerooms on a multiaged and heterogeneous ability basis.

Each unit has one teacher designated as a unit leader. Units meet at least twice each week for forty-five minutes to plan instruction and make decisions for the education of their students. In addition to the two regular units or teams, there are two special units: related arts, which includes personnel from physical education, art, music, and the IMC; and a special education unit representatives. Each of these units also has a unit leader and meets once or twice each week. Other specialists that are available to staff in the building include a guidance counselor, director of special education, psychologist, gifted and talented coordinastor, reading consultant, and a support staff of secretaries, custodians, playground supervisors, and cooks.

Decision making for the building is carried out in a meeting between the unit leaders and the principal. This group, the IIC, meets weekly for at least one hour to make building-wide decisions. Unit leaders bring input from their staff. The principal chairs the meeting. Specialists, parents, resource persons, and others are invited to IIC meetings as appropriate to the topics being discussed.

Principal Barnes feels that one secret to the success of the program is its variety. Another is the idea that "Children learn best in small groups that emphasize interaction." Today most students in this school spend about one-third of their time in cooperative groups. These groups are designed to accommodate low- and high-level learners in the same group. "Older kids helping younger kids" is another cohesive tradition. Older students work as tutors with at-risk students and as mentors for gifted students. They come to the instructional area and go on field trips and sometimes both adults and older students work with the same group. Special education students are mainstreamed into class groups whenever possible to achieve the "least restrictive environment where all kids can learn." Learning styles of students and teaching styles of staff are matched whenever possible and acceleration as well as enrichment opportunities are provided for students.

Since the philosophy of the school suggests that "the elementary school should focus on skills for lifelong learning," the curriculum must reflect this focus as well as promote reading and research and the fact that information changes. The staff, over the years, has written or rewritten most of the curriculum to meet the changing needs of students. Following is an overview of their current curriculum:

- The philosophy of *reading* is that "children learn to read by reading," so a whole language approach with language experiences for younger students uses multiple texts, trade books, and multiple materials.
- *Mathematics* focuses on using hands-on, concrete learning experiences within the process approach to actively solve problems and promote the idea that a child's point of view should be considered in the math program. The basis of the program consists of the six major strands of the Developing Mathematical Processes (DMP) program: fractions, addition and subtraction, place value and problem solving, multiplication and division, attributes/measuring, and geometry. Topics are assigned to third- and fourth-graders and each child progresses through the strands at his or her own rate. Students can work alone, in pairs, or as part of a group. Pre- and post-testing are used to place students in the program and to evaluate their progress.
- *Social studies* is an "interdisciplinary discipline" curriculum that is integrated into all classes and group experiences. The program was developed by the faculty. It focuses on getting along with self and others and caring for people and property with an emphasis on local, regional, and state environments. Since students are in multiaged groups, the social studies units of study are divided into Rotation I and Rotation II with one rotation taught

each year. Rotations, along with issues that are stressed in the curriculum on an ongoing basis, appear below:

Rotation I	*Rotation II*
1. Welcome Back	1. Welcome Back
2. McFarland Investigation/ Geography Review	2. Wisconsin Geography
3. Countries Around the World (I)	3. Countries Around the World
4. Native Americans	4. Explorers and Settlers
5. Madison/Government	5. Lumbering and Forests of the World
6. Careers/Consumers	6. Farming
7. Vacationland (Wisconsin)	7. Vacationland
8. Famous Wisconsin People	

Integrated Curriculum of Social Issues (on-going throughout the year)

Current Events (What's in the News?)
Martin Luther King, Jr., Day Observance
Black Studies
Women's Issues
Disability Awareness
Peace Awareness Month

• *Language arts* focuses on reading, grammar, usage, writing, speaking, listening, and related communication skills. Reading is an integral part of language arts learning and instruction. All of these skills are related to the use of various media used to communicate in our technological society. Language arts is taught on a rotation basis with the skills and processes for each rotation clearly stated.

• The basic *science* program is Science—A Process Approach (SAPA), which emphasizes the processes of science and hands-on experience. This program has been integrated with the four elements of science education suggested by the Wisconsin science guidelines—problem solving; science knowledge; nature of science; and science, technology, and society. The SAPA modules have been carefully selected and cross-indexed with teacher-developed materials to ensure students study environment, earth and space, and physical and biological science each year. Students in each unit complete six of the twelve modules and other lessons each year of a two-year rotation. Science is also integrated into reading through trade books and special activities such as Invent America and Odyssey of the Mind.

The basic curriculum also includes art, music, physical education, health education, library skills, and computer literary work. The curriculum is supported by many additional opportunities for staff and parents as well as students. Elementary students may select from the following according to their interests and needs:

- K–8 "young authors" program where students may write a book
- K–2 annual "reading motivation project," which increases interest and participation among primary readers; and a "language experience program" where parents are involved in student-generated stories
- K–4 "parent volunteer program" in all subject areas
- Superstar awards where students from grades 3 through 8 are recognized for improvement and excellence
- Annual Winterim for grades 3 and 4 features guest speakers and activities in art, science, industry, sports, and community awareness with a career education focus
- K–12 comprehensive summer programs in math, reading, science, computers, writing, foreign languages, and recreation
- K–6 music experiences where students are actively involved in programs
- Computer-assisted instruction; a curriculum for students to develop computer literacy has been written by local staff; basic programming starts at middle school level
- Dozens of other opportunities are available for middle school and high school students

What motivates staff and principals to execute and remain loyal to such a complex program? Principal Barnes listed several reasons and we have added others that were observed over several years of working with staff. They include support for the following:

- Recognition of special potential of staff by encouraging them to become "expert" in a subject matter area or a strategy such as Cooperative Learning or gifted education
- Encouraging staff to keep current in content and strategies by getting advanced training through workshops and university courses where the district pays 80 percent of the tuition cost and recognizes six-credit blocks of salary increments
- Opportunities to receive paid leave to work on a special university or state project, which include the social studies curriculum program and CMI (computer managed instruction)
- Participation in a national project such as the current *Project 2061*; McFarland staff, K–12, have been selected to write integrated science and math exemplary curriculum for the next century

- Unpaid leave for staff to participate in foreign exchanges and special personal travel opportunities and unpaid sabbaticals for a semester or year
- Job sharing, which is particularly helpful to staff members with young children
- Memberships in and time to work with and chair local, state, and national organizations, committees, and boards
- Recognition of individual differences among staff, including opportunities to lead, to mainly teach, or to do both, but to always give your best at whatever you choose in each "passage of life"

Putting all the elements of the multiunit school together at Conrad Elvehjem School is the task of the principal and the District Superintendent working with the local board of education. In McFarland it includes a combination of participatory management; high expectations for staff, students, and administrators; keeping an eye on the needs of students now and in the future; personal involvement by administrators in the everyday activities of the school; and creative and sound fiscal management. Integration of these elements "makes education happen" at Conrad Elvehjem and other schools in the McFarland district, has done so for over twenty years, and will continue to do so well into the future.

Personalized Instruction
Bowman School, Lexington, Massachusetts

When we entered the school, we were given a one-page description of the Bowman School Community. It set the tone for our visit to this exciting, stimulating learning environment. The school description is as follows:

> WE ARE THE BOWMAN SCHOOL COMMUNITY

We Are

474 Students
58 Staff Members
8 Student Teachers
106 School Volunteers
348 Families

We speak 19 different languages. And, as we learned from a fourth-grade social studies project, we wear shoes made in 14 different countries.

We read 13,763 library books each year.
And, we watch 39 clocks each day.

We read charts from 19 easels.
We jump 33 ropes.
And, we have 106 bulletin boards, each of them celebrating the hard work and learning of our 474 students.

But, we are much, much more.

We are a school community that is intellectually curious, motivated, responsible, and within our cooperative environment we continue to be lifelong learners who respect ourselves, each other, and the world. (Johnson, 1990b).

The goals of Bowman School are ambitious.

The first goal is to plan and implement a school-based management system. To achieve this goal, a Principal's Cabinet has been organized. The Cabinet represents Bowman's first attempt at site-based management. Classroom teachers, specialists, and parents meet biweekly with the principal to facilitate change within the school. Its first accomplishment was the establishment of the school's Core Value, which is printed above.

The second goal is to increase opportunities for meeting individual student needs through personalized instruction. To achieve this goal, the faculty has created a child-centered environment that emphasizes each student's work and self-esteem. When we entered the school, we quickly became aware that children are participants in their own education. Children's artwork, writing, science projects, maps, poetry, and social studies projects were displayed everywhere. Bowman is a hands-on, learn by doing school.

For example, on the bulletin board outside of one fourth-grade classroom was a display of "Wanted Posters." The posters were actually pictures of children disguised as criminals. The class members had to figure out who the children were. It was a neat display for their reading, writing, and creating unit on Mysteries.

Teacher JoAnn Wortman explained, "Kids love mysteries. This summer I did a lot of research and collecting. My classroom was filled with mysteries for children to read. Then we staged a crime while the kids were in the library. After the crime, a policeman came in and took eyewitness accounts. The point of this was to let the kids know what we think we see we don't really see. There were twenty-two different versions of the crime. The discussion that followed gave the kids the ability to work like a mystery writer. Their mysteries now contain clues and misinformation."

On the day we visited two boys were getting their mystery, "The Case of the Missing Surfboard" ready for binding. They had written, edited, and typed the story. Now they were cutting it and deciding where to place their illustrations. When bound, the mystery would be placed in the school library.

The "I Am Special" Awards Assembly was established to promote school values by recognizing individual achievements and improvement on the part of students and toward fostering self-esteem. Awards are presented weekly to K–3 students for reasons such as:

- Achievement of curriculum goals
- Appropriate school behaviors
- Improvement in risk taking
- Good citizenship
- Cooperative learning

Students receive a blue ribbon embossed with the words "I Am Special," a happy face, and Bowman School on the front. The reason for the award is written on the back. This idea received the Golden Achievement Award from the National School Public Relations Association (Johnson, 1990b).

The third goal of the school is to integrate computer technology into education-related activities. A computer team has been formed to keep Bowman on the cutting edge of informational technology for children. A computer lab, computers in upper grade classrooms, and a publishing center with word processors are available for students now (Johnson, 1990b). Curriculum strategies are being developed to integrate computer use in all content areas.

The fourth goal is to develop and maintain a positive school climate. This goal is achieved by giving special attention to faculty and to parents. Bowman has found that quality staff development provides an exciting and stimulating atmosphere in which to work, thereby enhancing the school climate. Last year twelve on-campus workshops, mainly on whole language, were scheduled. All faculty members were funded to attend off-campus workshops. Faculty forum is scheduled biweekly. It fills the need of teachers to encourage, inspire, or exhort one another to better teaching. Teachers can share an enlightened or a devastating moment from their classrooms. Teacher Steven Levy said, "As tired as any of us may have felt at 3:30 P.M., we all left the Faculty Forum at 5:00 P.M. refreshed and happy we stayed" (Johnson, 1990b).

The PTA is a very active organization at Bowman. Parent volunteers and PTA officers were busy in the building the day we visited. The *Bowman Banner*, the PTA newsletter, achieved national recognition by the National School Public Relations Association for its excellence. The Bear Week magazine drive and the Walk for the Arts raised almost $11,000. Bowman Arts Created Together (ACT), a committee of parents, teachers, and principal, was organized to integrate art into the curriculum. Some outcomes of the committee were a Poet-in-Residence who spent a month on campus, a Chinese New Year Celebration, an artist to enhance the unit "Medieval Times," and trips to the Boston Youth Symphony performances (Johnson, 1990a).

The story of Joe illustrates the caring climate of the Bowman School community. Joe was a special needs student who was assigned to the cooperative classroom of Mrs. Judith Rosenberg and Mr. Jim Hathaway. In these classrooms special needs students are integrated with regular fourth- and fifth-graders.

One day Joe's mother was visiting. She explained that she was busy planning for her elder son's bar mitzvah.

Mrs. Rosenberg said, "When Joe has his bar mitzvah maybe you can plan something else."

The mother replied, "Joe could never have a bar mitzvah. He's special ed."

"Yes, he could. He just needs some help and encouragement."

"Never!" the mother exclaimed.

Mrs. Rosenberg brought in a speech and language specialist to work with Joe. He concurred Joe had the capabilities to do it. After many long discussions, the mother agreed to let Joe try.

Three years later after the bar mitzvah, Joe stood in the pulpit and said, "I want to thank Mrs. Rosenberg for helping my mom realize I could do a bar mitzvah."

One can see that the goals of the school relate directly with its Core Value. It is a school community that is intellectually curious, motivated, and responsible. Within the cooperative environment of the Bowman Community, children, parents, and teachers are lifelong learners who respect themselves, each other, and the world. And it is personalized for students like Joe.

Summary and Reflection

In this chapter we described eight outstanding schools in action. Each school had structured an outstanding program for its students. Each school faculty chose to use a different approach to achieve its goals. At Lake George we saw family clusters with nongraded–continuous-progress curriculum sequence. The Meridith faculty treated all students like they were gifted and talented. At Montview brothers and sisters were placed in the same classrooms to provide stability for the children, the family, and the teachers. At Crawford the year-round calendar was designed so that children would not forget and thus need so much reteaching, and so that summer problems in urban neighborhoods would be minimized. At Lozano a carefully structured program and a faculty that valued children and their families helped disadvantaged students achieve and develop positive self-concepts. At Diamond we saw how a school can be restructured to meet the many needs of middle school students. At McFarland we saw the multiunit school in action and learned how content can be rotated to facilitate student learning in multiaged groups. And at Bowman we saw a personalized school that was structured so that all the members of the school community were viewed as learners. The schools were small enough (under 600 students) so that all students could be treated as special individuals. Each school restructured its instructional program in a different way to meet the needs of its children, teachers, and parents.

Each school was different and, yet, in many ways each school was the same.

We saw the qualities of good schools that had been identified in *Learning in America* (1990). Each school believed in the value of public education in a democracy. At each school we found a collegiality among the teachers and administrators. Each school found ways to circumvent the bureaucratic rules and regulations of their state and district. The principals shared much of their administrative authority with the teachers. At each school parents were regarded as crucial to the success of their children's education. And at each school there was a commitment to children — to their dignity, to their capacity to learn, and to their self-esteem.

We left feeling positive that restructuring can occur in many ways — that it is possible — and that as staffs become empowered so do the students. Schools can be restructured so that all children learn.

References

Barton, J. (1988). *Reading instruction in the accelerated school.* Palo Alto, CA: Stanford University.

Bennett, W. (1988). *James Madison Elementary School: A curriculum for American students.* Washington, DC: U.S. Department of Education.

Bingham, J. (1986). "Can-do" principal turns school around. *The Denver Post* (November 30): 12.

Crawford Elementary School. (1987). Autora, CO: Aurora Public Schools.

Critical skills. (1989). Aurora, CO: Aurora Public Schools.

Dixon, J. (1988). School goes beyond basics. *The Dallas Morning News* (September 2): 36A.

Duran, Y. (1990). *Lozano Special Emphasis School: Campus improvement plan 1990–91.* Corpus Christi, TX: Corpus Christi Independent School District.

George, M. (1990). Shorter summer vacation helps Crawford kids learn. *The Denver Post* (September 10): 4C.

Glickman, C. (1991). Pretending not to know what we know. *Educational Leadership,* 48(8): 4–10.

Hernandez, A. (1990). A page from a one-room school. *Rocky Mountain News* (June 3): 14–16.

Hernandez, A. (1989). Back from the brink. *Rocky Mountain News* (August 14): 4.

Johnson, M. (1990a). Grant awarded for children's publishing. Bowman Banner, 23(2): 1–2.

Johnson, M. (Ed.). (1990b). *State of the school report: Bowman Elementary School.* Lexington, MA: Lexington Schools.

Kollen, R., Olive, K., Attanucci, C., Neuman, C., & O'Conner, R. (1990). *Middle school student council: Inclusive, empowering.* International Conference of the Association for Individually Guided Education, Cambridge, Massachusetts.

Lake George Elementary School newsletter. (1989). Lake George, NY: Lake George Schools.

Learning in America: Schools that work. (1990). Public Broadcasting System.

Livingston, C., & Castle, S. (1989). *Teachers and research in action.* Washington, DC: National Education Association.

Lozano Special Emphasis School. (1990). Dissemination brochure. Corpus Christi, TX: Corpus Christi Independent School District.

Meridith Magnet National Exemplary School. (1990). Temple, TX: Temple Independent School District.

O'Connor, S. (1989). Crawford principal wins national award. *Rocky Mountain News* (August 20): 14.

Program of studies. (1990). Lexington, MA: Lexington Middle Schools.

Ramirez, M., & Rosales, S. (1983). A special emphasis school: A real success story. *TEPSA Journal.* Texas Elementary Principals Supervisors Association, May 27: 19–23.

Ross, R. (1990). *School cabinet: Shared decision making plus.* International Conference of the Association for Individually Guided Education, Cambridge, Massachusetts.

Schluter, D. (1990). Program keeps siblings together, gets rave reviews. *Aurora Sentinel* (September 12): 8.

We're on track: Crawford's year-round survey results. (1990). Aurora, CO: Aurora Public Schools.

Whitmill, J. (1988). What made a model Texas school. *The Saginaw News* (September 21): 4.

Year-round education at Crawford. (1989). A parent brochure. Aurora, CO: Aurora Public Schools.

CHAPTER FIVE

Effective Teaching Strategies

The most effective teaching machine ever invented is the teacher.

When we entered the model schools, we knew immediately that good things for students were happening here. The positive learning climate that had been established was readily observable. Teachers were teaching and students were learning. The students we interviewed seemed to be competent, confident, independent, and responsible. They were enthusiastic about their school, their own learning, their classmates, and their teachers.

Visiting schools has made us study, analyze, and evaluate teachers and teaching. Out of this has emerged an increased respect for teachers and the teaching profession. We know that good teaching makes a difference. Observing economically deprived children as they entered school and as they exited made us aware of the powerful and positive impact quality teaching has on students. Perhaps the heart of restructuring is a school organization in which good teachers can teach effectively.

Good teachers do two things well. First, they create in their mind's eye a clear picture of how the student will be different after their planned teaching. Second, good teachers know how learning takes place. They know what needs to be done to unleash the untapped potential of students and to let them emerge as capable learners (McClure, 1990).

One of these effective teachers explained why he gave up an administrative position to become a first-grade teacher (Nations, 1988). "My solution to my mid-life crisis was to return to the life that was most stimulating to me, that was most challenging to me, that gave me the most feedback of my worth as an individual. I became a classroom teacher again. Did it work? I am overworked, underpaid, never can keep up with all I have to do but, yes, it did work. I am stimulated. I am challenged. And every single day I receive messages of my worth as an individual from bright-eyed, eager little faces."

We agree that there is no work more rewarding than that of providing the best possible educational opportunity for each student.

Why is good teaching so exciting? Nations (1988) says it's exciting because it's a game. He explains that he doesn't mean this in a frivolous way. Being able to play the game well is important. In many families game playing is an important life skill. When you play bridge, you are dealt a hand. The first challenge is to assess what is in the hand; the second is to make the most of what's there. In bridge you don't do that alone. You enter into a partnership where communication is important.

Teaching involves the same set of game skills. Teachers are given a classroom of students. The first challenge is to assess the potential that is there. The second—the big challenge—is to make the most of what is there, to develop strategies that will help the teacher to make a human connection with those students—strategies that will help those students develop as human beings, develop new skills or new attitudes or new ways of life (Nations, 1988). There are many choices of teaching strategies available for use by teachers who are restructuring their instructional programs to provide for their students. That's why teaching today is an exciting game.

This chapter focuses on the strategies that effective teachers use to help elementary and middle school students to learn.

1. Two structured programs are described: the direct teach model and the mastery learning curriculum sequence. These models are based on the behaviorism learning theory.
2. Two instructional strategies that emphasize process learning are presented. These strategies—cooperative learning and whole language—are based on the cognitive learning theories.
3. The enriched basal textbook program at Meridith Elementary School is described. This program uses a combination from both behaviorist and cognitive approaches.
4. A series of strategies to provide for students' individual differences are presented.

The Direct Teach Model

The Direct Teach Model has existed for almost a century. Herbart (1904) was convinced that the learning process should proceed through a series of ordered steps. This was the approach to teaching that was stressed most in the early teacher colleges and normal schools. Behaviorist learning theories have refined this structured strategy and made it more scientific. Direct Teaching has been and is a primary teaching strategy in schools across the United States.

This model lends itself to well-planned, systematic, and intensive instruction. The Direct Teach lesson is designed so that the teacher gets immediate feedback, then corrective changes can be made during the lesson for increased student learning. When planning Direct Teach lessons, instructional and curriculum materials can be adjusted and modified to meet the individual differences of students (Hollingsworth and Hoover, 1991).

In 1984 we had the opportunity to visit twenty elementary schools in which minority students achieved in reading, writing, and mathematics. The study (Bechtol, 1984) only included schools whose student populations were over 50 percent minority and whose students had scored above the expected student population scores on a state test of basic skills in reading, writing, and mathematics. The findings from visiting these schools, from observing and scripting sixty-two classroom teachers, and from interviewing the teachers and principals showed that the Direct Teach Model was their primary teaching strategy.

These teachers emphasized that much of their success with students came from good use of instructional time. Their goal was to spend most of the class time in active teaching. To use time efficiently these teachers did the following (Bechtol, 1984):

1. Identified priorities and scheduled adequate time to achieve them
2. Planned well—they knew what they were going to do and they had the materials ready
3. Started immediately
4. Stayed on schedule
5. Kept transitions within and between lessons smooth and brief
6. Kept up with the paperwork

The teaching practices and the positive student learning results are consistent with Berliner's (1979) study of time on task. Effective teachers engage their students in appropriate instructional activities.

The Direct Teach Model requires teachers to use clear instructional objectives that identify what a successful learner should be able to do upon completion of the instructional activities. A good instructional objective is like a road map; it can tell teachers where they are going, suggest ways of arriving at the destination, identify materials needed, and tell teachers when they have completed the trip.

Clear instructional objectives contain three parts:

1. The behavior the learner is to achieve is stated.
2. The conditions under which the behavior can be expected to occur are given. For example, what the learner will be provided and what the learner will be denied; "given a map of the United States" or "without the aid of a map" are examples of conditions.
3. The criterion of acceptable performance is specified.

An example of an instructional objective that could be used by teachers who are studying this section is

Given ten multiple choice questions about the Direct Teach Model, the learner will answer at least eight correctly.

The behavior in the objective is "answer." The conditions are "Given ten multiple choice questions about the Direct Teach Model." The criterion is 80 percent or higher.

What does an objective like this tell teachers? It tells them that this instructional sequence will end with a test. Consequently, instructional activities must be designed so that students can score 80 percent or higher on a test about the Direct Teach Model. The objective becomes a road map that directs the instructional activities.

The Direct Teach Model was detailed in books and videotapes by Madeline Hunter (1982). This model was expanded in staff development materials by Donald Maas (1986) and Pat Wolfe (1987).

To help pre-service and in-service teachers to be able to understand and to use the Direct Teach Model, we have organized the lesson plan into three boxes (see Figure 5-1). Each box represents a part of the lesson: Focus, Teach, and Practice.

The Focus Box

The first few minutes of a lesson are prime time for teaching. When boys and girls come into a classroom they have many things on their minds — what happened before school or on the playground, a boy or girl that they just were holding hands with in the hall. What teachers want to do immediately is to get these thoughts out of their students' minds and to get their lesson into the students' life spaces.

The key purpose of the Focus part of the lesson is to get the students' minds focused on the lesson. Teachers focus their students by using an anticipatory set, by telling them the objective of the lesson, and by explaining the purpose of this learning.

The anticipatory set is a strategy teachers use to take students' minds off of other things and to focus their attention on the learning that is to come. There are many sets that teachers can use to hook students to their lessons. Novel beginnings, review of past materials, diagnosis of new material, pictures, and crossword puzzles are examples. Anticipatory sets are designed to:

1. Obtain active participation by the students
2. Give meaning by relating the lesson content to past learning
3. Give relevance by relating the content to the background of the learners

FIGURE 5-1 • *The Lesson Design for the Direct Teach Model*

Focus	Anticipatory Set Objective Purpose
Teach	Input Modeling Checking for Understanding
Practice	Guided Practice Closure/Summary Independent Practice

Source: Adapted from M. Hunter, *Mastery Teaching* (El Segundo, CA: TIP Publications, 1982); D. Maas, *Maintaining Teacher Effectiveness: A Workshop Guide* (Bloomington, IN: Phi Delta Kappa Educational Foundation Workshop, 1968); P. Wolfe, *Instructional Decisions for Long-Term Learning: Guidelines for Instructional Decisions,* Videotape series (Alexandria, VA: Association for Supervision and Curriculum Development, 1987).

An example of an anticipatory set in science follows:

"How many of you have eaten homemade ice cream?" Most students raise their hands.

"How many of you have eaten a McDonald's milkshake?
Most students raise their hands.

"Good. Now listen to this. If you try to eat a cone of homemade ice cream on a typical summer day, the ice cream will melt so fast that you may get some on your hands. But you can let your McDonald's milkshake sit out in the sun and it won't melt. You can put it in the oven and it won't melt. Why not?"
Teacher pauses.

"Because it's got emulsifiers in it. And that's what today's lesson is about."

The second part of the Focus box is the objective. Students will extend more effort and consequently increase their learning if they know what they will be expected to do. In the lesson that follows, the teacher presents to the student only the behavior of the objective:

> The learner will identify whether a person has committed a crime through omission of an act or commission of an act.

The teacher knows the conditions are "given 5 test items" and the criterion is "with 80 percent accuracy," but it is not necessary to share this information with students.

The third part is the purpose. Seldom do teachers teach content that has no relevance to a student's life, but frequently students do not make the connection. By explaining the purpose of the lesson, the teacher lets the students know how the learning will benefit them. It gives meaning to the lesson.

Let's look at how a middle school social studies teacher focused her class (Wolfe, 1987).

> "To begin our lesson today, I want you to think about what you've read or seen on TV about people being charged with a crime. You're aware of people in our community who have broken the law."
>
> "Let's brainstorm some crimes you're aware of. Think of them in your mind. Raise your hands and I'll write them on the board."
>
> The students raised their hands. The teacher wrote:
>
> "Possession of drugs."
>
> "Possession of weapons."
>
> "Assault."
>
> "Forgery."
>
> "Vandalism."
>
> "Murder."
>
> The teacher said, "Put your hands down and just think. Suppose your parents didn't pay their income taxes. Are there other crimes one can commit by not doing something? Can we add those to our list?"
>
> Brainstorming answers included:
>
> "Not paying a fine."
>
> "Tax evasion."
>
> "Not going to school."
>
> "Robbing a bank."
>
> The teacher stopped the brainstorming and said, "Look at our list. We've got two categories here: those things that are against the law and those things the law says we are to do." She uncovered a large sheet of newsprint. "Look at our objective. Read it silently while I read it aloud. *The learner will identify whether a person has committed a crime through omission of an act or commission of an act.* Jot down the objective in your note-taking guide."

After the students had copied the objective, the teacher said, "Look at the objective. What am I going to ask you to do?"

"Identify!" the students answered.

"Good for you!" responded the teacher.

The teacher explained, "The reason we're looking at this is to help you learn your rights and responsibilities as a citizen. It's important to learn from laws the things that we should do and those things we shouldn't do."

If we analyze this Focus part of the lesson, we can see that both the students and the teacher learned from this activity. The students were informed of the objective and purpose of the lesson. The brainstorming let the teacher diagnose what the students knew about crimes and what they didn't know.

Wolfe (1987) recommends the following:

1. Always involve students in the focus part of the lesson.
2. Make certain the beginning activities are related to learning.
3. Don't include something that isn't needed.

A few reminders about the Focus box. There is no sequence. In our example there was an anticipatory set, an objective, and the purpose. Any order is acceptable. When teachers believe that students are focused on the lesson, they move to the Teach box.

The Teach Box

The Teach part of a lesson includes input, modeling, and checking for understanding. This is the basic teaching cycle of Direct Teaching. The teacher provides information, models the information or the process, and checks for student understanding.

The input of information constitutes the foundation for learning and thinking. There are many ways to provide information. Teacher lectures, audio-visual presentations, and demonstrations are input examples. Careful planning is required for the input section. The teacher must determine which information is basic or essential to students' understanding of the content or process. The information must be presented in the simplest and clearest form. Organizing the information in small, sequential steps moving from simple to more complex understanding is one effective way of providing information. Giving older students advance organizers like note-taking guides is another helpful strategy.

A key component of the Teach box is modeling. A model may be concrete, such as a model of a human heart or a western town. A model may be a replication; for example, a picture or a symbolic item such as a diagram or a map. A model may be verbal, written or spoken, such as a sentence or a paragraph (Hunter, 1982). Written products such as essays, stories, and reports from past classes serve as excellent models for elementary and middle school students. These written models from the previous year's students set a standard and motivate the current students.

An effective model *highlights the critical attributes*. The teacher labels these critical attributes so that students know what makes a triangle different from other geometric shapes, for example. An effective model *avoids controversial issues*. The first models presented in a lesson must be *accurate and unambiguous*; and it *must be presented by the teacher*. This is an important concept. Teachers must choose clear models and present them or there will be errors in student learning.

Models *introduce nonexemplars*. Half of knowing what something is, is knowing what it is not (Hunter, 1982). After the teachers are satisfied that students can identify triangles and label their critical attributes, teachers can introduce other geometric shapes and have students explain why they are not triangles.

The sequence for teaching using models is important. The critical attributes of the concept must be identified:

1. A clear model should be presented and the critical attributes should be identified.
2. More examples should be presented with the teacher and then the students identifying critical attributes.
3. The teacher introduces nonexemplars and has the students contrast exemplars from nonexemplars.

We reemphasize this sequence because we have observed teachers teaching concepts such as honesty or sportsmanship by starting with nonexemplars; this is a teaching error that must be avoided.

In this section of the lesson teachers are trying to give their lessons meaning. If the teacher says, "Think of the word 'bat,'" students may be thinking of an animal, a baseball bat, the verb to hit a ball, or a disagreeable woman. Using a picture or an example gives meaning to this word. Meaning is the most important motivator for learning. If the teacher can relate a math problem to John buying a shirt and a pair of jeans, the problem has meaning. Models and examples should be selected that relate the learning to students' past knowledge and experiences (Hunter, 1982).

Sometimes it is not possible to relate the content of the lesson directly to the students' past experiences. In a case like this teachers find it effective to use a mnemonic device. The word HOMES is an artificial device that helps students remember the names of the Great Lakes. The sentence, "Keep Catching Apes And Silly Elephants" helps teachers remember the sequence of Bloom's Taxonomy. Putting the three blank boxes from Figure 5-1 on a chalkboard is a mnemonic device that helps teachers remember this Direct Teach Model.

The third component of the Teach box is checking for understanding. As teachers are teaching, they monitor students and adjust their teaching to ensure student success. Effective checking saves teachers from wasting time correcting poor quality tests and papers.

Signaled answers is a simple technique to check understanding. Teachers pose a question or statement and have every student signal a response. "Thumbs up if the statement is true, down if false, to the side if you're not sure." "A plus sign if it is add. A minus sign if it is subtract." "Use your Show-Me envelopes and show me the answer to problem 2." (Show-Me envelopes permit students to display numerals or letters; slates may be used in the same way.) Other signals include, "Hold up one, two, three, or four fingers," or "Raise your hand when you hear the s-s-s sound."

A second way of checking students' understanding is to ask the group a question and get a choral response. The strength as well as the correctness of the response can give the teacher valuable clues to determine if students have gained understanding. An advantage of this technique is that it allows students who do not know the answers to learn the correct response without visibility or humiliation. Two problems with the technique are (1) not all students will answer and (2) some students may be "coattailing" (making their mouths move without really knowing all the words). Even with these caveats choral responses are effective for checking student understanding (Hunter, 1982).

A third technique is for the teacher to beam a question to the whole class ("Be ready to give me a characteristic of a mammal."), and then call on individual students, making an inference on the basis of the strata of the class each student represents. Sampling the individual responses of one or two average students may give the teacher important information about student understanding. Another sampling technique is to pose a question and require students to write a brief response. While they are writing, the teacher can circulate among the students to check their understanding (Hunter, 1982).

There are three common teacher errors committed in checking students' understanding. The most common error is the noncommittal, "O.K.?" with the assumption that student silence means they understand. "Let's leave the War of 1812 and move on to the next section, O.K.?" What student will say, "No, it's not O.K., you're going too fast." A second common teacher error is the use of the statement, "You all understand, don't you?" Few students are willing to publicly admit they don't understand. A third common teaching error is to ask, "Does anyone have a question?" Often this query communicates that students should "understand" and would only have questions if they weren't listening (Hunter, 1982).

Teachers should avoid using all three of these dysfunctional methods. They should carefully check student understanding by using signaled answers, using choral responses, or sampling individual students.

Let's return to the lesson crimes (Wolfe, 1987):

"Now we have our two definitions for crimes. Let me model what I want you to do. Give the definition to your partner. Omission of an act. Something you didn't do that you should do to obey the law. An example of a crime by omission is not paying a fine."

"What I want you to do is this. The first person gives the definition. The second person gives an example. I'll walk around the room to check if we are getting this idea."

The teacher monitored the pairs for a short time and then checked understanding in a different way.

"Let's look at our list of crimes. If it is a crime of omission signal with an O. If it is a crime of commission, signal with a C."

"Ready. Tax evasion. O. Good."

"Murder. C. Good."

"On the next one say the word as you make the letter. Arson."

Students chorally said, "Commission," and signaled, "C."

The Practice Box

Hunter (1982) says that practice doesn't make perfect. If it did, freeway drivers would be much better than they are or older teachers would be much better than younger ones. We know that neither is true. Some people who have driven or taught for many years drive or teach poorly every day.

Let's look at the principles of practice before we study the Practice box. Hunter (1982) says there are four critical questions that teachers should answer so that students' practice does increase their performances.

1. *How much material should be practiced at one time? A short meaningful amount.* Content to be practiced should always be divided according to meaning. Short meaningful "chunks" should be introduced to students. Teachers should check for student understanding and accomplishment before new material is introduced.

2. *How long in time should a practice period be? A short time so that the student exerts intense effort and has an intent to learn.* A practice period on any one aspect of learning should be short. Several short, highly motivating

practice periods will yield more improvement than a long one that often deteriorates into lessening of effort and distraction. The key words in the answer are *intent* and *intense* effort. Short practice periods where students are highly motivated is what teachers should strive for. Rather than asking, "Have you finished?" teachers should ask, "Have you learned it?"

3. *How often should students practice? New learning, massed practice. Older learning, distributed practice.* There are two answers to the question. New learning is not very durable so massed practice—several practice periods scheduled close together—will produce rapid learning. Distributed practice may also be called review. Once something is understood or has been learned, the practice periods need to be spaced farther and farther apart. Increased time periods between practice yields long remembering. Practice should be massed at the beginning of learning, then changed to a distributed schedule.

4. *How will students know how well they have done? Initially, teachers provide feedback.* Students need to receive knowledge of how well they are doing as they practice. At first, the answer to the question "How am I doing?" needs to come from the teacher who sets the criteria for excellence in performance. Once students know the criteria for acceptable performances, they can evaluate their own performances or use materials to check corrections.

The principles of practice are reviewed in this short humorous skit. Royce, the elementary music teacher, is in the teachers' lounge with four other teachers. This is how they help him improve his practice sessions for the school musical program.

R: O.I.—I give up. I quit. It's over. I'm calling it off!

G: What's your problem?

R: What's my problem? My problem is this fiasco that's supposed to be a Christmas program. Here it is, only ten days until the program, and it looks and sounds like a train wreck.

M: Oh, come on, it can't be that bad.

R: Oh, yes it can. Every kid in this school is in that program. They can't remember the words to the songs, they can't remember the steps I've worked out, they can't remember their lines, they can't remember where to stand, they can't remember anything. It seems like it's getting worse every time we practice. I need more time. What am I going to do?

S: Well, you don't have much practice time left, and we can't postpone the program. It sounds as though you need to sit down and plan your practice time very carefully.

R: What do you mean? I always start at the beginning and try to go all the way to the end every time we practice.

M: Oh, I see what your problem is.

R: Oh, you do, do you? So, tell me, Miss Master Teacher, what am I doing so wrong?

M: It's not that you're doing anything so wrong—it's just that maybe you're trying to practice too much material at a time. My special education students need to have things broken down into short segments. If you give them too much to think about at one time, they'll never be able to remember it.

R: So what do I do?

M: Sit down and plan your practice time. Choose short sections to concentrate on during one practice session. Go over the same part several times until they get the hang of it. That will encourage them to want to learn some more.

G: Do you think you could break up your one long practice time into two or three shorter practice sessions?

R: I don't know. Why?

G: Well, I've noticed in my P.E. classes that after I've worked on an activity too long, the students get tired and quit trying. It's hard for kids to concentrate for a long time, and I get better results with shorter, intense practices.

R: I don't think it would be possible to get all these kids together for two or three practices a day. Their schedules are so hard to work around.

G: Well, then, try practicing one part for a while, then go to a different part and work on it for a while. Then go back and practice the first part again. Then try going to another new part. Don't make them dwell too long on any one part, or they'll get distracted and waste your practice time.

R: It seems like this is going to take a lot of my time planning.

S: It will take a little time, but it'll definitely be worth it. And there's something else that might make your practice time more efficient: when you're introducing something new, be sure to go over it several times. That will help them learn more quickly. Then, after they've learned it pretty well, you can practice it less often. They'll be able to remember for a longer period of time if you practice a certain skill often when it's new, then occasionally after it is learned.

M: Oh—one more thing: Always let the students know how they are doing.

G: Yes, if they're doing everything just right, be sure and tell them. They need to hear it from you.

S: Also, if they're not doing everything right, they need to know immediately. It's hard to unlearn something that was learned wrong.

R: O.K., already, I get the picture. I'll go right straight to my room and make plans for tomorrow's practice. I'll make sure I pick out short sections to work on, I'll make sure not to practice any one part for too long a period of time, I'll practice new parts several times and the parts they already know less often, and I will let them know exactly how they're doing. But if this doesn't work—I quit!

Now that Royce has a plan for using the principles of practice, we can return to our explanation of the Practice box.

The *guided practice* part of a lesson is very important. New learning is like wet cement; it can easily be damaged. A mistake at the beginning of a learning sequence can have long-lasting consequences that are difficult to eradicate. The mispronunciation of a new word or an error in the way a student holds a tennis racquet will take more time to remedy than it would have taken to learn it correctly in the first place. It is essential that students' initial attempts in any new learning or skill be guided by the teacher in order to minimize errors and to provide feedback essential to improve performance (Hunter, 1982).

The techniques for guiding the initial practice are similar to those used for checking for understanding. The difference is that the teacher has decided that the students are understanding and are ready to begin practice activities.

The first technique is *guiding the group through each step in practice.* It helps if the teacher breaks the practice into small steps, models how to complete each step, and explains the thinking processes as he or she completes the practice activity. The teacher's modeling alerts the students to critical points and helps them develop strategies to avoid making errors (Hunter, 1982).

The next technique is *monitoring group responses and giving feedback.* After the teacher has modeled the thinking process and guided the class through each step of that process, students need to practice and to receive immediate feedback. This can be done with choral responses or with signaled responses (Hunter, 1982).

The third technique is to *sample group understanding through an individual's response.* After modeling and having the group complete a practice activity, the teacher can call on individual students to do a practice activity. Checking to see if representative students can complete the activity lets the teacher know if the class is ready for independent practice (Hunter, 1982).

The final technique is *monitoring each individual's written response.* A brief written response by each student can be monitored as the teacher circulates throughout the class. If common errors exist, the material can be retaught (Hunter, 1982).

The dividends from carefully guided practice are realized in more accurate independent practice. When the teacher has determined that the students have an understanding of the subject, students engage in independent practice—this is practice completed without direct teacher supervision. Independent practice gives students the opportunity to display their knowledge or skills of the objective of the lesson. This practice helps move this knowledge or skill from students' short-term memory to their long-term memory.

Teachers should remember when assigning independent practice or homework to make certain that the assignment matches the objective of the lesson. In the Direct Teach Model new material should not be introduced with independent practice. Homework should contain a short, meaningful amount of material.

The final part of the Practice box is the closure or summary. In this part, students may complete a final practice activity, articulate the learning, or summarize the main ideas of the lesson. The teacher communicates that the lesson is over and that students can complete their independent practice later.

We like summaries best for closure. Good summaries permit students to think about the main ideas of the lesson. Summaries use one sentence for each main idea, present the main ideas in order, eliminate details, and use the summarizer's own words. After the teacher has modeled a number of summaries, students can be taught to summarize lessons (Christen, 1987).

Let's go back to the middle school social studies lesson (Wolfe, 1987) as the students work in the Practice box.

"I believe that you're ready for practice. I have a worksheet for you. You are to label the crimes on the worksheet as commission or omission. I'll do the first one. Shoplifting. I can see someone doing the act; it's commission."

"Now let's do the second one together."

The class worked the second example correctly.

"I think you've got it. Work the rest on your own."

The teacher monitored the class. When all the students had finished the worksheet, she read the answers and students checked their own papers. Almost all the students had labeled correctly.

"Good job! Let's summarize our lesson. Crimes can be committed two ways: through the omission of an act or the commission of an act. Good citizens should learn from the laws the things they should do and the things they should not do."

Then the teacher said, "I have another handout for your homework. This one has newspaper articles, but your job is the same as in the practice worksheet — to label the crimes as omission or commission. Look at it. What are you to do?"

"Label the crimes in the newspaper articles as a crime of omission or as commission," a girl answered.

"Thank you. Class dismissed."

The Direct Teach lesson contains three parts, which we've placed in boxes on our diagram. Students are motivated or focused on the lesson with an interesting anticipatory set, by the objective, and by the purpose. Input, modeling, and checking students' understanding are the components of the Teach part. The Practice part emphasizes guiding students' initial practice, assigning similar activities as independent practice, and summarizing the main ideas of the lesson.

Mastery Learning

Mastery Learning is an example of Direct Teaching over a longer period of time. It is an instructional process based on the belief that virtually all students have the ability to learn if teachers adhere to certain basic principles. Traditionally, educators have believed that students' individual differences in terms of intelligence and aptitude would yield a wide range of mastery levels in any given curriculum. They believed that some students would master the materials easily and quickly, that some would need extra instruction and practice to master the materials, and that some would make only limited progress — never achieving mastery. The notion that all students can learn and will learn is a new idea for many teachers.

Benjamin Bloom developed a working model for Mastery Learning in the 1970s. Bloom elaborated on the work of Herbart (1904), Morrison (1934), and Carroll (1963) to develop this model. Herbart had emphasized the importance of structure in teaching; he believed that if teachers could build *right* teaching sequences, *right* student learning would follow (Bigge, 1982). Morrison (1934) believed that content in each subject could be divided into units and that unit objectives could be presented with such thoroughness that mastery is achieved by most students. Carroll (1963) challenged the notion that student aptitude determined the level a student could learn a subject. He believed that all students have the potential to learn well if given enough time to do so. Bloom (1976, 1980) combined these ideas of structure, units, and time variance to develop the Mastery Learning Model.

An important component of Bloom's model is the careful consideration of the cognitive and effective characteristics of students in relation to learning tasks. Early achievement in school has a powerful effect on later achievement in school. By the end of elementary school the student who consistently succeeds has a general positive concept of self as a learner. Also, by this period students who have consistently failed (and who are reminded of this failure by teachers and parents) must come to view themselves with generally negative self-concepts as learners. Bloom believes that if students can be given appropriate time and quality of instruction they can exit from an instructional unit with cognitive skills and positive effective attitudes toward the next learning task.

How does Mastery Learning work? The content of a course is organized into instructional units that can be taught in a one- or two-week period. When the basic objectives of a unit have been taught, a formative test is given. This test is designed to give immediate feedback to students and to teachers. Those students who have mastered the basic objectives may choose to complete enrichment objectives or to serve as peer tutors. Those students who did not achieve mastery are assigned corrective activities. When students have completed corrective and enrichment activities, they are given a summative test. The primary purpose of a summative test is to assign a student grades or to assess competence in a particular skill. This sequence, which is illustrated in Figure 5-2, is as follows:

1. Organize the curriculum. The content of the course is divided into a sequence of instructional units, which are driven by clear instructional

FIGURE 5-2 • *The Mastery Learning Sequence*

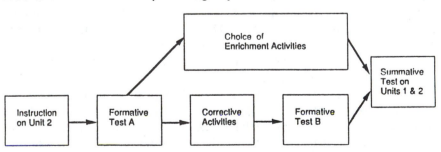

Source: Adapted from T. Guskey, *Implementing Mastery Learning* (Belmont, CA: Wadsworth, 1985); J. Block and L. Anderson, *Mastery Learning in Classroom Instruction* (New York: Macmillan, 1975); J. Block, H. Efthim, and R. Burns, *Building Effective Mastery Learning Schools* (New York: Longman, 1989).

objectives. The objectives specify the content or skill to be learned, what students must be able to do with this content or skill, and the level of proficiency to be achieved.

2. Construct the formative test. Test items (or tasks) are developed for each objective to be learned by all students and then the items are arranged into a formative test. The criteria of the objectives should set the standard for mastery on the test.

3. Develop an instructional sequence to achieve the unit objectives. This sequence will include a day-by-day outline of instructional activities and a list of instructional resources. At least two types of practice activities should be used for each objective. Equivalent activities are those in which the student actually practices the desired behavior identified in the objective. For example, if the objective is to add unlike fractions, the students are given practice problems and they add unlike fractions. Analogous activieies are those similar but not identical to the desired terminal behavior. With the objective mentioned, the student might use Cuisennaire rods to add unlike fractions. Corrective and enrichment activities will also be described.

Corrective activities: The essential characteristic of any corrective activity is that it teaches the same material in a way different from the way it was originally presented. The original instructional strategy had not worked with these students. A different corrective activity should give the students an increased opportunity to learn. This activity could match students' learning styles with an appropriate learning mode. Some types of corrective activities include reteaching using alternative textbooks and materials, using peer or volunteer tutors, and using computer-assisted instruction. Correctives should be chosen so that students feel confident and are successful when they are tested (Guskey, 1985).

Enrichment activities: Giving elementary and middle school students a set of limited choices works best for enrichment or extension activities. Students who master basic objectives on the formative test should see enrichment activities as a reward—not more of the same thing. Good enrichment activities should be fulfilling and exciting; they should challenge students to use high-level cognitive skills. Some types of activities that students like to choose include peer tutoring, developing instructional materials (practice activities, models, centers, games) to be used by other students, special projects and reports, more difficult games or problems, and advanced computer-assisted lessons.

4. Construct a summative test. The purpose of a summative examination is to gather cumulative information on students' learning so that grades can be assigned or competence in a particular skill or task can be determined. Guskey (1985) recommends that a summative test be broader in scope and

cover the content on a larger portion of the course, such as a grading period or two to four units. We like this idea. However, it does require that a parallel form of the formative test be developed to be used with students who are required to do corrective activities. Figure 5-2 illustrates this sequence.

Research on Mastery Learning approaches when compared with traditional instruction typically show that achievement levels are higher in mastery classes. Mastery approaches clearly can succeed in increasing the percentage of students who reach mastery on basic objectives, and they seem to have clear benefits for low achievers (Good and Brophy, 1991).

A criticism of the research is that many of the Mastery Learning experiments that had significant results were conducted for a short period of time — a few days to a month (Slavin, 1987). Long-term projects such as a semester ninth-grade general mathematics course in Philadelphia (Slavin & Karweit, 1984) and an elementary reading program in Chicago (Board of Education of the City of Chicago, 1982) did not achieve positive results.

We believe that Mastery Learning works. Most students can master any given subject or skill when given increased time and instruction. The results at Johnson City, New York, and by Jaime Escalante show how positive Mastery Learning can be.

Harry L. Johnson Elementary School in Johnson City has been making Mastery Learning work for over twelve years. The curriculum in reading and mathematics is based on Bloom's model. There is a special emphasis on reteaching so that students are successful. The results are outstanding. When children in this working-class community enter school, their achievement scores are similar to the national average. Their scores begin to skyrocket in fourth grade. Garmita Coles, basic skills coordinator, explained, "At a time when kids in other schools' enthusiasm for education wanes, ours are highly motivated. Mastery Learning builds on success." At the end of the eighth grade, Johnson City students' test results average 11.6 in reading and 12.5 in mathematics (*A + Schools,* 1984).

The successful teaching of Jaime Escalante and the high achievements of his students were documented in a television special and described in the movie *Stand and Deliver*. Heyman (1990) analyzed Escalante's teaching and found that he uses the principles of mastery teaching in his classroom. Heyman said, "Escalante believes his students can succeed. He teaches them carefully, tests them, and reteaches. He gives them extra time — two evenings a week and Saturday mornings — and sees them through to achievement."

Bloom's Mastery Learning strategies have been updated by two of his students, James Block (1975, 1989) and Thomas Guskey (1985). The strategies have been adopted by William Spady (1988) in Outcome-based Education. The works of these authors are useful for further study of Mastery Learning concepts.

The Mastery Learning sequence and the Direct Teach Models are structured, teacher-centered programs based on behavioristic teaching. The next section describes cooperative learning, a strategy based on cognitive learning processes — a more student-centered approach.

Cooperative Learning

In the elementary and middle schools that we visited all over the United States, we found the faculties engaged in cooperative learning. Students were no longer competing against one another in groups separated by ability or achievement. Instead, we found teachers structuring learning opportunities so that groups of students work cooperatively.

Why this change? Why have classrooms become places where one hears children's voices rather than teachers' voices? Why has cooperative learning become such a widespread innovation? There are three reasons:

1. Cooperative learning works. Teachers don't implement new teaching strategies unless they find them to be effective.
2. Cooperative skills are needed in today's society. Schools are mirroring the real world where people in fact work together to solve problems.
3. Cooperative learning fits the curricular and structural changes that are occurring in schooling. Curriculum changes that emphasize higher order thinking skills and learning for understanding and organizational changes that are responsive to student diversity require students to spend more time working democratically and collaboratively.

Let's look more closely at the reasons schools are using cooperative learning strategies. Does the research support the teachers' beliefs that cooperative learning works? The answer is a strong, "Yes." Slavin (1990, 1991) summarized most of the research on cooperative learning methods. He reports that the effects of cooperative learning on achievement are clearly positive: forty-nine of sixty-eight comparative studies were positive (72 percent); only eight (12 percent) favored the control group. Student achievement increases most when group goals and individual accountability are incorporated in the cooperative methods (Slavin, 1991).

In areas other than achievement, the findings are impressive. Cooperative learning arrangements have been found to promote friendship choices and prosocial patterns of interaction among students who differ in achievement, gender, race, or ethnicity and to promote the acceptance of mainstreamed handicapped students by their nonhandicapped classmates. Cooperative methods also have positive effects of affective outcomes such as self-esteem, academic self-confidence, liking for the class, liking and feeling liked by classmates, empathy, social cooperation, and psychological health (Slavin, 1983; Johnson, Johnson, Holubec, & Roy, 1984). Elementary and middle school teachers report that cooperative learning can benefit all students, even low achieving, gifted, and mainstreamed students (Augustine, Gruber, & Hanson, 1990).

Are cooperative skills needed in today's society? The answer again is a resounding, "Yes." In the real world of work, most jobs require workers with good interpersonal skills. Employers value those employees who can communicate clearly, assume responsibility, take initiative, and solve problems. Scientists, engineers, surgeons, and industrial managers don't work in isolation: they work in groups or teams. We find a socialization paradox: large bureaucratic impersonal schools that emphasize competition and pit students against each other produce alienated children, teenagers, and young adults. Most people lose jobs not because they lack basic or technical skills but because they lack the interpersonal skills that are promoted in cooperative learning. The ability of all students to learn to work cooperatively with others is the key to building and mainstreaming stable careers, marriages, families, and friendships (Johnson & Johnson, 1985).

Do cooperative learning structures facilitate the curriculum and the structural changes that are being implemented in today's schools? The answer again is "Yes." Steffens (1990) identified some common themes of schooling. Three of the themes — an emphasis on active learning, higher order thinking skills, and learning for understanding — are curriculum goals that can be achieved in the cooperative learning structure. Two organizational themes — heterogeneous grouping and an environment responsive to student diversity — are not only more effectively implemented with cooperative learning, but they are also supported by over ten years of research findings.

The common positive thread running through the reforms in curriculum and school organization is a commitment to prepare students to be informed and participating citizens in a democracy. Restructured schools prepare students not only for the world of work but also for life in a democratic society. The promise of restructuring is to enable and empower students, to teach them how to learn and do significant things, to teach them how to work together, and to give them confidence in themselves and their peers. In heterogeneous groups students can learn to work democratically and collaboratively (Steffens, 1990). Cooperative grouping provides an appropriate structure for students to become competent, confident, independent, and responsible school citizens.

In cooperative grouping, students work together in small groups to achieve a common goal. Having students work in groups is not a new concept in education. However, small group work has been plagued with the problem of one or two students doing all the work while everyone got the credit. An even greater problem and concern was the question of how much, if anything, the nonworking members of the group learned. What had been missing in small group strategies was a structure that involves all students in the work and ensures that each student learns the materials (Vasquez, Slavin, & D'Arcangelo, 1990).

Cooperative learning provides a structure for group work based on the following three elements (Vasquez et al., 1990):

- *Positive interdependence:* The success of the group depends on the efforts of all its members. "We're in this together." Tasks are structured so that group members depend on one another to contribute to the success of the group's effort. This structure promotes a caring atmosphere where students help one another learn.
- *Individual accountability:* Students are individually accountable for mastering the materials. Each student has objectives for which he or she is held accountable; it is not possible for the brighter or harder working member to "cover" for other members who are ignored or who fail to do what they are supposed to do.
- *Social skills:* Interpersonal and communication skills can promote successful group interaction. Students are taught interpersonal and small group skills, such as how to communicate accurately, how to accept and support one another, and how to solve conflicts constructively.

Let's look at cooperative learning in action. A fifth-grade teacher has organized his students into five heterogeneous teams to complete a report using the Group Investigation model (Sharon & Sharon, 1990). Each team has selected a different section of the country; they will present a report explaining why the great cities of the United States exist where they do.

Everyone's learning is the responsibility of the team. Each student in the team has a city. After completing their individual tasks, the individual team members will prepare a group report with a map to communicate their findings to the class. All team members will be evaluated on the quality of the report—all for one and one for all. Therefore, Harold, who has a stutter and reads below grade level, is no longer an object of ridicule. The other team members encourage him to speak up in discussions. They cheer him on. They help him if the reading passages are hard. And they have good reason to do so. Harold is a whiz in math. Everyone turns to him for help with fractions and decimals. Then he becomes the tutor.

Harold and his friends are active learners. They are seeking answers to some hard questions. They are answerable to each other, and a 10-year-old can put a lot of pressure on another 10-year-old who is "goofing off." They organize information, help others with team responsibilities, create a product, and present it publicly.

Notice that what has just been described—gathering information, making sense of it, interacting with groups, and developing a product — is not terribly different from the work adults do in top-notch organizations and businesses. Experience in cooperative learning gives students a feel for the real world (McClure, 1990).

There are many cooperative group structures. We will briefly describe a few of these strategies. These methods and many others are described in detail in *Cooperative Learning: Theory, Research, and Practice* (Slavin, 1990).

Jigsaw

The Jigsaw method (Aronson, Blaney, Stephan, Sikes, & Snapp, 1978) ensures active participation and group cooperation by arranging tasks so that each student possesses unique information and has a special role to play. In other words, each group member has a part of the puzzle. The group task cannot be completed unless each student does his or her part. For example, information needed to compose a biography might be broken into early life, first accomplishments, major setbacks, later life, and world events occurring during a person's lifetime. One member of each group would be given relevant information and assigned responsibility for one of the five sections of the biography. The other group members would be assigned to the other sections. Students who were working on the same section would work together in "expert groups" to discuss their sections. Then they would return to their regular groups and take turns teaching their group mates about their sections. Since the only way that students can learn about sections other than their own is to listen carefully, they are motivated to support and to learn from each other. The students then prepare biographies or take quizzes on the material individually. Jigsaw is a good strategy for beginning cooperative learning. It also works well for staff development.

Learning Together

The Learning Together Model of cooperative learning was developed by David and Roger Johnson (1985). This approach calls for students to work together in four- or five-member heterogeneous groups on a group assignment. The method emphasizes four elements:

1. *Positive interdependence:* Students work together to achieve a successful group project.
2. *Face-to-face interaction:* Tasks that require significant interaction, rather than those that can be accomplished by group members working their own, are assigned.

3. *Individual accountability:* Students must demonstrate individually that they have mastered the material.
4. *Interpersonal and small-group skills:* Students are taught effective means of working together and of discussing how well their group is working to achieve their goals.

The Learning Together Model can be used with group assignments and products. One special use is called *cooperative controversy*. Students study materials on a controversial issue. Two group members take one side of the issue and two take the other. Then they switch roles and argue the opposite side. Finally the group comes to a consensus. Some of the rules the group follows include: "I am critical of ideas, not people" and "I remember that we are all in this together." Research has generally found this method more effective than traditional debate or individual study methods in increasing retention of information or in changing attitudes (Slavin, 1990).

Student Teams—Achievement Divisions (STAD)

STAD has five major components: class presentations, teams, quizzes, individual improvement scores, and team recognition. Class presentations are most often direct instruction conducted by the teacher. Teams are composed of four or five students who represent a cross-section of the class in terms of academic performance, sex, race, and ethnicity. The teams study presentation notes and work on worksheets in the team to master the material. Quizzes are given after one or two periods of teacher presentation and one or two periods of team practice. Students take individual quizzes. Every student is accountable for mastery of the material. The idea behind Individual Improvement Scores is to give each student a performance goal that the student can achieve by working harder. The students can contribute points for their team by exceeding their base score. Team recognition is based on team members' improvement scores, and individual certificates or class newsletters are used to recognize high scoring teams. Slavin (1990) recommends STAD as a good model for teachers who are new to the cooperative approach.

Teams—Games—Tournament (TGT)

TGT is the same as STAD in every respect but one: instead of quizzes and the individual score system, TGT uses tournaments. Games are composed of content-relevant questions designed to test the knowledge students gain from class presentations and team practice. The tournaments usually take place on Friday. Students are assigned to three-person tables composed of students from different teams who are similar in achievement. Students earn points by correctly answering questions or by successfully challenging and correcting the answers of the other two students at the table. Team recognition is based on team members' tournament scores.

Upper elementary and middle school students like the challenge of TGT; their teachers are pleased with their students' improved achievement (Slavin, 1990).

Team Assisted Individualization (TAI)

TAI combines cooperative learning with individualized instruction to meet the mathematics needs of students in the heterogeneous classroom. It is a structure that combines the motivation and peer assistance of cooperative learning with an individualized curriculum plan. The curriculum has a nongraded–continuous-progress sequence covering addition through algebra with a consistent emphasis on problem solving.

Students are assigned to four- or five-member heterogeneous teams. At the beginning of the program students are pretested with a Placement Test and are placed at an appropriate point in the curriculum continuum. In Team Study, students from pairs or triads work practice exercises, have teammates check answers, and take formative tests. When students make a satisfactory score on the formative test, they receive a unit test from a monitor from another team. The monitor scores the unit test. At the end of each week the teacher computes a Team Score; Team Recognition is based on the number of units covered by each team member and the accuracy of the unit test. Everyday the teacher works with Teaching Groups, small groups of students drawn from the different teams who are at the same point in the curriculum. Mainly teachers use these mini-lessons (ten to fifteen minutes) to introduce new concepts to the students. Twice each week students take Facts Tests. Some units in the curriculum, such as geometry and measurement, are designed to be taught as whole class units.

The advantage of TAI is that most of the checking, recordkeeping, and filing is done by the students. Teachers are free to provide assistance and/or Teaching Group instruction (Slavin, 1990; Slavin, Madden, & Stevens, 1990).

Cooperative Integrated Reading and Composition (CIRC)

CIRC includes three principal elements: basal-related activities, direct instruction in reading comprehension, and integrated language arts and writing. Students are assigned to a Reading Group according to their reading level. Within the reading group, the students are assigned to pairs or triads. Teams are made of pairs or triads from two reading groups.

Most of the basal-related activities are done in pairs or in teams. These include Partner Reading, Treasure Hunts, Words Out Loud, Word Meaning, Story Retell, and Spelling. The teacher teaches reading groups or individuals while the teams work independently. Once each week students receive direct instruction in reading comprehension. In the integrated language arts and writing curriculum, students work as teams on language arts skills that lead directly to writing activities. The writing program uses both writer's workshops and Direct Teach lessons. For independent reading, students read a trade book of their choice twenty minutes every evening. Parents initial forms indicating that students have read the required time. Students complete at least one book report every two weeks.

Students' scores on quizzes, compositions, independent reading, and book reports contribute to team scores, which result in team recognition.

Initial results from CIRC are quite positive. Teachers report that students enjoy CIRC because they're so involved with the processes of reading and writing (Slavin, 1990; Slavin, Madden, & Stevens, 1990).

Groups of Four

Groups of Four (Burns, 1981) has worked successfully in many elementary and middle school classrooms in mathematics. Students are assigned to groups randomly by drawing a card from a deck of playing cards. Tables are labeled Aces, Twos, Threes, and so on. Teachers like the randomness of this system.

There are three rules that are in operation when students are in groups of four:

1. You are responsible for your own work and behavior.
2. You must be willing to help any group member who asks.
3. You may ask for help from the teacher only when everyone in the group has the same question.

Burns (1981) recommends that a good beginning is for each group to find all the ways to write the numbers from one to twenty-five as the sum of consecutive numbers. She explains what "consecutive" means and models nine because is it the sum of more than one set of consecutive numnbers ($9 = 4 + 5$ and $9 = 2 + 3 + 4$) to get the groups started.

Students stay in the same group for two weeks. They are not allowed the option to change groups. Burns wants all students to benefit from all their classmates' thinking; therefore, they are expected to work with whomever draws the same cards.

Values in Physical Education

DeLine (1991) has developed a sequence of lessons to teach cooperative values such as honesty, sportsmanship, sharing, and teamwork. The lessons include both physical education objectives and values objectives. DeLine (1991) teaches these value lessons early in the school year so that students can use them throughout the school year.

The lesson sequence is as follows:

1. *Focus word:* The teacher clarifies the definition of the target concept, making certain children know what it means. For example, honesty — the ability to be truthful, fair, and trustworthy.
2. *Discussion:* The importance of the focus word is discussed. Questions for "honesty" would include, "Can you think of a time when you've been honest?" and "Would you enjoy a game in physical education if you knew everyone would play fair?"
3. *Strategies:* The teacher explains how students can participate in the physical education activity and also demonstrates the target value. For example, in the activity toe fencing, all touches by the wand must be declared verbally. When a student feels that his or her foot has been touched by the opponent, he or she says, "Touch!" or "You got me." A touch may not be declared by "I got you."
4. *Activity:* Students play the game and practice the value concept. In this example, students toe fence and also demonstrate "honesty."
5. *Reinforcement and feedback:* The teacher checks to see if the concept was practiced by asking questions. "Has your partner been honest?" "How many times?" "Did you have problems?" "Did you work it out?" are examples of feedback questions for the concept of "honesty."
6. *Nice time:* This is a time for peer praise and reinforcement. "Who in your group said nice things about your efforts?" and "Who did you notice that always seemed honest?" are questions that help students reinforce one another for "honesty."

As we said earlier, in our school visits we found teachers using cooperative learning strategies at all grade levels. We can understand why. Students learn more, develop friendships, work together more efficiently, and like school more. Cooperative learning helps students to develop the skills needed for future employment. Cooperative settings work to free the students from the academic and social constraints that characterize so many classrooms by fundamentally changing the relationships among the participants. It allows students to take more responsibility for their own learning.

One teacher explained: "I was tired of being the only teacher in my classroom. Cooperative teams are now serving as 'teacher assistants' in my room. We send our students out into a world where they must be able to communicate and work with their peers, but yet so often in our classrooms we keep them from doing that" (Walters, 1989).

When one thinks of a traditional classroom setting, the teacher was the primary audience for student talk — when it was permitted. Cooperative learning provides new and changing audiences for students, drawing them into conversations with their peers in settings structured by the teacher. Student talk is the major means by which learners explore the relationship between what they know and the new information they receive in the classroom. The emergence of real conversation about academic matters within the classroom is an important feature about cooperative learning (Barrett, 1989).

Are there legitimate objectives that should not be taught cooperatively? Absolutely. Students need to learn to compete. They need to learn to work independently. There must be balance in learning activities. The problem with the traditional classroom is that it almost never includes any cooperative activities. Students need opportunities to work both together and alone.

Teaching Students to Read and Write Effectively

In our study of the teaching of language arts or reading, writing, English, and spelling or whatever the school calls it, we think of Rick Masten's (1988) thoughtful musing, "Good Lord! It just came to me. My shoes are older than almost everyone in this building." The authors have been teachers, administrators, or teacher educators for over thirty years. During our professional careers there has been a constant controversy about how to teach children to read and write effectively. Jeanne Chall called it the Great Debate. The debate continues in the 1990s. Phonics? Whole language? Basal readers? Grammar? Reading readiness?

The neat thing that happens when one visits a number of excellent schools, as we have, is that you have the opportunity to see many outstanding programs. We have chosen to describe some distinctly different programs. Each of the programs meets these criteria:

1. There are measurable test results that demonstrate that students are learning to read and to write well.
2. The teachers believe in the program.
3. The reading and writing classes are stimulating.
4. There is evidence that students are reading independently.

The schools that we have chosen to describe relate positively to all the criteria. Their reading and writing scores are outstanding; all the schools had received recognition for their achievement. The teachers not only believed in their programs but were busy disseminating information about them in a missionary-like fashion. The classrooms were exciting and stimulating; they were fun to visit. This excitement was important to us because we had observed reading lessons in other schools (not those included in this book) that were dull and blah, much as Goodlad (1984) described in *A Place Called School,* without joy or enthusiasm. Finally, the students were reading trade books in these exciting classrooms and were enjoying them.

The Whole Language Approach

When you walk into primary classrooms at Bowman Elementary School in Lexington, Massachusetts, you will see the following (Johnson, 1990):

- Teachers sharing big books with the whole class as they gather around the easel
- Children generating ideas for a poem or story, which the teacher writes down on language experience chart paper before the group
- Choral reading of a poem or chant displayed by the teacher on a large chart paper mounted on an easel
- Pairs of children reading to each other from a big book or other trade book
- Small clusters of children enjoying a shared book experience together as they listen to the tape that accompanies the text
- Children and teacher reading from individual trade books during a Drop Everything and Read (DEAR) period
- Selected children individually or in groups of two or more engaged in reading and discussing a story with the teacher. The teacher has drawn from the children their own experiences about the story subject and has extended their knowledge to be able to better enjoy and understand the story to be read; predictions about the story events are drawn from the children periodically by the teacher in order to stimulate their continued interaction with the story text
- Children reading stories, singly or in pairs, from bound books that they have written and published for class sharing
- Children writing stories, as part of their writing workshop, using ideas that may have been sparked by listening to a story by a special author
- Children using a word processing program on the computer for the purpose of story or letter writing
- Children illustrating a story or participating in some other story-related

activity or project to further enhance appreciation and understanding of the literacy experience

As a visitor, you will notice that there are (Johnson, 1990):

- A rich supply of children's literature in the form of trade books (both large and small)
- Storage racks holding a volume of experience charts containing poems, chants, and stories that have been written by both students and teachers
- Bookcases and book racks overflowing with a rich and varied assortment of children's books (fact and fiction)
- Easels displaying big books
- Easels displaying chart paper for class or group story writing

When you walk into an upper-grade classroom you will see the following (Johnson, 1990):

- The entire class reading a common literary piece with the teacher reading aloud; discussion is a major part of the preliminary and ensuing activities along with stimulating and provocative questions calling for each pupil's individual written response to be shared at a future meeting
- Children and teacher reading from individual trade books during a DEAR period
- Children writing stories, as part of their writing workshop, the ideas for which may have been sparked by listening to a story by a special author
- Children using a word processing program on the computer for the purpose of story or letter writing
- Students researching and taking notes on information from texts relating to the curriculum they are studying
- Bookcases and book racks overflowing with a rich and varied assortment of children's books (fact and fiction)

The teachers at Bowman are very enthusiastic about the whole language approach. "The children love to read by themselves, to each other, and to other adults. They enjoy writing. The first-graders know book titles, authors, and chants" (Johnson, 1990).

The writing program at Bowman begins in kindergarten. Kindergartners, in the very early weeks of school, are given the tools, encouragement, and guidance to express themselves through drawings and "writings" using invented spelling. This is an approach to early writing in which children sound out words for themselves and write without concern for standard spelling. Inventive spellers' errors do not interfere with their learning to spell correctly later. Like early attempts to walk, talk, and draw, initial attempts to spell do not produce habits to be overcome. Invented spelling is not so much an approach to writing, as it is a way of removing obstacles in the path of a young writer (Johnson, 1990).

Children dictate and write stories based on their experiences; these materials are then used along with books and poetry as the basis of the reading program.

The Bowman writing program is especially strong because it connects a primary student's oral language, which is more highly developed, with the written language.

Teaching writing as a process looks somewhat different in the upper elementary grades, but the fundamental principles are the same. At the beginning of each writing period, the children are gathered together for a brief mini-lesson; here the teacher presents something that will inspire the children and/or help them to develop their writing. Mini-lesson topics range from improving peer conference to examining the use of voice in a narrative to introducing new punctuation skills.

After reporting on their work in progress, the students settle down to it. Students are strongly encouraged to write narratives based on their own experiences; most authors produce significantly better writing when they write about what they know well, and for children this means writing about their own lives. Writing is indeed a process for these children and at any given time in the classroom individual writers will be working along the continuum from first draft to published product.

In a typical classroom you will find that Marissa is working on her first draft (a story about a party she had last weekend), while Jon is working on his story (another adventure of Brer Rabbit, inspired by the Julius Lester version he had enjoyed in read-aloud time). Reading and writing become unavoidably connected in wonderful ways, and this is always encouraged!

Matt has just finished a peer conference about his story and has gone back to make a few revisions.

Leslie is now editing the final version of her story; she checks it for each item on her individual skills list. For Leslie, this includes, among other skills, marking new paragraphs and punctuating dialogue correctly. She must also check for spelling of any words she should know or suspect are incorrect. Invented spelling is still encouraged when children are stuck on a word during the draft stage, so that they do not lose their train of thought. Correcting to standard spelling is a required part of the editing process, however.

Gina and Shelley are both working on publishing their stories. These published stories will then be shared with the class and added to the growing Bowman collection of works by classroom authors. These collections are prominently displayed in the library.

The Bowman faculty believe that children should choose their own topics. Choosing gives them a chance to express what is important to them. Their investment in these stories is immense and they work to develop their writing with natural motivation and enthusiasm. This is certainly not the only writing children do. To broaden their writing skills and repertoire, topics — both specific and general — are assigned. But to this writing as well, the children bring two valuable things they have learned: a sense of writing as a process and, perhaps more importantly, confidence in themselves as writers (Johnson, 1990).

Portfolios

At Montview School in Aurora, Colorado, all students keep portfolios. These portfolios contain lists of books read at school and at home. These portfolios emphasize the home's role in a student's reading development. The portfolio includes writing samples, tests, checklists, personal spelling lists, journals, published stories, and many other items.

Teachers evaluate portfolios and students' progress in the whole language curriculum by completing profiles. Figure 5-3 shows the K–2 Whole Language Individual Profile. Figure 5-4 shows the K–2 Whole Language Individual Writing Profile. This information is printed on the front and back of a sheet of paper so both profiles can be filed easily. Teachers also complete a class profile of the same data. This permits them to check children's progress quickly and efficiently. Figure 5-5 shows the Whole Language Portfolio Evaluation (3–5) form. These forms provide an indication of the changes that are occurring in schools using the whole language curriculum.

A change is also occurring in teacher evaluation at Montview. Teachers keep personal class portfolios. The class profile is a key component of the portfolio. Also included are samples of the best children's writing and the worst. By monitoring the progress checks of the class profile and studying the children's writing progress, the principal can supervise instruction in a new way. Principal Debbie Backus reports, "I know where the kids are. I can help a teacher fine tune her teaching to meet children's needs. I can make certain that a teacher's successes are celebrated. I can provide coaching to strengthen a teacher's weakness and develop a network among staff for peer support and improvement."

Enriched Basal Textbook Programs

At Meridith Elementary School in Temple, Texas, students have language arts instruction in both homogeneous and heterogeneous groups. The students are homogeneously grouped for a daily two-hour language arts

FIGURE 5-3 • *K–2 Whole Language Individual Profile, Montview Elementary Aurora, Colorado*

Name _____   Year _____

Teacher _____

K–2 WHOLE LANGUAGE INDIVIDUAL PROFILE

Code:

+	Consistently
✔	Progressing
–	Not Yet
☐	Not Assessed

Quarter			
1	2	3	4

TALKING AND LISTENING

1. Tells a story using pictures
2. Retells the story
3. Comments on story
4. Stays focused on discussion topic
5. Is becoming more active listener, but sensitive

READING

1. Likes to read
2. Uses story mapping
3. Comprehension
4. Uses strategies for unknown words
5. Uses strategies for meaning
6. Increases sight vocabulary
7. Reads with fluency and expression

WRITING

1. Selects topics
2. Writes appropriate amount for writing
3. Spelling stage at each quarter
   1. _____
   2. _____
   3. _____
   4. _____
4. Shows growth in editing

Comments (if any) on the reverse side.

Source: Used with permission of Debbie Backus.

FIGURE 5-4 · *K–2 Whole Language Portfolio Evaluation (3–5) Montview Elementary School, Aurora, Colorado*

Name _____ Year _____

Teacher _____

K–2 WHOLE LANGUAGE INDIVIDUAL WRITING PROFILE

	1	2	3	4

Format:
   Picture
   Picture and Writing
   Writing

Form:
   (Level of Writing)
    Scribbles
    Mock Writing
    Printing
    Cursive
   (Level of Representation)
    Letter
    Word
    Sentence(s)
    Paragraph(s)

Invented spelling:
   Precommunicative
   Semiphonetic
   Letter–Name (Phonetic)
   Transitional
   Conventional

Graphophonic representation:
   Initial Consonant
   Final Consonant
   Vowels
   Blends
   Diagraph
  Chooses topic with confidence
  Shares own writing
  Shows growth in editing

Themes: _____

Comments: _____

Source: Used with permission of Debbie Backus.

FIGURE 5-5 · *Whole Language Portfolio Evaluation (3–5), Montview Elementary School, Aurora, Colorado*

WHOLE LANGUAGE PORTFOLIO EVALUATION (3–5)

Code: 1 Consistently 2 Generally 3 Sometimes 4 Not Yet	1	2	3	4
TALKING AND LISTENING Active listener and sensitive to waiting for others.				
Maintains discussion with ease, joins in class discussion.				
Speaks out clearly and with confidence.				
Speaks with acceptable grammar and tone.				
READING Reads silently for increasing periods of time.				
Reads silently whenever it is possible and without prompting.				
Oral reading of familiar text fluent and expressive.				
Interest in literature beginning to broaden.				
Reads strategically to learn in content areas.				
Seeks opportunities to discuss reading with others; works co-operatively in discussion groups.				
Beginning to use table of contents, index, catalogues, etc., aware of way in which text is arranged in books.				
WRITING Able to write about self-directed topics.				
Able to write about teacher-assigned tasks/topics.				
Writes sufficient relevant ideas and connects them in logical sequence.				
Familiar with drafting and revising strategies; actively searches for better ways to express things; understands that revision is important.				
Publishes with correct spelling, acceptable grammar and appropriate punctuation.				

Source: Used with permission of Debbie Backus.

block. They are scheduled by heterogeneous homerooms for rotating classes in reading lab and theater arts; these classes meet two times each week. Regularly scheduled during the year are Reading Olympics and two Fun in Reading celebrations. The achievement test scores reported in Chapter 4 (Table 4-2) showed that Meridith scores on the Metropolitan Achievement Test were two years above the expected grade equivalent score. Let's look at this language arts program in which student mean scores are in the seventieth percentile or higher at all grade levels.

In reading classes at Meridith the goal is to instill a love of reading in students by providing numerous positive reading experiences. Using a basal textbook as well as supplementary materials, reading comprehension, vocabulary, and word attack skills are stressed (*Meridith Magnet National Exemplary School,* 1990).

Each reading class begins with a whole group skill lesson. The lessons taught during this time are directly related to an annual skill timeline, which is prepared at each grade level. After the initial warmup activity, the class breaks into groups to allow the teacher to work with small groups of students.

There is an emphasis on the reading of stories to build a strong foundation of comprehension skills. All stories that are read apply the skill that is being studied in class. Due to the varying reading abilities of the Meridith students, two basal readers are used in most reading classes. For example, every student in the fifth grade at any given time works on the same skill. However, these skills will be practiced and applied by reading stories at different levels of difficulty. Home reading plays an important part in the reading program. Every student in the school has a home reading assignment for the week. Regular homework is a key component of the instructional programs of restructured schools.

Another vital area of importance in the language arts curriculum is the use of core book units. Enrichment opportunities are available to all students regardless of ability levels and background experiences.

Through reading and discussing the books, students participate in many spin-off activities; research projects and presentations are also incorporated into the lesson to supplement learning. Language arts skills are applied to core books, complementing the facilitation of higher level thinking skills. This participation and involvement in reading gives students a sense of accomplishment in studying the entire book. Thus, we emphasize our schoolwide goal: "Reading Success Begins With Books." Figure 5-6 shows the core books used at Meridith Elementary School, a school for students in grades 3 through 5.

The language arts curriculum focuses on grammar, composition skills, vocabulary enrichment, and spelling.

Grammar skills are often taught within the composition lesson. The typical grammar instruction during a writing exercise focuses on labeling parts

FIGURE 5-6 · *Core Books Used at Meridith Elementary School, Temple, Texas*

Third Grade

A Taste of Blackberries
How To Eat Fried Worms
Bunnicula
The Best Christmas Pageant Ever
Caps For Sale
Alexander and the Terrible Horrible No Good Very Bad Day
*Mrs. Frisby and the Rats of NIMH
*Davey Crockett's Earthquake
*21 Balloons
*Ben and Me
*Stuart Little
*The Enormous Egg
*Chancy and the Great Rascal
*Can't You Make Them Behave, King George?

Fourth Grade

Charlotte's Web
Dear Mr. Henshaw
Mr. Popper's Penguins
The Great Brain
*King of the Wind
*The Borrowers
*Island of the Blue Dolphins
*The Helen Keller Story
*Myths and Their Meanings
*D'aulaire's Book of Greek Myths
*Old Yeller

Fifth Grade

The Incredible Journey
Misty of Chincoteague
Where the Pirates Are
*The Adventures of Robin Hood
*Treasure Island
*The Secret Garden
*Follow My Leader
*A Wrinkle In Time
*The Gammage Cup
*The Files of Mrs. Basil Fulwiler

Used with permission of Bonnie Martin.
Note: Books with an asterisk are used by the gifted/talented classes.

of speech, understanding the word-order nature of sentences, and even understanding the way in which different words function in sentences. Grammar is also taught using basal supplementary materials, as well as audio-visual materials.

Another weekly goal is to introduce vocabulary words. These words are taken from the Texas Assessment of Academic Skills vocabulary list. Numerous activities and games are used to make vocabulary learning fun and challenging.

Throughout the school year there are many different types of writing taught: descriptive, time-order, persuasive, informative, narrative, and classificatory. In the classroom the students are taught prewriting skills, organization, and rewriting skills. The students are required to keep journals and are encouraged to maintain fluency charts. Group activities enable the students to share and edit their papers.

In conjunction with grammar and composition skills, spelling is a necessary element of a complete language arts program. The spelling program is based on an individualized approach. Basal-text word lists, as well as enrichment word lists, are the core of the weekly spelling unit activities. Included in the weekly spelling assignments are exercises in vocabulary, handwriting, phonics, proofreading skills, reading skills, and writing/composition skills. Challenge lessons are provided for above-average spelling students.

The language arts program at Meridith stimulates creative thought and provides positive learning experiences. The program focuses on both written and verbal experiences to develop and expand mastery of the communication skills (*Meridith Magnet National Exemplary School*, 1990).

A unique component of the Meridith language arts program is the Reading Lab. This lab provides supplementary and enriching reading opportunities for all students. Each student, including those in the gifted/talented and special education programs, is scheduled for two lab lessons per week.

The lab program is individualized. The reading teacher bases the instructional program on students' individual needs. The goal of the Reading Lab is to remediate, supplement, and enrich the reading experience for each student.

The lab uses hands-on machines such as the guided speed reader, the language masters, and computer and reading software that correlate with the basal programs.

Instruction in the lab ranges from individual teacher-pupil teaching sessions to group instruction. At times, the Reading Lab teacher directly reteaches skills such as main idea, sequencing, and other essential elements of reading. This review helps students maintain these important reading skills. The Reading Lab promotes increased reading comprehension and skill mastery for each child who attends Meridith.

All students are also scheduled for two *Theater Arts* lessons each week.

Expressive use of the body and voice is the main objective of these classes. But much more seems to occur. Students have the opportunity to achieve higher level thinking skills as they develop and role play solutions to various situations. As students learn to express different solutions, they become more self-confident.

While the major thrust of the Theater Arts program is not directed at public performance, children have extensive opportunity to perform in three operatic and one Broadway musical productions yearly.

Having Theater Arts classes with a teacher who is involved with these productions has had a positive effect on students. Meridith students have increased language fluency and also presentation skills.

Once each semester Meridith has a Fun In Reading weekly celebration. A book fair is held. Each student gets three free books. The students or their families can purchase more. An assembly featuring an author or illustrator of children's books is held. However, the super week is the Meridith Reading Olympics.

Reading Olympics is held to coincide with winter or summer international competition. This is a week filled with both schoolwide and classroom activities to promote excellence in reading.

An opening ceremony is scheduled on a Monday morning with a Parade of Flags. The theme, "A Quest for Excellence," is instilled in the student body as they witness the lighting of the Olympic torch. A week-long Reading Marathon takes place in the foyer where students and celebrity readers read in shifts to accumulate continuous blocks of reading time. Super Silent Reading is also incorporated into each day's lesson. Olympia trivia questions are asked daily, culminating at the end of the week.

In addition to the schoolwide Olympic activities, the Reading Department at each grade level holds Olympic events in the classroom. Medals are awarded by teachers to all reading champions. These are worn with pride and Meridith school spirit by participants during the entire event. The celebration is concluded on Friday with an exciting assembly where students are recognized for their achievements (*Meridith Magnet National Exemplary School,* 1990).

Both the whole language programs at Bowman and Montview and the enriched basal program at Meridith meet the criteria of being effective. Their test results are outstanding. The teachers believe in the programs. The reading and writing classrooms are exciting. Students can read on their own and *they do read on their own.*

Getting Students Started Reading:
Early Intervention Programs

It hardly seems possible that one could be a failure at 6 or 7 years old, but that is exactly what happens to some first-graders. They experience confusion, frustration, and anxiety over something that is fairly natural for most children: learning how to read. In a few short but critical months, educational life passes them by and they begin a pattern of thinking that tells them they can't do things in school very well. This pattern may last for years. It may be reinforced by labels like remedial, Chapter 1, or special education (*Reading Recovery 1984–1989,* 1990). Or it may result in failure. In some urban districts, as many as 20 percent of first-graders are retained each year. These students who fail begin to have poor motivation and poor self-expectations. This causes continued poor achievement. For many, the result is a downward spiral that results in despair, delinquency, and dropping out (Madden, Slavin, Karweit, Dolen, & Urasik, 1991).

The best way to get children reading effectively is to get them started effectively. The first-grade prevention programs are built on that proposition that success in reading in first grade is a prerequisite for success later in school. These programs apply intensive resources including tutors and other additional staff to try to enable every child to succeed in beginning reading. In this section, three early intervention programs will be presented. They are Reading Recovery, Success for all, and Accelerated Learning.

Reading Recovery

The major goals of Reading Recovery are to reduce reading failure through early intervention and to assist each student to develop as an independent reader who has an internal system for self-improvement. Reading Recovery helps children who are off track in learning to read to get on track quickly (Pinnell, 1990).

Reading Recovery is a one-to-one intervention program for the poorest readers in the first grade and an intensive training program for teachers. Students receive tutoring for thirty minutes every day with a trained teacher until they develop the independence and self-correcting skills needed to return to the regular classroom instructional program (Tierney, Readence, & Dishner, 1990).

This program was developed by Marie M. Clay in New Zealand as she worked to help young readers with reading difficulties. She found that good reader have a self-improving system of reading. Poor readers learn words one at a time with the goal to get through the assignment. This is why Reading Recovery teachers emphasize a self-improvement system instead of remediation. In 1979, Reading Recovery became a nationwide program in New Zealand. In 1984, it was introduced in the United States (Pinnell, 1990).

The program targets the poorest readers in first-grade classrooms. Children from the lowest 20 percent of their classrooms are selected for Reading Recovery using classroom teacher judgment and results from the Diagnostic Survey (*Reading Recovery 1984–1989,* 1990).

The following six measures comprise the Diagnostic Survey (*Reading Recovery 1984–1989,* 1990):

1. *Letter identification:* Children are asked to identify upper- and lower-case letters.
2. *Word test:* Children are asked to read down a list of twenty words drawn from the most frequent words from the pre-primers in use in the school or from the Dolch list.
3. *Concepts about print:* Children are asked to perform a variety of tasks during book reading. These book handling tasks are used to check significant concepts about printed language, such as directionality and concept of word.
4. *Writing vocabulary:* Within a ten-minute period, children are asked to write the words they know.
5. *Dictation sentence:* Testers read a sentence to the children who are to write the words. This gives data about the child's ability to analyze the words for sounds.
6. *Textbook reading level:* Children are checked to see their highest level of reading at 90 percent or better. Levels are drawn from a basal reading system.

The results of the Diagnostic Reading Survey and the first ten days of the child's thirty-minute daily lesson are used in special ways in Reading Recovery. The survey results show what the child has been able to learn. The first ten lessons are called "roaming around the known." The teacher does not teach but rather explores reading and writing with the child. It is a time when the two get to know each other. They can talk with each other, enjoy books, and write collaboratively. "Roaming through the known" allows the teacher and the child the opportunity to develop a relationship of trust. This time allows the teacher to see what the child initiates as well as what the child can and cannot do (Tierney et al., 1990). It also helps the student feel good about what he or she knows (Noyes, 1991).

A typical tutoring session might include reading two or more familiar books and taking a running record; writing messages and stories, then rereading them as a cut-up story; listening to sounds; and introducing, then attempting new books. These activities help the child develop fluency in reading and writing, using phonetic structures, understanding sequence, and learning new vocabulary. These instructional procedures are described in *The Early Detection of Reading Difficulties* (Clay, 1979), which is the primary source for Reading Recovery information.

The research results of the program in New Zealand indicate that children at risk of failure made accelerated progress while being tutored. After twelve to fourteen weeks in the program, almost all (80 percent) of the

Reading Recovery children *caught up with their peers and needed no further help*. Three years later, children still retained their gains and continued to progress at average rates. They were able to function successfully on grade level. Similar results were achieved in a five-year study in Columbus, Ohio (*Reading Recovery 1984–1989*, 1990), and in a three-year study in San Antonio, Texas (Noyes, 1991).

Success for All

The idea behind Success for All is to use everything known about effective instruction so that students at risk leave the third grade above or on grade level in reading and other basic skills. The goal is to prevent children from developing academic deficits. Children are provided a rich and full curriculum that enables them to build a firm foundation of basic skills. If a deficit does appear, the student is provided immediate help so that the deficit is corrected (Madden et al., 1991).

Most schools using Success for All provide a half-day preschool and a full-day kindergarten program. These early childhood programs provide a balanced and developmentally appropriate learning experience for young children. Emphasis is placed on language development. The curriculum also provides a balance of academic readiness activities with music, art, and movement activities (Madden et al., 1991).

The grouping for Success for All is similar to the Joplin Plan described in Chapter 2. During most of the school day, students in grades 1 through 3 are assigned to heterogeneous, age-grouped classes of about twenty-five students each. During the ninety-minute reading period students are regrouped into reading classes of fifteen to twenty students, all at the same level of reading performance. Regrouping allows teachers to teach the whole class without having to break the class into reading groups. This system increases the time devoted to direct instruction and reduces the time students spend in seatwork. Reading teachers begin each class by reading good children's literature to the students and engaging them in a discussion of the story to enhance their understanding of what has been read, their listening and speaking vocabulary, and their knowledge of story structure. When students reach the primer reading level, they use CIRC as an instruction strategy (Madden et al., 1991). This cooperative group model was described earlier in the chapter. At eight-week intervals, reading teachers assess the students' progress. The results are used to determine who needs tutoring, who should change reading groups, and who needs other types of assistance, such as family intervention or screening for vision and hearing problems (Madden et al., 1991).

Another important tenant of Success for All is the family support team. The philosophy is that parents are an essential part of student success. The members of the student support team usually include the program facilitator, the Chapter 1 parent liaison, and the counselor. The team works to support their children's success in school. The family support staff, teachers, and parents work together to solve learning and behavior problems. The team works with parents so that students attend regularly, receive adequate sleep and nutrition, and receive support from other social agencies. Parent education is a key component of this program (Madden et al., 1991).

At most Success for All schools there is a program facilitator who works with the principal to oversee the program. Facilitators work directly with teachers and tutors, helping them to implement the Success for All curriculum. They lead staff development and coach teachers. Facilitators organize sessions to share professional problems and solutions and to discuss individual students (Madden et al., 1991).

The findings from the evaluation of Success for All indicate that the program works. Madden (1991) reports that students in Success for All outperformed the control group in reading at all grade levels. In grade-level equivalent terms, the differences between Success for All students and those in the control group rises from three months in first grade, to five months in third grade.

Accelerated Learning

Curtis is a nervous 10-year-old boy who has moved to Colorado from a small town in Kentucky. After his mother completes the enrollment forms for Montview Elementary School, she and Curtis are invited into the principal's office. Mrs. Backus, the principal, studies the forms and Curtis' materials from his former school. She reads that Curtis has been placed in Chapter I classes in both reading and mathematics because he is over a year below grade level in each subject. Mrs. Backus says, "Tell me about your reading, Curtis."

"It's not very good," said Curtis. "Do you have 'medial' reading here?"

Mrs. Backus thought about what he said and then answered, "No, we don't have remedial reading here. We're going to place you in accelerated programs in both reading and math. You'll like Montview."

"You mean I'm going to get to read regular books, not baby stuff?" asked Curtis.

"You bet. Ms. Enlow, our Instructional Support Teacher, will test you this morning. Then she'll get you into your classes quickly. And she'll work with you and your teacher so you get off to a good start."

"This is a neat school," Curtis said to his mother.

Montview, like many other schools, uses accelerated learning so that at-risk students are able to achieve at grade level by the time they leave elementary school. Table 4-2 shows that the program has been quite successful. Ninety percent or more of Montview's students are leaving elementary school on or above grade level. Curtis will be tested, placed in appropriate materials, and given a time schedule designed to get him functioning at grade level quickly.

Remediation has not worked. The sad fact is that once students are assigned to remedial or compensatory classes, they seldom can enroll in regular classes again. This is because remedial classes move at a slower that normal pace, making these students get turned off to schooling. They crawl through endless repetition of drill-and-practice exercises emphasizing rate skills. Able students are introduced to challenging problems and stimulating materials. Remedial students get to practice basic skills and memorize them (Hopfenberg, Levin, Meister, & Rogers, 1990).

The basic premise of the accelerated school strategy is that at-risk students must learn at a faster rate—not a slower rate. An enrichment strategy, rather than a remedial one, offers the greatest hope to achieve this goal. Instead of perceiving disadvantaged students as lacking the learning behaviors associated with middle-class students, Levin (1989) views these students as having unique assets that can be used to accelerate their learning. He recommends acceleration, not remediation.

Levin (1989) has identified five basic objectives crucial for program success:

1. Placing high expectations on students, teachers, and parents
2. Giving teachers the power to make decisions concerning the students and their classroom based on their best judgment
3. Providing stimulating and exciting instruction through active learning
4. Setting deadlines so that students will have a firm completion date
5. Involving parents and the community in children's learning processes

Does accelerated learning work with at-risk students? In the fifty schools that have implemented this program, the answer is "Yes." For example, Daniel Webster Elementary School, a school with many ethnic groups, made the greatest gains in language and the second greatest gains in mathematics among the seventy-two elementary schools in San Francisco. Hollibrook Elementary School, a school in a predominantly Hispanic working-class neighborhood, in the Spring Branch School District of Houston, Texas, had dramatic achievement gains scoring above district average in math at all grade levels. In a rural school in Springfield, Missouri, 39 percent of Chapter I students tested out of remedial reading and mathematics programs (Levin & Hopfenberg, 1991).

The findings of evaluations of Reading Recovery, Success for All, and Accelerated Learning indicate that focusing on prevention and early intervention can significantly increase the reading performance of disadvantaged and at-risk students, as well as reduce retentions and special education placements. These programs also help students achieve at grade level in language arts and mathematics.

We recommend that the restructured school provide early intervention teaching so that students who need intensive help can achieve success in language arts and mathematics.

Maintaining Basic Skills

Practice strategies described earlier in this chapter indicated that for new learning practice should be massed and for old learning practice should be distributed.

Two of the schools that we visited had structures so that reading skills were carefully reviewed. At Meridith, students had two lessons each week in the Reading Laboratory. Reading skills were carefully reviewed. At Lozano, there was daily supplemental instruction in the media center in both reading and mathematics. This instruction was designed to review skills and to give students reinforcement in learning. Test scores in both schools indicate that these instructional programs are effective. Review seems to be especially important for students from low-income homes.

We recommend that the restructured school provide a supplemental instruction program so that students have the opportunity to review basic skills and processes regularly.

Accelerating Able Students

Good language arts and mathematics programs should be organized so that able students are encouraged and enabled to increase their skills and understanding.

This can be achieved with a structure that provides able students learning opportunities in materials and with instruction above their age or grade level. It can be accomplished in many ways. The multiaged setting with nongraded–continuous-progress curriculum sequences at Lake George Elementary School is a structure in which able students do excel. The Lake George faculty has adopted some of the key ideas of the Joplin Plan and Success for All. The whole language program at Bowman Elementary School permits able students to read very challenging fiction and nonfiction trade books. Able students achieve more because the program enables them to increase their vocabulary and learn to comprehend material much more difficult than a basal reading series.

Research findings have positively supported accelerated curriculum sequences.

We recommend that the restructured school provide a curriculum that facilitates able students to accelerate so that they increase their skills and understanding of language arts and mathematics.

Summary

Good teaching can make a difference in the lives of both children and teachers. Disadvantaged children enter school with few skills; they can exit both skillful and confident. This process has a positive effect on their teachers who chose teaching because they wanted to see their students achieve.

In this chapter, we have described a number of effective teaching strategies and curriculum choices that are available for teachers. Two structured strategies were described. In the Direct Teach Model, students are focused on the lesson objective, taught carefully, and helped to practice correctly. Mastery Learning is a way to organize the curriculum so that students have increased opportunities to learn.

Next, strategies emphasizing cognitive learning processes were presented. Cooperative Learning is an effective way to help students learn school curriculum goals and also to help them improve their social skills. Whole language is an effective way to teach reading and writing.

Then three early intervention strategies were presented: Reading Recovery, Success for All, and Accelerated Learning. All have proved effective for getting at-risk students started effectively and keeping them achieving on grade level.

Finally, a number of strategies to provide for students' individual differences were presented. Strategies are available so that teachers can provide their students two kinds of TLC: Tender Loving Care and Teaching, Learning, and Curriculum. In both sequences emphasis must be placed on the "L" words. When students find themselves with a *Loving* and *Caring* teacher who has access to effective teaching and curriculum strategies, *Learning* occurs.

When students learn, both the students and the teachers feel successful.

References

A $^+$ schools: Portraits of schools that work. (1984). *Instructor,* 93(9): 18–20.

Aronson, E., Blaney, N., Stephan, C., Sikes, J., & Snapp, M. (1978). *The jigsaw classroom*. Beverly Hills, CA: Sage Publications.

Augustine, D., Gruber, K., & Hanson, L. (1990). Cooperation works! *Educational Leadership*, 47(4): 4–7.

Barrett, P. (1989). Finding their own voices: Children learning together. *Doubts and Certainties*, IV(4): 1–5.

Bechtol, W. (1984). Effective practices in the multicultural elementary classroom. San Marcos, TX: Southwest Texas State University.

Berliner, D. (1979). Tempus educare. In P. Peterson & H. Walberg (eds.). *Research on teaching: Concepts, findings, and implications*. Berkeley, CA: McCutchan, pp. 120–135.

Bigge, M. (1982). *Learning theories for teachers*. New York: Harper and Row.

Block, J., & Anderson, L. (1975). *Mastery learning in classroom instruction*. New York: Macmillan.

Block, J., Efthim, H., & Burns, R. (1989). *Building effective mastery learning schools*. New York: Longham.

Bloom, B. (1976). *All our children learning*. Hightstown, NJ: McGraw-Hill.

Bloom, B. (1980). *Human characteristics and school learning*. New York: McGraw-Hill.

Burns, M. (1981). Groups of four: Solving the management problem. *Learning*, 10(2): 46–51.

Board of Education of the City of Chicago. (1982). *Chicago mastery learning reading implementation model*. Watertown, MA: Mastery Learning Council.

Carroll, J. (1963). A model of school learning. *Teachers College Record* 64: 723–733.

Clay, M. (1979). *The early detection of reading difficulties*. Auckland, New Zealand: Heinemann Educational Books.

Christen, W. (1987). *The A.T.L.A.S.S. program: The application and teaching of learning and study skills*. Dubuque, IA: Kendall/Hunt.

DeLine, J. (1991). Why can't they get along? *Journal of Physical Education, Recreation, and Dance* 62(1): 21–26.

Good, T., & Brophy, J. (1991). *Looking in classrooms*, 5th ed. New York: HarperCollins.

Goodlad, J. (1984). *A place called school*. New York: McGraw-Hill.

Guskey, T. (1985). *Implementing mastery learning*. Belmont, CA: Wadsworth.

Herbart, J. (1904). *Outlines of educational doctrine*. New York: Macmillan.

Heyman, E. (1990). Intensive care: Observations of Jaime Escalante. *Kappa Delta Pi Record*, 26(3): 90–91.

Hollingsworth, P., & Hoover, K. (1991). *Elementary teaching methods*. Boston: Allyn and Bacon.

Hopfenberg, W., Levin, H., Meister, G., & Rogers, J. (1990). Accelerated schools. Stanford, CA: School of Education, Stanford University.

Hunter, M. (1982). *Mastery teaching*. El Segundo, CA: TIP Publications.

Johnson, M. (1990). Editor. *State of the school report: Bowman Elementary School*. Lexington, MA: Lexington Schools.

Johnson, D., & Johnson, R. (1985). Cooperative learning and adaptive education. In W. Wang & H. Walberg (eds.). *Adapting instruction to individual differences*. Berkeley, CA: McCutchan, pp. 105–134.

Johnson, D., Johnson, R., Holubec, E., & Roy, P. (1984). *Circles of learning: Cooperation in the classroom*. Alexandria, VA: Association for Supervision and Curriculum Development.

Levin, H. (1989). *Accelerated schools: A new strategy for at-risk students*. Bloomington, IN: Consortium on Educational Policy Studies.

Levin, H., & Hopfenberg, W. (1991). Don't remediate: Accelerate! *Minority Education* (January): 11–13.

Maas, D. (1986). *Maintaining teacher effectiveness: A workshop guide.* Bloomington, IN: Phi Delta Kappa Educational Foundation Workshop.

Madden, N., Slavin, R., Karweit, N., Dolen, L., & Urasik, B. (1991). Success for all. *Educational Leadership,* 72(8): 593–599.

Masten, R. (1988). The poet goes into the elementary school. *Doubts and Certainties,* II(4): 2–3.

Meridith Magnet National Exemplary School. (1990). Temple, TX: Temple Independent School District.

McClure, R. (190). The coming paradigm shift in American schools. Paper presented at the education Week Lecture Series, Chautaqua Institute, Chautaqua, NY.

Morrison, H. (1934). *Basic principles of education.* Boston: Houghton-Mifflin.

Nations, J. (1988). Thoughts from a bewhiskered pedagogue. *Doubts and Certainties,* 2(4), 5.

Noyes, D. (1991). Interview reading recovery teacher. San Antonio, TX: Colby Glass Elementary School, Northside ISD.

Pinnell, G. (1990). Reading recovery: A focus on an answer. International Conference of the Association for Individually Guided Education, Cambridge, MA.

Reading recovery 1984–1989. (1990). Columbus, OH: The Ohio State University, College of Education. National Diffusion Network, No. 4.

Sharon, Y., & Sharon, S. (1990). Group investigation expands cooperative learning. *Educational Leadership,* 47(4): 17–21.

Slavin, R. (1983). *Cooperative learning.* New York: Longman.

Slavin, R. (1987). Mastery learning reconsidered. *Review of educational research,* 57: 175–213.

Slavin, R. (1990). *Cooperative learning: Theory, research, and practice.* Englewood Cliffs, NJ: Prentice Hall.

Slavin, R. (1991). Synthesis of research on cooperative learning. *Educational Leadership,* 48(5): 71–82.

Slavin, R., & Karweit, N. (1984). Mastery learning and student teams: A factorial experiment in urban general mathematics classes. *American Education Research Journal,* 21: 725–736.

Slavin, R., Madden, N., & Stevens, R. (1990). Cooperative learning models for the 3 R's. *Educational Leadership,* 47(4): 22–28.

Spady, W. (1988). Organizing for results: The basis of authentic restructuring and reform. *Educational Leadership,* 46(2): 4–8.

Steffens, H. (1990). Reform: The third wave. *Doubts and Certainties,* V(2–3): 1–5.

Tierney, R., Readence, J., & Dishner, E. (1990). *Reading strategies and practices: A compendium.* 3rd ed. Boston: Allyn and Bacon.

Vasquez, B., Slavin, R., & D'Arcangelo, M. (1990). *Cooperative learning: Facilitator's manual.* Alexandria, VA: Association for Supervision and Curriculum Development.

Walters, S. (1989). The MIL conference on realizing renewal: A reporter's first impressions. *Doubts and Certainties,* IV(3): 1–5.

Wolfe, P. (1987). *Instructional decisions for long-term learning: Guidelines for instructional decisions.* Videotape Series. Alexandria, VA: Association for Supervision and Curriculum Development.

CHAPTER SIX

The "Learning How to Learn" Curriculum

The challenge of restructuring is the development of independent learners who have the skills to think and to solve problems.

To help students develop the skills to become lifelong independent learners is one of the major goals of the restructured school. The phrase "learning how to learn" has traditionally been associated with process skills such as problem solving and higher level thinking in specialized subject areas. As we view today's students living and working in the technical world of the twenty-first century, we envision students needing more than basic process skills. They need to know how to learn and manipulate a wide variety of thinking skills and to solve multistep problems; how to learn new content; how to develop, use, and evaluate new products; and how to learn and to live in new and different environments. It's the challenge of this future that demands school restructuring.

This chapter focuses on a curriculum that helps students learn how to learn. It's a nuts-and-bolts chapter that contains many options for practical ideas, strategies, sample lessons, and learning activities. The chapter describes how one school staff restructured its curriculum. We encourage readers to use the Lawton School strategies as a resource for their own instructional planning to help their students become independent learners who are able to live effectively in a technological society.

Lawton School draws its characteristics and restructuring strategies from several of the model schools described in Chapter 4. Roles and responsibilities of the staff in planning and preparing for restructuring as well as in restructuring the curriculum are discussed. In order to provide options for readers, more ideas than any one school might accomplish in a given time frame are presented.

Lawton School includes grades K–8 with 460 students, eighteen classroom teachers, three clerical/instructional aides, and six to eight student teachers from nearby universities. The school was organized into three regular units or teams that were multiaged/graded as follows: K–2, Primary Unit; 3–5, Intermediate Unit; 6–8, Middle Level Unit. Each team had about 155 students and six teachers, one of which was designated as unit leader; one aide; and two or more student teachers. They met weekly for one hour to make decisions for the students in the unit. In addition, specialists such as special education, Chapter 1, art, music, physical education, and technology teachers along with the media center director, school counselor, and school psychologist provided a support system for the school program. This support group met as a team once each month, but met with the unit or units in which they provided special services during other weekly planning meetings.

The unit leaders met with the principal and assistant principal as an IIC for one hour each week to make decisions for the staff and students in the building. The organizational pattern at Lawton allowed all staff to have input into decisions such as selecting the theme for curriculum restructuring for the coming school year.

To get started on restructuring, the IIC and units analyzed their curriculum for strengths and weaknesses. From the data produced by the analysis, they identified the thinking skills and problem-solving theme for four reasons:

1. Local and national standardized test data indicated that Lawton students scored lower in language arts subareas such as "perform a persuasive writing task" or "make inferences from written material" than they did in basic comprehension. In math, they scored higher in computation than they did in conceptual understanding and multistep problem solving. Test data from social studies and science were less precise, but in all subcategories dealing with problem solving, scores were lower than in the more fact-oriented areas. Although this trend was pretty much the same nationwide, the staff at Lawton wanted to do something about it.

2. A survey of all teachers indicated that they judged their students to be more efficient at regurgitating factual information and working one-step problems than they were at solving how-to problems and interpreting more complex concepts. Teachers felt that the back-to-the-basics emphasis of the last decade had caused textbooks and other instructional materials to focus too heavily on the *what* rather than the *how* and *why* of learning. Also, instructional materials failed to provide enough opportunities for students to connect things together and to work in different modes — alone or with others — on projects that related several subject matter areas.

3. Teachers felt that the curriculum lacked opportunities for students to create products or carry out projects to apply their learning inside and outside the school setting.

4. "Learning how to learn" strategies could apply to all subject matter areas and all age/grade levels as well as provide opportunities for interdisciplinary learning.

The IIC at Lawton had taken all this information into consideration along with the philosophy that they wanted students to start at a level where they would have success, yet challenge them to go as far as they could toward more complex and abstract work in all curriculum areas.

The four elements of the "learning how to learn" curriculum that they had selected to guide their restructuring were *content, process, product,* and *environment* (Sorenson, Engelsgjerd, Francis, Miller, & Schuster, 1988; Maker, 1982; Kaplan in Renzulli, 1986).

In this discussion, these elements are defined as follows:

- *Content* refers to kinds and levels of knowledge students are expected to learn in terms of facts, principles, concepts, and theories.
- *Process* relates to the ways students go about learning, including encountering, storing, and retrieving information. Discussion here focuses on five sets of thinking skills—Bloom's cognitive taxonomy, creative thinking, inquiry processes, critical thinking skills, and single-step problem-solving skills—and their use in multistep problem solving.
- *Product* refers to kinds of outcomes students are expected to produce as evidence of learning; real problems that relate to real audiences and undergo real evaluation should be considered.
- *Environment* includes physical sites from the classroom to the community, state, and nation; human resources; teaching styles; learning styles; technology; and personal characteristics of students.

These four elements along with their related skills or concepts are shown in Figure 6-1. The elements are summarized in the center block with related strategies and conditions to help students learn how to learn around the perimeter. The structures of Figure 6-1 underlie the philosophical and practical basis for the curriculum discussions in this chapter.

It should be noted that "learning how to learn" content, process, product, and environment is only one phase of curriculum restructuring. Attention to subject matter content and structure as well as the affective and psychomotor curriculum also need to be considered.

Content

The staff at Lawton School had often discussed ways to handle content in the "learning how to learn" curriculum. At the IIC meeting, they looked at

FIGURE 6-1 • *Elements of a "Learning How to Learn" Curriculum*

		[ ] Knowledge [ ] Comprehension [ ] Application [ ] Analysis [ ] Synthesis [ ] Evaluation	[ ] Facts [ ] Principles [ ] Concepts [ ] Theories		
		Bloom's Process—Cognitive Taxonomy	Content		

[ ] Compare/contrast
[ ] Fact/opinion
[ ] Relevant/irrelevant
[ ] Reliable/unreliable
  sources
[ ] Cause/effect
[ ] Sequence/prioritize
[ ] Bias/stereotype
[ ] Point of view
[ ] Consistent/inconsistent
[ ] Assumptions/
  generalizations
[ ] Analyze arguments
[ ] Induction/deduction
	PROCESS—Critical Thinking Skills	**CURRICULUM**
		
		Content refers to kinds and levels of
		knowledge students are expected
		to learn in terms of:
		* facts, principles, concepts,
		  and theories
		
		Process relates to the ways students go
		about learning; focus is on thinking
		skills and their use in solving problems
		* Bloom's cognitive levels
		* creative thinking
		* inquiry processes
		* critical thinking skills
		* single-step problems-solving techniques
		* multistep problem solving
			Process—inquiry	Observe [ ]
				Classify [ ]
				Infer [ ]
				Predict [ ]
				Communicate [ ]
				Measure [ ]
				Interpret data [ ]
				Formulate operational [ ]
				definitions
				Formulate questions [ ]
				and hypotheses
				Experiment [ ]
				Formulate models [ ]	

			Process—Creative Thinking	Fluency [ ] Flexibility [ ] Elaboration [ ] Originality [ ]	
[ ] Work backwards [ ] Simplify/reduce [ ] Recognize patterns [ ] Organize lists [ ] Guess and test [ ] Form analogies [ ] Make drawing, figure [ ] Make table, graph [ ] Make a model [ ] Act it out	PROCESS—Single-Step Problem-Solving Techniques	Product refers to kinds of outcomes students are expected to produce as evidence of learning, such as: * problems, audiences, transformations, evaluations Environment includes intellectual, psychological, and physical settings in which learning occurs	Process—Multistep Problem Solving	State problem [ ] Generate solutions [ ] Implement design [ ] Evaluate results [ ]	
		PRODUCT	ENVIRONMENT		
		[ ] Problems [ ] Audiences [ ] Transformations [ ] Evaluations	[ ] Physical sites [ ] Human resources [ ] Teaching styles [ ] Learning styles [ ] Technology [ ] Student characteristics		

many definitions of content and its role in the curriculum to derive their own useable definition.

Charles Suhor (in Brandt, 1988, pp. 31, 43) defined content as "knowing" and process as "doing"; content is "that which is to be processed." Maker (1982, p. 3) suggested that curriculum content consists of ideas, concepts, descriptive information, and facts. Coleman (1985, p. 317) said content can take many forms and vary in its degree of abstractness, complexity, and organization. It is knowledge to be learned and is related to broad issues and themes that integrate the disciplines. Sandra Kaplan (in Renzulli, 1986, pp. 185–187) suggested that content is knowledge and information that is useful, important, timely, and interesting for students to learn as they progress through an educational program. Sorenson et al. (1988) defined content as a body of understandings that includes facts, principles, theories, and concepts. Lawton's staff developed its own working definition: *"Content describes the knowledge base of the subject matter areas or disciplines we teach."*

To restructure content, the Lawton staff considered four topics: selecting content, organizing content, forming concepts, and teaching concepts. Strategies that teachers can use to help students learn content more thoroughly and effectively are emphasized here.

Selecting Content

The selection of content often involves controversy and concerns, so it can be a difficult part of restructuring and developing a curriculum. Kaplan (in Renzulli, 1986) has suggested some rules to consider:

- Select content related to the organizing element or theme.
- Designate topical areas within the theme that are multidisciplinary.
- Select topics for the theme that include those that are mandatory for all students to learn, as well as those to meet the needs, interests, and abilities of the more able learners.
- Select topics that provide for a time perspective, showing how past, present, and future are related.

Organizing Content

A curriculum can organize content or knowledge in any discipline in a hierarchy relating facts, principles, theories, and concepts (Haney & Sorenson, 1977; Sorenson et al., 1988). Facts are based on sensory experiences and relate to particular objects and events.

Principles (laws) are more general and relate several facts. An example of a principle in science: "The volume of a confined gas varies inversely with the pressure if the temperature is held constant." A basic principle in economics: "When a product has a short supply and high demand, the price increases; when it has low demand and ample supply, the price decreases, if other factors remain stable."

Theories, which represent the highest level of generality, normally relate several principles. For example, the principles governing the behavior of gases can be explained using the kinetic molecular theory of gases, which contains statements about molecules and their interactions.

Concepts appear in statements at all levels of generality — facts, principles, and theories. Concepts are abstractions or ideas based on many encounters with similar objects and events. Math concepts include divisor, subtraction, and fraction; social studies concepts include government, exchange, and democracy; and language arts concepts include noun, consonant, and paragraph.

Figure 6-2 illustrates the relationships among facts, concepts, principles, and theories. Here, the base shows an array of factual information. Located between the theory and facts are certain principles, and concepts appear in statements at all three levels. Thus, reasoning deductively, it can be said that the theory explains principles, which in turn explain facts, and that a concept at any height in the cone can be explained from concepts or ideas at a higher level. Conversely, reasoning inductively, several facts can be related to form a principle and several principles related to form a theory, using individual concepts at all levels.

Forming Concepts

Thinking should not be limited to facts because the type of learning that enables us to profit from past experiences and to cope more readily with new experiences would be lacking. Structured knowledge becomes possible only when generalizations are made from the specifics of people's experience and abstractions are formulated. These generalizations and abstractions range from the informal concepts and principles of common sense to precisely defined concepts, principles, and sophisticated theories of a discipline such as math, science, language arts, or social studies.

No two experiences are identical. Everything changes, yet people can find regularity in nature. An individual may never encounter the same robin, apple, or parallel circuit twice, yet that person recognizes new robins, apples, and parallel circuitrs when he or she comes in contact with them.

To communicate, humans represent concepts by words, sounds, and other symbols. People develop their own private concept of something by the idea a symbol brings to mind as well as by the thing itself. Chair, automobile, house, dog, cloud, melting, dissolving, and bending are all

FIGURE 6-2 • *A Hierarchical Arrangement of Facts and Principles, Correlated by a Theory That Uses Concepts at All Levels*

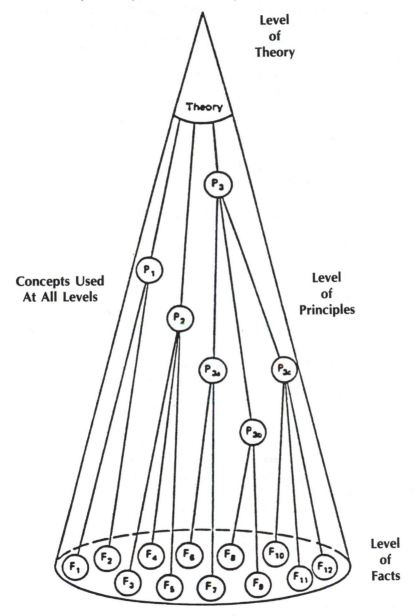

Source: R. Haney and J. Sorenson, *Individually Guided Science* (Reading, MA: Addison-Wesley Publishing Company, 1977), p. 20. Reprinted with permission.

everyday concepts. The first five words represent classes of objects, and the remaining three represent classes of events. Certainly, for many purposes people find it easier to think chair than to list descriptions of many individual chairs, such as kitchen chairs, upholstered living room chairs, wooden chairs, dining room chairs, and folding chairs. All of these objects have features in common that make up the concept of chair. Similarly, people's concept of melting depends on numerous encounters with material undergoing this physical change. The richness of people's concepts depends on their range of experiences with the objects and events that the concepts represent.

Students can learn concepts in a discipline by placing the concepts in a hierarchy that incorporates the following features (Harris & Harris, 1973):

- Criterial: relevant and irrelevant attributes
- Examples and nonexamples of the concept
- Definition of the concept
- Subordinate, supraordinate, and coordinate concepts to the one under study
- Relationships between the concept of interest and other concepts.

For example, the concept *planet* can be analyzed in this way:

- Criterial relevant attribute(s): revolves around the sun
- Relevant attributes that related concepts share: is located in space, motion is affected by other heavenly bodies, shines by reflected light
- Irrelevant attributes: visibility to the naked eye, surface temperature and apparent color (to the earthly observer), may support life
- Examples: (picture of a body orbiting the sun)
- Nonexamples: (picture of a body orbiting the earth)
- Subordinate concept(s): major or minor planet
- Coordinate concept(s): moon, meteor, and so on
- Supraordinate concept(s): heavenly body, solar system
- Definition (includes name of supraordinate concepts, criterial attributes): A planet is a heavenly body that revolves around the sun and shines by reflected light.
- Relationships: *Planets* travel in paths called *orbits*.

For teachers, the most important things to help students learn concepts are the relevant criterial attributes that separate the concept under study from all other concepts.

Teaching Concepts

The features discussed in forming a concept in the previous section are presented in diagram form in Figure 6-3. They are arranged in a suggested

FIGURE 6-3 • *The Anatomy of a Concept*

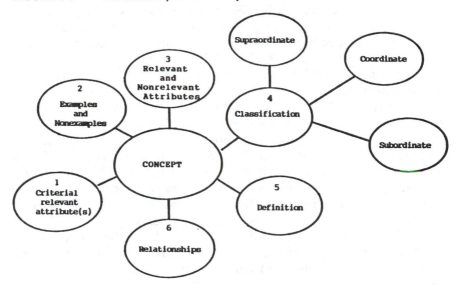

order to use in teaching important and difficult concepts to students at varying age/grade levels. The steps are illustrated here using the concept *bird* (Voelker, Sorenson, & Frayer, 1971, pp. 46–47).

1. Be sure the students understand the criterial attribute(s) of the concept to be taught. For *bird,* the criterial attribute is "covered with feathers." The teacher needs to be sure all students can distinguish between covered with feathers and other common animal coverings, such as hair, scales, and skin.

2. Focus on examples and nonexamples of the concept *bird.* It is often useful to include pictures as well as words in teaching examples and nonexamples and this is possible with the concept *bird.* Pictures for students to identify as birds and nonbirds might include pictures and descriptions of mammals, amphibians, reptiles, or fish in addition to a variety of birds from robins to chickens to ostriches. With more abstract concepts such as government, sentence, or gravity, the concept cannot be readily pictured, so words are used to describe these examples and nonexamples.

3. Identify relevant attributes that this concept shares with related concepts. For example, bird shares being warm-blooded, female lays eggs, and has a backbone (vertebrate) with several other members of the vertebrate group; bird also shares being an animal and a living thing with large numbers of others. Irrelevant attributes for bird might include size, coloration, habitat, and types of food.

4. Classify, identifying supraordinate, coordinate, and subordinate concepts to the concept being studied. For bird, supraordinate or higher groups to which bird belongs include vertebrate, animal, living things; coordinate or parallel concepts to bird include mammals, amphibians, reptiles, and fish. Subordinate concepts under bird can be varied, such as habitat—water, woods, prairie—or food they eat, or specific kinds of birds such as robins, chickens, flamingoes, and so on.

5. Teach the definition. Most definitions in textbooks, dictionaries, or references include the name of the concept (bird); the supraordinate group to which the concept belongs (vertebrate, animal, living thing); and the criterial attribute(s) separating this concept from all others (covered with feathers). Therefore, the definition for bird would be "a bird is a warm-blooded, vertebrate animal that is covered with feathers; the female lays eggs." A definition is a result of understanding a concept, not the starting point of learning as is so often the case in our classrooms.

6. Relate the concept to other concepts. These relationships can be simple or complex according to the age/grade level of the students. Some examples: Many birds migrate from colder to warmer climates during the winter season (bird and migrate); birds and mammals form the two warm-blooded classes of vertebrates (bird and mammal); birds use a gizzard to help digest food (bird and gizzard).

One of the important parts of "dissecting" a concept in this fashion is the natural ways in which attributes of related concepts (e.g., fish, reptile, amphibian, mammal) come into the discussion to differentiate birds from them.

An example of teaching a concept such as *sentence* in language arts is presented here for contrast to the concept *bird* from science (Golub, Frederick, Nelson, & Frayer, 1971).

1. Identify the criterial attributes: Subject and predicate, begins with a capital letter, ends with a punctuation mark, tells something or asks something.
2. Provide examples and nonexamples of the concept. Examples include: We saw a flower. Cats like to chase mice. Why does a deer run so fast? After school, the students played ball. Nonexamples include: Since you went away; at the bottom of the box; across the street; leaning on a locker.
3. Identify relevant and irrelevant attributes. A relevant attribute shared with other concepts includes a group of words. Irrelevant attributes include: type of punctuation (for example, periods, question marks, exclamation point); long or short or number of words in a sentence; and position of subject and predicate.

4. Classify by the three subgroups: supraordinate—group of words; coordinate—phrase, clause; subordinate—question, command, statement.
5. Teach the definition. The definition of sentence is: "A sentence is a group of words with a subject and predicate, which begins with a capital letter and ends with an end-punctuation mark."
6. Relate the concept to other concepts. Examples include: A paragraph is made up of one or more sentences. Sentences can be made up of several clauses.

When teachers actually "dissect" a concept to teach it to students, they would probably start with the definition from a reliable source. Then, they would identify the items for the other five steps. The six-step teaching sequence presented in Figure 6-3 is suggested so that students gain understanding of a concept before they memorize the definition. In certain situations, the teacher may wish to present the definition to the students and have them share the dissection process by asking them to help identify the elements of the concept. Also, older students might work alone, with a partner, or as a part of a small group to develop their own dissection of important or difficult concepts in various subject matter areas.

Process

Lawton School would focus much of its restructuring in-service and planning efforts on process since it ws the weakest of the four elements in its current instructional program. Process has been previously defined as the "ways in which students go about learning, including encountering, storing, and retrieving information." In this discussion, process focuses on five thinking skills clusters—Bloom's cognitive taxonomy, creative thinking, inquiry processes, critical thinking skills, and single-step problem-solving techniques—and their use in multistep problem solving. These clusters with subskills are outlined on the perimeter in Figure 6-1.

Here, they are defined and their use illustrated with sample activities from several subject matter areas. Relationships to content, product, and environment, the other three basic elements of learning how to learn, are pointed out as appropriate to the discussion. A multistep problem-solving process is presented and illustrated according to the model and narrative in Figure 6-7. Two very different, multistep problems—one in science and one in social studies—illustrate the versatile use students can make of this model from one situation to another. Details on how the unit teams and the building-wide IIC share responsibility to implement the thinking skills and problem-solving program are also a part of the narrative of this section.

Bloom's Cognitive Taxonomy

At the meeting of the IIC, Tom, leader of the Intermediate Level Unit, mentioned that his team wanted to emphasize Bloom's cognitive taxonomy, especially use of the higher levels, as one of the "learning how to learn" processes this year. Karen, another team leader, suggested that most teachers knew about Bloom's taxonomy and probably didn't need to go over it again. The principal, Jim Black, said, "Let's survey the teachers on all of the teams to find out (1) if they are familiar with Bloom's taxonomy and (2) if they use it regularly in their teaching and lesson planning. Bring this report back to our next meeting and we'll discuss Bloom again."

A tally of the survey indicated that most teachers knew about Bloom's levels, but few of them used the taxonomy regularly in their lesson planning, classroom teaching, and selection of practice activities. So the IIC decided to prepare a handout for all teachers, which included an overview of Bloom's cognitive levels and sample instructional objectives to help teachers review the kinds of objectives and activities that could be used to illustrate the hierarchy of levels in the classroom. Following is the content of the handout:

A Brief Overview of Bloom's Cognitive Taxonomy

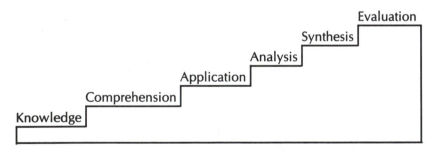

This diagram illustrates the hierarchical arrangement of the taxonomy (Bloom, 1959). Students need to learn the information on the lower steps or levels before proceeding to the higher ones. It also suggests that lessons should allow for students to progress from the lower levels (knowledge and comprehension) to the higher levels (application, analysis, synthesis, and evaluation). Following is a listing of the levels along with a brief definition, sample verbs, and general activities for each (Sorenson et al., 1988, pp. 5–6):

1. *Knowledge:* This level is the lowest level of learning. It includes recall and memory; learners recall specifics with concrete references. Knowledge includes specific facts, dates, events, persons, places, and so on.

Verbs: Define, recall, identify, label, collect, observe
Activities: Defining terminology and symbols; recalling facts, names, examples, rules, and categories; recognizing trends, causes, and relationships; acquiring principles, procedures, implications, and theories

2. *Comprehension:* At this level, the learner can use materials or ideas without relating them to other ideas or materials.

Verbs: Infer, paraphrase, explain, give examples, summarize, extrapolate

Activities: Rephrasing definitions; illustrating meanings; interpreting relationships; drawing conclusions; demonstrating methods; inferring implications; predicting consequences

3. *Application:* Learners use information in specific situations. The information may be in the form of general ideas or concepts, principles, and theories, which students remember and apply.

Verbs: Demonstrate, modify, change, use, rearrange
Activities: Applying principles, rules, and theories; organizing procedures, conclusions, and effects; choosing situations and methods; restructuring processes, generalizations, and phenomena

4. *Analysis:* This level calls for taking apart information to make new relationships. Learners clarify by discovering hidden meaning and basic structure.

Verbs: Interpret, solve, discriminate, break down, sequence
Activities: Recognizing assumptions and patterns; deducing conclusions, hypotheses, and points of view; analyzing relationships, themes, evidence, causes, and effects; contrasting ideas, parts, and arguments

5. *Synthesis:* This level recombines ideas to generate a new pattern or structure not previously apparent. Learners reassemble the component parts of an idea to develop new or creative ideas.

Verbs: Create, compose, design, construct, propose
Activities: Producing products and compositions; proposing objectives, means, and solutions; designing plans and operations; organizing taxonomies, concepts, schemes, and theories; deriving relationships, abstractions, and generalizations

6. *Evaluation:* This is the highest level of cognition. It calls for judging material, information, or a method for specific purposes and using a distinctive criterion as a basis for a decision. It relates to the problem-solving process of selecting one of several proposed alternatives for action.

Verbs: Appraise, judge, evaluate, justify, criticize
Activities: Judging accuracy, consistency, and reliability; assessing errors, fallacies, predictions, and means and ends; considering efficiency, utility, and standards; contrasting alternatives and courses of action.

Bloom's cognitive taxonomy is useful in planning, teaching, and questioning for all students in a classroom. It provides a vehicle to move from lower levels (knowledge and comprehension) to higher levels (application, analysis, synthesis, and evaluation) as a lesson or unit of instruction develops. It also provides for ways to meet individual student needs. Some students will need more practice at lower level skills, while others, who have already mastered them, can spend more time on higher levels. Also, many students can learn to use the taxonomy in their own writing and questioning in lessons and discussions. Some sample objectives to illustrate Bloom's cognitive levels at several grade levels are presented here.

Grades K-2; topic, A Farm Field Trip in October in Minnesota

Knowledge: Identify the characteristics of the weather in October.
Comprehension: Explain in your own words how you feel outside at that time of year.

Application: Predict what kinds of outer clothing you would want to wear on the field trip.

Analysis: Differentiate between the kinds of outer clothes you would wear in October and in July; give reasons for your choices.

Synthesis: Make a drawing showing several students on the field trip at the farm wearing the proper outer clothing for October.

Evaluation: After the field trip, judge whether or not the students wore the proper types of clothing; give reasons for responses.

Grades 3-5; topic, Water Pollution

Knowledge: Name three substances that pollute water.
Comprehension: Give examples of what has happened to rivers in your community or state that have a lot of water pollution.

Application: Predict what would happen if there were an oil spill into your local water supply or a nearby river.

Analysis: Illustrate how oil pollutes the water.
Synthesis: Propose a program that would eliminate water pollution in the local river.

Evaluation: Appraise the quality of water in your local river at the present time in relation to state water standards.

Grades 6–8; topic, Zip Codes

Knowledge: Define a zip code.

Comprehension: Explain the meaning of the five digits in your school zip code.

Application: Show the ten geographic distributions of the zip code areas of the United States along with the initial digits for each area on a map of the United States.

Analysis: Compare the zip code system in the United States with those in Canada, Europe, Japan, and other countries.

Synthesis: Devise a new set of zip codes for all of the countries in the world that is uniform throughout; give logical reasons for your choice of system.

Evaluation: Judge your new set of uniform codes in terms of ease of use and understanding, number of digits, coverage of areas for population growth, population shifts, and any other applicable criteria.

Creative Thinking

In order to get the "learning how to learn" restructuring off to a good start, the Building-Wide In-service Committee at Lawton School selected the topic of creative thinking for its first in-service meeting of next year. John, a long-time member of the committee and intermediate unit teacher, said, "Teachers love creativity and creative thinking. They always teach it in language arts." Mary Ellen, a middle school unit teacher who was new to the building, replied, "That's just the trouble. We teach creative writing in language arts and then we fail to carry it over to the other subject areas where students can apply it to many different kinds of situations." Nancy, the chair of the In-service Committee, decided to appoint a subcommittee to develop a plan and an agenda. The committee suggested they select a series of activities to introduce the teachers at Lawton to the topic of creative thinking. The committee also suggested that the teachers have hands-on experiences. John and Mary Ellen, who had shown an interest in the topic, along with Pat, a primary unit teacher, were appointed as a subcommittee to study "creativity."

They decided the in-service meeting should be about two hours long and should be held early the following fall. This was a real challenge since they needed to accommodate the needs of teachers and students, K–8, and also to illustrate ways to use creative thinking in several subject areas.

At the first subcommittee meeting, Pat agreed to be chair. All three teachers gladly accepted their challenge to develop the agenda and plans for the meeting. They decided to start by consulting several resource teachers in the district as well as a variety of instructional materials. Pat indicated that she had taken a course in creativity at a nearby university the previous year and had accumulated several activities she thought would be useful for the meeting. Each member took on an assignment and they scheduled another meeting in three weeks to develop the meeting agenda. They also agreed to bring along copies of activities so they could review them and decide which ones to use for the in-service meeting.

At their second meeting, they were excited about what they had found. After discussing their needs and reviewing their resources, they developed the following agenda for the two-hour in-service meeting. The philosophy behind the agenda was to have teachers experience the activities they would use with students and adapt the ideas in the activities to the age/grade level and other characteristics of their students.

Agenda for Creative Thinking In-service Meeting (2 hours)

Approximate Time	*Content and Activity*
(5 min)	1. "Ice Breaker" — Introductory Activity
(10 min)	2. Presentation — Definitions of creativity and four creative processes
(15 min)	3. Hands-On Experiences — Fluency
(30 min)	4. Hands-On Experiences — Flexibility
(30 min)	5. Hands-On Experiences — Elaboration
(30 min)	6. Create an Activity — Originality

Excerpts from the agenda above and from the activities the teachers participated in during the in-service session are presented below. Copies of the complete activities are available in the appendix.

Agenda item 1 was an introductory activity, Ding-A-Ling Definitions in Math and Science. It was designed to get participants thinking in creative, different ways and to alleviate some of their fears and traditional ways of approaching situations. Some of the ding-a-ling definitions included:

- What little acorns say when they grow up (math, **geometry**)
- What to call a dead parrot (math, **polygon**)
- A huge purple flower (science, **ultraviolet**)
- What does a barber do? (science, **eclipse**)

Agenda item 2 dealt with definitions of creativity and creative thinking and characteristics of creative processes that are useful to teach creativity. The presentation is summarized in the following narrative.

Creative thinking calls for recognizing the existence of a problem, generating and testing a variety of ideas to solve it, and communicating possible solutions (Torrance, 1977). During creative thinking, students learn a great deal by exploring, trying out, manipulating, experimenting, questioning, and modifying ideas. Students should have the freedom to inquire, search, and speculate without fearing penalties for "wrong" answers. Creative thinking and action should be a planned part of lessons and instructional activities in all subjects of the curriculum.

Four creative processes — fluency, flexibility, elaboration, and originality — are useful in all creative endeavors, particularly in creative thinking (Klein, 1982; Sternberg, 1986):

- *Fluency:* To think quickly and in quantity, generating a large number of ideas or possibilities, including relevant responses
- *Flexibility:* To think in different modes, ideally using different categories and mind-sets
- *Elaboration:* To think in detail — magnifying, minifying, simplifying, adapting, substituting, and so on; embellish or embroider upon an idea
- *Originality:* To think in new, unique, clever, unusual terms

Brainstorming, listing, and collecting activities encourage fluency. Activities that incorporate role playing, decoding, using symbols, and forecasting help develop flexible thinking. Designing, editorializing, illustrating, and inventing rely on elaboration skills. And, though true originality is very difficult to achieve, originality within a given situation is easy to recognize.

Divergent thinking is essential to creative thinking. It can be defined as "the kind of thinking required to generate many different responses to the same question or problem" (Costa & Pressein, in Costa, 1985, p. 310). Creative thinking also helps people express creative, innovative, and nontraditional ideas. Isaksen and Treffinger (1985) and Davis (1983) have suggested guidelines for divergent thinking. They include deferring judgment, generating many ideas or options, accepting all ideas, reaching for limits, not jumping to conclusions, taking risks, and letting one idea lead to another.

Agenda item 3 focused on *fluency* activities. Here teachers generated ideas in several subject matter areas. In science, they might use an outline of an animal and have the students indicate as many words or phrases as they could in relation to it. They could use the same technique for monuments, scenes, and other pictures in social studies. In language arts, students could generate ideas in relation to pictures of situations such as those related to joy, danger, sadness, and so on.

Several activities illustrated different ways to look at *flexibility* in agenda item 4. Examples from the Number and Word Jumble activities are

24 H in a D   (24 hours in a day)
435 M in the H of R   (435 members in the House of
                            Representatives)

| the B of R | (the Bill of Rights) |
| 90 D in a R A | (90 degrees in a right angle) |

Looking at things in other ways and from different points of view were emphasized in a second flexibility activity, Common Sayings Arranged in Unusual Ways. Following are some examples:

F r i e n d s Standing Miss F r i e n d s	O — M D Ph D B A	deal	world world world

Sweet Lover's Delight is a third activity to encourage flexibility. It relates unusual descriptions to common candy bar names, such as nickname for a common pet (Kit Kat), several small hills (Mounds), state of euphoria (Joy), a well-known planet (Mars).

After the teachers had completed each flexibility activity, the leader asked them to share examples of where they could use the activity and others similar to it in their own classes. It was amazing how teachers at different age/grade levels could use the same activity depending on the complexity and abstractness of the subject they were introducing or the point of view they wanted to emphasize.

Agenda item 5 dealt with *elaboration.* Two activities of very different kinds were used to illustrate this creative process. They were

1. Generating words from names of body parts: Teachers formed groups of four and each group was given the name of a body part, such as head, foot, arm, hand, leg, eye, knee, finger, thumb, heart, brain, and so on. They were given two minutes to generate as many words, including hyphenated words, as they could that used the name of the body part. Then the groups shared their results.

2. Teachers completed the activity, Football Fun, which asked them to name the professional football team brought to mind by an unusual phrase such as:

Indian leaders (Chiefs)	King of Beasts (Lions)
Seven squared (Forty Niners)	Boeing 747 (Jets)
Rodeo horses (Broncos)	Helpers to relocate (Packers)

Then teachers were asked to "extend Football Fun" by generating other activities related to sports in the content areas of social studies, science, math, and language arts that would be appropriate for students at the age/grade level they taught. Some of the ideas they generated included the following:

- Identify the city and state where each of the professional football teams played this year (for example, Vikings in Minneapolis, Minnesota) on a U.S. map. (Grades 3–5)
- Search out the derivation of the name of each team (for example, Bears, Forty Niners) and explain how it relates to the geographical location of the team. (Grades 3–5)
- Make your own list of "sports-o-whats" (like Football Fun) for:

> Major league baseball teams
> National Basketball Association teams
> National Hockey League teams
> Big Ten, Big Eight, and other college or university teams
> Other sports teams and leagues (Grades 3–5 and 6–8)

The last agenda item dealt with *originality*. Before the leader asked teachers to complete an activity, she talked about techniques such as SCAMPER (Eberle, 1977) that all students and teachers can use to help them create original ideas. Here, "S" is for substitute where one person, place, or thing can take place of another; "C" is for combine; "A" for adapt; "M" for modify, magnify, or minify; "P" for put to other uses; "E" for eliminate, remove a part of the whole, and elaborate to add details; and "R" for reverse and rearrange.

Finally, teachers were asked to create an original activity for their own students. They could use elements of SCAMPER or do it in any way they wished. They were also asked to identify which creative process or processes the activity emphasized and to relate the activity to science, social studies or math in order to encourage them to use creative thinking in areas other than language arts.

To be creative is one of a human being's most widely held dreams. All students and teachers can participate in creative thinking. A chart listing more than one hundred activities and products for students that teachers can use when planning lessons is presented in Figure 6-4. These activities are listed at three levels: "A" level activities focus on fluency as well as on the knowledge and comprehension levels of Bloom's cognitive taxonomy, "B" level activities emphasize flexibility and the application and analysis levels of Bloom, and "C" level activities encourage elaboration and Bloom's synthesis and evaluation levels.

Inquiry Processes

"Inquiry processes are fun to teach to young children because they just love to work with real, hands-on materials." This comment came from a

FIGURE 6-4 · *Student Activities and Products at Three Levels of Difficulty*

A Kaleidoscope of Student Activities		
Level A	*Level B*	*Level C*
Assignments, Class Projects, Individual Challenges		
Agendas	Associations	Advertisements
Announcements	Biographies	Arguments
Autobiographies	Book jackets	Articles
Character sketches	Bulletin boards	Brochures
Classifications	Captions	Cartoons
Collections	Charts	Casts (news and so on)
Completions	Checkerboard techniques	Codes
Data sheets	Clues	Compositions
Definitions	Comparisons	Conclusions
Descriptions	Computations	Court trials
Dramatizations	Contrasting	Critiques
Drill and practice	Conversations	Debates
Example giving	Criteria for evaluation	Dioramas
Explanations	Deductions	Editorials
Games or quizzes	Demonstrations	Evaluations
Glossary entries	Diagrams	Experiments
Guides	Directions	Filmstrips/films
Information search	Discussions	Games development
Invitations	Drawings	Goals/objectives
Journal entries	Encyclopedia entries	Headlines
Just supposing	Graphs	Idea or product changes
Lists	Interviews	Illustrations
Log entries	Letters	Inventions
Memorizations	Manipulations	Itineraries
Memos	Newspaper production	Judgments
Morning talk (show/tell)	Opinions	Keys (development)
Observations	Outlines	Machines
Odes	Posters	Menus
Paraphrasing	Presentations	Models
Peer teaching	(individual/class)	Myths
Programmed instruction	Problem identification	New combinations
Puzzles	Puns	Pantomimes
Questions and answers	Questionnaires	Peer presentation
Reading assignments	Questions	Peer project evaluations
Recitations	Rebus stories	Plans
Repetitions	Relationships	Play writing
Rules	Reports	Poems
Structured poems	Rhymes	Problem definition
Summaries	Role playing	Product development
Telegrams	Role reversals	Programs
Worksheets	Sequences	Recipes
	Simulations	Research projects
	Skits	Self ideas
	Solutions	Slogans
	Story writing	Songs
	Surveys	Tales
	Tongue twisters	Testimonials
	Warnings	Weather reports

Source: J. Sorenson, J. Engelsgjerd, M. Francis, M. Miller, and N. Schuster, *The Gifted Program Handbook* (Palo Alto, CA: Dale Seymour Publications, 1988), p. 99. Reprinted with permission.

teacher in the primary unit at Lawton Elementary School. Actually, it could have come from any teacher, kindergarten through university level. Students at all ages learn best from a combination of reading, working with visual materials and media, discussing information, and hands-on examining of objects and situations to draw their own conclusions. Learning how to learn by using inquiry processes helps them to develop their own strategies to seek, organize, and subsequently store information in all subject matter areas and in daily life.

Inquiry processes have been a formal part of learning for several decades. Various sets of processes have been emphasized in science, social studies, and math textbooks and in many curriculum materials and reference books. One set of inquiry processes, sometimes called processes of scientific inquiry, along with their definitions are presented here (Sorenson et al., 1988, pp. 79–80):

- *Observing:* Gathering information directly using the human senses and indirectly using instruments and other extensions of the senses
- *Classifying:* Clustering of objects or events based on likenesses and differences in arbitrarily selected attributes or characteristics
- *Inferring:* Identifying patterns and relationships among observable facts
- *Predicting:* Guessing what will happen in the future based on what we know has happened in the past
- *Measuring:* Comparing properties and conditions of objects directly or indirectly with arbitrary units; units can be standardized
- *Communicating:* Sharing observations and data so that others can verify and use them
- *Interpreting data:* Analyzing and sifting data relevant to a given problem or situation; limiting interpretations to data
- *Making operational definitions:* Generally describing the physical characteristics of object(s) or phenomena and the conditions under which the descriptions are made, as well as intended uses of the object
- *Formulating questions and hypotheses:* Asking questions on the basis of observations and data and setting hypotheses based on answers to questions; hypotheses should be simple and testable
- *Experimenting:* Testing hypotheses through observing, identifying, and controlling variables; gathering, sorting, and interpreting data
- *Formulating models:* Developing representations of states, objects, and events; models help explain and describe ideas and events in the present and predict future events or phenomena not yet explained

These inquiry processes are presented in a triangular arrangement in Figure 6-5. Here, observing forms the base of the triangle. Each process above observing uses those below it to carry out the process. For example,

FIGURE 6-5 • *Inquiry Processes in a Hierarchy*

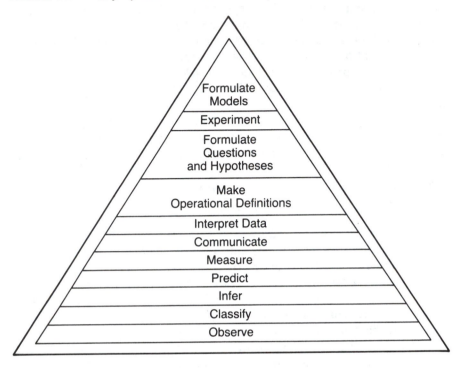

Source: J. Sorenson, J. Engelsgjerd, M. Francis, M. Miller, and N. Schuster, *The Gifted Program Handbook* (Palo Alto, CA: Dale Seymour Publications, 1988), p. 79. Reprinted with permission.

when students conduct an experiment, they use most or all of the processes below experimenting in the diagram. The order of use is not rigid, however, and sometimes a process above the one being emphasized is used to solve a problem. It is most important to remember that no single process is used in isolation. A lesson or situation that focuses on a certain process or two or three processes offers an opportunity to review, use, and reinforce several other processes as well.

The team leaders in each unit at Lawton School asked their team members to review and discuss the Inquiry Processes and Stamps activity presented below. Each team focused on the activities for the age/grade level of its students. This interaction helped the team to identify ways to incorporate inquiry into teaching.

Inquiry Processes and Stamps Activity

Teacher Input

Purchase a large bag of 300 to 500 used stamps at a hobby or craft specialty store. Give each student, pair of students, or cooperative group of students, 20 to 40 stamps that have been randomly selected from the bag. Have students carry out some of the activities listed below as appropriate for their age/grade levels and abilities. The inquiry process(es) that are emphasized in the activity are listed in parentheses.

Student Activities

K–2

1. Observe the stamps with eyes alone and then with a hand lens or magnifying glass. What can you see with the magnifying instrument that you couldn't see with eyes alone? (observation)
2. Divide the group of stamps into two subgroups based on one characteristic. Then redivide each subgroup into two groups using another characteristic. Keep a list of which characteristic is used first, second, and so on. (observation, classification)
3. What characteristics, such as color, shape, size, and cost do you find among your stamps? Make a simple chart to identify differences in each characteristic. (observation, classification)
4. How many ways can you divide your stamps into two groups based on a single characteristic? What are these characteristics? (observation, classification)

Grades 3–5

1. Observe the stamps with eyes alone, then with a magnifying instrument. Identify characteristics in which stamps differ, such as color, size, shape, cost, or denomination. (observation, classification)
2. What can you tell from postmarks on the stamps? Which stamps came the greatest difference? Why? (inference)
3. Measure several different sizes of stamps in metric units. Why do you think stamps come in different sizes? (measurement, inference)
4. What are the different kinds of categories of designs you can find on your U.S. stamps? Why do you think these categories are so popular? How many different presidents did you find? Write a one-page report on one of the presidents you found on a stamp. (observation, classification, inference, communication)
5. Design a stamp to honor an important person, place, or event from your state or region of the country. Research the background on your

selection to incorporate it into your design. (interpreting data, inference, making models)

Grades 6–8

1. Make and chart observations on at least forty stamps, including color, size, shape, cost, denomination, and any other characteristics you find. Divide them into two groups, then two more groups, and so on until each group has identical members. Chart your characteristics used to divide the groups. (observation, classification)
2. From your groups in 1 above, identify the following:

    a. Which stamps probably traveled the greatest distance? Why?
    b. Which stamps cost the most money in U.S. currency?
    c. Why are stamps that cost the same amount of money issued in different sizes?
    d. Why are many stamps reproductions of fine art works?
    e. What kinds of topics are the most popular on stamps? Why? (inference, interpreting data, formulating questions)

3. Design a stamp to commemorate a significant event in science or history in the United States and another country that you or the group selects. Research your topic to incorporate appropriate and important information about each country into your design. (communication, interpreting data, experimenting, making models)
4. Pretend you are one of the foreign stamps and tell of your travel experiences from your home country to another country (for example, from Japan to Argentina). Research background materials to make your story accurate and interesting. (communication, interpreting data, formulating questions)

Some of the items listed above are adapted from Barrow (1979).

Critical Thinking Skills

The middle level team at Lawton School had selected critical thinking skills as an area of emphasis for the upcoming school year. These skills were a part of the "learning how to learn" theme for the entire district. Sue, the team leader, had been to a thinking skills workshop in February and had gleaned many practical ideas and activities on this topic to use with the sixth-, seventh-, and eighth-grade students in the unit.

Critical thinking can be defined as "reasonable, reflecting thinking that is focused on deciding what to believe or do" (Ennis in Costa, 1985, p. 54). Another definition suggests that critical thinking is "essentially evaluative in nature. It involves precise, persistent, and objective analysis of any claim, source, or belief to judge its accuracy, validity, or worth" (Beyer, 1988, p. 60–64).

Critical thinking skills are not used in a particular sequence. They are a collection of specific operations that can be used alone or in combination with others in any order. Critical thinking skills can be integrated into every curriculum subject from kindergarten through high school and are best learned when students have the opportunity to practice the skills until they become a part of their everyday thinking.

After discussing the definitions and information about the skills, team members reviewed several lists of critical thinking skills that Sue brought to share with them and decided to emphasize the twelve skills shown in Figure 6-6. Here, a brief definition and an example to illustrate each skill are also presented.

After reviewing the definitions and examples for each skill in Figure 6-6, the team decided on the following teaching sequence:

1. Review the skills with the students because some students had been introduced to several of the skills previously while others had not been exposed to them.
2. Teach the elements of each critical thinking skill in a subject matter class. For example, bias and stereotype, compare and contrast, reliable and unreliable sources, consistent and inconsistent, and analyzing arguments would be taught in social studies; sequence and prioritize and deductive and inductive reasoning in math; and fact and opinion and point of view in language arts.
3. Introduce, define, and illustrate each skill with a class-size group. Have the students practice the skill with an example from the subject matter area. Then, after the students became familiar with the elements of the skill, have them practice it as a part of a small group.
4. Make an effort to use the skills in all subject matter disciplines on an everyday basis whenever appropriate.

The team felt that such a sequence would allow for a continuous flow and application of critical thinking skills throughout the year.

In addition, members of the team selected and/or developed a series of activities that students could carry out to use critical thinking skills along with other "learning how to learn" processes in interdisciplinary activities. An example from "Christopher Columbus and Critical Thinking" is presented here.

"In 1492, Columbus sailed the ocean blue." Some historians remind us that other explorers visited North America before Columbus

FIGURE 6-6 • Critical Thinking Skills

Critical Thinking Skill	Definition	Example
Compare and contrast	Determine similarities and differences.	How are ants and ticks alike? How are they different? Compare and contrast the causes of World War I and World War II.
Fact and opinion	Separate statements that can be verified (facts) from those that can not (opinion).	The fire started at 1:30 A.M. while the three children and the mother were asleep. No one called the fire department until 1:50 A.M. when the fire was raging out of control. Which statements are facts, which opinion?
Relevant and irrelevant	Decide whether something is related (irrelevant) to the item or situation under discussion or not (irrelevant).	In selecting a band instrument, the following items may be considered: shape of your mouth, dental structure, your willingness to practice, your interest in being in the color guard and/or marching band, the instrument your friend is going to play, cost of the instrument, the color of the lining in the instrument case, your physique. Which items are irrelevant, and why?
Reliable and unreliable sources	Decide whether a source is believable based on the author's expertise and reputation, and the publication's reputation, accuracy, and agreement with other sources.	An automobile manufacturer advertised that its "Zinger" model got more miles per gallon than its competitor, "Xerkes." Consumer Reports magazine ranked Zinger's mileage lower than its competitor, Xerkes. Which source is more reliable? Why?
Cause and effect	Identify the cause, reason, or motive for a condition or action; and the effect, result, or outcome of the cause.	What were the major causes and effects of the stock market crashes of 1929 and 1987?
Sequence and prioritize	Sequencing involves determining the logical order of tasks or events to produce a product, complete a project, or attain a goal; prioritizing involves ranking each step according to its importance in the situation.	Determine the steps an individual needs to take to get a job. Then, put the steps in order from least important to most important.
Bias and stereotype	Recognize bias, a slanted view in favor or against something, often formed unfairly, and stereotype, a form of bias in which certain characteristics are considered common to a group without respect to individuals and their differences.	In settling playground disputes, one teacher always take the side of the girls (bias); third world countries are unable to maintain a democratic form of government for more than a few years (stereotype).
Point of view	Identify the position or situation from which something is presented, observed, or considered, and identify which elements of bias might be present.	The Republicans considered the Supreme Court candidate to be a moderate while the Democrats considered the candidate conservative.
Consistent and inconsistent	Decide whether the line of reasoning is logical (consistent) or contradictory (inconsistent).	The family always said their ancestor came to the United States from England in 1856. His naturalization papers indicate he came in 1859.
Assumptions and generalizations	Identify and explore the validity of assumptions, beliefs, or ideas we take for granted or tend to accept as true, and generalizations, general statements, laws, or principles drawn from specific cases.	"The gifted student is ensured acceptance at a highly rated university" is an assumption that may or may not be true depending on other characteristics of the individual. On the other hand, "when the pressure on a confined gas increases, the volume decreases if temperature is held constant" is a scientific generalization that is true.
Analyzing arguments	Identify the elements of an argument and determine the strength or weakness of each element.	The teenager says, "Mom and Dad, everyone else in our class gets to go. You are the old-fashioned parents." What elements are evident in this argument: Which elements are strong and which are weak?
Deduction and induction	Make deductive inferences that are conclusions drawn from general principles or given promises; make inductive inferences that are conclusions drawn from specific instances.	Deductive: The small creature you found in the grass has six legs. Since you know that insects have six legs and mites and ticks eight legs, you reason it must be an insect. Inductive: You are given four different shapes and sizes of triangles—right angle, obtuse, isosceles, equilateral. You measure the angles in each one and add them up. The sum is 180 degrees for each. From this, you reason that "the sum of the angles of any triangle will be 180 degrees."

Source: Summarized from J. Sorenson, J. Engelsgjerd, M. Francis, M. Miller, and N. Schuster, *The Gifted Program Handbook* (Palo Alto, CA: Dale Seymour Publications, 1988), pp. 71–72.

"discovered" it . . . and they did. But, the struggle to get to America that was led by Columbus remains the best-documented source of America's discovery and was an integral part of a worldwide awakening known as the "renaissance." Columbus was a part of this movement that shook the beliefs and attitudes of European society and strained the technology of the day to its breaking point. Columbus and his discoveries contributed to scientific and sociological information of the world and fired up people's imaginations about exploring, exploiting, and settling in a "new world." They also brought slavery, plunder, and destruction of civilizations to many of the native inhabitants of the Americas.

Some sample activities on Columbus and his life are presented below. A series of activities at a variety of learning levels on this topic can be developed by teachers for their students. Critical thinking skills that are emphasized in this activity appear in parentheses.

- Research to find out how Columbus conceived the dream of "finding a new world." Find the dates of his long and difficult search for money to indicate his encounters with his family, royalty, and others. Focus on the final months of his search. (*Skills emphasized:* cause/effect, sequence/prioritize, reliable/unreliable sources, bias/stereotype, point of view, assumptions/generalizations)
- Sailors at the time of Columbus had many superstitions, such as fear of sea monsters, sailing on Friday, spilling salt, whistling aboard ship, rainbows in the morning, cutting their hair while at sea, and so on. Compile a list of these superstitions, reasons for them, and identify which ones still exist today. Develop the information into a radio or television talk show (*Skills emphasized:* cause/effect, bias/stereotype, fact/opinion, point of view, analyze argument, relevant/irrelevant).

Single-Step Problem-Solving Techniques

Another set of thinking skills that students can practice to help them learn how to learn are single-step problem-solving techniques. At Lawton School, several of these techniques had been stressed in the K–8 math texts and in math supplementary materials (for example, in *Problem-Solving Experiences in Mathematics,* Addison-Wesley) they had used over the previous five years. Therefore, the IIC decided to only review the techniques with the entire staff and encourage them to use those techniques wherever appropriate in all subject matter areas, not just in math. The techniques are easy for students to learn, have self-explanatory titles, and are very useful in everyday living. They can be introduced in primary grades and expanded in complexity and difficulty for a variety of situations as the students progress through elementary and middle school.

The IIC selected ten techniques. Work backward, simplify and reduce, recognize patterns, organized listing, guess and test, and form analogies are techniques that are fairly precise. Make a drawing or figure, make a table or graph, make a model and act it out give students more opportunity to explore. Following are definitions along with examples and suggestions of appropriate situations in the curriculum to teach and use the techniques (Sorenson et al., 1988, pp. 74–76):

* *Work backward:* This technique works best when the answer is known. For example, if a library fine is $2.40, and the library charges $.10/day for each day that the book is overdue, then $2.40 divided by $.10/day = 24 days overdue. (In an everyday example, Tom has to catch the school bus at 7:35 A.M. He can work backward from this time to decide how much time it takes to get up and dressed, eat breakfast, and gather his books. Then, he knows when to set the alarm!)

* *Simplify and reduce:* Simplifying and reducing is especially effective in working math problems. When large numbers distract students from the process, they can reduce the size of the numbers to see the process more clearly. For example, suppose a family drove 2,100 miles on a recent vacation, their car averaged 28 miles/gallon, and the average price of a gallon of gasoline was $1.29. How many miles did they travel and how much did the family spend for gasoline? This is how the technique works: Reduce the trip size to 100 miles, change the miles/gallon to 10, assume the cost of gas is $1.00/gallon. Then the process is simpler. The family used 10 gallons of gas (100 divided by 10) and paid $10.00 (10 times $1.00). Once the process is clear, the student can plug in larger numbers. In this example, the family used 75 gallons of gas (2,100 miles divided by 28 miles/gallon) and paid $96.75 (75 gallons at $1.29/gallon).

* *Recognize patterns:* Pattern recognition is a skill that students can use in many areas and transfer to other areas as needed. Patterns can appear in numbers, letters, words, shapes, and forms. For example, extend the pattern for each of the following examples and give a rule.

   1. 2,4,6,8,10 . . . <u>12,14,16,18</u> . . . ; Pattern rule: <u>Counting by two</u>
   2. A,B,A,C,A,D,A, _____ , _____ , _____ ; Pattern rule: _____
   3. Bob, Carla, David, _____ ; Pattern rule: _____

* *Organized listing:* Arranging information in columns or categories makes it easier to see relationships and interpret data. For example, if the problem were to find as many ways as you can to make change for 25 cents, the data could be listed under the following columns:

Pennies (1)	Nickels (5)	Dimes (10)	Quarters (25)
25	–	–	–
20	1	–	–
15	2	–	–
10	3	–	–
5	4	–	–
5	–	2	. . . and so on.

• *Guess and test:* Using the guess-and-test technique, students can make an appropriate approximation of an answer, then test the approximation to see if it works. Wild or random guessing is not very effective and teachers should discourage it. The following examples offer opportunities to try this technique.

1. Use the following chart to find a word worth thirty-five points. The points appear at the top of the chart and the letters that represent these point values appear below each one. Note that some values are negative.

1	2	3	4	5
– A	B	C	D	– E
F	G	H	– I	J
K	L	M	N	– O
P	Q	R	S	T
– U	V	W	X	Y

2. Draw only one straight line to divide each of the following figures into a triangle and a four-sided figure:

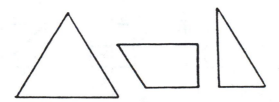

• *Form analogies:* Analogy formation is an extension of pattern recognition. To solve analogies, students must recognize relations between relations. For example,

(A) lawyer : (B) client :: (C) doctor : (D) patient

Element D is usually the unknown in the analogy.

Steps to solve analogies have been suggested (Sternberg, 1986, pp. 112–122; Beyer, 1988, p. 133):

1. Look at the A and B side of the analogy to identify or translate the key terms or elements, recall knowledge associated with each of these key terms, and infer the appropriate relationship between these key terms.
2. Look at the C and D side of the analogy to map and apply the inferred relationship between A and B to elements C and D, remembering that D is usually the unknown, and complete the analogy based on your inferences and decisions.

Analogies may be either verbal or figural. Following are examples of each type, in the format in which they might appear in an exercise or test. Students should be able to explain the reasoning behind their choices.

Verbal

1. George Washington : 1 :: Abraham Lincoln: _____

    (a) 4 (b) 8 (c) 16 (d) 20

2. 30 : 15 :: 12 : _____

    (a) 9 (b) 10 (c) 4 (d) 6

    ### Figural

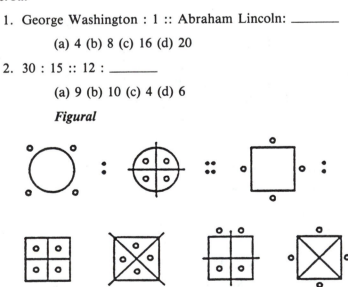

(a)   (b)   (c)   (d)

The four remaining techniques in this set — make a drawing or figure, make a table or graph, make a model, and act the situation out — allow for more open-ended operations. The student must first limit the situation and information and then become involved in creating the result such as a table or model, or actually performing the acting to illustrate the situation.

- *Make a drawing or figure:* We often ask young children to draw what they see and feel. Yet, we too seldom use this technique with older students. For example, if you want to give directions to your home to someone who is not familiar with your geographical area, you can write down the streets that should be taken from the starting point, but a good accompaniment to the street listing is a simple map showing the relationships of the streets with arrows to show the person where to turn.

- *Make a table or graph:* Making tables and graphs helps us organize and summarize numerical and verbal data so we can draw inferences and make evaluations of past situations or projections for future actions. Examples of tables or charts with letters and numbers have been presented in this section under organized listing and guess and test. Review of these tables shows how much easier the reader can see relationships in the information compared to reading it in sentences.

- *Make a model:* Designing or formulating an original model is considered one of a human's highest levels of intellectual performance. Yet, young children often make a model of sorts when they "show us how it is or was." Students need to practice using models and then making their own. Models help us visualize a situation, explain complex and abstract situations, relate to hands-on activities, and illustrate relationships and parts of simple and complex information. Three types of models have been identified — iconic, analogue, and symbolic.

  - *Iconic* models are large- or small-scale representations of states, objects, or events. They are the most concrete type because they represent the important properties of the real thing with only a difference in scale. Examples are aerial photos, atoms, planetary systems, airplanes, insects, or deoxyribonucleic acid (DNA) models. Flow charts, floor plans, or a series of steps in a process are also iconic models.

  - *Analogue* models use one property to represent another. For example, if we want to show elevation on a map, we usually do not produce a three-dimensional map, but use color and/or contour lines to convey information about the elevation. Also, if we want to show the kind of road, we use color, thickness of line, and shading to explain our scheme in the map legend.

  - *Symbolic* models are those in which properties and things are expressed with symbols; arrangement of things can also be a part of that symbolism. For example, in a chemical equation such as $2H_2 + O_2 \rightarrow 2H_2O$, hydrogen, oxygen, and water are substances that are represented by symbols. The subscripts below the symbols for the atoms and numbers in front of molecules ($2H_2O$) also represent quantity relationships in this reaction. The arrow pointing to the right indicates which direction the reaction goes. Computer programs today are written in symbolic language and many basic functions are expressed in a symbolic fashion. Symbolic models are the most abstract of the three types of models.

• *Act it out:* Today's students seem to learn particularly well if they can be involved in a situation. Acting isn't just for plays and skits. Acting it out can be achieved in all subject matter areas and can usually be done right in the classroom. For example, two terms that students often confuse or fail to understand are rotation and revolution in relation to the solar system and other situations. The teacher should model and then have each student stand up and *rotate*—by putting one leg on the floor and moving the body around on it like a spinning top. *Revolution* can be illustrated by having each student move around a globe or other object at a set distance to form a path around the object.

Mathematics has long been considered an individual subject, but acting out and getting involved helps many students understand concepts and operations. For example, basic division can be illustrated by starting with a class-size group of twenty-six students on one side of the room. Ask students to leave the group five students at a time. Then count how many groups of five left. This makes a concrete way to show that 26 divided by 5 equals 5 plus a remainder of 1. This can lead to working with remainders, fractions, decimals, and so on.

Multistep Problem Solving

The IIC and each of the teams—primary, intermediate, and middle school—agreed that students at Lawton needed more emphasis on ways to solve multistep problems and more opportunities to practice problem solving. Here, they could also apply skills from the five clusters of thinking skills they had studied or reviewed earlier. The committee also concurred with the idea that "the ability to solve problems—academic, personal, professional, or social—is one of the most important skills students can take with them from their twelve years of schooling."

A summary of comments and suggestions from several committees who had worked on the curriculum indicated that staff development/in-service sessions to be held over the next year should present straightforward and practical information on problem solving as follows:

- Definitions of problem solving
- Guidelines to help students solve problems in any situation or subject matter area in both formal and informal situations
- Samples of problems at several difficulty levels from several subject matter areas along with appropriate teaching strategies
- Strategies to infuse problem solving into the existing curriculum
- Resources for problems in language arts, math, science, and social studies at a variety of difficulty levels

The information presented below deals with these areas of need in relation to the process of problem solving. Each area looks at some differing points of view and relates to more than one subject matter area.

Definitions of Problem Solving

Problem solving can range from simple to complex and concrete to abstract. It is a kind of thinking that involves appropriate skills from creative thinking, Bloom's cognitive levels, critical thinking, single-step problem solving, and inquiry processes, which were discussed in detail earlier in this chapter. In fact, many authors call each of these sets "kinds of problem-solving skills," and many of these skills overlap each other in the problem-solving process. This discussion focuses on more complex, multistep problems and situations where choices must be made by the problem solvers. Some formal definitions of problem solving include the following:

- "In simple terms, problem solving is a process of asking questions, collecting data, analyzing data, and explaining" (Wisconsin Department of Public Instruction, 1986, p. 22).
- "Problem solving is a process. It is a means by which an individual uses previously acquired knowledge, skills, and understanding to satisfy the demands of an unfamiliar situation." (Krulik & Rudnick, 1987, p. 4).
- Problem solving is a complex thinking process "to resolve a known or defined difficulty, assemble facts about the difficulty and determine additional information needed; infer or suggest alternate solutions and test them for appropriateness; potentially reduce to simpler levels of explanation and eliminate discrepancies; provide solution checks for generalizable value" (Presseisen in Costa, 1985, p. 45).

A summary of these definitions suggests that problem solving is a process by which the problem solver, consciously or unconsciously, moves systematically or randomly through a series of operations, gathering more data as needed, making choices and selections to arrive at one or several solutions. The next section discusses a series of guidelines to help students carry out the problem solving process.

Guidelines for Problem Solving

Education literature abounds with sequences or models for solving problems in all subject matter areas. The practical problem-solving model presented in Figure 6-7 is derived from four of these previous models: inquiry problem solving (Sorenson et al., 1988, p. 81; Haney & Sorenson, 1977, p. 20), decision-making process (Wales, Nardi, & Stager, 1986, p. 38), creative problem solving (Isaksen & Treffinger, 1985, pp. 2–4), and creative processes (Wallas in Davis & Rimm, 1985, p. 215). This model is simplified to four basic steps with two operations, divergence and convergence, at each step. It is applicable to problems in all subject matter areas and to those in daily life. It can be used by students at all age/grade levels with approximate adjustments for language difficulty, teacher input, and content.

The model incorporates both graphic and verbal forms. The shape of the numbered blocks (1, 2, 3, and so on) indicates that each of the four basic steps in the model has a divergent ◹◸ , and a convergent ◺◹ , phase. The divergent phase allows for fluent, free, brainstorming and asks students to consider a wide range of ideas. The convergent phase requires students to prioritize and select the "best" of the ideas they generated to apply to the problem to be solved. The four basic steps in this model are:

1. State the problem (steps 1 and 2).
2. Select the best solution(s) to the problem (steps 3 and 4).
3. Select the best design and try it out; gather data (steps 5 and 6).
4. Evaluate the results of the solution to determine whether or not the problem as stated is solved (steps 7 and 8; steps 9 and 10 indicate alternatives).

Sample Problems to Illustrate Uses of the Model

Two problems — one from science and another from social studies — are presented here. The discussion details how the teacher and a group of students might proceed through the steps of the model in Figure 6-7 to solve each problem. A worksheet for students that correlates with this model is shown in the appendix.

PROBLEM 1 · *Egg in a Bottle*

The teacher brought a flask with a hard-boiled egg (or water balloon) inside it to class and asked the students to "solve the problem." Using the ten steps of the model, they identified the divergent and convergent part of each step (Figure 6-7).

FIGURE 6-7 • *Practical Problem-Solving Model*

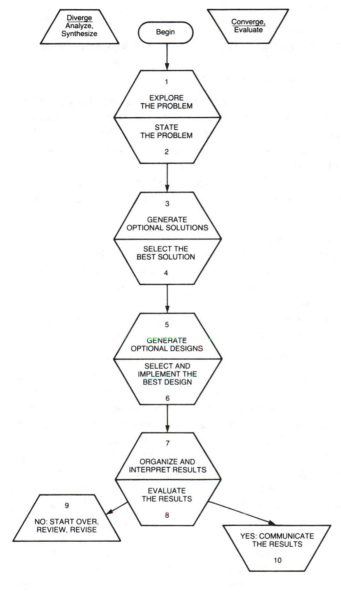

Problem-Solving Steps

1. EXPLORE THE PROBLEM
   Pool experiences and knowledge to make several problem
   statements that include
   criteria; seek outside
   information as needed.

2. STATE THE PROBLEM
   Select the best statement to
   solve the problem.

3. GENERATE OPTIONAL
   SOLUTIONS
   Generate alternative ways to
   solve the problem; predict the
   feasibility of each solution
   according to the criteria and
   problem statement.

4. SELECT THE BEST
   SOLUTION
   Select the best solution to the
   problem as it was stated.

5. GENERATE OPTIONAL
   DESIGNS TO TEST
   SOLUTION
   Make several alternative
   designs, including sequential
   tasks, to investigate and
   implement the solution.

6. SELECT AND IMPLE-
   MENT THE BEST DESIGN
   Select the best design and
   implement it; gather data from
   the implementation.

7. ORGANIZE AND
   INTERPRET RESULTS
   Organize and interpret the
   results from the implementation in several appropriate
   formats.

8. EVALUATE THE
   RESULTS
   Select the best interpretation
   of the results and evaluate
   whether or not it solves the
   problem. If "YES",
   go to step 10; if "NO",
   go to step 9.

9. NO: START OVER,
   REVIEW, REVISE
   Return to step 1 to review the
   action at each step; revise as
   necessary to solve the
   problem.

10. YES: COMMUNICATE
    THE RESULTS
    Share the results with others
    so they can repeat, verify, and
    accept them. The problem is
    solved, at least temporarily.

1. They *explored the problem* and arrived at these following possibilities for "problem statements:"

a. Get the egg out of the bottle.
b. How can we get the egg out of the bottle without breaking the egg or the bottle?
c. Ways to get the egg out of the bottle.

2. After discussing the three statements, they selected problem statement b as the best *problem statement* because it clearly stated the situation and included criteria that had to be considered in formulating solutions. (This could also have been written as a statement such as, "Getting the egg out of the bottle without breaking it or the bottle."

3. *Generating optional solutions* to solve the problem is probably the process the students like best. Some of the solutions the class suggested were

a. Fill the bottle with water.
b. Shake the egg very hard against the neck of the bottle.
c. Put more air molecules inside the bottle than are outside the bottle.
d. Warm the molecules of air inside the bottle with the egg "sealed" against the neck of the bottle.
e. While holding the bottle vertically with the egg "sealed" against the neck of the bottle, blow very hard directly under the neck of the bottle.

4. *Selecting the best solution* offers the most exciting teaching opportunities. Here, students need to accept or reject each solution from step 3 on the basis of what they already know, or they need to gather new information and use it. They must give verifiable reasons for their answers. This part of the problem-solving process automatically uses analysis, synthesis, and evaluation skills from Bloom's cognitive txonomy, inference, and prediction skills from inquiry processes and combinations of several creative thinking, critical thinking, and single-step problem-solving skills. For this problem, they eliminated solution a because they tried it and the egg did not come out; they accepted solution b because they tried it and the egg came out; and they decided to consider solutions c, d, and e further, but needed to gather more information to set up a design to carry them out.

5. For solution 3c, the students *generated optional designs* "to put more molecules into the bottle" with a tire pump; by blowing very hard into the bottle; or by blowing air in with a straw. For solution 3d, they figured they could warm the air molecules by heating the outside of the bottle or by putting burning paper into the bottle. For solution 3e, they decided to try blowing very hard under the neck of the bottle by holding their hands on one side to direct the molecules under the neck.

6. *Selecting and implementing the best designs* held student interest.

For solution 3c, they decided to blow very hard directly into the neck of the bottle with the lips in a "trumpet blowing formation," let the egg slide down into the neck, and then suddenly move the lips away; the egg came out of the bottle. For solution 3d, they decided to warm the bottle with hot water from the faucet while holding it at a downward angle with the egg "sealed" in the neck; the egg came out of the bottle. For solution 3e, they decided to blow very hard under the neck of the bottle; the egg started down the neck, but didn't come all of the way out of the bottle.

7. The students *organized the results* in both narrative and chart form, using diagrams in both formats as appropriate. Drawing information from both formats, they arrived at these interpretations of results:

   a. Shaking will get the egg out of the bottle, but it's a matter of using physical force and gravity.
   b. Filling the bottle with water does not work since the egg did not come out of the bottle when they tried it; they need to seek reasons for why it did not come out.
   c. Blowing hard into the neck of the bottle to add more molecules brought the egg out of the bottle because when the greater number of molecules inside the bottle tried to reach equilibrium, they pushed the egg out ahead of them; molecules move from areas of greater to lesser concentrations.
   d. Warming air molecules inside the bottle by warming the bottle itself, gave the air molecules more energy causing them to move faster and exert greater pressure to "push" the egg out of the bottle when the air molecules tried to move from areas of greater to lesser pressure.
   e. Blowing very hard underneath the neck of the bottle was only a partial success, but investigation of the literature indicated the idea was feasible. Reducing the number of air molecules under the neck by blowing hard leaves a greater concentration of molecules inside the bottle; when molecules try to reach equilibrium by moving from greater to lesser pressure areas, they push the egg out ahead of them. The students needed to blow harder to reduce the air pressure a bit more, or get a smaller egg, or put water on the egg and inside the bottle neck to reduce friction. Further experimentation was needed here.

8. In *evaluating the results,* they selected "blowing very hard directly into the bottle" and "heating the bottle by running hot water from the faucet over the bottle" as equally effective methods to solve the problem of "getting the egg out of the bottle."

9,10. The students decided to *communicate* and ask another class to try their solutions and verify them. Also, the teacher suggested that they might like to work in small groups the next day to solve a new problem—how she got the egg in the bottle in the first place.

The "egg in the bottle" problem was solved with rather precise results. The strategy the teacher used was to present a stimulus, the egg in the bottle, to the students and then use the inquiry teaching style to guide the entire class-size group through the problem. They used many of the inquiry thinking skills, as well as several critical thinking skills, such as cause and effect, identifying relevant and irrelevant data, inductive and deductive thinking. She also encouraged creative thinking — fluency in all steps of the model, flexibility in generating solutions, and elaboration in going from the first problem, "getting the egg out of the bottle" to the obvious second problem, "getting the egg into the bottle." Several single-step problem-solving techniques, such as guess and test, recognizing patterns and forming analogies, as well as thinking at Bloom's higher levels were used constantly. An interesting feature of this problem was that it automatically led to a second problem, "getting the egg into the bottle," which the students could solve in cooperative or other groups. Here the teaching style could change to cooperative and/or student-centered rather than inquiry. This is a good example of using teaching styles appropriately — starting students out with guidance in the inquiry style, then moving to more student responsibility in the cooperative and student-centered styles. The teacher can provide guidance to the groups if they run into difficulty in keeping the problem-solving process moving along.

PROBLEM 2 · *Too Much Trash*

The floors in the hallways and cafeteria of Lawton School were littered with candy wrappers, lunch papers, parts of old assignments, occasional bits of food and other waste materials to the point they were nearly unsafe to walk on. Repeated announcements by the principal, student council members, and others reminding students to put their trash in the containers provided for it had not solved the problem. One of the intermediate unit social studies classes, Miss Black's group, had decided to try to solve this problem using the guidelines of the practical problem-solving model shown in Figure 6-7. They would first work on the problem with the teacher as a class-size group and then break into cooperative groups to work on more specific aspects of the problem. The following narrative summarizes their work. The numbers refer to the steps of the model in Figure 6-7.

1. In their attempt to *state the problem* meaningfully, they suggested four choices:

   a. Ways to keep litter off the floors
   b. Ways to persuade students to put their litter in the trash cans provided

c. Putting trash in containers

d. A strategy to encourage students to put their trash in containers instead of on the floor

2. They eliminated problem statements a, b, and c as too weak, too mild, or too negative and agreed to use d as the *statement of their problem.*

3. They *generated several solutions* to the problem:

a. Reposition trash cans in areas where the most trash was found.

b. Identify students who were doing the most littering and fine them.

c. Station "trash detectives" near stairways and areas of heavy littering to remind students who littered to put their trash in containers.

d. Identify the heavy litterers and make them pick up the trash each day.

4. In *selecting the best solution* they decided to eliminate solution b because they didn't want to identify peers if they had to pay money, and fines had not worked very well to get students to return library books on time. Likewise, they eliminated solution d because they thought it would take too much effort to get these students to do the pickup effectively. They couldn't choose between solutions a and c so they decided to combine the best elements of each into the solution they would implement.

5. Before they could *generate designs,* they needed to form subgroups from the class to do several investigations.

a. Identify the areas where most of the trash was deposited. They obtained a map of the school and collected data for one week. They used "items of trash regardless of size" as their criteria for counting.

b. Explore ways and locations appropriate for stationing "trash detectives." They decided to use the other subgroup's survey data on the "heaviest trash locations" to help find the best locations for the detectives. And they visited the counselor to ask for ways to word the "reprimands" from the detectives to the trash-droppers in a positive, yet "we mean business" manner.

c. Identify ways to select "trash detectives" and reposition the containers. They went to the principal who met with them and the custodians to be sure everyone would agree on moving containers to the heavy-use areas. They met with Miss Black on the "detective selection" process. She suggested they use leadership inventories and/or data from the sociogram they had completed earlier in the year. One of the students suggested starting with students from the unit who had been identified as leaders by their peers. They also thought an equal number of boys and girls should be detectives. If the detective idea were successful, they would develop a pool of students to select from or perhaps select students from the intermediate unit on a random basis.

d. Determine the length of shifts of detectives. The survey group had gathered data for one week to determine high discard areas in fifteen-minute shifts — one shift before school, two shifts at noon, and one shift after school. This seemed to work well and it would allow lunch time for detectives.

6. From the information they gathered from conversations with peers and others, new ideas they generated, and data from the survey group on discard areas, they went ahead and *implemented the design* as follows:

    a. Trash containers with new glow-in-the-dark "TRASH" signs were moved to the ten heaviest discard areas as indicated by the survey.

    b. Twenty students, ten girls and ten boys, who were identified as leaders, were stationed about three feet from a trash container for two, fifteen-minute shifts — one group of ten before school and at noon, and the other group of ten at noon and after school. Detectives did *not* wear any signs or uniforms.

    c. The plan was outlined and explained by the chair of the subcommittee that identified heavy use areas. The chairs of the four subcommittees also explained the plan and how they had arrived at their decisions. The council endorsed the plan wholeheartedly. This information was also shared with the entire student body and faculty during the announcements over the loudspeaker on the Friday morning before they started the plan on Monday and on each morning during the first week of the implementation.

7. *Results were interpreted* from the first, two-week tryout as follows:

    a. The amount of trash on the floors decreased about 60 percent. This was determined by the same committee that had completed the initial survey, using a map to identify heavy discard areas.

    b. The detectives found the job tolerable and a good opportunity to develop positive leadership in a peer–peer situation. These attitudes were determined through interviews with all twenty detectives.

    c. While most students reacted positively to more strategically placed containers and a gentle reminder to pick up what they dropped and use the cans next time, there were a few chronic "trashers" who seemed untouched by the campaign. These trashers were identified by the detectives as mostly older boys with a few girls who sometimes mocked what the detectives said, and did exactly as they pleased.

8,9,10. *Evaluation of the results* indicated that, generally, the problem was on the way to being solved, but reducing trash by 60 percent was not enough. They still needed:

    a. More cooperation from the entire student body

    b. Some way to change the attitude or habit of chronic trashers

c. Some ways to make the detective job more satisfying
d. Strategies to sustain the program after the "newness wears off"

As is often the case, working on the solution to one problem leads to the identification of other problems. These new problems can be solved by using the same guidelines (see Figure 6-7) as were used to solve the initial problems. In a second attempt, more information is already available to the students and they can probably work much more efficiently and effectively to solve the problems. Also, they can learn from their earlier mistakes or misjudgments, which is a very useful skill for all of us.

It should be remembered that repositioning trash containers and having students act as trash detectives is only one way to solve this problem. The characteristics of the student body and school community might lead to other ways to better solve the problem.

Strategies to Infuse Problem Solving into the Existing Curriculum

After teachers have identified resources that will provide strategies and practice for students at various age/grade levels and appropriate to different subject matter areas, they can start keying problem-solving activities into the appropriate objectives in their lessons and units of study in their curriculum. If they do not have appropriate objectives for problem solving, those objectives need to be added. Many teachers already include many problem-solving opportunities in their existing curriculum and these should be identified in the activities related to the lessons they teach.

Further refinements to infuse problem solving into the existing curriculum could include (1) identifying the problems as easy, medium difficulty, or challenge difficulty so they can be matched more directly to student needs; (2) identifying which grouping strategy—individual, pair, small group, or class-size group—would best accommodate a particular problem-solving situation; and (3) determining whether the problem is primarily disciplinary or interdisciplinary in nature.

Perhaps sets of problems could be compiled to form a master file from which teachers could take copies to put into their teaching files. These problems could be duplicated for individuals, groups, or the entire class as appropriate to the needs of the students. The source of the problem sets should be included so teachers can refer to the source if they need more problems or want to share the information with other teachers. And, remember, real problems from the classroom academic work or from "real life" are probably the best ones to solve.

Resources for Problems in Several Subject Matter Areas

Teachers can get help to locate problem-solving resources from their media center director, from appropriate central office personnel, and at professional meetings. Book reviews, advertisements, and articles in subject magazines and journals such as *The Arithmetic Teacher, Science and Children, Science Scope,* and similar publications in other disciplines for elementary and middle school teachers are also good sources. Publications and recommendations from regional and state organizations along with the teacher's manuals from textbook series are additional sources of information about problem-solving books and materials. A list of twelve resources on problems and products appears in the next section of this chapter.

Products

An emphasis on having students produce products in all subject matter areas was another thrust of Lawton's "learning how to learn" focus for the coming school year. The staff agreed that the creation of products allowed students to have input into their learning. It also provided the students the opportunities to take the initiative to investigate the background and literature, manipulate real materials, collect data, and organize and report results to a real audience to get real evaluations of their work. Also, products allowed teachers to guide students' progress and to help students learn how to learn.

Products are often called the "ends" of instruction. They can range from simple to complex and concrete to abstract according to the needs of students. The difficulty level of a product can fall in any quadrant of the chart below:

	Concrete	*Abstract*
Simple	A	B
Complex	C	D

For example, an A product would be appropriate for young students and those just getting started on a topic; a B product could be geared to introduce students to dealing with abstract ideas; a C product could help students learn to deal with more variables in several settings, yet keep the work at a concrete level; and a D product would provide a challenge to students to deal with both abstract and complex ideas.

Products provide many other positive experiences for students. These include the following:

- Students can work on a product alone, with a partner, or in a small group.
- Products can be short term (one to a few hours at a learning station),

intermediate term (during a unit of instruction or several lessons), or long term (a semester or a year).

- Products allow students to incorporate their special interests and skills.
- Product development involves several subject areas and the opportunity to practice many basic skills.
- Product development often reaches out to parents and community for resources and assistance.
- Products can promote affective as well as cognitive development when they are selected, developed, displayed, and explained by the students.
- Product development automatically encourages students to use higher level thinking skills (for example, analysis, synthesis, evaluation, elaboration) and problem-solving techniques.
- Products can relate to units of study, such as astronomy, World War II, a Shakespearean play, or to general topics or problems not usually a part of any subject, such as "How can we solve the growing population of elementary school pupils in our community at the lowest cost to taxpayers?"

Products that students develop should relate to real problems, be shared with real audiences, and involve transformation and manipulation. They should not be just summaries of information. Products should undergo real evaluation by peers, teachers, community, and experts. These "real" aspects of products are explored in detail here.

Problems from Authentic Situations

Students often need help from teachers and others to select and investigate authentic problems. One technique applies a series of "W" questions—Who? When? What? Where? Why important?—which can be used to investigate a historical or current topic or personality (Maker, 1982). The "where" narrows the focus to local, state, region, national, or world geographical location; the "who" is biographical and helps students limit the person(s) of interest within the "where"; the "when" is chronological and relates the person, event, or situation to a period of the past, present, or future (for example, eighteenth century, last year, or 2025); the "what" is functional and helps students focus on an area such as literature, sports, economics, or government; the "why important" helps students relate the significance of the topic to world events within the period of study as well as its impact on future time periods (Sorenson et al., 1988).

A second way to help students start to investigate a problem for a product is to develop a set of "real world" questions under a variety of general headings, such as the following (Sorenson et al., 1988):

Medical

- What is the impact of junk food on growth and development of teenagers?
- How do diseases such as acquired immune deficiency syndrome (AIDS) affect our society and its laws?

Business and Industry

- How can we create more jobs for people in our city?
- How will a decrease in capital gains taxes affect the stock market?

Cultural

- How is communication technology (television, videocassette recorders, satellite transmission, and so on) changing family life?
- How has music influenced our lives during [select a time period]?

Historical

- What part have women played in the development of labor unions?
- Why do you think so many outstanding politicians and scholars were involved in the framing of the U.S. Declaration of Independence and the Constitution?

A third way to get students at the intermediate and middle school levels involved in developing a product from a problem is through competitions from the classroom or through the school, district, region, state, and national levels. A wide variety of these competitions in all subject areas is available. Many of them provide teachers and facilitators with topics, resource ideas, and problems. Some of these events are: Odyssey of the Mind, Future Problem Solving, Young Astronauts, Invent America, MATHCOUNTS, Math Pentathlon, and Academic Decathlon. A listing of catalogs and directories and a description of more programs along with a listing of the address, group for which the program is intended, cost, and requirements in language arts, mathematics, science, and general topics is available in *The Gifted Program Handbook* (Sorenson et al., 1988, pp. 149–154). Information on competitions is also available from school counselors and in subject matter publications.

A fourth source of problem and product ideas include lists of ideas in teacher and student resource materials in general or specific subject matter areas. Many of these materials include questions and more sources of information for the students to use in developing their products or places to write to secure up-to-date information on a particular topic. Some resources for teachers and students are listed below. Each of these also refers the reader to more sources.

Problems and Products Resources

Bartch, M.R., & Mallett, J.J. (1986). *Math motivators: Grades 1-3 and math motivators: Grades 4-6.* Glenview, IL: Scott Foresman.

Caney, S. (1985). *Invention book.* New York: Workman.

Clements Z.J., & Hawkes, R.R. (1985). *Mastermind: Exercises in critical thinking, grades 4-6.* Glenview, IL: Scott Foresman.

De Bruin, J. (1986). *Creative, hands-on science experiences.* Carthage, IL: Good Apple.

Eberle, B. (1985). *Warm-up to creativity: Word games to kindle divergent thinking.* Carthage, IL: Good Apple.

Krulik, S. & Rudnick, J.A. (1987). *Problem Solving.* Newton, MA: Allyn & Bacon.

Kruse, J. (1989). *Resources for teaching thinking: A catalog.* Philadelphia, PA: Research for Better Schools.

Levenson, E. (1985). *Teaching children about science: Ideas and activities every teacher and parent can use.* New York: Prentice-Hall.

Nelson, L.W., & Lorbeer, G.C. (1985). *Science activities for elementary children.* Dubuque, IA: Wm. C. Brown.

Prutzman, P. (1988). *The friendly classroom for a small planet: A handbook on creative approaches to living and problem solving for children.* Philadelphia, PA: New Society Publishers.

Sobel, M.A., & Maletsky, E.M. (1988). *Teaching mathematics: A sourcebook of aids, activities and strategies.* Englewood Cliffs, NJ: Prentice-Hall.

Stanish, B. (1990). *Mindanderings: Creative classroom approaches to thinking, writing and problem solving.* Carthage, IL: Good Apple.

Teachers' manuals to accompany textbooks and idea books for students in the school media center are also good sources of product development ideas and suggestions.

A fifth source of ideas for student products is presented in Figure 6-4, which lists more than one hundred products that students can develop to practice thinking and problem solving, and in the appendix, which contains several sets of activities.

All of these ideas lead students into several disciplines — language arts, science, math, and social studies. They also present a series of ideas for products covering a range of simple–complex, concrete–abstract levels.

Audiences for Student Products

Students need an authentic audience with which to share their products. One way to find out about audiences is to ask the question, "What do professionals such as scientists, writers, and artists do with the products they create?" Some answers might include the following (Sorenson et al., 1988, pp. 91–92):

- They use their products to influence the general public through the media and local, state, and national legislative bodies.

- Artists, writers, and composers create products to bring enjoyment into people's lives or to send a message to promote understanding.
- Scientists might investigate to find a cure for a life-threatening disease, such as cancer, or they might seek additions to the body of knowledge.

In addition to classroom teachers, audiences who can help students with projects are peers, teachers with special expertise, professional groups (engineers, artists, or writers), social service groups (for example, Lions or Rotary clubs), governmental groups (for example, committees or entire city councils, county boards, town councils, or special interest groups such as the Environmental Protection Agency), media (newspapers, radio or television), clubs (for example, Scouts, Brownies, or 4-H), and religious groups. Students need to recognize, develop, and practice a variety of communication skills to relate to any audience.

Transformations

When students develop products, they need to do more than summarize information. They need to interact with and manipulate the ideas and information. They need to change known information in terms of its meaning, significance, use, interpretation, mood, or sensory qualities. They also need to understand its implications in terms of "expectancies, anticipations, and predictions" (Guilford, 1967, p. 104). Not all of these desirable qualities can be accomplished in every product students produce, but teachers and others can guide students to use thinking skills and problem-solving strategies such as those described earlier in this chapter to ensure a result that includes "something of the student" that is more than a summary or compilation of the work of others.

Evaluations of Student Products

Audiences can also act as evaluators for the students' products, but students and teachers should be aware that an authentic audience may look at a product differently depending on their area of interest. For example, in the case of "seeking a way to solve the overpopulation in elementary schools at the lowest cost to the taxpayer," the school board may be most interested in providing quality education and keeping the teacher–student ratio low; the taxpayer may be most interested in keeping costs low; and the state might emphasize the safety of the children in terms of space and facilities. The point of view of the audience may influence the evaluation.

Since students are not professionals at presenting, they should practice sharing the product to a simulated audience and their teacher(s) before they take it to outside groups. Students should be encouraged to self-evaluate as well as receive feedback from the simulated audience.

Evaluators should take the following steps when evaluating a product (Sorenson et al., 1988, p. 93):

- Develop criteria as the basis for judgments.
- Develop methods to assist in evaluation — such as checklists, scales, and so on — and, where appropriate, assign values to each item on the scales or checklists.
- Decide when the evaluation should take place and who should do it.
- Apply the criteria consistently.

Students can develop products and receive evaluations from class projects; from products related to local, regional, and state competitions such as those mentioned earlier in this section; through internships with businesses and industries; through work as assistants at newspapers, television, or radio stations; or through work as guides or helpers at museums, zoos, or national government offices. Regardless of where the student experiences evaluation, it should be done in a positive manner that deals with both the strengths and weaknesses of the students' product and/or its presentation. This opportunity for students to reach out to the world around them should convey a partnership with education and be one that the students learn from and want to repeat.

Providing opportunities for students of all ages to develop products was one of the most satisfying ways Lawton staff could restructure the curriculum. Products could be individualized to meet student interests and abilities as well as foster independence and a sense of pride and responsibility.

Environment: The Support System for Learning

At the district-wide staff development meeting in the fall of 1991 the teachers and administrators at Lawton School were impressed with the speaker who talked about preparing students for the twenty-first century. One of the things the speaker had emphasized was getting students out of that unnatural and limited setting — the classroom. As part of their emphasis on the "learning how to learn" curriculum, they wanted to look at possibilities within their school, district, and community to offer more varied learning environments for their students. One of the first outcomes of this effort was a summary report that provided an overview of the elements of environment along with some ideas about ways to weave them into the existing instructional program.

Instructional environments play a major role in providing an appropriate learning program for all students. Environment has several facets:

physical sites and conditions in which instruction and learning take place; a variety of teachers, specialists, and facilitators who act as the human resources to guide learning; styles of teaching or ways in which teachers convey learning to students or present situations with specific learning goals; the learning styles of students appropriate to their needs and preferences and to the material to be learned; technology; and the personal characteristics of the students. Each of these facets of environment, along with suggestions of ways to infuse them into the curriculum, is discussed briefly in the following pages (Sorenson et al., 1988).

Physical Sites

Learning takes place both inside and outside the classroom. As students progress from skill-oriented activities to those requiring in-depth investigation, special equipment, and real-life situations, they should also move out of the classroom where they are under the direction of one teacher to other facilities in the district and community and work with other adult "teachers."

Physical sites in the school setting besides the classroom include media centers, classrooms at other grade levels and in other buildings, resource rooms, specialized rooms, and computer and other laboratories. In the community, learning sites include businesses, industries, libraries, cultural facilities such as museums and theaters, medical facilities, and the facilities of other education institutions such as technical schools, colleges, and universities. Student involvement with specialized sites might be as casual as a field trip or as involved as a mentorship. Regardless of the complexity of the involvement, variety and appropriateness of learning sites increases student interest and provides more "real" learning opportunities.

Design of a building and arrangement of the furniture and instructional equipment within classrooms, labs, and other specialized areas should reflect the activity that will take place in them, allowing flexibility wherever possible. For example, the traditional egg-crate room arrangement — in which rows of chairs face the front of the room — is designed for teachers to tell students information and for students to recite answers or passages in return. It is not conducive to science work that requires two to four students to work together using equipment or for small problem-solving groups in language arts or social studies. Schools should select furniture that teachers can change from rows to groups to provide table-type space, put in a circle for discussions, and so on. Many teachers provide variety, comfort, and atmosphere for students by carpeting a corner of a room, building a tree house, or providing study carrels. Several physical sites for learning are elaborated in Chapter 9.

Human Resources

In addition to their contact with the classroom teacher in elementary school and specialized class teachers in middle and high schools, students need exposure to other adults and specialists. When students move to a learning environment in other school sites, they have an opportunity to interact with the media director and other teachers. When they move into the community, they can learn from people working in businesses, industry, medicine, cultural organizations, and other fields. These experiences, casual or intensive, can enrich the learning environment and also provide career education opportunities.

Mentorships and internships provide extensive experiences with community resource people, but larger numbers of students should have contact with a variety of specialized personnel, too. Field trips provide these opportunities. Or teachers can bring speakers into the classroom and school to provide variety and reality in learning. By surveying family and school personnel about their interests and expertise, the school staff can develop lists of community human resources. Also, chambers of commerce, community groups, and universities often have lists of people who are willing to work with students. Many examples of using parents and community members as resources are detailed in Chapter 9.

Teaching Styles

Authors have classified teaching or instructional styles in many ways, but most experts suggest a continuum from more teacher control to more student control in the learning process. Five teaching styles predominate: teacher-centered, self-instructional, inquiry, cooperative, and student-centered. Teaching styles need to be appropriate to the material to be learned and to the needs and characteristics of the students who are doing the learning. Teaching styles are discussed in detail in Chapter 7.

Learning Styles

What is learning style? Rita Dunn and Kenneth Dunn (1975, p. 74) have defined learning style as "stimuli that affect a person's ability to absorb and retain information, values, facts, or concepts." William Bechtol (1973, p. 47) has defined it as "those factors that ease and facilitate learning for an individual student in a given situation." Elements of learning style may include grouping, learning modes, instructional materials, media, physical environments, and many other personal factors. Learning style is discussed in detail in Chapter 7.

Technology

"Today the technologies in most of America's schools have not kept pace with those used in the larger society. For example, telephones and typewriters, films and videotapes, computers and optical data storage have scarcely affected the operation of schools, while they have transformed the operations of most businesses. Schools today reflect their nineteenth-century roots (when they themselves were a technological innovation to educate the masses). Even when schools use twentieth-century technologies such as film, they tend to be "add-on" rather than an integral part of the school program. Today electronic learning makes feasible new patterns of organization other than the classroom" (Mecklenburger, 1990, pp. 106–107). Can schools adapt to technologies to make electronic learning techniques part of their offering, bringing the world into the school setting?

Cost has been both an excuse for and a real obstacle to using technology in the schools. There seems to be a resistance to using technology in the schools that is not found in the general society. Technologies are not widely used in schools that have them in place or they are not used properly to relate learning to technologies. We hesitate to abandon the traditional learning forms to center around electronic learning. Widespread use of computers was observed in only three of our model schools. Whatever the financial and attitudinal barriers to technology in the schools, the fact remains that we are approaching the twenty-first century and we cannot long keep the schools in a nineteenth century learning mode. Change is inevitable and technology will play a major part in this change. Using technology is a challenge and a promise for the future that all teachers must meet.

Personal Characteristics of Students

Many personal factors enter into the student's learning process, including intrinsic motivation, persistence, responsibility, attention span, self-directedness, locus of control, and self-evaluation. An investigation of these characteristics by major authors in the field (Dunn et al., 1984) indicates that students who score in the ninetieth percentile and above and who have an intelligence quotient between 120 and 130 (and above) show consistent patterns of independence, self-motivation (internal), persistence, and strong perceptual strengths. We need to encourage all students to develop these characteristics. Appropriate learning environments are key elements of this process. Personal characteristics of students are discussed in more detail in the learning style section of Chapter 7.

Summary

This chapter focused on ways the Lawton School staff went about restructuring its "learning how to learn" curriculum. The elements of the curriculum were content, process, product, and environment. Under *content,* selection and organization, along with forming and teaching concepts were emphasized.

After an introduction to the basic ideas of *process,* six kinds of process thinking were discussed and illustrated with examples. There were Bloom's cognitive taxonomy, creative thinking, inquiry processes, critical thinking skills, single-step problem-solving techniques, and an extensive review and illustration of multistep problem solving.

Products are the "ends of instruction." Here students can apply processes and content in an interwoven format in a real world situation according to their abilities, interests, and motivation.

In this book, the traditional view of one teacher with 25 to 30 students in a classroom is challenged by the concept of several teachers with one identified as a team leader and 75 to 150 students working together with aides, student teachers, and others in a group called a team or unit. Likewise, the learning should occur in a variety of *environments.* Physical sites within the school and in the community, not just a classroom, should be used. Other facets of environment include human resources — that is, other instructors from the school and community as well as teachers from the school — teaching style, learning style, uses of technology, and the personal characteristics of the students.

It is the interface and integration of the content, process, product, and environment of a curriculum that produces "learning how to learn" appropriate to the needs of our children in school today and into the twenty-first century.

References

Barrow, L. (1979). Science, stamps and learning. *Science and Children,* 16(5): 22. Washington, DC: National Science Teachers Association.

Bechtol, W. (1973). *Individualizing instruction and keeping your sanity.* Chicago: Follett.

Beyer, B. (1988). *Developing a thinking skills program.* Boston: Allyn and Bacon.

Bloom, B.S. (1959). *Taxonomy of educational objectives.* New York: David McKay.

Brandt, R. (Ed.). (1988). *Content of the curriculum* (1988 ASCD Yearbook). Alexandria, VA: Association for Supervision and Curriculum Development.

Coleman, L. (1985). *Schooling of the gifted.* Reading, MA: Addison-Wesley.

Costa, A. (Ed.). (1985). *Developing minds: A reference book for teaching thinking.* Alexandria, VA: Association for Supervision and Curriculum Development.

Davis, G., & Rimm, S. (1985). *Education of the gifted and talented.* Englewood Cliffs, NJ: Prentice Hall.

Davis, G. (1983). *Creativity is forever.* Dubuque, IA: Kendall/Hunt.

Dunn, R., Bruno, A., & Gardiner, B. (1984). Put a cap on your gifted program. *Gifted Child Quarterly,* 28(2): 70–72.

Dunn, R., & Dunn, K. (1975). *Educator's self teaching guide to individualizing instructional programs.* West Nyack, NY: Parker.

Eberle, R. (1977). *SCAMPER: Games for imaginative development.* Buffalo, NY: D.O.K. Publisher.

Golub, L., Frederick, W., Nelson, N., & Frayer, D. (1971). *Selected analysis of language arts concepts.* Madison: Wisconsin Research and Development Center for Cognitive Learning, The University of Wisconsin.

Guilford, J. P. (1967). *The nature of human intelligence.* New York: McGraw-Hill.

Haney, R., & Sorenson, J. (1977). *Individually guided science.* Reading, MA: Addison-Wesley.

Harris, M., & Harris, C. (1973). *A structure of concept attainment abilities.* Madison: Wisconsin Research and Development Center for Cognitive Learning, The University of Wisconsin.

Isaksen, S., & Treffinger, D. (1985). *Creative problem solving: The basic course.* Buffalo, NY: Bearly Limited.

Klein, R. (1982). An inquiry into the factors related to creativity. *Elementary School Journal,* 82(3): 264–265.

Krulik, S., & Rudnick, J. (1987). *Problem solving: A handbook for teachers.* Boston: Allyn and Bacon.

Maker, C.J. (1982). *Teaching models in education of the gifted.* Rockville, MD: Aspen.

Mecklenburger, J. (1990). Educational technology is not enough. *Phi Delta Kappan,* 72(2): 104–108.

Renzulli, J. (Ed.). (1986). *Systems and models for developing programs for the gifted and talented.* Mansfield Center, CT: Creative Learning Press.

Sorenson, J., Engelsgjerd, J., Francis, M., Miller, M., & Schuster, N. (1988). *The gifted program handbook.* Palo Alto, CA: Dale Seymour.

Sternberg, R. (1986). *Intelligence applied: Understanding and increasing your intellectual skills.* Chicago: Harcourt Brace, Janovich.

Torrance, E.P. (1977). *Creativity in the classroom.* Washington, DC: National Education Association.

Voelker, A., Sorenson, J., & Frayer, D. (1971). *An analysis of selected classificatory science concepts.* Madison: Wisconsin Research and Development Center for Cognitive Learning, The University of Wisconsin.

Wales, C., Nardi, A., & Stager, R. (1986). Decision-making: New paradigm for education. *Educational Leadership,* 45(8): 37–41.

Wisconsin Department of Public Instruction. (1986). *A guide to science development.* Madison, WI.

CHAPTER SEVEN

Learning and Teaching Styles

Learning style means that each person has a preferred way that makes learning new materials or tasks easier for him or her.

"Why has Diamond Middle School, one of our model schools, decided to provide for students' different learning styles?"

"All of our teachers took an assessment on styles so they were knowledgeable about their own learning style and aware that their students had many learning styles. So when restructuring caused an instructional problem, we looked at learning styles research for some answers."

"Problem! How did restructuring cause a problem?" we asked Principal Joanne Hennesay.

"As a staff we decided that tracking was not effective for our students. We restructured so that there were heterogeneous groups in language arts, social studies, and science."

"What happened?"

"We had to find ways to provide for students' individual differences. Our classrooms have changed."

"How have they changed?"

"The strategies used in the classroom are different. There's more cooperative learning. Teachers now incorporate a variety of assignments. Students may choose the assignment that fits their learning style best."

"Has it worked?"

"You bet. Our achievement is high. But I believe there's more. Our students are happier. They leave us more ready for high school."

We were delighted with this dialogue. The Diamond faculty was using the research findings on both teaching and learning styles to provide for the individual differences of their middle school students.

People have long been fascinated by how they and others learn or do not learn skills and knowledge. Why can my brother play the violin and organ without lessons and I can barely play a tune after many lessons? How can two people study with the same teacher—with one making great strides while the other seems to learn very little? Is it chance? Inheritance? Destiny? Talent? Environment? Or are there other variables such as styles of learning and teaching that can help all of us learn more effectively and efficiently?

The relationship of styles to learning has interested educators for decades. But the current situation of U.S. students—lowest among the achievement scores among the developed nations of the world, illiteracy, and lack of skills to be employed in our current society—has raised style to a high degree of concern. Current thought on styles is summarized as follows: "As dropout and student 'disengagement' rates persist at alarmingly high levels, attending to style is being viewed as one way to expand teaching methods and curriculum to reach more students" (O'Neil, 1990, p. 5). Also, the styles movement goes along with a more personalized version of education in an increasingly diverse student population. Learning styles are also being investigated because they emphasize student strengths rather than weaknesses (Guild in O'Neil, 1990, p. 5).

Helping the at-risk student is another factor. These students often reject the standard teaching practices of lectures and textbooks, classroom design, and grouping. Carbo (in O'Neil, 1990, p. 5) believes that students who drop out of the system have styles that are severely mismatched with what normally goes on in the school. These students are put under more stress because they like to work with peers and are made to work alone; they like to work under soft light and in an informal design, but aren't offered these opportunities.

Dunn (in O'Neil, 1990, p. 6) suggests that all children have strengths, but classroom design and rules that restrict student movement are primary reasons many are called underachievers and problem students. Students succeed at difficult work who never did it before because they can lie on their stomachs on the floor rather than sit restricted at a desk or table.

Silver (in O'Neil, 1990, pp. 5–6) suggests that at-risk students learn best through concrete experiences, collaboration, cooperation, and high levels of interaction, but our classrooms become more competitive, independent, and abstract as students move through the grades. Have we designed schools that work against the success of these students?

While experts agree that most students have the brain power and can learn if they are taught in ways that allow them to work to their strengths, the experts disagree on how to translate this belief into reality in the schools. Many researchers claim to achieve amazing success with groups of underachieving and problem students using their own style models and methods, but usually fail to convince their peers of the merit of their programs. Some experts accept style as a learning variable only cautiously. Others label it a fad or frill. Maybe we don't yet know enough about styles and related brain research to have widespread agreement on how to use style—learning or teaching—in the classroom. Yet, most everyone agrees, styles hold great potential for improving education of students.

Both learning and teaching styles will be considered here. The discussion includes learning and teaching in different styles; summaries of research, models, and programs currently in widespread use; strategies to assess styles; and sample lesson plans and units of study to accommodate and relate a variety of teaching and learning styles.

Learning in Different Styles

Educators define learning style in many different ways. Yet all definitions include the idea that students and adults have preferred ways to make their learning easier—particularly when they are trying to learn something for the first time or are tackling difficult material.

Dunn and Dunn (1975, p. 74) define learning style as "stimuli that affect a person's ability to absorb and retain information, values, facts, or concepts." They identify four basic stimuli—environmental, emotional, sociological, and physical—and eighteen style elements. Bechtol (1973, p. 46) defines learning style as "those factors that ease and facilitate learning for an individual student in a given situation." He considers variables such as group size, sensory factors, learning tempo, and how the individual goes about solving problems. Keefe (1988, p. 3) defines learning style as the composite of "characteristic, cognitive, affective, and physiological factors that serve as relatively reliable indicators of how learners perceive, interact, and respond to the learning environment."

Recognition that individuals learn differently is not new. An Old Confucian proverb states: I hear, I forget; I see, I understand; I do, I remember. Like all proverbs, it contains exaggerations, but it does recognize differences in the ways people learn. The work of Barbe and Swassing, Dunn and Dunn, and others reflects this proverb in their discussion of three modalities—auditory, visual, and kinesthetic or hands on (Guild and Garger, 1985, pp. 63–66).

Auditory learners use their voices and their ears as the primary mode for learning. They not only want to hear to remember, but they also want to discuss what they are learning with others and verbally express the way they interpret the material. Visual learners want to see things written down as well as view pictures and diagrams to help them better understand the material to be learned. Kinesthetic learners prefer and actually learn better when they are involved in the learning process through some kind of physical activity. They like to make a product, act out a situation, or handle as many things as possible. They also like to carry out simulations and experiments.

In the classroom, teachers have students with all of these mode preferences. From her work with the Learning Style Inventory (LSI), Dunn suggests that about 20 to 30 percent of students learn best from what they hear (auditory); another 40 percent learn best by seeing things (visual); and the remaining 30 to 40 percent rely heavily on touching and being involved with physical things (kinesthetic) to learn best and remember (Sorenson, Engelsgjerd, Francis, Miller, & Schuster, 1988).

Concern for these broad-based modalities, of course, indicates that teachers must provide for learners with a wide variety of preferences in everyday teaching. Loper (in Dunn, Beaudry, & Klavast, 1989) suggests that teachers who teach and evaluate in only one mode serve only students who prefer to learn in that mode. She also believes that if teachers are to give all students the chance to succeed, they need to (1) include a variety of learning modes in their lessons, (2) be aware of their own learning styles and how they affect their teaching styles, and (3) help students move from one preferred mode to several modes so they can benefit from a variety of instructional styles.

Overview of Current Research and Programs on Learning Style

Learning style is a complex subject that relates to a variety of areas such as the psychological, sociological, philosophical, neurological, emotional, physical, and interaction of these areas with the environment. Research on learning style has been difficult. It has been characterized by three major problems (Curry, 1990).

1. There is confusion in definitions, which vary widely in scale and scope of learning, school achievement, and other behaviors predicted by learning style concepts. Some definitions deal mainly with simple preferences while others try to predict habitual responses across all learning.
2. Research instruments tend to be weak in reliability and validity. Based on only one or two sets of data, many researchers have printed and marketed their results prematurely.
3. Relevant characteristics in learners and instructional settings and their relationships have varied widely and have often been checked out only on small groups of students.

While researchers have explored style for decades, the search has intensified in the past ten years as U.S. efforts to produce students who can compete successfully in an increasingly technological and complex society have increased. The immediacy of this search is expressed by Dunn (1990, p. 18): "When students cannot learn the way we teach them, we must teach them the way they learn."

The work of four research groups will be reviewed here. They are: Rita Dunn and Kenneth Dunn's work with learning style elements; Bernice McCarthy's 4MAT system; Anthony Gregorc's learner styles; and Herman Witkin's work on field dependence–independence.

Learning Style Elements: Rita Dunn and Kenneth Dunn

The Dunns, with Gary Price, have researched learning style for more than twenty years, have written widely in the field, and developed a commonly used assessment instrument, the LSI. In their work, they identified four stimuli and eighteen elements as indicated in the following chart (Dunn, 1983, p. 61; Dunn & Dunn, 1975, p. 77):

Stimuli	*Elements*	
Environmental	Sound	Light
	Temperature	Design
Emotional	Motivation	Persistence
	Responsibility	Structure
Sociological	Peers	Self
	Pair	Team
	Adult	Varied
Physical	Perceptual	Intake
	Time	Mobility

To assess these eighteen elements in four stimuli areas, they produced the LSI for three different age/grade groups: grades 3–5, grades 6–12, and adults—a version often used by teachers, the Productivity Environment Preference Survey (PEPS). Respondents react to straightforward items such as those listed below from the grades 6 through 12 instrument. The five-point scale moves from "strongly agree" to "strongly disagree" (Guild & Garger, 1985, pp. 44–46; Dunn, 1983, pp. 60–62).

Sample items	I study best when it is quiet.
	I like to be told exactly what to do.
	I concentrate best when I feel warm.

Data from these inventories can be computer scored and learning style preferences for both individuals and groups of students are available and easy to understand. Teachers can use these data to get students involved in the learning process at their preferred style and also to counsel students to move them from one style to another. The adult version can be taken by teachers to identify their own preferred learning style and can initiate a discussion of how their learning styles influence their teaching styles.

The 4MAT System: Bernice McCarthy

The 4MAT system was developed by Bernice McCarthy in 1972 to help teachers organize their teaching around the different ways people learn. It is based on research from education, psychology, neurology, and management. McCarthy has carried out nearly two decades of research on the 4MAT system in many school districts focusing on its use in instruction and staff development planning (McCarthy, 1990).

The 4MAT system has two major premises: (1) people have major learning styles and hemispheric (right-mode/left-mode) processing preferences, and (2) designing and using multiple instructional strategies in a systematic framework to teach to these preferences can improve teaching and learning (McCarthy, 1990). Two major dimensions—perceiving and processing—form the heart of the 4MAT system. People perceive differently, particularly in new situations. Some respond mostly *by sensing and feeling their way* (concrete) while others *think things through and reflect on them* (abstract). People also have preferences in how they process information and experiences and how they internalize them. Some people are *watchers* first while others are *doers* and act on new information immediately. When the perceiving and processing dimensions are juxtaposed, they form the quadrant model shown below and produce four types of learning styles (McCarthy, 1990, p. 32):

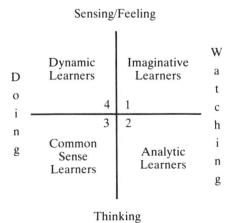

Type 1, imaginative learners, perceive information concretely and process it reflectively. They tend to listen and share ideas to learn, believe in their own experiences and need to be personally involved in learning. They often find traditional school too fragmented and disconnected from personal issues and struggle to connect the content of the curriculum to their need to grow and understand the world.

Type 2, analytic learners, perceive information abstractly and process it reflectively. They learn by thinking through ideas and come up with theories by combining their observations into what they know. They value sequence, need details, and are thorough and industrious. They usually enjoy traditional classrooms and sometimes enjoy ideas more than people. They have good verbal skills and are good readers.

Type 3, common sense learners, perceive information abstractly and process it actively. They combine theory and practice by testing theories and applying common sense. They are good problem solvers and want to find answers to questions. They like to experiment and manipulate to find out how things work and prefer to work on real problems. They often find school frustrating because they want to know how learning is of immediate use.

Type 4, dynamic learners, perceive information concretely and process it by doing. They learn by trial and error. They are enthusiastic, adaptable, and flexible people. They often reach accurate conclusions in the absence of logical justification. They seek to influence others and are sometimes seen as pushy or manipulative. Since they want to pursue their interests in different ways, they are often frustrated with the structure of traditional schools.

McCarthy (1990) developed her ideas on learning style into the 4MAT system approach for the school setting. She has identified the tasks of students, teachers, and principals, again using four quadrants. Quadrant 1 relates to the question, Why? Here the students attempt to connect personal life and the content of schooling. The teachers connect meaning to content, and the principals try to articulate the meaning of school through their vision.

In quadrant 2, the students are comprehenders of content, and the question, What? The teachers become instructional leaders as specialists in content; and the principals are instructional coordinators who align curriculum with the school or district mission statement.

In quadrant 3, the students become users of content and skills and ask, How does this work? The teachers become coaches and the principals facilitate resources, including multiple methods of instruction, time, money, and materials.

In quadrant 4, students become the innovators and ask, If? Teachers become facilitators of creative options and principals refocus and coordinate evaluations and enlarge diffusion networks.

At a practical level, many individuals and school districts have used the 4MAT system as the basis for different kinds of programs including an interdisciplinary program (Blair & Judah, 1990); ways to improve staff development, curriculum assessment, and planning (Kelley, 1990); and as a guide to improve student presentations (Weber & Weber, 1990). Many science teachers and science educators have adapted the 4MAT program to their teaching particularly because of the concrete–abstract and observation (reflective) and experimentation (active) dimensions of the model (Samples & Hammond, 1985).

Learner Styles: Anthony Gregorc

Gregorc developed his interest in style from his own comfort and frustration in the jobs he held in education and from practical experience with students in a high school for exceptional children. His work includes a balance of practical, philosophical and psychological implications. He suggests that style in behavior comes from the qualities of our mind (Guild & Garger, 1985).

Gregorc defined *perception* as going from abstract to concrete on a continuum. He believed that everyone is capable of using both kinds of perception, but has a tendency to prefer one over the other. His other dimension is *ordering* within the extremes of sequential and random with each person again having a preference. He combined the possibilities of the two extremes of perception and ordering into four patterns of learner styles (Guild & Garger, 1985, p. 38).

- Concrete sequential (CS): perceive in a concrete way and order in a sequential pattern
- Abstract sequential (AS): perceive in an abstract way and order sequentially
- Concrete random (CR): perceive in a concrete way, order randomly
- Abstract random (AR): perceive in an abstract way and order randomly

Gregorc and others have related these four style patterns to both learning and teaching. Some characteristics of learners with each style are presented below. It should be remembered that everyone exhibits all styles to some extent, but most people prefer one or two styles (Phi Delta Kappa, 1980; Butler, 1984; Guild & Garger, 1985).

Concrete Sequential

- Their world is objective and predictable
- Naturally structure things and appreciate order and logical sequence in materials
- Have a desire for perfection and strive to achieve it

- Can be resistant to change and accept it slowly
- Are patient, hardworking, responsible
- Like tangible rewards for good efforts
- Prefer lectures accompanied by handouts and visual aids
- Learn best from hands-on materials; respond well to computer-assisted instruction
- Are sometimes inflexible and rigid; often critical of others

Abstract Sequential

- Enjoy thinking and all kinds of mental activities and constructs
- Like to surround themselves with knowledge and documents
- Use reason and logic to explain things and situations around them
- Are easily distracted and like to work alone rather than in a group
- Handle verbal and symbolic materials well
- Are sometimes absent-minded

Concrete Random

- Are not afraid of change
- View words as concrete and physical
- Are quick and intuitive thinkers; impulsive, optimistic, adventurous
- Are creative risk-takers and like to find answers on their own
- Sometimes jump to conclusions; do not read directions or instructions
- Often forget—out-of-sight, out-of-mind
- Don't accept can't or don't
- Are outgoing, friendly, and aggressive; have a natural curiosity
- Like to manipulate and try things out; learn by trial and error

Abstract Random

- Live today to the fullest; let future take care of itself
- Easily absorb ideas, information, and impressions
- Like to receive information in an unstructured way; dislike rules and guidelines
- Sometimes have an inflated self-image
- View learning experiences globally and prefer lecture with discussion
- View procedures and orderliness as boring and unimportant

Field Dependence–Independence: Herman Witkin

Witkin and fellow researchers began looking at perceptual characteristics among people in the 1940s to find out to what extent a person's perception of any item was influenced by the content or "field" in which it appeared. In other words, were there people who saw the tree while others saw the forest? They worked with piots and disorientation in space and developed experiments to test orientation in the laboratory. These experiments led Witkin and his group to define two extreme indicators of the extent to which the field influenced an observer's perception of something within it. A person with a field-dependent (FD) perception mode is strongly influenced by the prevailing field, while the field-independent (FI) person experiences items more or less separate from the field. It should be noted that most subjects the researchers tested scored along a continuum from FI to FD, tending toward one or the other pole (Guild & Garger, 1985).

While Witkin's work was replicated in hundreds of studies, its application in education is not well documented. Yet, it contains a fascination for educators, especially in terms of the many students today who are having difficulties learning effectively in our traditional school environment. Some of the implications that have been identified (Guild & Garger, 1985, pp. 29–30) are that field relationships are independent of intelligence and more related to the "how" than to the "how much" of cognitive function; since cognitive style is neutral, both field-dependent and field-independent people make good students and good teachers; and, perhaps most significantly, teachers and others need to be sensitive to these style-related demands of learning and teaching. Characteristics of field-dependent and field-independent learners are described below (Guild & Garger, 1985).

Field-dependent learners tend to perceive globally and work within the parameters the teacher presents. They have a social orientation to their surroundings and learn best when material has a social content. They want experiences to be relevant, they seek externally defined goals, and they want the teacher or materials to provide structure and organization. They are sensitive, strongly affected by criticism, and use a spectator approach to learn concepts.

Field-independent learners tend to perceive analytically. They put structure on their own experiences, define their own goals, and have an impersonal orientation to their surroundings. They are interested in information for its own value. And they are not strongly affected by criticism and tend to use a hypothesis-testing approach to learn concepts.

It is easy to predict that students with these two very different learning styles would have difficulty learning successfully in the same classroom unless the teacher provided learning opportunities to accommodate their differences.

Strategies to Assess Student Learning Styles

Assessing learning styles has been difficult and the results have caused controversy among experts particularly because the instruments used often have had weak reliability and validity. Nonetheless, valuable information can be gained from assessing the learning styles of students and, in some instances, of staff. Learning style assessment can range from formal to informal. Brief descriptions of several instruments representing varying degrees of formalness are discussed here.

Learning Style Inventory (LSI)

The learning style inventory (LSI) is available commercially for two grade levels of students: 3–5 and 6–12. It also has an adult version, PEPS. The LSI was developed by Rita Dunn, Kenneth Dunn, and Gary Price (1989 Edition, Price Systems, Lawrence, KS 66044). The instruments are designed around the Dunns' eighteen learning style elements in four stimuli areas. These were described earlier in this chapter.

Learning Style Inventory

The commercially available inventory was developed by David Kolb (1986, McBer and Co., Boston, MA 02116) to assess learning styles of individuals by presenting four words to be ranked. The resulting numerical scores relate to the four dimensions of Bernice McCarthy's 4MAT model. Differences in scores on the perceptual and processing dimensions are calculated and output provides a visual picture of an individual's placement in a particular quadrant of the 4MAT model. Kolb calls Type 1 learners, "Divergers"; Type 2 learners, "Assimilators"; Type 3 learners, "Convergers"; and Type 4 learners, "Accommodators" (Guild & Garger, 1985, p. 57). Elements of McCarthy's 4MAT model to which this inventory relates were discussed earlier in this chapter.

Learning Styles Checklist

Less complex, noncommercial instruments to assess learning style are also available. The Learning Styles Checklist, which includes elements from several authors, is shown in Figure 7-1. This instrument is intended for use with students in intermediate grades, middle school, or junior and senior high school. It can also be used with teachers. It is easy to use, simple to score and interpret, and can be duplicated inexpensively. Staff can also rephrase, add, or delete items to adapt the instrument to the needs of their students and the local situation.

Staff in one middle school team used this instrument to assess learning style preferences of the eighty students in their unit. The results are shown

FIGURE 7-1 · *Learning Styles Checklist*

Directions: Check the box between the two words or phrases that best describes your reaction to the item on the left.

		1	2	3	4	5	
1. Alertness	morning						afternoon
2. Attention span	continuous						short bursts
3. Noise tolerance a. amount	absolute quiet						high-level conversations
b. type	random (foreground)						organized (background)
4. Grouping patterns a. alone	like						dislike
b. one-to-one (adult)	like						dislike
c. one-to-one (peer)	like						dislike
d. small group	like						dislike
e. medium-sized group	like						dislike
f. large group	like						dislike
5. Learning environments a. (1) learning center (IMC)	like						dislike
(2) instructional area	like						dislike
(3) isolated study area	like						dislike
b. structure	low						high
6. Self-directedness (task completion)	low						high
7. Media a. print	like						dislike
b. visual	like						dislike
c. audio	like						dislike
d. manipulative	like						dislike
e. kinesthetic involvement	like						dislike
8. Self-evaluation	well developed						undeveloped
9. Mode of operation	inductive (parts to whole)						deductive (whole to parts)

Source: J. Sorenson, M. Poole, and L. Joyal, *The Unit Leader and Individually Guided Education* (Reading, MA: Addison-Wesley Publishing Company, 1976), pp. 431–432. Reprinted with permission.

214

in Figure 7-2. Review of these data reveal several interesting preference patterns and suggestions for change in teaching strategies. These preferences are discussed below according to the nine variables presented in Figure 7-2. The percentages of the two "agree" responses and two "disagree" responses have been combined in this discussion.

On the topic of alertness (1), students indicated they were more alert in the afternoon (41 percent) than in the morning (24 percent) and many (35 percent) showed no preference. These findings are contrary to a long-held idea among teachers that reading and math should be taught in the morning because they are very important and because students "learn better" at that time.

Attention span (2) ratings showed about equal responses to continuous and short bursts with 41 percent rating this factor as neutral. No conclusion can be drawn here except variety in length of span exists.

Noise tolerance considered amount (3a) and type (3b). Preferences on amount, quiet and high-level conversations, were nearly equal: quiet, 38 percent; high-level conversations, 31 percent; and no preference, 31 percent. Organized background type noise was strongly preferred (60 percent) over random foreground noise (23 percent). These responses indicate a need for learning opportunities using a variety of media and types of student interactions that generate varying amounts of different kinds of noise.

Among learning or grouping patterns, the two strong preferences were one-to-one with a peer (4c, 72 percent) and working in a small group of peers (4d, 48 percent). Preferences on working alone (4a) were nearly evenly distributed between like and dislike. Working one-to-one with an adult (4b), in a medium-sized class group (4e), and in a large group (4f) were generally disliked. These preferences provide a strong argument for teachers to offer many learning opportunities in all subject areas for peer tutoring or helping. Opportunities for students to work in pairs and small groups in the learning environment in all subject areas are essential. These data also indicate that traditional class-size and large group instruction are probably not very effective with today's students and should occupy only a small portion of the instructional time.

Sixty-three percent of students preferred to learn in an isolated study area 5a (3) or the learning center (5a (1) 45 percent). Students indicated a dislike (34 percent) or no preference (37 percent) for learning in the classroom instructional area. Low structure (5b) was also strongly preferred (55 percent). This suggests students should spend more of their school time in carrels or other isolated locations or in an informal media center area. Student activities with a minimum of structure should also be available. Currently, most students spend most of their learning time in a highly structured classroom or study area. This is particularly true in middle school or junior and senior high schools.

FIGURE 7-2 • *Learning Styles Checklist Completed by Middle/Junior High Students*

Directions: Check the box between the two words or phrases that best describes your reaction to the item on the left.

		1	2	3	4	5	
1. Alertness	morning	10	14	35	34	07	afternoon
2. Attention span	continuous	10	23	41	07	19	short bursts
3. Noise tolerance a. amount	absolute quiet	13	25	31	18	13	high-level conversations
b. type	random (foreground)	16	07	17	18	42	organized (background)
4. Grouping patterns a. alone	like	21	21	22	21	15	dislike
b. one-to-one (adult)	like	21	11	22	17	29	dislike
c. one-to-one (peer)	like	43	29	18	06	04	dislike
d. small group	like	29	19	34	06	12	dislike
e. medium-sized group	like	11	14	22	25	28	dislike
f. large group	like	17	09	09	15	50	dislike
5. Learning environments a. (1) learning center (IMC)	like	34	11	15	15	25	dislike
(2) instructional area	like	12	17	37	11	23	dislike
(3) isolated study area	like	37	26	15	12	10	dislike
b. structure	low	39	16	17	08	20	high
6. Self-directedness (task completion)	low	09	07	32	16	36	high
7. Media a. print	like	18	11	26	15	30	dislike
b. visual	like	63	21	10	04	02	dislike
c. audio	like	60	16	20	02	02	dislike
d. manipulative	like	49	20	23	04	04	dislike
e. kinesthetic involvement	like	48	25	20	04	03	dislike
8. Self-evaluation	well developed	23	40	24	07	06	undeveloped
9. Mode of operation	inductive (parts to whole)	18	12	40	18	12	deductive (whole to parts)

On self-directedness (6), students gave themselves a high (52 percent) or neutral (32 percent) rating. One objective of all educational programs, is, of course, to produce more self-directed and independent learners, and opportunities in the learning programs need to direct students toward this goal.

Students liked visual (7b, 84 percent), auditory (7c, 76 percent), manipulative (7d, 69 percent), and kinesthetic (7e, 73 percent) learning media. Only 29 percent liked and 45 percent disliked print media (7a). Traditionally, print media has been the cornerstone of student learning in our schools. This practice is changing with wider use of television, videotapes, interactive computer programs, and satellite transmissions directly into schools. There is now more initiative for change, but funds for new technology and training for teachers to use it are necessary to meet student needs for education appropriate not only to their preferences but for the demands of the twenty-first century.

Sixty-three percent of the students indicated that they had well-developed evaluation skills (8). More opportunities for students to evaluate their own work should be available in our school curricula. Teachers and specialists often argue over whether they should present information in a deductive or inductive format (9). Students here showed no preference (30 percent like, 30 percent dislike). These responses suggest that teachers should offer opportunities for students to learn in both modes of operation in a variety of situations as appropriate to the subject matter to be learned.

Perhaps the most important conclusion that can be drawn from the responses of this group of students was that they had a wide range of learning preferences that need to be considered in planning and implementing instruction in the restructured education program. To gain this variety, schools need to use appropriate technology, media, and strategies.

Learning Style Preferences for Younger Students

For younger children, a teacher-made instrument such as the one shown in Figure 7-3 can be used to assess learning style preferences. While many of the items are similar to those in the Learning Styles Checklist, in this instrument, the young students can respond to a face rather than trying to understand the more abstract vocabulary. Also, direct questions make it easier for young students to respond. This instrument is easy to use, simple to duplicate, inexpensive, and can be adapted to meet the needs of students and situations.

Observation of Student's Learning Style

For a small number of students, teachers might want to carry out observations using an instrument such as the Observation of Student's Learning

FIGURE 7-3 • *Learning Style Preferences for Younger Students*

Directions: Everyone likes to do some things and does not like to do others. Also, sometimes we are neutral—we neither like nor dislike to do something. For the questions below, put an "X" on the face that best describes your reaction to the question. The smiley face ☺ means "like"; the reverse smile face ☹ means "dislike"; and the straight-mouthed face means neutral. 😐 There are no right or wrong answers. It is the way you feel about the questions that is important.

1. How do you feel about working alone on school assignments?

2. How do you feel about working one-on-one with an adult?

3. How do you feel about working on an assignment with another student?

4. How do you feel about working as a part of a small group?

5. How do you feel about using a computer to learn new information?

6. Do you think you do your best work in the morning?

FIGURE 7-3 · *Continued*

7. When you are working, how do you feel about someone disturbing you?

8. How do you feel about having a teacher check on your work?

9. How do you like working at a desk?

10. How do you feel about working in the IMC or media center?

11. How do you feel about using books, papers, and magazines to learn new information?

12. How do you feel about using videotapes, filmstrips, and transparencies to learn new information?

13. How do you feel about working on the carpeted floor or other informal area?

Source: Adapted for younger children from the Learning Styles Checklist (Figure 7-1) by P. Rossman, McFarland, Wisconsin, Elementary School.

Style (OSLS) (Figure 7-4). This instrument should be used by an adult. Three students can be observed at once, rotating observations among them, in a forty-five-minute period. This amounts to devoting about fifteen minutes to each student. It is easy to use, inexpensive to duplicate, and can be adapted to student and situation needs. Activities and materials listed at the bottom of the OSLS have been grouped to make observing easier: 1a through 1h refer to listening and speaking activities; 2a through 2h to reading and writing activities; and 3a through 3f to miscellaneous activities.

For more information on assessing student learning styles, refer to summaries of instruments by Keefe (1987, pp. 16–25). These instruments, which assess cognitive, affective, and psychological style elements or combinations of these, are titled:

- Edmonds Learning Style Identification Exercise (ELSIE)
- Group Embedded Figures Test (GEFT) (Witkin and others)
- Cognitive Profile (Letteri)
- Paragraph Completion Method (PCM) (Hunt)
- I/E Scale (Internal/External locus of control) (Rotter)
- NASSP Learning Style Profile (Keefe and Monk)
- Time Questionnaire (Dunn and Dunn)
- Myers-Briggs Tyle Indicator (MBTI) (personality dispositions and preferences)
- Cognitive Style Mapping (Hill)

Teaching in Different Styles

Teaching, like learning, is never done in exactly the same way by any two individuals. Each teacher has preferences in what tasks he or she will perform and what tasks he or she will ask the students to carry out. Yet, similarities among many individual teachers usually fall along a continuum from a teacher-controlled situation to a student-controlled one.

Teaching style has been defined in several ways. Butler (1984, pp. 51–52) defines it as "a set of attitudes and actions that open a formal and informal world of learning to students. It is a subtle force that influences a student's access to learning and teaching by establishing perimeters around acceptable learning procedures, processes, and products." Butler suggests further that the teachers' attitudes are as powerful a force as the instructional activities they use to help students learn.

Mosston and Ashworth (1990, pp. 2–3) suggest that teaching styles are decision patterns. Decisions are made by both the teacher and the learner. They have identified a spectrum of teaching styles according to the decisions

FIGURE 7-4 • *Observation of Student's Learning Styles (OSLS)*

Minute Number	1 Activity	2 Number of Students in Room	3 Number of Students in Some Activity	4 Interaction with Adult—Specify Whom	5 Materials Being Used	6 Number of Students Using Same Material	7 Check if Activity Is Assigned by Teacher	8 Comments

1. *Listening and Speaking Activities:*
   a. Listens to teacher speak
   b. Listens to teacher give directions
   c. Listens to teacher read
   d. Listens to student speak
   e. Listens to student read
   f. Asks question
   g. Answers question or contributes point to discussion
   h. Makes a report
   i. Other—specify

2. *Reading and Writing Activities:*
   a. Reads silently in textbook
   b. Reads other material silently—specify
   c. Follows oral reading in book
   d. Reads orally
   e. Works in workbook
   f. Works on worksheet
   g. Works with programmed materials, computer
   h. Answers questions based on assignment
   i. Other—specify

3. *Miscellaneous:*
   a. Uses an educational game or kit
   b. Works in another subject—specify
   c. Exhibits nonacademic behavior (talking to neighbor, doing nothing, etc.)
   d. Uses audiovisual material
   e. Waits for materials
   f. Draws or paints
   g. Other—specify

Name _____ School _____

Date _____ Teacher _____ Grade _____

Source: J. Sorenson, M. Poole, and L. Joyal, *The Unit Leader and Individually Guided Education* (Reading, MA: Addison-Wesley Publishing Company, 1976), p. 433. Reprinted with permission.

made by the teacher and the learner as learners move from one style to another along the teacher-centered to student-centered continuum.

A simple, practical definition of teaching style is implied by Sorenson et al. (1988, pp. 94–95): teaching style relates to which elements the teacher and learner control in the teaching–learning process. Elements include goals and objectives, media, materials and activities, schedule for time and space for instruction, method of presentation, and evaluation of student performance. Control of elements denotes a style from teacher-centered to student-centered control.

How important is teaching style? Goodlad (1984, p. 108) believes that "teaching style governs the reality of the classroom. While no teachers will use a program or text in the same way, each teacher conveys attitudes toward curriculum's content and process." He calls the teacher "coach, quarterback, referee, and even rule-maker." From his study of schooling and interaction with teachers, Goodlad indicates that about two-thirds of teachers at all levels perceived that they had complete "control" in the selection of teaching techniques and students' learning activities (pp. 188–189).

Overview of Current Research and Programs on Teaching Style

The discussion here will examine several views of teaching style that range from teacher oriented to student oriented. Specific programs reviewed include Gregorc's teaching styles, the spectrum of teaching styles, and five practical teaching styles.

Gregorc's Teaching Styles

Gregorc's style patterns were discussed earlier in this chapter. They are concrete sequential (CS), abstract sequential (AS), concrete random (CR), and abstract random (AR). Here these styles are related to teaching (Guild & Garger, 1985; Phi Delta Kappa, 1980; Butler, 1984).

For example, a teacher who prefers concrete perception and sequential ordering will exhibit the CS style of teaching. Some of the personal and classroom characteristics related to this teaching style are:

- Uses practical and hands-on learning experiences.
- Expects students to answer the question, "How does this work?"
- Encourages students to create real and practical products.
- Uses a variety of manipulative materials available in the classroom.

- Expects students to be task oriented and to show all steps in completing their work.
- Manages the classroom in a structured and logical way.
- Makes school practical, realistic, predictable, and a secure place for students.

A teacher who perceives in an abstract way and orders sequentially will have an AS teaching style. Characteristics include:

- Encourages students to be analytical—to evaluate what they are learning and to support their ideas with logical evidence and data.
- Encourages students to carry out research in an impersonal and structured setting.
- Expects students to be patient learners.
- Expects students to gather information accurately and learn material thoroughly.
- Makes many abstract resources available, especially books and other printed materials.
- Encourages students to be intellectually curious and to build a strong knowledge base.

A teacher who perceives concretely and orders randomly exhibits the CR teaching style. Characteristics include the following:

- Emphasizes practical, realistic work that is expressed in original, creative ways.
- Encourages students to invent and solve problems by producing useful and original products.
- Is active, enthusiastic, flexible, and spontaneous in the classroom.
- Uses a variety of methods and promotes active student involvement in learning.
- Encourages students to make choices, to think for themselves, and to ask, "How many different ways can I?"
- Challenges students to go beyond traditional learning to invent and discover new products.

A teacher who perceives abstractly and orders randomnly, will have an AR teaching style. Characteristics of this style include the following:

- Focuses on individual students, their interests and their needs.
- Responds to the moods, feelings, and sensitivity of the students and reacts spontaneously.

- Provides opportunities for students to create artistic and creative products.
- Displays students' work, including materials reflecting students' interests.
- Educates the whole child and develops esteem and self-confidence in students.
- Encourages students to cooperate and share with each other.
- Makes content personal, suits the curriculum to the individual child, develops a child-centered classroom.
- Uses themes to teach knowledge and skills.
- Inspires students and brings joy and enthusiasm to learning.
- Encourages students to ask, "How can we interpret this?"

Mosston and Ashworth's Spectrum of Teaching Styles

Mosston and Ashworth's approach to teaching considers eleven different styles ranging from the command style, where the teacher makes nearly all of the decisions, to the learner initiative and self-teaching styles, where the learner makes virtually all of the decisions in the learning process. These eleven styles (Figure 7-5) are clustered into two general human capacities: reproduction and production. The first five styles — command, practice, reciprocal, self-check, and inclusion — represent reproduction, since they ask students to foster the reproduction of past knowledge. The guided discovery, convergent discovery, divergent production, learner-designed individual program, learner-initiated, and self-teaching styles are production because they encourage students to gain new knowledge by solving problems, reasoning, inventing, and going beyond the data given (Mosston & Ashworth, 1990, pp. 3–6). A brief summary of the eleven styles, including purpose of the style, role of the teacher, and role of the learner are presented in Figure 7-5.

Mosston and Ashworth (1990) elaborate on these eleven styles in considerable detail in their book. They also discuss anatomy of the style; objectives of the style; how to implement the style in the classroom, including student and teacher tasks; how to select and design subject matter lessons and units, with specific classroom examples in several subject matter areas; an analysis of tasks that deviate from the style; how to design a learner task sheet, with examples; lesson planning; implications of the style; and, where appropriate, teacher and learner hazards related to the style.

An overview of how one style — guided discovery, style F — functions with a teacher and students is presented here (Mosston & Ashworth, 1990, pp. 193–216). This style is located midway between teacher-centered and student-centered style on the style continuum (see Figure 7-5).

Here, two sets of *objectives* apply.

FIGURE 7-5 · *An Overview of* The Spectrum of Teaching Styles

Style	Purpose	Role of Teacher	Role of Learner
A. Command	Learner completes tasks accurately and within a short period of time following all decisions by teacher	Makes all subject matter decisions Make all impact decisions on subject matter, order of task, start time, pace and rhythm, stop time, interval, appearance, initiation of questions for clarification	Follow and perform task when and as described
B. Practice	Offer learner time to work alone and privately Provide teacher time to offer learner individual and private feedback	Be available to answer learner's questions Gather information about learner's performance and offer individual and private feedback	Do task Make decisions on order of tasks, start time, pace and rhythm, stop time, interval, posture, location, appearance, and initiation of questions for clarification (nine impact decisions)
C. Reciprocal	Work with partner Offer feedback to partner based on criteria prepared by teacher	Monitor observers Give feedback to observers Answer observer's questions	Select roles of doer and observer Does task (as in Style B) Observer compares work of doer with criteria, draws conclusions, and offers feedback to doer Doer and observer switch roles at completion of task by doer
D. Self-Check	Learn to do a task Check your own work	Prepare subject matter and the criteria Answer questions by learner Initiate communication with learner	Perform task Make decisions (as in Style B) Check own task performance
E. Inclusion	Learn to select a level of task learner can perform Check your own work	Prepare task and levels within task Prepare criteria for task levels Answer questions by learner Initiate communication with learner	Make decisions (as in Style B) Examine different levels of the task Select level appropriate for self Perform task Check your own work against teacher criteria Ask teacher questions for clarification
F. Guided Discovery	Discover a concept by answering a sequence of questions presented by the teacher	Design a sequence of questions Present questions to learner in a sequence Provide feedback to learner Acknowledge "discovery" of concept by learner	Listen to teacher's questions in sequence Discover answers for each question in the sequence "Discover" the final answer or concept
G. Convergent Discovery	Discover solution to problem, clarify issue to arrive at conclusion, employ logical procedures, verify process and solution against appropriate criteria	Present the problem or issue Follow the learner's process of thinking Offer feedback or clues (if needed) without giving answer	Examine problem, issue Evolve own procedures to solve Use mini hierarchy to lead to solution Verify process and solution by checking them against appropriate criteria
H. Divergent Production	Engage in producing (discovering) multiple responses to a single question	Make decisions about question to be asked; Accept the responses; Serve as verification source (in some subject matter tasks)	Make 9 impact decisions of style B; Produce divergent responses (multiple responses to the same question); Ascertain validity of the responses; Verify responses in some subject matter tasks
I. Learner-Designed Individual Program	Allow learner to design, develop, and perform a series of tasks organized into a personal program	Select general subject matter area from which learner chooses topic Observe learner's progress Listen to learner's periodic questions and answers	Select topic to be focus of study Identify questions, issues for topic Organize questions to organize tasks and design a personal program Collect data about topic to answer questions and organize answers into framework Verify procedures and solutions based on criteria intrinsic to subject matter
J. Learner Initiated	Provide learner with opportunity to initiate learning experience, design it, do it, and evaluate it	Accept learner's decision to initiate learning experience Provide general conditions for learner's plans Accept learner's procedures and products Alert learner to discrepancies between intent and action	Initiate the style Design the program for self Do it Evaluate it Decide how to use the teacher
K. Self-Teaching	Learner makes all decisions	Learner takes over the role of the teacher	Learner makes all decisions

Source: Summarized with permission from M. Mosston and S. Ashworth, *The Spectrum of Teaching Styles: From Command to Discovery* (New York: Longman, 1990), pp. 49, 83, 108, 124, 158, 215, 226, 264, 274, 281, 283.

1. Subject matter objectives include discovering the interconnection of steps within a given task and discovering the "target" — the concept, principle, or idea.
2. Behavior objectives include crossing the discovery threshold, engaging the learner in the discovery of the target (convergent thinking), and engaging the learner in a unique cognitive relationship with the teacher.

In the *anatomy of the guided discovery style,* the teacher makes all the decisions in introducing the student to the process (pre-impact set) including those about objectives, the target of the episode, and the sequence of questions to guide the student to the target. But, during the act of discovering (impact set), more decisions are shifted to the learner because questions and decisions come from both the teacher and the student. In the final part of the activity (postimpact), the teacher verifies the learner's response to the questions, but, hopefully, with experience, the learners can verify the responses themselves. This sequence of continuous, corresponding decisions in the impact and postimpact sets is unique to this style.

During *implementation of this style,* teachers and learners have specific roles, which are summarized in Figure 7-5. In addition, the teacher must never tell the answer, always wait for the learner's responses, offer frequent feedback, and maintain a climate of acceptance and patience.

In *selecting and designing the subject matter,* the teacher follows several specific steps. The first is to *select the task.* Here, several guidelines apply: learners can discover concepts, principles, relationships, cases, limits, and "how to's"; the target or topic to be discovered must be unknown to the learner; the target to be discovered must not be a fact or specific word, name, or term — these are best learned by being told; this style may not be appropriate for some sensitive topics such as religion, sex, or politics because it may bring out conflict and embarrassment, which is not its purpose.

Designing the task for guided discovery also needs guidelines: the process is initiated by a specific series of stimuli — questions and statements to set the scene; questions to promote discovery with each question bringing about a small discovery; questions proceed in a specific sequence; and small discoveries build on each other and accumulate until the learner "discovers" the target. The number of steps needed to set the scene and discover the target may vary according to the complexity and nature of the subject matter and the age/grade level of the learners.

Designing the sequence of questions is the most difficult step. Questions need to include the following four points:

1. What is the objective or target of the exercise?
2. How do the questions or statements set the scene?
3. What is the first question in the discovery sequence after the scene is set?

4. How can the teacher be sure the size of the step is not too large or too small?

An example of a *guided discovery episode* that might occur in a science classroom follows:

Objectives: Which has the larger volume, a quart or a liter? How much larger is one than the other?

Equipment: A 1-quart clear container and a 1-liter clear container each with its own overflow dish; a 250 ml or other standard measure; about six cups of water in a bucket; a 50 ml clear graduate

Sequence of Questions and Activities

1. Please look at each of the containers. Which one do you think is larger? Look at the 250 ml measure. How many measures do you think it will take to fill the quart container? The liter container? (Students make estimates in response to these teacher questions.)
2. How can you find out which container is larger? (Students suggest filling each container with water using the 250 ml measure.)
3. The teacher asks a student from the class to fill each container with water using the 250 ml measure. Other students observe. The teacher asks, "What happened?" (Four, 250 ml measures of water overflowed the quart container; four measures just filled the liter container.)
4. "How much larger is the quart than the liter? How can we find out?" (A student suggests using a 50 ml graduate to measure the overflow from the quart container and proceeds to measure it as about 50 ml.)
5. "Discovered answers" or the targets are (1) the liter is larger than the quart (students discovered this because the fourth 250 ml of water overflowed the quart container), and (2) a liter is about 50 ml larger than a quart (when students measured the overflow, it was about 50 ml).

In addition to discovering answers, this style often leads to or illustrates other information such as the following: a liter is 1,000 ml; a quart is about 950 ml; a liquid takes the shape of its container, but its volume is constant regardless of shape.

Practical Teaching Styles

Teaching styles and student learning styles are endlessly interwoven. A practical way to look at teaching styles is to determine who sets and controls a number of variables in the teaching–learning process. One set of variables includes goals and objectives, materials and activities, time and space, presentation method, and how evaluation is determined. These variables can be coordinated with five practical teaching styles — teacher-centered, self-instructional, inquiry, cooperative, and student-centered styles (Sorenson et al., 1988). These variables and teaching styles along with who controls the variables — student, teacher, or both — are presented in Figure 7-6 and are discussed below.

In the *teacher-centered style,* the teacher makes most of the decisions. The main job of the student is to execute the directions in the five variables. This style is applicable to all subject matter areas at all age/grade levels. It is probably the most traditional style of teaching and focuses on an active teacher and a passive learner. While this style will always be useful for conveying necessary information and directions to a group of students efficiently, many educators feel it has numerous shortcomings. Many of today's students cease to function in the classroom when taught in this style. It may not be an effective style to convey the learning necessary for students to function in a technological society since it does not involve the learner actively in the learning process.

In the *self-instructional style,* the student would work at a computer or with programmed printed material. While the objectives and goals are set by the materials in the software or other programs, the teacher and student can work together to select programs most appropriate to the student's learning needs. The student has wide options and involvement in all of the other variables. One of the unique facets of this style is the immediate feedback the student gets in the evaluation variable. While the presentation method and evaluation are indirectly determined by materials, both teacher and student can provide supplemental support. Generally, the teacher acts as a resource person in this style beyond the selection of goals and objectives. The greatest advantage of this style is that materials can be easily matched to student needs at any age/grade level and for a variety of purposes — remediation, regular instruction, enrichment, or acceleration. Once selections have been agreed upon by teacher and student, the teacher does not have to be immediately available to the student. This allows the student to develop a sense of independence in learning, too.

In the *inquiry teaching style,* the teacher forms a partnership with the students as individuals, pairs, or in small groups. The idea behind this style is for the teacher to present materials to motivate the students to think and learn. A lesson is often started in a class-size group. The teacher encourages

FIGURE 7-6 • Roles and Relationships among Teaching Styles and Learning Variables

Learning Variables

Practical Teaching Styles	Goals and Objectives	Materials and Activities	Time and Space	Presentation Method	Evaluation
Teacher-Centered	Teacher determined	Teacher selected	Teacher scheduled	Teacher directed	Teacher determined
Self Instructional	Set by materials	Selected by student from a list-menu	Cooperatively scheduled by student and teacher	Student follows direction of materials	Immediate feedback from materials
Inquiry	Set by teacher and materials	Cooperatively agreed upon	Selected mainly by student	Teacher presents, but student takes initiative	Cooperatively between student and teacher
Cooperative	Selected by students and teacher	Selected by students; teacher monitors	Selected by students; teacher monitors	Students take initiative; teacher guides	Cooperatively determined by students and teacher
Student-Centered	Selected by student; teacher guides	Selected by student; teacher guides	Selected by student; teacher guides	Student takes initiative; teacher guides	Student determined; teacher guides

students to seek answers to questions by asking yet more questions. Then students usually work in pairs or small groups to seek answers to their questions through manipulation, experimentation, surveys, or other active means. The teacher does not give the students answers to memorize or verify. The teacher encourages the students to discover the answers on their own. Students are highly involved in the variables of media, materials, and activities; time and space; and evaluation. Elements of inquiry were also discussed under the topic of thinking skills in Chapter 6 of this book. When students work in inquiry groups, each person has a specific task, such as leader, scribe, information organizer, presenter to the total group, and so on. Of course, all students are involved in gathering information and discussion.

The *cooperative learning style* can be thought of as an extension of the inquiry style. Some of its major tenets include the following:

- Students working together in a small group on a cooperative, not competitive basis
- Groups are usually structured in a heterogeneous manner, although groups of students with homogeneous abilities have worked out well in some gifted programs
- The development of social skills and other effective qualities such as self-esteem and independence as well as cognitive achievement are expected outcomes.

Cooperative learning groups also provide a structure for group work based on positive independence—the success of the group depends on the efforts of its members and individual accountability where students are individually accountable for mastering skills and concepts. Cooperative learning is described in more detail in Chapter 5 of this book.

The *student-centered style* should be the ultimate goal of every teacher—the development of a life-long, self-motivated, independent learner. Here, the student takes the initiative in all five instructional variables. The teacher acts as a resource and provides direction and support to the student's learning. This style borrows generously from all other styles. Students may learn alone, in pairs, small groups, or, on occasion, in class-size or large groups. As all experienced teachers know, not all students have the motivation, academic skills, and personal discipline to function in this style. But many do and all students should have the opportunity to move toward using this style as they progress through the educational system.

Every classroom in a school has students who function well with teachers who use one, two, or all five teaching styles discussed here. Every lesson and unit of instruction a teacher plans should provide opportunities for students to learn in more than one style—preferably, three or four different styles. When these opportunities are built into the learning plans, the idea of teaching styles has true meaning. And student learning styles can easily be matched to these five practical teaching styles.

Strategies to Assess Teaching Styles

Several commercial and teacher-made assessment instruments are available. They present the assessment material in an interesting and nonthreatening manner and lead to beneficial and positive discussions by the teachers who participated in the assessment. Instruments that will be discussed here are Gregorc's Style Delineator, The Teaching Performance Profile, and Practical Teaching Style Patterns.

Gregorc's Style Delineator

Gregorc's Style Delineator, an instrument for assessing teaching styles, has been widely used by many school districts during the past decade. It is available (in the 1985 version) from Gregorc Associates (Box 351, Columbia, CT 06237).

Data collected on this instrument relates the four dominant teaching styles suggested by Gregorc—CS, AS, AR, and CR—to twelve categories. These categories are:

World of reality	Creativity
Ordering ability	Approach to change
View of time	Approach to life
Thinking processes	Environmental preferences
Validation process	Use of language
Focus of attention	Primary evaluation words

For example, a teacher who exhibited the CS style might be slightly adverse, speculative, hesitant, and slow in relation to the category of "approach to change." A teacher who had a dominant AR style would probably use super, fantastic, out-of-sight, and dynamite as "primary evaluation words." In the instructional setting, teachers who exhibit dominance for each of the four styles might use the following mechanical media and techniques:

CS dominant	Computer-assisted instruction, workbooks, lab manuals, field trips, work study applications
CR dominant	Independent study, games and simulations, problem-solving situations, mini lectures, and exploration

| AS dominant | Lectures, audio tapes, books, texts, syllabi, guided individual study |
| AR dominant | Videotapes, television, movies, assignments with reflection time, group discussion |

This output and more from Gregorc's instrument is presented in graphic and descriptive form and is related to many aspects of teaching. More background information on Gregorc's styles was provided earlier in this chapter.

The Teaching Performance Profile

The Teaching Performance Profile, a commercial instrument to assess teaching styles, is available (in the 1988 version) from Digicator Systems, Inc., through Donald Barnes (3502 Highway MN, McFarland, WI 53558). It assesses the following twelve teaching styles:

Classic	Director	Guide
Coacher	Energizer	Mentor
Constructive critic	Evaluator	Professor
Demonstrator	Facilitator	Technician

Output from this instrument includes scores, graphs, and descriptions of which styles are dominant for the respondent. Guidelines for interpretation, personalization, and discussion of the preferred teaching styles are also available. Output categories include general characteristics, teaching, philosophy, interaction, strength, and ways to increase teaching effectiveness.

Practical Teaching Styles

A less complex instrument for assessing teaching styles is shown in Figure 7-7. The content in this instrument relates to the five practical teaching styles that were summarized in Figure 7-6 and discussed earlier in this chapter. This instrument's output provides a visual picture or scatter pattern of the teacher's preferred teaching style—teacher-centered, self-instructional, inquiry, cooperative, and student-centered. It is easy to use, inexpensive to duplicate, and staff can add, delete, or alter both the questions and variables to meet their needs.

Matching Learning and Teaching Styles

Perhaps the most important thing about reflecting on learning and teaching styles is how to match them to each other. This is not an easy task (Hunt,

FIGURE 7-7 • *Practical Teaching Styles Patterns Assessment Instrument*

Person(s) who Controls the Learning Variables

	Student	Student with Input from Teacher	Student and and Teacher Cooperatively	Teacher with Input from Student	Teacher
Who should determine or select goals and objectives for instruction?					
Who should determine media, materials, and activities for instruction?					
Who should determine the time schedule and space for instruction in the classroom, school, and community?					
Who should determine the method of presentation—structured or unstructured—for instruction?					
Who should determine the method of evaluation for what the student learned from the instruction?					
Other:					

1979; Joyce, 1981). Some guidelines to help set the tone for this match include the following:

- Students in any group have a variety of dominant learning styles. Even though a teacher may have a dominant teaching style, the students in each class have a wide range of learning styles. Thus, the teacher must provide a variety of options and choices for students with different learning styles to meet the same goals and objectives in lessons and units of study.
- Student learning styles and teacher teaching styles are most easily matched in a team setting. When students and teachers are part of a multigraded team, students with structured, unstructured, or any other combination of learning styles can be assigned to teachers with compatible types of teaching styles — at least part of the time.
- Students should be encouraged to learn in other styles than their dominant one. While teachers should try to accommodate a student's preferred learning style, particularly when learning new or difficult material, students should also be encouraged to "stretch" to become comfortable and efficient in learning in more than one style. As students go through life and into careers, they must be able to adapt to changes.
- The nature of the subject matter to be learned needs to be considered in terms of learning and teaching styles. Even though some students might have a strong preference for learning in a small group, there are some situations, such as giving instructions, safety directions, daily schedules, and announcements that are best presented in a structured, teacher-directed manner. Conversely, some material is best learned alone or in pairs.

Two examples — one for intermediate level students and one for middle school and junior high level students — of how learning and teaching styles can be "matched" are presented here. Strategies used in both examples are practical and can be used in a team or self-contained classroom organizational pattern.

Intermediate Level: Math and Science

The following math and science lessons relate learning style preferences from the Learning Styles Checklist (see Figure 7-1), and teaching style preferences from the five Practical Teaching Styles (see Figure 7-6). The math lesson deals with the precise topic of multiplication in which one correct answer is desired for any problem; the science lesson deals with the more open-ended topic of explaining differences in bounce height for several kinds of balls and does not focus on any one answer. The styles that are matched are listed in parentheses following each numbered item. The learning styles are listed before the semicolon and the teaching styles after the semicolon.

Math

The interrelationship of learning and teaching style here relate to fourth-grade students who are encountering formal multiplication for the first time or who are reviewing multiplication that was learned earlier. The lesson focuses on giving the students choices of different activities to meet the same multiplication objective. One possible set of procedures follows:

1. The entire class or group starts out together. The teacher demonstrates the idea that multiplication is repeated addition with 1's and 2's using plastic peanuts on the overhead projector. The teacher controls the pace and asks the students to answer questions as she proceeds. (hands-on media; teacher-directed style)

2. The students from the group break into pairs to replicate what the teacher has done on the overhead projector with plastic peanuts. They are encouraged to talk to each other as they work. After they have had a chance to work through the 2's, they share their results and questions with the entire group. The teacher once more reinforces the idea that multiplication is repeated addition. (small group, varied noise tolerance; cooperative teaching style)

3. Now the teacher moves through the 3's and 4's using the plastic peanuts on the overhead projector, asking the students to interact and talk along with her as she groups the peanuts to get answers. (structured environment; teacher-directed)

4. For practice, the teacher has prepared a worksheet for the students to use their newly learned multiplication. The students have the following choices:

- Complete the worksheet alone or with a partner (varied group sizes, structured environment, varied attention spans; self-instructional).
- Work out answers to problems on worksheet with paper and pencil or use hands-on plastic peanuts or a combination of the two (varied media; self-instructional).
- Check their own work or have the teacher check it; where students have made errors, they are encouraged to use plastic peanuts to arrive at the correct answers. (self-evaluation, teacher-evaluation; student-centered).

5. After the students have mastered multiplication through 4's, the teacher illustrates multiplying up through 10's on the overhead projector.

At this point, a wide range of choices for learning and practicing are available to the students.

- Work on a computer program or at a practice center that includes choices for paper and pencil and manipulative activities; students can work alone, with a partner, or in a small group of three or four students. (varied media, self-directedness, varied noise tolerance; self-instructional, cooperative)
- Work on a computer program or at a center to interact with more advanced materials; this is for students who mastered the basics quickly. (varied learning environments, self-directedness, self-evaluation; self-instructional)
- View a videotape—alone, with a partner, or in a small group—that illustrates the multiplication process using different colors, sizes, and shapes of manipulatives along with a narrative of each step in the process. (varied media, structured environment, inductive mode; inquiry, self-instructional)
- Schedule a ten-minute teacher-led or aide-led group to explain the multiplication process from the beginning for students who need or want to attend. (structured learning environment; teacher-directed)
- Work in a small group to explain multiplication by developing a simulation or other activity for their fellow students to carry out. (small group; cooperative, inquiry, student-centered)
- Make assignments in math book or worksheets for students to complete—allowing hands-on manipulatives as an option to develop and explain how they arrive at answers. (structured learning environment, varied media; inquiry, self-instructional)
- Have students develop materials to help others learn multiplication through 10's; work in small groups in media center, classroom, other space. (varied learning environments, self-directedness; student-centered)

6. Once students have mastered single digit multiplication, move to two-digit by two-digit multiplication. Many of the same processes and options suggested in steps 1–5 can also be used here. Division can be taught in much the same structure, emphasizing that division is repeated subtraction. Accommodating several kinds of learning styles of students is particularly important in the initial stages of learning new material.

Science
The matches for learning styles and teaching styles are illustrated here in a situation where the objective is to focus on the processes of inquiry, such as observation, classifying, predicting, inferring, formulating questions

and hypotheses, and experimenting rather than on learning how to obtain a precise answer as was the case in the math example above. This is an open-ended activity where the doing is just as important or more important than getting an answer. Steps are listed here. The dominant learning styles appear on the left of the semicolon and the dominant teaching styles on the right within the parentheses following each procedure.

1. The teacher bounces three different kinds of balls (for example, tennis ball, table-tennis ball, golf ball) from the same height onto the same surface. The teacher asks the students to make observations. After discussion in the total group, the teacher records agreed-upon observations on a transparency or blackboard. Then the teacher asks the students to explain why differences in bounce height occurred, records the responses, but does not give the students any answers. (structured environment; inquiry, teacher-directed)

2. Students break into cooperative groups of four to five students to develop a list of reasons for bounce height differences and, among themselves, discuss each reason presented. They include those from the common list in step 1 plus others they generate to decide which ones are most plausible. One student acts as a motivator or discussion leader, another as a recorder, and so on. After five to seven minutes, another student, who acts as explainer, shares the decisions of the small group with the class-size group. The teacher adds the plausible reasons from all groups to the list from step 1, but does not evaluate any of the reasons as right or wrong. (self-directedness, varied sizes of groups, self-evaluation; inquiry, cooperative, student-centered)

3. Now the small group is asked to repeat and, if the students wish, expand the experiment with the three balls that the teacher performed initially. To verify the explanations or reasons they selected, they can use the same kinds of balls as the teacher used or they can work with different kinds of balls to a limit of three, or they can do both. They send one student to get the equipment they need from the central supply table. They can also send one or two students to the media center to search for more information (print, video, diagrams, and so on) about their topic. Their goal is to develop an explanation to defend or reject their original reasons according to their further experimenting and information they gathered. (varied learning environments, small group, varied attention spans, varied noise tolerance; student-centered, cooperative, inquiry)

4. One student from each small group will share an oral explanation, with visuals if they wish, with the entire group. The students will grade themselves and the teacher will also grade them, not on their original explanation, but on the quality of the work they did to defend or reject their reasons. (self-evaluation; student-centered, teacher-directed)

This kind of open-ended activity might not be completed in one class session. It could lead to more experimentation, information seeking, and so on. Hopefully, several students would try out many kinds of balls at home or at a center in the classroom. And, isn't this, after all, the main purpose of learning and teaching?

Middle/Junior High Level: Integrating Geography into the Curriculum

For several years, people who live in the United States have been frequently reminded that among the developed nations of the world they least "know where in the world they are." In 1985, the National Geographic Society established a Geography Education Program to revitalize geography education in our schools. This program provides support for teachers to use new classroom materials and technologies with their students to help them learn geography. Also, many curriculum initiatives have been launched to increase interest in the study of geography and many ideas that teachers have used in their classrooms have been shared with others through magazine articles, workshops, and meetings. Programs of two schools, one in California and one in Spain, that carried out activities to integrate geography into their middle school and junior high level curriculum using several teaching and learning styles are described here.

Students at the American International School in Mallorca, Spain, took a trip around the world without leaving the school. For two weeks, they lived and breathed geography in all subject areas in an event titled "Geography in a Fortnight" (Pajares, 1989). The staff established a set of general concepts and categories such as countries, capitals, major cities, major rivers, mountain ranges, seas, and specific places before the project began as a basis for integrating geography into all areas of the curriculum. They also gave a pretest to determine the students' level of geography knowledge—which they found to average 34 percent correct. And they added concepts as they went along, such as NATO, EEC, Pacific Rim, and planned a game show similar to a Geography College Bowl at the end of the fortnight.

Everyone got involved in the Geography Fortnight. Administrative offices became classrooms with globes as paperweights and maps on the wall. The library displayed maps and atlases, the "quote of the day" involved geography, and each student was given an atlas. Students who had high scores on the pretest acted as aides and instructors and tutored students who were having problems learning geography. And every subject centered around geography. For example, English grammar and composition assignments involved geography, as did art and science work. On the posttest, the students scored an average of 84 percent correct (a jump of 50 percent from the pretest average). Students who scored less than 80 percent were tutored to meet the minimal 80 percent level. The attitudes and spirit of both students and staff were as positive as the test scores. The fortnight was a great success and it allowed for a wide variety of learning and teaching styles.

Because of their unique location in North San Juan, California, students of a rural middle school were able to visit a cargo ship, the *President Kennedy,* in Oakland harbor and then follow its route from there to Yokohama, Japan, and around Asia as it discharged its cargo. They used their computer, modem, and a satellite communications system that linked them with the ship (Mociun, 1989).

At the harbor, they met the crew. They visited crew living quarters, navigation and safety equipment on the bridge, the engine room, and so on. They also saw the cargo being loaded onto the ship and were surprised by its diversity—electronic goods, industrial machines, food, clothing, lumber, and automobiles.

When the ship sailed, the first communication the students got was weather and the ship's course, speed, latitude, and longitude. The *Kennedy* was being routed by a service that guides ships on the best route according to existing weather conditions. The ship was sent north to the Bering Sea through the Aleutian Islands. The class plotted the ship's course on maps and charts. In the classroom, all facets of weather were studied and each student was to complete a report plus a hands-on project on a topic related to Pacific Rim countries. These activities helped acquaint the students with the Pacific Rim area and made the world smaller and more real. Activities also provided opportunities for students to learn in many styles and have many options in styles of teaching.

Other ways to make geography come alive for middle school students is to relate it to everyday things and events that interest and involve them. These include sports, things students see on television such as weather and action, and what they read about in daily newspapers. And, perhaps most of all, they need to be involved and have choices. Two activities, Sports and Geography and Taking a Trip in the Classroom, that meet these criteria are outlined below. They include a wide range of choices in learning and teaching styles that can be related to Gregorc's learner patterns—CS, AS, CR, and AR. The dominant styles emphasized in each part of the activity are indicated in parentheses following the statement of the activity.

Sports and Geography: Activity

1. a. On an outline map of the United States, locate cities or areas and write in the name of the team for

- Major league baseball teams
- National Football League teams
- National Basketball Association teams

   b. Are the teams in any of these three leagues equally distributed around the United States? What factors do you think are related to their locations? Explain. (CR, AS)

2. a. On an outline map of the world, locate the sites and list the names of the teams in the World Soccer League. (AS, CS)

   b. What factors relate to the locations of teams in this very popular sport? Explain. (CR)

3. a. Obtain a list of countries that participated in the most recent *winter* Olympic Games. Locate and identify these countries on an outline map of the world. (CS, AS)

   b. After you have completed the map on countries that came to the winter games, note their latitudes north or south of the equator. Do you think their latitudes had anything to do with their participation in the winter games? Explain. (CR)

4. a. Locate and identify the countries that took part in the most recent *summer* Olympic Games on an outline map of the world. (CS, AS)

   b. Review the latitudes of the summer game participants. Did their latitudes have anything to do with their participation? Explain. (CR)

Taking a Trip in the Classroom: Activity

The one hundred students in the middle school unit divided into four divisions. Then, within each division, they divided into small groups of five or six students. Their project was to "take a thirty-day trip from New York to San Francisco." Within each division, one small group would travel by car or van; another by train; a third by air; and a fourth by ship; and, if they wanted to have a fifth group, that group would travel by some combination of transportation as they selected. This activity integrates geography with reading, language arts, social studies, science, and math and features student involvement through inquiry or cooperative group work. Some activities the students could carry out are the following:

1. Read in travel books, textbooks, and other sources about possible routes, sites to visit on the route, time it would take to travel the distance, events that might occur, weather, and so on. (AS)

2. Listen to audio tapes and lectures about the routes, sites, travel time, and so on. (AS)

3. View videotapes, films, and other visuals that relate to routes, sites, travel time, and so on. (AR)
4. Play games such as "Global Pursuit" (from National Geographic Society) that relate to the project. (CR)
5. Take a field trip to a travel bureau to ask questions and obtain more printed and other information about the trip. (CS, AR)
6. Study maps, manuals, workbooks, and computer programs that would relate to the topic of the project. (CS)
7. Calculate the following:

   a. Time needed to complete the trip comfortably and meaningfully in the thirty-day period, according to the mode of transportation. (CR, AS)
   b. Costs for the group for

      • transportation (CS)
      • food and lodging (CS)
      • admissions to parks, museums, and other sites of interest (CS)

8. Carry out group discussion and problem solving to develop

   a. A schedule for daily travel, including lodging sites each night (CS)
   b. Sites and events to visit each day (CS)
   c. Responsibilities for each member of the group (CS)
   d. Other information

9. Vicariously take the trip and

   a. Keep a daily written and/or oral diary that tells what each group does on the trip. They might want to add slides, photos, or video or audio material to illustrate the diary. The diary could be put on computer. The diary format can be poetry or prose or a combination of several literary forms, including plays. (CS, AR)
   b. Keep a ledger of all costs on paper or on a spreadsheet on the computer. (CR)
   c. Record weather conditions for each day. (CS)

10. Each group of five or six students presents a summary of their travels to the division group using visual, audio, hands-on materials, drama, or whatever format or combination of formats—formal or informal— they choose. (AR, CR, CS, AS)
11. After the groups in the division have presented the trip via each transportation mode, the trips are evaluated according to the strengths and weaknesses or advantages and disadvantages of each transportation mode. Is there one best way to travel? Why? Why not? (AR, CR)

12. Representatives from each division compare notes with the other divisions to find out if conclusions reached in the evaluation concerning the advantages and disadvantages of the different modes of transportation were the same or different across divisions. The summaries from each division and across divisions are prepared as a newspaper article or television program to share with all one hundred students on the middle school team and with parents and the community at a meeting later in the year. (CR, AR, AS, CS)

Summary

Several definitions of learning style and teaching style were presented in this chapter. In addition, an overview of current research and programs on learning and teaching styles, along with strategies to assess them, were discussed. Finally, strategies to match learning and teaching styles were illustrated with activities for intermediate and middle/junior high school level students.

References

Bechtol, W. (1973). *Individualizing instruction and keeping your sanity*. Chicago: Follett.

Blair, D., & Judah, S. (1990). Need a strong foundation for an interdisciplinary program? Try 4Mat! *Educational Leadership, 48*(2): 37–38.

Butler, K. (1984). *Learning and teaching style in theory and practice*. Columbia, CT: The Learner's Dimension.

Curry, L. (1990). A critique of the research on learning styles. *Educational Leadership, 48*(2): 50–56.

Dunn, R. (1983). Can students identify their own learning styles? *Educational Leadership, 41*(1): 60–62.

Dunn, R. (1990). Rita Dunn answers questions on learning styles. *Educational Leadership, 48*(2): 15–19.

Dunn, R., & Dunn, K. (1975). *Educator's self-teaching guide to individualizing instructional programs*. West Nyack, NY: Parker.

Dunn, R., Beaudry, J., & Klavas, A. (1989). Survey of research on learning styles. *Educational Leadership, 47*(6): 50–57.

Goodlad, J. (1984). *A place called school*. New York: McGraw-Hill.

Guild, P., & Garger, S. (1985). *Marching to different drummers*. Arlington, VA: Association for Supervision and Curriculum Development.

Hunt, D. (1979). *Student learning system: Diagnosing and prescribing programs*. Reston, VA: National Association of Secondary School Principals.

Joyce, B. (1981). *Flexibility in teaching*. New York: Longman.

Keefe, J. (1987). *Learning style theory and practice*. Reston, VA: National Association of Secondary School Principals.

Keefe, J. (1988). *Profiling and utilizing learning style*. Reston, VA: National Association of Secondary School Principals.

Kelley, L. (1990). Using 4Mat to improve staff development, curriculum assessment, and planning. *Educational Leadership,* 48(2): 38–39.

McCarthy, B. (1990). Using the 4Mat system to bring learning styles to schools. *Educational Leadership,* 48(2): 31–37.

Mociun, T. (1989). Geography by cargo ship. *Educational Leadership,* 47(3): 33–34.

Mosston, M., & Ashworth, S. (1990). *The spectrum of teaching styles: From command to discovery.* New York: Longman.

O'Neil, J. (1990). Making sense of style. *Educational Leadership,* 48(2): 4–9.

Pajares, F. (1989). Geography in a fortnight. *Educational Leadership,* 47(3): 35–37.

Phi Delta Kappa. (1980). On mixing and matching of teaching and learning styles. *Practical Applications of Research,* 3(2): 1–4.

Samples, B., & Hammond, B. (1985). Holistic learning. *The Science Teacher,* 52(8): 41–43.

Sorenson, J., Poole, M., & Joyal, L. (1976). *The unit leader and individually guided education.* Reading, MA: Addison-Wesley.

Sorenson, J., Engelsgjerd, J., Francis, M., Miller, M., & Schuster, N. (1988). *The gifted program handbook.* Palo Alto, CA: Dale Seymour.

Weber, P., & Weber, F. (1990). Using 4Mat to improve student performance. *Educational Leadership,* 48(2): 41–46.

CHAPTER EIGHT

Management and Motivation

The key to successful classroom management is prevention. Teachers do not have to deal with misbehavior that never occurs.

Students are harder to teach today. For the past ten years either "lack of discipline" or "use of drugs" has been identified by the Gallup Poll as the biggest problem that public schools must face (Elam, 1990). In one survey, two out of three teachers reported that unmotivated and undisciplined students were a serious problem in their classrooms. (Baker, 1985). The following statements are typical of the management problem:

"Kids are harder to teach. This year I have more students with problems in my class. It's more difficult to be a classroom teacher than ever before."

"There's an absence of emotional nourishment for many children in my classroom. They live in a throw-away society that discards husbands, wives, children, and things. Many come to school more concerned for basic security needs than for learning. It's hard to motivate insecure kids."

"I was taught if your curriculum is good you would have no behavior problems. That isn't true. What I've learned is that before you can teach a student you must get his rear end on a chair."

"It is unfair to the students who want to learn to have continual disruptions from others."

"I can't seem to manage my class. The students don't respect me and aren't interested in school. They are bored. The parents don't seem to care. I don't have enough time or materials to meet all the needs. I'm failing and I'm afraid."

Some teachers have difficulties managing their classrooms. Other teachers do not. Many schools have apparent management and discipline problems. Other schools, like the model schools we visited, do not have management and discipline problems. However, good classrooms and good schools do not run smoothly by chance; effective teachers and school staffs must work carefully to attain efficient classrooms and buildings. The first step in restructuring is to make certain that an effective classroom management system is in place.

The purpose of this chapter is to present some effective management and motivation techniques that good teachers use and also to present some schoolwide strategies that are working in restructured programs.

Teacher Expectancies

Whatever we do in teaching depends on what we think students are like. Teachers who believe students can learn will try to teach them. Teachers who expect to be obeyed are more likely to be obeyed. Teachers who like and respect their students usually will find that their students like and respect them. The teachers' expectations of how students will learn or behave often become a self-fulfilling prophecy. This idea has profound implications for teaching. In all the schools that we visited, teachers had high expectations for their students.

Two stories illustrate the effect of teacher expectations. The first anecdote is from an elementary classroom. The children had read a story that had been translated from an Aztec myth and were now doing a written assignment. The story was filled with many proper nouns that were difficult for some of the students to read. One boy came up to the teacher and said, "Ms. Enemark, I can't do this. It's too hard."

"How many arms do you have, Frankie?" the teacher asked.

"O.K., O.K., I'll do it," the boy replied and returned to his desk.

We couldn't figure out what had happened. When the students left the classroom, we asked Ms. Enemark what "how many arms do you have?" was about.

She smiled and said, "During the first week of school I show the kids a videotape about a woman who was born with no arms. The tape describes how she works and all that she's been able to accomplish. When a child says, 'I can't' I ask him or her, 'How many arms do you have?' It works. The children will try."

We, too, had seen the *60 Minutes* presentation about the handicapped woman but had not ever thought of using it to motivate students.

The second anecdote is based on an interview with a student who had grown up in a Spanish-speaking home and was now a university honor student. We asked, "Maria, how do you explain your success in school?"

She blushed and said, "I've never told this story to anyone. It's too embarrassing. When I was in the fourth grade, I had a crush on a male teacher. The only problem was that he taught the top group of the fifth grade and I was in the middle group. So the entire fourth grade I worked my tail off so that I could move up to his room. In the fall on the first day of school I got to the building just as it opened. I wanted to see if I'd been placed in Mr. Contreras' room. There was my name on his class roster. I was so excited. I ran down the hall to his room. I hurried into the room and said, 'Mr. Contreras! Mr. Contreras! I worked hard all last year so I could be in your room. I'm so excited that I'm on your class list!' He looked at me rather sternly and said, 'I'll expect you to get all A's.' That started it. I got all A's that year, in middle school, and in high school. I've gotten one B in art since I've been in college."

We asked, "Does Mr. Contreras know the effect he's had on you?"

"I don't think so. Maybe I could tell him now. But my parents don't understand me. They can't understand why I'm going to school instead of being married and living in the valley like my sisters."

Teacher expectations made a difference in the lives of these two students.

Teachers who are going to do their jobs successfully must have the following set of basic attitudes and expectancies:

1. Teachers should enjoy teaching. We believe that this can be tested best by checking to see how a teacher feels when he or she gets in the car to drive to school on a Monday morning. Those teachers who have a positive attitude about their teaching, students, content, and school get better results. As one teacher explained, "If I'm positive about my students and their learning, it motivates them."

2. Teachers should expect students to enjoy learning. When teachers have an appropriate attitude toward schoolwork, they present it in ways that make their students see it as enjoyable and interesting. Tasks and assignments are presented as meaningful activities that are valuable in their own right. Students value mastering school tasks and gaining skills. They enjoy classrooms where they can see their skills in reading, writing, and mathematics improving.

3. Teachers should expect to deal with individual students, not groups or stereotypes. Each student is a unique individual. Children, like fingerprints, are all different. Teaching is a very personal act. Teachers should think, talk, and act in terms of individual students, not classes.

4. Teachers should assume that all students want to be cooperative, respectful, fair, and responsible. However, these values must be taught A

student who behaves in a disrespectful way may not know how to behave with respect. Prosocial skills must be taught.

Although we selected the values *cooperative, respectful, fair,* and *responsible* for our classrooms, we encourage each teacher to select three or four values that fit the particular class setting and to teach them directly. These values may relate to the age of the student, the subject, or the teacher's beliefs. For example, teachers of young children might select *sharing,* while middle school teachers may choose *citizenship.* Writing teachers may choose *creativity* and science teachers could select *curiosity.* Whatever the values are, they need to be carefully taught. Later in this chapter lessons teaching the values *respect* and *encouragement* are described.

5. Teachers should expect to be obeyed. Teachers who give directions that students obey must use careful communication. Careful teacher talk is assertive. The teacher looks directly at the student, speaks clearly and confidently, and states what is needed. Examples of assertiveness are, "Please raise your hand so that I can call on you," and "Joe, your wandering around the room disturbs the class."

Many beginning teachers are nonassertive. Their directions are not obeyed. These teachers ask students to "Try to be good." rather than giving clear directions. Nonassertive teachers seem passive, nervous, and unsure of themselves. They nag: "How many times do I have to tell you to stop talking?" instead of assertively communicating, "Follow directions the first time they are given."

Some teachers are aggressive or hostile. They shout, threaten, glare, and call students derogatory names. They begin their school year by saying, "My name is Miss Applegate. One false move and I'll clobber you." Hostile teachers maintain a negative class climate: "Just you wait, Miss Smarty Pants, I'm going to get you. I know you've been passing notes." Since hostile teachers don't respect their students' rights, students in their class often become aggressive and hostile.

An example of careful teacher talk follows: On the first day of school Miss Brown taught her children that they may sharpen their pencils when she is not teaching. On the second day of school Doug and Bob decide to test Miss Brown by sharpening their pencils while she is teaching. Miss Brown sees Doug and Bob walking toward the pencil sharpener. She gives them her "discipline look." Bob sits down. He decides not to test her. "Doug, be seated, please." Doug sharpens his pencil. Miss Brown watches Doug at the pencil sharpener and says, "Doug, listen to me. I'm not sure you heard what I told you. I told you to sit down, and you sharpened your pencil. So we understand each other, the next time I tell you to sit down I want you to sit down. Are you with me?" This careful teacher talk communicates to the student that the teacher is in charge and should be obeyed.

6. Teachers should expect some difficulties. Expectations are not

automatically self-fulfilling. There are no perfect classes or perfect teachers. There will inevitably be some difficulties. Mistakes are normal and tolerable. Teachers should be forgiving. They should focus on the students' progress and past successes, not on their misbehaviors.

Motivation

Many teachers complain that unmotivated students are their major management problem. The research agrees with this complaint. Nearly half of the eighth-graders in the United States report being bored in school half or most of the time (O'Neil, 1991). Many students spend little time on homework and reading. Even gifted students who were voracious readers in elementary school are hard to motivate in middle school (Giddings, 1991). There is peer pressure in most middle schools to do enough work to get by but no more. Doing well in schools is acceptable; doing great is not.

Motivation is a serious problem. Restructuring will achieve little unless students are motivated to put more effort into their schoolwork. We believe that there should be a dramatic increase in homework if U.S. students are to be competitive with those from other countries. Upper elementary and middle school students should have forty-five to ninety minutes of homework each evening. High school students should have two to three hours of homework each evening. To accomplish these major changes in student behavior teachers and principals in restructured schools must understand the principles of motivation.

Motivation is a student's intent to learn. It is not a generic skill. People are not born motivated or unmotivated. It is a learned skill. Hunter (1982) says that what is learned can be taught. Teaching is our business. She recommends that the teacher who carefully uses motivation strategies can increase students' efforts and intent to learn.

Hunter (1982) has identified six variables of motivation. They are level of concern, feeling tone, success, interest, knowledge of results, and rewards. Following are descriptions of these motivational variables along with examples that we observed in the model schools:

Levels of Concern How much do students care about whether they learn? When students become concerned about their learning, they will do something. Reviewing for a test causes students to become concerned about preparing for a test. Giving time limits causes students to become concerned about finishing. Setting high standards ("We're the best first grade in Corpus Christi.") makes students work harder. A moderate level of concern stimulates students' efforts to learn. When there is no concern, there is little or no learning. When there is too much concern (test anxiety or fear of failure), students may have no energy available for learning. When a teacher says, "This next question is going to be a little bit more difficult," she is raising students' levels of concern (Hunter, 1982).

Feeling Tone   The way students feel in a particular situation affects the amount of effort they are willing to put forth to achieve learning. Feeling tone exists on a continuum from positive to negative. Positive feeling tones motivates students, so do negative tones. Most of us can remember the best meal we've ever had—and the worst! Neutral feeling tones don't motivate. Few of us can remember what we had for lunch last Thursday (Hunter, 1982).

Pleasant feeling tones motivate students. Students are inclined to try to learn when the classroom situation is pleasant and they believe they have a high probability of being successful. A teacher's enthusiasm and positive attitude makes the class feeling tone pleasant and motivates students toward higher achievement. As one teacher said, "If I'm excited about teaching and enjoy seeing students learn, it stimulates them." Another said, "I brag on them. It makes them feel worthy. If a student feels good about himself, he'll do what his teacher wants him to do."

Unpleasant feeling tones also activate learners to put forth effort. A teacher comment such as, "If that assignment isn't finished, there will be unpleasant consequences" is effective in stimulating effort; however, it may have undesirable side effects. Students may learn, but they may also avoid the content or the teacher in the future. When it is necessary to use unpleasant feeling tones as motivators, the teacher must return to pleasant feeling tones as soon as students put forth the effort to learn. An example is, "I've really put a lot of pressure on you to learn decimals. You've responded magnificently! You should be proud of your improvement."

Success   One of the strongest variables of motivation is success. To use this motivation strategy, teachers must diagnose students carefully and select materials appropriate for their performance levels. Materials should be selected so that students have high success rates (80 to 90 percent correct). Careful diagnosis of new students at Crawford and Montview Elementary Schools has helped these students become immediately successful in their new school. Success is a strong motivator.

Helping students become successful requires efficient teaching and adequate practice before testing. When students experience success, they gain confidence and are willing to try harder materials. If a teacher is excited and pleased when a student is successful, it is motivating to the child. Students feel successful when teachers recognize their quality performances and display their good work.

We observed a teacher who may once have been a cheerleader, passing back a set of math tests. She was so pleased with her students' scores she was chanting, "Are we great? Yes, we're great!" The students were pleased because they had been successful on the test. The teacher was pleased because her teaching had been successful.

Interest   There are two ways to promote students' interest in the learning task. The first is to use the students' interest in themselves. Relating the materials to be learned to the student's life, use of the student's name, and examples that refer to a student's interest or ability are a few possibilities a creative teacher can use to make material more interesting.

For example, students were having difficulty with the concept of an unknown, X. The teacher said, "Look at the equation $2X + 30 = 80$. John, let's suppose X is a pair of jeans and $30 is the cost of a shirt. So 2 times the cost of a pair of jeans plus $30 equals $80. How much does a pair of jeans cost?"

"Oh, I see," said John. "You can subtract 30 from 80 and divide the answer by 2. A pair of jeans costs $25. It's simple."

A second way teachers can make materials more interesting is by accentuating the novel or vivid — that which is different or unexpected. A social studies teacher who wears a tie that has geographic significance will motivate the class to find what country the tie represents and why. Teachers who dress as historical or literary characters motivate their students. Caution: Don't make things so novel that students forget what the lesson is about. Hunter (1982) warns us not to bring an elephant into the classroom to teach the color gray. Use novelty and vividness to attract students' attention to learning, not to distract from the learning.

Knowledge of Results   Feedback is a strong motivator for students of all age levels. It's not very satisfying when a teacher gives students another assignment when they don't know how well they did on yesterday's similar assignment. When the students find out what they did well, what needs to be improved, and what to do to improve it, they are motivated to improve their work on the next assignment.

Specific feedback motivates. For example, the writing teacher says, "Your first two paragraphs are very descriptive. If you used adjectives like that in the rest of the paper, it would be ready to publish."

Strategies for giving the students knowledge of results include the following:

1. Make specific comments on students' papers, in addition to grades.
2. Assign short written papers that can be checked and returned promptly.
3. Correct short-answer papers or tests in class. Provide self-check opportunities. Students can mark and correct their own papers.

4. Monitor and give specific feedback when students are practicing independently.
5. Grade and return tests quickly.

One teacher explains: "Learning about the importance of knowledge of results has fouled up my life. I have to grade tests and return them the next class period. Sometimes the grading interferes with social activities. But I know it's a key to students' learning, so I grade them."

Cool Seat (Allen, 1986) is an activity that gives feedback to students and also improves classroom morale. The teacher arranges six chairs in a circle. He asks four students to help him give feedback. They sit on the chairs. The teacher sits next to an empty chair—the Cool Seat. The teacher says, "In a minute we will go around the circle and each of us on the chairs will say one nice thing about the person in the Cool Seat. I'll go first. It can be something we like about the way the person acts or something we like that they're wearing. While we do this, the person in the Cool Seat can answer, "Thank you" or "I appreciate that." That's all the response they can make. Now let's start with you. Please come over here and sit beside me in the Cool Seat while I begin."

Rewards and Recognition   Students will work to receive a reward. Stickers, stars, stamps, candy, pretzels, raisins, and pencils motivate students to work.

While visiting in a middle school, we sat next to a girl who looked like a high school student. She was angry. We asked, "What's the matter, Andrea?"

"It's not fair. We are having the Olympics. Mrs. Miller gives us a gold star if we have a perfect paper. If we miss one or two, we get a silver star. She doesn't give bronze stars. I've missed three in language arts everyday this week. It's not fair."

We were surprised. Here was a girl who looked like a high school student angry about not getting a star by her name on an Olympics chart.

The teachers we visited rewarded students with personal notes; coupons worth one free math assignment; choices; extra time for art, music, or recess; reading by the teacher; and gifts of all kinds.

One principal said, "We buy the candy wholesale. I worry about their teeth. But our kids will work and behave for a piece of candy."

Of course, we wish that students were intrinsically motivated. In many restructured schools students do begin to find learning satisfying and rewarding. Reading becomes their hobby and stops being a school activity. Even these students are motivated by the possibility of getting a T-shirt that says "Super Reader" by reading fifty books in the fifth grade.

Teachers should use external rewards only when they are needed. The more discouraged a student is, the more external reinforcement is needed. If a student is internally motivated, don't spoil this motivation by using a reward.

Recognition at School Level was a strategy that motivated students at the schools we visited. Honor rolls, attendance awards, top spellers awards, high test scores, most improvement recognition, and citizenship awards stimulated some students to work and to behave. This recognition also promoted school spirit and a sense of community.

One strategy that we especially liked was the Super Student awards. Students initiated the process by completing the Super Student Quiz (Figure 8-1). The student had to answer "Yes" to each question in the quiz. Two teachers had to verify that the student's answers were true. When students could answer "Yes" to all the questions for a grading period, they were recognized at a special assembly. At this assembly they received a Super

FIGURE 8-1 · *Super Student Quiz*

Yes	I have two sharpened pencils in my desk.
Yes	I have notebook paper ready to use.
Yes	I get to all classes on time and with the supplies I need.
Yes	I turned in *all* my homework last week.
Yes	I keep things in my desk orderly.
Yes	I keep my books covered.
Yes	I have a ruler in my desk.
Yes	I have crayons in my desk.
Yes	I have a red pen or pencil in my desk.
Yes	I have been considerate of other students this past week.
Yes	I study at least four nights a week every week.
Yes	I read at home every day.
Yes	I write down my assignments.
Yes	I have a good attitude toward my schoolwork.
Yes	I try not to hurt others' feelings.
Yes	I can control my temper most of the time.
Yes	I do not cheat.
Yes	I am good at staying out of other people's business.
Yes	I go to bed at a reasonable time every night.
Yes	I behave well in class.
Yes	I behave well in the cafeteria.
Yes	I look at the teacher shen she is talking.
Yes	I am respectful of others and their property.

Source: Adapted from Lozano School, Corpus Christi, Texas. Used with permission of Kathy Bregenzer.

Student badge and a certificate. If they could answer "Yes" for another grading period, they were recognized at the assembly and a ribbon was attached to the badge. If they could answer "Yes" for a third grading period, they received a T-shirt with the school name and motto. Students and their teachers wore the T-shirts during *school spirit* days.

Super Students received privileges such as lunch with the principal (frequently off campus), freedom to be in the halls without passes, pictures posted on the bulletin boards, and discounts at the student store. Since the students had begun the process to become a Super Student, they had ownership to all the activities and responsibilities.

What we like about the Super Student Quiz is that all questions measure citizenship. Any student in the school could become a Super Student. The other thing we liked is that the list is adaptable. Teachers and principals at all levels have adapted the Super Student Quiz to fit their school settings. Most have shortened it so there are approximately ten key questions. Super Student is a strategy that has worked well with elementary and middle school students.

In summary, six variables of motivation were discussed. These included (1) raising or lowering students' *level of concern,* (2) using positive or negative *feeling tones,* (3) helping students experience *success,* (4) relating instruction to students' *interests,* (5) using feedback *(knowledge of results)* to motivate student learning, and (6) giving *rewards* to recognize quality work or appropriate behavior. Teachers who use these variables will motivate their students to achieve more and to behave better.

Preventive Discipline Strategies

The key to successful classroom management is prevention. Teachers do not have to deal with misbehavior that does not occur. Kounin (1977) and Evertson, Emmer, Clements, Sanford, and Worsham (1989) have studied the behaviors and strategies of teachers who were effective classroom managers. This section describes these preventive discipline behaviors and strategies.

Preventive discipline techniques include the following:

1. *Productivity.* Students are engaged in productive classroom work most of the time. Since students are busy and industrious in the classroom, time for misbehavior is minimal.

2. *Clarity.* Communicating information and directions in a clear, comprehensive manner is an important teaching skill. Clarity is the precise communication to students regarding what they are to learn and how they are to behave.

3. *Firmness*. A firm teacher projects an "I mean it" attitude. These teachers are prepared to back up their words with action. Firmness produces better student behavior and conformity to classroom norms.

4. *With-it-ness*. The "with-it" teacher is aware of what is going on in all parts of the classroom. The students say, "She's got eyes in the back of her head." "With-it" teachers do use their eyes well. They can monitor student behavior by going around the classroom with their eyes. They have a "discipline look" that they use to cause students to behave properly.

5. *Overlapping*. This is the ability to attend to two issues at the same time. A teacher who is working with a small group in reading demonstrates overlapping when she responds to a student's request for help while keeping track of the recitation by the members of the small group.

6. *Ripple effect*. When a teacher spots a potentially disruptive problem in the early stages, such as whispering, she can walk to the offending students, thus nipping whispering in the bud — before it ripples through the classroom. Teachers can also use the ripple effect by identifying a desired behavior, such as, "Good, I see many of you already have your dictionary and paper ready," causing this behavior to ripple through the classroom.

7. *Proximity*. Teachers use proximity by moving close to the problem. As in the whispering incident noted above, the teacher's proximity did stop the misbehavior. This is a good technique. Problems are quietly corrected by a teacher's touch or whisper; the other class members continue to be productive workers.

8. *Monitoring*. When a teacher methodically moves through the classroom to monitor students during the practice part of a lesson, students' behaviors change. They are more focused on the practice assignment. Monitoring gives the teacher the opportunity to praise those students who are working successfully and to give brief help (fifteen to twenty seconds) to those who need it.

9. *Signals*. Teachers need a signal so they can get their students' attention quickly. Effective signals can be ringing a small bell; raising the right hand; saying, "Eyes on me" or "Sit tall"; or turning off the lights. Whatever the signal selected, the teacher must have the students practice responding to the signal until their response becomes automatic.

Teachers find that a *visual symbol* such as a sign that says "Quiet" on one side and "Silence" on the other also works. When the "Quiet" side is shown, students may whisper or talk in their "six-inch" voices. When the "Silence" side is shown, no talking is allowed. Using the *visual signal* during cooperative learning or science experiments reminds students of appropriate behavior.

Preventive discipline doesn't just happen. Smoothly running classrooms where students are productive and that are free from disruption and chronic misbehavior do not happen accidentally. These classrooms exist because effective teachers have a clear picture of the kinds of student behaviors they want. They have planned carefully to achieve a well-managed classroom (Evertson et al., 1989).

10. (Avoid) *Roughness*. Roughness is a teacher's noisy, angry, frustrated response to student misbehavior. Effective teachers avoid roughness. When the teacher yells, "Stop whispering, Mary!", all the students stop their productive work to see why the teacher is yelling at Mary.

Organizing Your Classroom

Arranging the physical setting of the classoom is a logical starting point in preventing discipline. The room arrangement should not cause a management problem. The guidelines for good room arrangement are (1) keep high traffic areas free of congestion; (2) be sure students can easily be seen by the teacher (so a discipline look can be used); (3) be certain students can easily see instructional presentations; (4) keep frequently used teaching materials and student supplies readily accessible; (5) be certain students are not facing distractions (windows, hallways, and so on); and (6) organize the classroom so that the teacher can monitor the students (Evertson et al., 1989).

Choosing Rules and Procedures

A carefully planned system of rules and procedures makes it easier for teachers to communicate their expectations to students. A rule identifies general expectations or standards for behavior. "Treat others with respect" is an example of a rule. Procedures are ways of accomplishing a specific activity. "Form a line to walk to lunch" is an example of a procedure.

Rules are social agreements to help students accomplish the goals and objectives of the class. Rules provide students a set of predictable boundaries for behavior. They also set expectations to gain student cooperation. Rules give students guidelines so they can become more accountable and self-directed (Wolfe, 1988).

A sample set of rules for elementary students is

1. Respect other people and their property.
2. Take care of your classroom and the school.
3. Raise your hand when you wish to speak.
4. Be polite and helpful.
5. Obey all school rules.

A sample set of rules for middle school or secondary students is

1. Bring all needed materials to class.
2. Be in your seat and ready to work when the bell rings.
3. Treat fellow students and the teacher with respect.
4. Follow all rules and regulations in the school handbook.
5. Laugh with anyone but at no one.

Teachers should consider the following guidelines when choosing class rules:

1. *Select three to five rules.* Students have difficulty remembering more than five rules. Some teachers believe that one rule, "Follow directions the first time they are given" is the only one needed.
2. *State rules clearly and in positive terms.* "Walk inside the school building" is better than "Don't run in the halls."
3. *Make certain class rules are consistent with school rules.*

Is it reasonable for students and teachers to make rules together? Yes. It's a good way to teach the principles of democracy. It gives students an opportunity to discuss rights and responsibilities. Yes, students can help make the rules when they are reminded of one essential idea: Rules must always reinforce the basic notion that students are in school to study and learn.

Rules developed by teachers and students together will vary according to the age of the students and the subject. For example, a third-grade class decided on the following rules:

1. Always listen to the teacher.
2. Raise your hand to talk.
3. Complete all work.
4. Follow "Quiet" and "Silence" signs.
5. Be kind to others.

A middle school physical education class decided on the following:

1. Be on time.
2. Dress correctly.
3. Play safely.
4. Practice sportsmanship.
5. Take care of equipment.

The fifth- and sixth-grade classes at Hunt School in Hunt, Texas, have demonstrated that students can accept responsibility. The class is organized as a corporation with class officers who maintain straight A averages. The class objectives and rules have been modeled after the U.S. Constitution.

The students originally made these rules. Each new class re-adopts or revises the constitution every fall. These enterprising youngsters have organized bake sales, product sales, and raffles that have resulted in annual sales of $15,000 to $25,000. They have received state and national recognition for their hard work, politeness, and dependability ("A Class by Itself," 1985). The preamble to their class constitution is the following:

Preamble

We, the students of Hunt 5th & 6th Grades, Inc., are organized to promote the following ideals: To do things to help us in the future; to take our time and do things right; to honor our country and be patriotic; to keep up our grades; to try to learn how to best deal with money and deal with people; to conduct our business in a business-like way; to always try to help others; to always work together as a team; to be able to take criticism; to respect our elders and our parents; to always be truthful, honest, and dependable; to see that everyone has something to offer to make things run better; and to make sure that everyone has an equal opportunity.

Managing Student Work

In good schools each day of the school year teachers give their students assignments that they will be expected to complete in the classroom or at home. These assignments are important for student learning and retention. Consistent and accurate completion of assignments is a critical goal for effective management (Evertson et al., 1989).

Getting students to complete their assignments is a problem for many teachers. Many students do not feel accountable for their work. Teachers must have strategies to make certain students consistently complete assignments. There are three major strategies that effective teachers use (Evertson et al., 1989).

Clear communication of assignments and work requirements is the first strategy. Students need a clear idea of what their assignments are and what is expected of them. This means that the requirements of each assignment must be explained carefully. Standards for form, neatness, and due dates are made clear.

Early in our teaching career we worked for a superintendent who believed that good assignments were the key to good teaching. "That's the student's part of the lesson," he would explain to new teachers. The teachers' lounge talk in that district was, "When Mr. Ball visits, he wants to see you give an assignment. When he comes into your classroom just stop what you're doing and give an assignment; he'll leave. Oh, yes, write that assignment on the chalkboard so that the students can get it into their notebooks." What happened in that school district was that teachers always had carefully prepared assignments. Mr. Ball's supervision strategy was effective; the students in the district were recognized for their high achievement.

In some of the schools we visited, students were taught to use an assignment sheet or assignment book. Figure 8-2 shows the weekly assignment sheet used at Meridith Elementary School in Temple, Texas. An assignment sheet is a standard form on which students write their assignments on a continuing basis. When each assignment has been completed and handed in, the student checks it off on the assignment sheet. Teachers can check to see if students have recorded their homework assignments correctly. Parents can study the sheet to see what the students' assignments are. The teacher can have the parents initial the assignment sheet to indicate they have seen the written assignment (Gall, Gall, Jacobsen, & Bullock, 1990).

FIGURE 8-2 · *A Weekly Assignment Sheet Used by Third-, Fourth-, and Fifth-Graders at Meridith Elementary School, Temple, Texas*

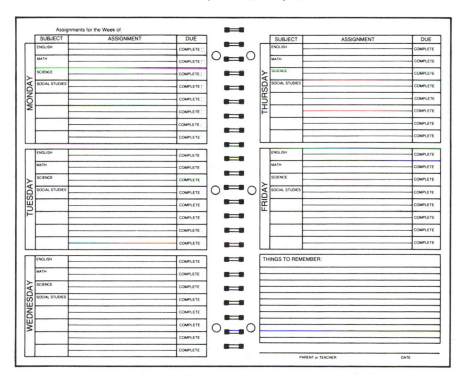

Source: Used with permission of Bonnie Martin.

Monitoring progress on and completion of assignments is a second strategy (Evertson et al., 1989). Once teachers have made an assignment, they should pay careful attention to student work. A quick monitoring trip through the classroom works. A good strategy is to monitor student work during the guided practice part of the lesson. If teachers don't check, some students will not even start the assignment and others may begin it incorrectly.

Monitoring the completion of assignments is also important. Teachers need to establish procedures for students to turn in completed work. Grade book records should be used to monitor completion rates and performance levels on assignments. One school we visited had an after school study center that students who are having difficulty completing homework could use. This was a positive place where students could go for help, for encouragement, and for a quiet place to work.

Keeping up with student papers can be overwhelming. Teachers must develop efficient systems to look over, grade, record, and return assignments quickly. Student teachers and volunteer aides can help with this task.

Providing feedback to students is a third strategy. Frequent and regular feedback is required because it reduces the amount of time students spend making errors if their performance is incorrect. This means that students' assignments must be checked and returned promptly.

Explaining the grading system is a key part of this strategy. Grades are very important to most students (and to their parents) because they are tangible evidence of student accomplishment. A handout explaining the basis for grading is especially helpful for upper elementary and middle school students. When students understand how completing an assignment by the due date helps their grades, they will work to complete their assignments.

In the restructured schools that use team teaching or departmentalization, feedback is crucial. One strategy that works is the student accountability meeting. Once each grading period each homeroom teacher or advisor reviews his or her students' progress with all the other teachers who teach them. The process is simple. The homeroom teacher or advisor presents each student in the homeroom to the other teachers who teach them. Each teacher explains how the student is doing in the particular class. The homeroom teacher or advisor takes notes. Later the teacher or advisor will meet with the students and tell them how they are doing. Having the student do a self-analysis before this conference makes the feedback more useful. It helps the student accept responsibility.

An example of a conference after a student accountability meeting follows.

"Mary, have a seat here by my desk. The team met yesterday. We discussed your progress. I'm happy to report they think you're doing good work this grading period. You're doing well in math, reading, and science and in social studies with me. Mr. Leigh is especially pleased with your progress in physical education. He said that learning to juggle was hard for you, but you've mastered it. Congratulations!"

Mary was beaming. She smiled and said, "Thank you for the good report. He's right. Juggling was really hard for me. I can do it now. Wow! Thank you!"

The neat thing about student accountability meetings is that good students, like Mary, get good reports. One teaching error is failure to give positive feedback to good students. Feedback, like Mary just received, will help her keep working the next grading period.

All students are not like Mary. One middle school teacher reported to us that his students would not do their homework. He told us that he gave 70 D's and F's the first grading period.

"Did it work?" we asked.

"No," he replied. "I told my wife our phone is going to ring all evening. I got one phone call from the mother of a girl that got a B⁺. She wanted to know how close her daughter was to an A."

He continued, "What I discovered is that the parents and the students accepted my low grades. If these students were going to work and achieve in social studies and English, I had to help them."

"What did you do?"

"Two things worked. I stood at the door and collected assignments when they came in the room. Most of them could not walk by me two days in a row without having a paper to give to me. The second thing was peer pressure. I said that we'd have no Friday assignment and would do something fun that day if all the Monday through Thursday assignments were completed. The kids called it Funny Friday."

"Did it work?"

"Yes, it took about a month and lots of help, tutoring, and encouragement. Now the kids do their assignments and get reasonable grades. It's funny how hard they'll work for ten minutes of their music or rap time on Friday."

One way to keep students completing their assignments is not to let them get in the habit of missing them. Once students start handing assignments in late or fail to complete them, they are unlikely to be successful in class (Soloman & Rothblum, 1984). Teachers should make certain their assignment system gives students an opportunity to start over each week so they don't get into a "no hope" cycle. A sample of a homework letter is included in the appendix.

Why should teachers make such a big deal about homework? Because students who regularly do academic homework learn more and behave better (Rutter, Maughan, Montimore, Austen, & Smith, 1979). Homework is an effective instructional technique. Homework can have positive effects on achievement and character development. Meaningful assignments can serve as a vital link between the school and the family (Cooper, 1989a). *All students should complete homework assignments regularly.*

Cooper (1989a, p. 7) defines homework as "tasks assigned to students by school teachers that are meant to be carried out during nonschool hours." He reports that regular homework has both immediate and long-term positive effects on students' achievement and learning. The completion of homework causes the student immediately to understand and remember the material studied. The long-term academic effects of homework are students who have better study skills, who have more positive attitudes toward school, and who are willing to learn during leisure time. Positive nonacademic effects include greater student self-direction, self-discipline, and time management (Cooper, 1989b).

Homework causes students to develop study skills and independent learning skills. Gall et al. (1990) reports that there is a tremendous difference in student responsibility for doing assignments at home from doing seatwork at school. Homework requires students to take responsibility for transporting their textbooks and other materials from school to home and back again. Students are responsible for organizing their home environment so that their assignments can be completed. Students must accurately record the directions for the assignment so that they can follow them when they are at home, working on their own. At school, students' time is managed by teachers or the daily schedule. At home, students must learn to manage time on their own, allocating enough time to get their homework done. Students who successfully complete homework assignments also learn self-discpline and time management skills. There is a tremendous difference in students' learning in a restructured school where homework is assigned regularly from a school where students only complete seatwork.

Homework should have different purposes for different age levels of students. For younger students, it should foster positive attitudes, habits, and character traits and promote independent reading skills. For upper elementary and middle school students, it should facilitate knowledge acquisition and also promote independent reading skills.

All the model schools had regular homeroom assignments. The Lozano faculty emphasized homework the most. Students in grades 3, 4, and 5 had several homework assignments each day. These assignments usually required students to work for one hour to one and a half hours independently. The Lozano staff believed that one reason that their student achievement results were so positive was because homework helped students develop good work habits and it increased students' vocabulary and reading comprehension.

Daily homework should average approximately fifteen minutes for younger children; twenty to forty-five minutes for grades 3 through 5; forty-five to seventy-five minutes for middle school students; and seventy-five to

120 minutes for high school students (Cooper, 1989b; Gall et al., 1990). If students are economically deprived or are from non-English speaking homes, more homework may increase student learning.

School programs that help inner city students become successful in college both extend the school day and increase homework demands. Joyce Oatman motivated her high school students to come in early in the morning, to stay late in the afternoon, and to come in on Saturdays. Her demanding homework assignments not only helped students in reading and mathematics but also got them to think critically about diverse issues such as philosophy and the environment. Oatman treated her black inner city kids as if they were gifted and they began to perform as if they were gifted (Ryan, 1991). Her program and success rate is similar to Jaime Escalante's with Hispanic students. Economically deprived students need more homework and more quality instruction.

Homework should include both mandatory assignments and voluntary assignments. Mandatory assignments should be graded and counted toward the student's total course grade. Voluntary assignments should involve tasks that are intrinsically interesting to students (Cooper, 1989b). Independent reading, projects, and reports are examples of voluntary assignments. T-shirts awarded to students stating, "I Read 100 Books in First Grade" encourage students to read independently.

Parents will rarely be asked to play a formal instructional role in homework. Instead, they will be asked to create a home environment that facilitates student self-study (Cooper, 1989b). As restructured schools grow, family activities will change (as they have at Lozano) so that time is made available in the home for students to complete their assignments.

We believe that this change is a beginning step in helping U.S. schools become more competitive with those in other countries. Management strategies to make certain that students complete all their assignments are extremely important.

Using Rewards and Penalties

Elementary and middle school students need incentives to encourage them to work hard, to complete assignments and homework, and to follow class rules and procedures. Whether students will consistently follow classroom rules and do their work depends in part on the consequence — both positive and negative — of cooperating or not cooperating. Rewards and penalties are two major kinds of consequences (Evertson et al., 1989).

A reward is something desirable that students receive in return for accomplishment, effort, or appropriate behavior (Evertson et al., 1989).

Positive reinforcement is the process of supplying a reward that the student wants when the student completes an assignment or follows a rule or procedure. The teacher can reinforce the student by providing some type of a reward.

Rewards may simply be the *social reinforcers* that good teachers have always used. Social reinforcers are words, gestures, and facial expressions. Many elementary and middle school students work diligently just to get a smile, pat, or kind word from the teacher. Examples of verbal reinforcers are words like "Wow!", "Excellent!", "Nice going," "Thank you," and "Super work!". Nonverbal reinforcers include smiles, winks, eye contact, nods, thumbs up, touches, pats, handshakes, standing near, and walking beside.

Rewards may be *grades and other symbols*. Good grades are a powerful incentive for most students, especially when they are perceived to be a reflection of the students' efforts, achievement, and competence (Emmer, Evertson, Sanford, Clements, & Worsham, 1989). Elementary students also respond positively to stars, stickers, and happy faces.

Recognition rewards involve some means of giving attention to students. Examples are displaying students' work, awarding a certificate for achievement, improvement, or good citizenship. Recognition rewards may be given on a weekly, monthly, or grading period basis using strategies like Super Students, honor rolls, or 100 percent clubs. It is effective not only to recognize outstanding achievement but also to recognize effort; awards for improvement, excellent effort, and good conduct are effective (Emmer et al., 1989).

Activities rewards permit students to do something that they perceive as special or enjoyable. Elementary students will work very hard for extra art, music, physical education, free reading, or playtime. Middle school students like activities such as "our music," free reading, and social time. All students are motivated by any activity called a party.

Material incentives include rewards of some value to students. These may include food, out-of-date classroom materials, pencils, and books.

We suggest using rewards like these sparingly. In the long run a teacher's goal is to have students working intrinsically; accomplishing the activity is rewarding because the student has achieved his or her goal.

Students also behave to avoid penalties. A penalty is something undesirable that students must receive or do because their behavior was not appropriate (Evertson et al., 1989). Penalties should be selected in advance. When students are aware of the consequences of not following rules and procedures, they behave more appropriately. Planning ahead for penalties allows teachers to give a standard, consistent response to particular types of student misbehaviors.

Penalties must be something that the students do not like. During our visits we observed some penalties that were especially effective. These included loss of recess time, loss of lunch time (waiting in the outer office five minutes), and loss of privileges (not allowed to move freely in the classroom).

Most schools have some system of detention or in-school suspension for those students who would not conform to classroom teachers' behavior expectations.

We especially like the "White Owl" strategy that is used at Crawford School. Instead of sending a misbehaving student to the principal, the teacher calls the office on the intercom and says, "There's a White Owl in Room 108." The principal or assistant principal immediately goes to Room 108 and asks "Who?" The student is identified and the administrator stays with that student until the problem is resolved.

While we were visiting, the principal received a White Owl call from the physical education teacher. We went to the gymnasium immediately. April, a defiant twelve-year-old girl, had refused to dress for class. This was the third consecutive day that April had not dressed for physical education. Her teacher said that her behavior was unacceptable. After the teacher left, April said angrily, "I don't like that teacher, anyway." The principal told April that he was working with us and that she could just sit in the office while we interviewed him. He later told us that he wanted her to cool off before they talked.

About thirty minutes later, April asked, "When can I go back to my room? Physical education is over."

Principal Martin said, "When you decide that you'll dress appropriately for P.E."

The defiant girl became quiet and tearful. She said in a low voice, "I don't have any shoes."

"Have you talked with Mr. Brown, our community liaison director?" April shook her head.

"I'll take you to him. He'll help your mother get you some tennis shoes."

Mr. Martin left with April. When he returned, he said, "She'll be all right. She agreed to make amends with the P.E. teacher. She was embarrassed because she didn't have shoes."

The White Owl strategy seems to work.

At Meridith School the students who are most likely to misbehave are assigned an in-school mentor. All the administrators, counselors, and special teachers have one student whom they treat as their school son or daughter (most were sons). The mentors see their students every day; they hug them, talk with them, and give them candy. No negative words are ever said to these students by the mentors.

The principal says when one of these students misbehaves and is sent to the office she asks, "Who gets treated the best in this school?"

"Me."

"Why is the most favorite kid in the school in the office? Who's fault is it that you're here."

"Mine."

By now the student is crying and the principal says, "Write down what happened and what you can do to be a better student."

The student has a chance to correct his behavior with only a minimal penalty. Usually the students will behave. The Meridith staff has high expectations. They will not accept misbehavior.

Assertive Discipline is simply a system of rewards and penalties. Many of the model schools (Crawford, Lozano, and Meridith) had adapted Assertive Discipline strategies to fit their school programs.

Canter (1976) developed Assertive Discipline. The main focus of this model is assertively insisting on proper behavior from students. The components of the model include the following:

1. A set of rules
2. The rewards or positive consequences students will receive for following the rules
3. The penalties or negative consequences students will receive for not following the rules; the penalties are arranged in a hierarchy beginning with a warning and ending with a severe clause (parents meet with the principal or the student is suspended)
4. Careful communication to the students and the parents

The letter to the parents from the Meridith staff (Figure 8-3) shows how Assertive Discipline can be implemented.

The Assertive Discipline system is a good beginning management strategy for teachers. Its structure stops student misbehaviors and allows teachers to teach efficiently without losing a large amount of instructional time. Assertive Discipline worked well as a system during the initial years that school staffs worked to restructure their instructional programs. In the long run the emphasis should be placed on systems that help students become more self-disciplined.

One final comment on penalties: *corporal punishment does not help students.* Glickman (1991) reports that there is no research that shows long-term benefits from paddling students. The least successful schools are the most punitive. What corporal punishment does is make students comply out of fear. What students learn is that physical might is the best way to solve problems. Older students may rebel and physically retaliate. Eliminating corporal punishment helps students to focus on self-control and self-discipline.

Beginning the School Year

The beginning of school is a critical time for classroom management because during this time students will learn behaviors, attitudes, and work

FIGURE 8-3 · *Discipline Letter, Meridith Elementary School, Temple, Texas*

MERIDITH-DUNBAR MAGNET SCHOOL
School of Excellence

Dear Parents:

We at Meridith are looking forward to a very special year of teaching your children. We believe that each student is capable of behaving in our classrooms. There are certain behaviors we need and want from each child so that we can do the best possible job. To ensure quality education, we will not allow any student to interfere with the teaching process.

In order to guarantee for your child the best possible learning atmosphere, we will use the following Discipline Plan.

Each teacher will establish guidelines or rules for his/her class in accordance with the following schoolwide rules:

1. Keep hands, feet, and all objects to yourself.
2. Follow all directions the first time they are given.
3. Listen to who is speaking.
4. Stay in your seat unless you have permission to get up.
5. Bring supplies to class including assignments and homework.

Each teacher will develop a meaningful system for students who behave appropriately to be rewarded. Some of the rewards may include positive notes to parents or students, no homework, line leader, good citizen award, educational games, TV activities, special bonus points, stickers, movies, etc.

If a student chooses to break a class rule, the consequences are as follows:

1st consequence—*Name on board.* This is a warning to the student.

2nd consequence—*Check by name.* Student will stop all classwork and sit for ten minutes. All work missed during this time will be made up during free time or at home.

3rd consequence—*Second check by name.* Student will sit twenty minutes by the teacher's desk and parent will be called.

4th consequence—*Third check by name.* Student will leave the room and report to the office.

Students who severely disrupt classes will be immediately subject to the *fourth consequence.* Severe disruptions are categorized below:

1. *Physical harm to another.* This includes any form of fighting.
2. *Willful destruction of property.*

FIGURE 8-3 · *Continued*

3. *Refusal to obey.*
4. *Any disturbance that prevents instruction and normal procedure.*

It is in your child's best interest that we work together in relation to his/her schooling. We know we can have a very productive year and we will be in close contact with you regarding your child's progress in his/her classroom. Please sign the form below and return it tomorrow. If you have any questions or comments, please call or write them in the space provided.

Sincerely yours,

The Meridith Staff

_____

To the Meridith Principal and Teachers:

I have read and understand the Discipline Plan being used at Meridith School.

_____

_____
Parents/Guardian Signatures

_____
Student's Name

Comments:

Please list home phone number and/or work numbers where you can be reached. Thank you.

_____
Home Phone Number

_____
Work Phone Number

Source: Used with permission of Bonnie Martin.

habits that will affect their performance the entire year. A teacher's major goals for beginning the school year are to obtain student cooperation in (1) following rules and procedures and (2) successfully completing all work assignments. Attaining these goals will establish a classroom climate that supports learning during the rest of the year (Evertson et al., 1989; Emmer et al., 1989).

Getting off to a good start requires teachers to give careful attention to teaching rules and procedures and to planning lessons and assignments. Teachers must resolve student uncertainties. When students arrive on the first day, they will not be certain of the teacher's expectations for behavior or of the course requirements. Students are more comfortable once rules and procedures have been clarified. Teachers can help students be successful by planning uncomplicated lessons those first days of class. This helps students to feel secure and optimistic about their ability to do well in the class.

Good teachers are available, visible, and in charge. They are "with it!" during the beginning of the school year (Emmer et al., 1989). For example, super teacher Harry Wong (1983) describes how he begins his first day of school in middle school science: "My room is ready. All the materials and equipment are in place. I'm standing at the doorway dressed as a professional. As students enter the room, I greet them, shake their hands, and hand them an index card with D-4, A-3, etc., written on it. I tell the students to find their seats. The kids are saying to themselves, 'What's a D-4?' 'What's this guy Wong up to?' As they enter the classroom, they see a seating grid displayed on the overhead projector. They use their index cards to find their seats. They're so pleased to find their seats that I never have requests for changing seats. When the bell rings, I greet the students and tell them how glad I am to be working with them. I give them a copy of the grid and start filling out the one on the overhead by asking who's seated in A-1. Middle school students are pleased to know the names of the other students in science class."

Wong (1983) explains, "Then I introduce myself to the class. I show them my diplomas. I tell them that I've been teaching over thirty years, that I'm good at it, and that I enjoy teaching. I tell them not to worry. Even though science has some difficult concepts, I will teach them well and they will learn."

He stops describing teaching and says, "Picture this. It's your son's birthday. You take him and his grandparents to a restaurant to celebrate. The waiter says to you, 'I've been a waiter for over thirty years; twenty-two at this restaurant. I especially like birthday parties. Don't worry. I'll take good care of you.' How would you feel? Relaxed. Not worried. That's how I want my students to feel those first days of school."

Wong (1983) smiles and says, "As soon as they relax, I hit them with my discipline plan. I teach them my rules and procedures quickly. They immediately know what is expected of them. Then I give an assignment. My first assignments are designed so that students can do them successfully. I help each of them who needs assistance during the guided practice part of the lesson. What I want to happen that first week of school is for students to successfully complete three assignments and to do well on their first science test."

Wong (1983) continued, "Then I can call parents and tell them something like this. 'Barbara is off to a good start in science. Her assignments have been done on time and they are good quality work. Her first test score was 92. Barbara made a neat comment in science today. Ask her about it.' Then I hang up."

We can see why, with a careful start like this, Wong's students do so well and why he has been given so much recognition for quality teaching.

Deliberate planning is required to teach rules and procedures carefully. The first step is to describe and demonstrate the desired behavior. For example, one teacher allowed students to whisper when the "Silence" sign was displayed. She demonstrated for the students a voiceless whisper. The second step is rehearsal. This means the students practice the behavior. In the previous example each student whispered to the teacher, "I know how to whisper." This deliberate teaching helps students learn the appropriate behavior and lets the teacher know if the students can correctly follow the procedure. The final step is feedback. After teachers have asked students to follow a procedure for the first time, they should tell them if they did it properly and praise them. If improvement is needed, specific feedback should be given and students should practice the procedure again (Evertson et al., 1989).

A meaningful activity that helps pre-service and in-service teachers conceptualize their management role is the classroom management plan. This plan is a detailed description of the first two days of school. It is written prior to the beginning of the school year.

The classroom management plan includes the following:

1. A short description of the school assignment (i.e., grade level(s), subject(s), students)
2. A diagram of the room arrangement
3. A list of rules
4. A list and brief description of the procedures that will be taught the first day of school
5. A list of motivation strategies that will be used
6. A description of Day One as the teacher teaches rules and procedures and gives assignments
7. A description of Day Two as the teacher reteaches rules and procedures and evaluates assignments

A sample classroom management plan is included in the appendix.

Writing a detailed classroom management plan requires teachers to rethink their instructional and management strategies. It requires them to become more precise and positive as they talk with students. A middle school teacher explained, "When I was given this assignment, it made me mad. I had been teaching for over ten years. I didn't want to go to the trouble of describing how I would start the school year. But I did it. And, you know what? It makes sense. Last week I read my plan to the entire Language Arts team. I know more about how I'm going to start next year than how I'll be finishing this one."

A pre-service teacher said, "The classroom management plan was a relevant and challenging assignment. I spent more time thinking about my "First Day" than any other body of work in my teacher preparation. Visualization is a critical component of teaching and this is precisely what this exercise allowed me to do."

Teaching rules that contain *value* words requires special care. For example, on the second day of school as a teacher was reteaching the classroom rules to her intermediate students (Wolfe, 1988), she said, "Let's look at Rule Two. Treat others with *respect*. Think about the word *respect*. What does *respect* look like? What does it sound like? What does it feel like? Let's make a list."

She wrote on the chalkboard "What Is Respect?" Then she said, "I'll do the first one. Sharing." She wrote the word on the board. "Let's make a list of what respect is."

The students brainstormed and discussed respect. Their list looked like this:

What Is Respect?
Sharing
Helping
Being polite
Caring
The Golden Rule
Honesty
Assisting

The teacher stopped the brainstorming and said, "We've got a pretty good list. What I want you to do now is think about a time in your life when someone showed you *respect*. I'll go first. This morning when people came in the door and followed my directions, I thought they showed me respect. Can you give me an example of someone showing you respect?"

A girl raised her hand. She said, "A girl asked me to be her friend."

"Lucky you. A friend does show respect. Another example?"

A boy answered, "My niece and nephew got out of my room when I asked them to."

The teacher said, "Their listening to you did show respect. Very good. I think that you're getting the idea. You seem ready to practice observing. I'll distribute a worksheet to you. What I want you to do is observe at lunch today. Look for examples of respect in the lunchroom, in the restrooms, in the hall, and on the playground. Record four different examples. Explain how each situation showed respect (Wolfe, 1988)."

The Social Skills Model

Another way to teach value words is with coperative grouping. The social skills model is a sequential plan so that students master the social skill and can use it in the classroom and in other settings. In the social skills lesson that follows, a primary teacher teaches her students how they can *encourage* each other to participate and to achieve. There are five steps in the social skills cooperative group lesson (Vasquez, Slavin, & D'Arcangelo, 1990).

1. Help students see a need for the skill.

   The teacher began: "The idea that I want to teach you today is encouragement. In social situations such as parties or games, how do others respond when you encourage, compliment, or congratulate them?"

   "They like you."

   "They want to be near you."

   "Right," responded the teacher. "That's the reason that we're working on this skill. Other people like you more when you know how to encourage and to support them. People with these skills get invited to birthday parties."

2. Define the skill clearly and specifically.

   The teacher explains: "My dictionary states that encouragement means to inspire with hope, courage, and confidence. What I want you to do is to watch a short role play from our study about Rosa Parks. Nicole will play Rosa Parks. David will be Mr. White Gentleman. Shannon will be the Audience. When the role play is over, Shannon will encourage and support the role players. Watch what Shannon does carefully.

Mr. White Gentleman: Hey, Lady, get up. I want to sit down.

Rosa Parks: No, Sir. I worked hard all day. I have the right to sit down.

Mr. White Gentleman: Lady, if you don't get up, I'll call the police.

Rosa Parks: No! I won't get up. I'm tired of being treated different just because I'm black.

Audience: Bravo! Bravo! You were both fabulous. I was so impressed! (Walked to Nicole). Nicole, you were fantastic. I could really tell that you had had enough (Hugged Nicole). Congratulations! (Walked to David). David, you were so good. If I were Rosa Parks, I'd have flown out of my seat. You're such a good actor. (Patted David on the shoulder). You both were awesome."

The teacher asked, "How did Shannon encourage Nicole and David?"

"She complimented them."

"She said 'Awesome.'"

"She gave them a pat on the back."

The teacher smiled and said, "Good observations. Now what I want you to do is help me make a T-Chart about encouragement. On the left side of the T let's list what encouragement looks like and on the right side what it sounds like" (Vasquez, 1990).

The group made a T-Chart (see Figure 8-4).

3. Set up practice sessions and encourage mastery.

Once the social skill *encouragement* has been introduced, students need to practice it in cooperative groups. Teachers usually choose a simple activity that allows students to focus on *encouragement* without having to deal with mastering academic content.

The teacher explained the cooperative group activity: "In your trios I want each person, one at a time, to work on an art design,

FIGURE 8-4 · *T-Chart for the Value Word* Encouragement

ENCOURAGEMENT

Looks Like	Sounds Like
pat on the back	"way to go!"
smile	"awesome."
high fives	"good try!"
hugs	"okay!"
thumbs-up sign	"excellent!"
applauding	"super!"
nodding the head	"nice job!"
touching the shoulder	"neat!"

Source: Adapted from B. Vasquez, R. Slavin, and M. D'Arcangelo, *Cooperative Learning* (videotape series) (Alexandria, VA: Association for Supervision and Curriculum Development, 1990).

and the other two to encourage and compliment the design. I will be moving around the classroom monitoring your groups. I will be observing each group. Each time I hear you encourage someone, I will put down a tally mark. Your group will earn bonus points if I hear everyone in your group encourage others at least three times" (Vasquez, 1990).

Another strategy to teach a social skill is to assign roles within the cooperative group. A student in the encourager role sees that everyone participates. A student in the observer role checks the number of times the social skills were practiced.

4. Provide time for students to process.

The teacher stopped the groups and said, "Now what I want you to do is talk in your group about what went well and where work is needed. How did you *encourage?* What did it sound like? What did it look like? Rate your group on a scale of one to five."

The groups began to discuss the activity. In a few minutes the teacher approached one group.

"What's the score that you gave yourself?"

"Four."

"What's the reason? Why a four?"

The students replied, "We didn't compliment enough."

"OK," said the teacher. "That can be in your improvement section. What I observed was that the group members moved very close together. Moving in like that also demonstrates encouragement and support. And you did compliment. You're off to a good start."

Processing takes time, but it's worth the time. It's the step that causes the kids to decide to improve.

5. Encourage continued use of the skill.

"Congratulations! I believe that we're off to a good start in using *encouragement* strategies!" exclaimed the teacher. "I want you to think about *encouragement.* How it felt when someone complimented you. How it felt when someone encouraged you. Did you want to do more work on your design? Did it boost your ego? I'm seeing lots of heads nodding 'Yes.' What I want you to do is to continue to encourage and support others in the classroom and out of the classroom."

Teaching social skills like encouragement and respect works better when teachers remind children to practice these skills at home.

Letters to parents help children learn the social skills because it gives parents opportunities to reinforce their child's learning. After social skills instruction parents comment that their children are more polite, understanding, encouraging, and supportive. They are especially pleased because sibling relationships improve.

Transitions

At the end of the reading group, the teacher asked the 6- and 7-year-olds, "What is willpower?"

A boy replied, "You want to hit someone, but you don't."

A girl said, "You save some candy to eat later."

The teacher smiled and said, "Use your willpower. Return to your seats quietly and start working on your reading assignments."

The students returned to their seats and began working.

This is an example of an effective transition. The interval between any two activities is a transition. At first, transitions may seem to be minor concerns. Kounin's (1977) research concluded that teacher's abilities to manage smooth transitions and to maintain instructional momentum were more important to student productivity and classroom control than any other preventive discipline technique. He found that there was an important relationship between student behavior and movement within and between lessons.

In many classrooms a surprisingly large amount of time is spent in transition from one activity to another. What causes these time wasting transitions (Kounin, 1977)?

1. *Poor planning*—the teacher is not ready for the next activity
2. *Jerkiness*—the failure to move smoothly from one activity in the lesson to another
3. *Slowdowns*—overdwelling or spending too much time on directions and explanations, or lecturing about inappropriate behaviors.

Good movement within and between lessons is achieved through momentum and smoothness. Momentum refers to pacing and is indicated by lessons that move along briskly. Smoothness means a smoothly flowing lesson that has continuity, as opposed to jerkiness.

The following are examples of smooth transitions that we observed in our school visits.

"You're doing well for the second day of division." Stand up and stretch." Students stretched for fifteen seconds. "OK. Be seated. Get out two pieces of paper. We're ready for writing." We then observed this group stay on writing tasks for forty minutes.

Six middle school students were working math problems at the chalkboard; the remainder of the class was working the same problems at their seats. "OK. Switch. Boys, give your chalk to girls. Girls, give your chalk to boys." The transition was very smooth and quick.

"Put your hands over your mouth and exchange your papers." This teacher told us that students can only whisper with their hands over their mouths.

Students were taking a timed test. "Stop. Put all pencils away. Red marking pencils only. We're going to mark our own papers with our grading pencils."

One teacher had an unusual (and effective) technique for handing in papers. She said, "May I have the papers in alphabetical order, please." The students quickly lined up and filed by the teacher. The teacher made a comment—mostly praise—to each student. She later told us, "Young children can quickly learn to line up alphabetically. Movement like this lets me see how the kids have done. It takes the place of standing and stretching time."

The students returned quietly to their classroom from physical education. They stood in silence behind their chairs. After forty seconds, the teacher said, "Thank you for waiting so quietly. Be seated. Please get out your language arts books." This teacher told us that her students were "hyper" when they came back from physical education and that standing quietly calmed them down. We observed a very creative and on-task lesson after that transition.

Methods for making smooth transitions include the following (Evertson et al., 1989):

1. Arrange the classroom for efficient movement.
2. Have materials ready for the next lesson.
3. Establish beginning-of-lesson and end-of-lesson routines with clear expectations for student behavior.
4. Do not relinquish students' attention until you have given clear instructions for the next activity (i.e., "You are going to underline the nouns in these sentences. Now get in groups of three to complete this task.").
5. Usher transitions (i.e., "You will have five minutes to finish your math assignment. At 2:15 we will begin science.").
6. Don't wait for one or two students and hold up the rest of the class. Monitor the dawdlers to find out why they are having trouble. Then give them individual feedback and close supervision.

Summary of Preventive Discipline Strategies

Much emphasis in this chapter has been on preventive discipline strategies. A key to successful management is prevention. Teachers do not have to deal with misbehavior that never occurs.

The first set of preventive strategies relates directly to teacher behavior. These include teacher behaviors such as clarity, firmness, with-it-ness, ripple effect, proximity, avoiding roughness, monitoring, and signals. All these behaviors are designed to keep students on task and productive.

The second set of strategies relates to teacher planning. These include (1) organizing the classroom so that the room arrangement does not cause management problems, (2) developing a set of rules and procedures that communicates behavior expectations to students, (3) preparing accountability strategies to make certain students complete assignments and homework, (4) using rewards and penalties to encourage students to work hard and to follow class rules and procedures, and (5) beginning the school year by carefully teaching rules and procedures and by getting students to complete all work assignments.

The importance of transitions within and between lessons was also emphasized.

Careful Teacher Talk

In an early childhood center there is a covered play area so that young children can have outdoor activities even on rainy days. Children are allowed to play in all parts of that play area except a bricked area near a large plate glass window. On the day we observed, a young child was riding a tricycle on the bricked area.

"What are you doing?" the teacher asked.

The boy replied, "I'm riding my tricycle." The boy suddenly looked down, "on the bricks."

"Is that against the rules?"

"Yes, I'm going to ride way over there."

This simple dialogue reflects careful teacher talk. By asking the question, "What are you doing?" correcting the behavior becomes the student's problem. The child's simple solution, "I'm going to ride way over there," is a satisfactory solution. However, careful teacher talk like this is not easy to achieve.

Most teachers would say, "Stop riding on the bricks!" Stopping the tricycle rider becomes the teacher's problem. A tug-of-war may develop: "Can't catch me" or "Can't make me." Careful teacher talk using the question, "What are you doing?" causes the student—not the teacher—to own the problem. This is an important difference. In this situation the teacher's careful dialogue with the student had prevented a discipline problem from occurring. Learning to speak appropriately while handling a discipline problem is an important teaching technique.

The preceding dialogue was based on Glasser's (1969) reality therapy approach to school discipline. This eight-step model provides an appropriate structure for talking with misbehaving students. The questions from the first few steps, "What are you doing?" and "Is it helping you?" are very useful for talking with misbehaving students. The steps of the model are as follows:

1. *Be personal.* This recommendation relates to the relationship between teachers and students. Glasser (1969) encourages teachers to become friends with their students. Once this relationship has been established, the classroom can be viewed as a personal, friendly, caring place. The teacher who is a friend can say, "I accept you but not your behavior."

2. *Refer to present behavior.* What are you doing? This is the key in reality therapy. Deal in the present. Nothing in the student's past will make any difference once the student learns to behave properly in the present. "What" is the important word. "What are you doing?" "What is the problem?" Questions like this help teachers work with students' present behavior, not past mistakes.

3. *Stress a value judgment.* It is critical that the student "values" changing the behavior. When the teacher in this step asks questions such as, "Is it against the rules?" "Is it helping you?" "Is it helping me teach the lesson?" The student must answer, "No, it's not helping me or you."

4. *Make a plan.* Plans usually work best if they are made jointly by the teacher and the student. If a student can choose from alternate plans, the process works better. For example, a student wants to stop bothering students as he walks through the classroom. One plan might be to stay at his desk; another could be to walk with his hands at his sides. The student would probably choose to walk with his hands at his sides.

5. *Get a commitment.* The student should commit to the plan for a short period of time. A day. Three days. A short time frame allows the plan to be achieved quickly and allows the discipline sequence to end.

6. *Do not accept excuses.* All teachers have heard excuses: "The dog ate my homework." "I was late because I was kidnapped." Glasser (1969) recommends that no excuses be accepted. The teacher should say, "No excuses. We made a plan. You said you were going to do it. When are you going to do it?" In careful teacher talk, questions with "why" should not be used because they are usually answered with excuses.

7. *Do not punish.* If a student does not follow the plan, Glasser (1969) recommends no punishment. He says students should suffer the natural consequences for the misbehavior.

8. *Never give up.* Glasser (1969) believes that teachers who make a difference work with students longer than the students expect them to. Achieving results with misbehaving students takes time.

An example of careful teacher talk using the reality therapy model follows. Mr. Hubel has personal, friendly relations with his middle school students. During social studies he observes Damon poking Anna with a pencil. Mr. Hubel walked to Damon. "What are you doing?"

"Nothing."

"What I saw was you poking Anna with your pencil."

"Sorry."

"Is it helping you to poke Anna?"

"No, I'm in trouble now."

"How could you stop bothering Anna?"

Damon thought and then answered, "I could move my desk away from her or I could change seats."

"Choose one."

"I'll move my desk."

"We'll try your plan for two days."

Careful teacher talk also prevents future discipline problems.

Cooperative Discipline

The theoretical basis for Cooperative Discipline is that children and youth *choose* different behaviors to feel significant and important in different groups—the class, the family, the Scout troop, the Little League team. By recognizing this need to belong, Alpert (1989) says teachers have a strategy to help students choose appropriate behavior to achieve their special place in the classroom. Cooperative Discipline has adopted the works of Rudolf Dreikurs (1968; Dreikurs & Cassel, 1972; Dreikurs, Grunwald, & Pepper, 1982) for today's classrooms.

Cooperative Discipline is an approach that teachers use with individual students. It is not a group strategy. We encourage teachers to use the approach to help the students who keep them awake at night because they can't figure them out.

The basic concepts of behavior are the following (Alpert, 1989):

1. Students choose their behavior.
2. The ultimate goal of student behavior is to fulfill the need to belong.
3. Students misbehave to achieve one of four mistaken goals: attention, power, revenge, and avoidance of failure.

Students choose their behavior. All students want recognition; most behavior or misbehavior occurs when students attempt to get recognition. This concept is illustrated by the behavior of Katie in language arts and mathematics classes.

In her 8:30 language arts class Katie pays attention, contributes to class discussion, and completes her assignments. Katie's language arts teacher describes her as a bright, cooperative eighth-grader who works well with her peers. The next period in math Katie is sullen, mutters obscene words, talks out of turn, and refuses to complete her assignments. The math teacher describes Katie as a nuisance who interferes with his teaching and distracts the other kids.

Why the difference in Katie's behavior? The school rules have not changed. Katie's family background has not changed. In both classes Katie has *chosen* the behavior that makes sense to her. In language arts she receives recognition by cooperative behavior. In mathematics she receives recognition by misbehaving. When teachers remind themselves that both of Katie's behaviors are based on choice, they have some strategies to help her choose her behavior.

The ultimate goal of student behavior is to fulfill the need to belong. The need to belong means to feel significant and important in the group. It's a basic need of students in elementary and middle schools.

To experience a sense of belonging in school, students must satisfy the "three C's" (Alpert, 1989). They need to feel *capable* of completing assignments in a manner that meets the standards of the school. They need to feel that they can *connect* successfully with teachers and classmates. They need to know they *contribute* in a significant way to the group. Classrooms must be structured so that students can achieve, feel successful, and develop quality relationships.

One can see how Katie easily achieved the three C's in language arts. Katie *connects* because her teacher believes she is bright and has good relations with her peers. She *contributes* by exchanging ideas and participating. She feels *capable* because her work is sastisfactory. In mathematics she achieves recognition by misbehaving. She *connects* with the math teacher by making him respond to her misbehavior. She satisfies her need to feel *capable* by refusing to do the work. If she had completed the assignment and failed, she would have felt incapable. Unfortunately, the math class is not structured so that Katie can *contribute* in a significant way.

Students misbehave to achieve one of four mistaken goals. They are seeking attention, power, revenge, or avoidance of failure. What do they hope to gain with this misbehavior? In time, their place in the group. At the present they are frustrated because they can't achieve the three C's in a positive manner; so they misbehave in an attempt to achieve immediate gratification. What they want usually corresponds with one of four goals (Alpert, 1989).

The big idea in Cooperative Discipline is not to try to make Katie behave in math but to use techniques designed to convince her she'd be better off by choosing to behave. A five-step school action plan is designed (Alpert, 1989).

1. Pinpoint and describe the student's behaviors that are causing the most concern.
2. Choose the goal of the misbehavior.

3. Choose intervention techniques. Intervention had a double purpose: to stop the behavior occurring at the moment and to influence the student to choose more appropriate behavior in the future.
4. Select encouragement techniques that build student self-esteem. These encouragement techniques are ways to assure the student that he or she is capable, can connect, and can contribute.
5. Involve parents as partners. The redirection of the student's behavior becomes a joint effort of both the teacher and parents.

Lozano Elementary School uses this discipline strategy with its students.

While observing Dreikurs working with elementary and middle school students, we were amazed at his diagnostic skills. he could quickly pinpoint the behavior to be changed and identify the student's goal for misbehavior. Learning these two steps are the keys to successful implementation of Cooperative Discipline. In the next sections we will describe student misbehavior and appropriate corrective action strategies.

Attention-Seeking Behavior

Attention-seeking students are like stage performers; they require an audience. In the lower grades the attention seekers usually perform for the teacher. In the upper grades and middle school they prefer a wider audience. They perform as much for their classmates as for their teacher (Alpert, 1989).

Active attention-seeking students do all kinds of behaviors that distract teachers and classmates. They disrupt, ask special favors, continually need help, use four letter words, make noises, and ask irrelevant questions. Passive attention-seeking students dawdle and work at slow, slower, and slowest paces (Alpert, 1989).

Why do students misbehave to get attention? Because it works. Parents and teachers tend to pay more attention to misbehavior than to appropriate behavior. They nag, scold, or coax the student to behave. Giving attention like this to misbehaving students does not improve their behavior; it reinforces it.

In diagnosing misbehaving students, teachers should note their own responses to the misbehavior. If teachers feel annoyed or irritated, it indicates attention-seeking behavior.

Dreikurs et al. (1982) recommends that teachers ask, "Could it be that you want me to pay attention to you?" Questions like this open up communication between the teacher and student, remove the fun of provoking the teacher, and allow the teacher to implement the school action plan.

Some intervention strategies for attention-seeking behaviors are as follows:

1. *Minimize the attention* to negative behavior. Ignore the behavior, give the student the "discipline look," or use proximity.
2. *Legitimize the behavior.* Make a lesson out of the behavior, have the whole class do it, or use a diminishing quota (If I give you attention ten times, will that be enough?)
3. *Do the unexpected.* Lower your voice, talk to the wall, or cease teaching temporarily.
4. *Distract the student.* Ask a favor, ask a direct question, or change the activity.
5. *Notice appropriate behavior.* Thank students who are well-behaved.

The silver lining of attention-seeking behaviors is that the student wants a relationship with the teacher and his or her classmates. To prevent attention-seeking behavior, teachers should give lots of attention for appropriate behavior and teach students to ask directly for attention ("I need a hug.") when they think they need it.

Power-Seeking Behavior

Power-seeking students feel that defying adults is the only way they can get what they want. Their mistaken belief is; "If you don't let me do what I want, you don't approve of me." These students constantly challenge teachers. They argue, lie, have temper tantrums, and exhibit hostility. Through their words and actions, they try to prove that they are in charge, not the teacher or the principal.

Unfortunately in today's schools, power-seeking behavior is on the rise. In a society where almost no one models unconditional compliance to authority, students do not assume a subservient attitude. For children of controlling parents, school may be the only place they can express power. Teachers must have strategies for dealing with this classroom behavior.

The first thing teachers can do is identify the student's mistaken goal by examining their responses to the student's misbehavior. If teachers feel threatened, angry, frustrated, or fearful, it indicates power-seeking behavior. If their diagnosis is correct, students will refuse to stop or will increase the behavior.

Most teachers respond to power struggles by doing the wrong thing — fighting back! That's what power-seeking students want. If they can get the teacher to fight with them, they win. Success is getting the teacher into the power struggle. Whether students get what they wanted does not matter. What does matter is that they upset the teacher. Dreikurs et al. (1982) believes that the best thing for teachers to do is not to get involved in power struggles in the first place. He suggests that teachers ask, "Could it be that you want to prove that nobody can make you do anything?" Allen (1986) calls it a tug of war. He suggests that teachers "throw the student the rope." A student cannot meet a goal of power if there is no one with whom to fight.

The silver lining of power-seeking behavior is that these students do have some desirable personal characteristics. They are potential leaders and independent thinkers. These students will never be human doormats who are walked on or pushed around. By wanting to think for themselves and to control their own lives, they are exhibiting signs of a mentally healthy person. Power-seeking students are a challenge, but their potential makes them worth the extra teacher time (Alpert, 1989).

To prevent power-seeking behaviors, teachers should avoid and diffuse direct confrontations. They should grant students some independence and legitimate power.

Revenge-Seeking Behavior

When students misbehave to get revenge, they are retaliating for real or imagined hurts. Their mistaken goal is, "I can only feel significant if I hurt others." Hurting others makes up for being cruel, and violent. When they are not lashing out, these students often sulk and scowl. They seem ready to explode at the slightest provocation.

Students who seek revenge set themselves up to be punished. When teachers punish them, revenge-seeking students have renewed cause for action. They feel justified for the trouble that they caused. To be disliked is a victory for them.

Underneath the bravado of revenge-seeking students is hurt, devastation, and dislike. Being the target of a student's hostility is highly unpleasant. A teacher's first impulse is to strike back or to escape from the situation. Dreikurs et al. (1982) suggests that the teacher ask, "Could it be that you want to hurt me or others?" Confronting a revenge-seeking student like this is better than the "fight or flight" approach.

Is there a silver lining in revenge behavior? There is if the teacher looks at the situation through the eyes of the student. The student sees the hurting of someone else as a means of protecting themselves from being hurt. It does show a spark of life and hope for improvement (Alpert, 1989).

To decrease revenge-seeking behavior, teachers must build caring relationships with these students. This is a difficult task—to care for students who are out to hurt them. It's hard to react positively to a student who has just torn up your wedding pictures. Ginott (1972) advises that the teacher should "separate the deed from the doer." A teacher who can say, "I accept you but I cannot accept what you're doing" can be successful with these students.

A super teacher told us how this approach worked for her. She explained that she had to go a step further than expected. "You must accept the students and show them that they are really cared for. That's the tough part—liking them. When I can use that approach, amazing results occur."

She continued, "One day a student yelled at me and said 'I hate you!' I said, 'I'm sorry that you hate me because I love you and want you to do well.' It was the first step of a positive teacher–student relationship."

In working with students whose mistaken goals are power or revenge, teachers who avoid confrontations and who remain calm are much more effective.

Avoidance-of-Failure Behavior

Teachers may fail to recognize avoidance of failure as a goal of misbehavior because these students do not distract or disrupt. They just don't try. They don't do their schoolwork and passively refuse to participate in class activities, quietly hoping that their teacher will not notice them. Their mistaken goal is, "If others believe I am inadequate, they will leave me alone."

Avoidance-of-failure students procrastinate, fail to complete projects, develop temporary incapacity (fake illness and so on), and assume behaviors that resemble a learning disability (Alpert, 1989).

What causes this behavior? Students display inadequacy for many reasons. Some fear papers covered with red marks so they don't work. Others feel that they can't meet the expectations of their parents or teachers. Young children who seek perfection stop trying when they can't achieve it. Others won't compete in classrooms where awards are only given to winners, not to students who try hard. Whatever the cause, these students feel discouraged, worthless, and inadequate.

When a teacher feels powerless because a student refuses to cooperate or to participate, it indicates a student displaying avoidance-of-failure behavior.

The silver lining for avoidance-of-failure students is that most of these students want to succeed. They need a structure that provides encouragement and gives them some status. Cooperative learning works well with these students.

Our super teacher friend says, "Encourage! Encourage! Encourage! Because when a teacher gives up on a student their own sense of helplessness is confirmed. It may take three years and three teachers to encourage before this student can change."

To help avoidance-of-failure students achieve, teachers

- Modify instructional methods

- Provide tutoring
- Teach positive self-talk
- Make mistakes okay
- Build confidence
- Recognize achievement.

Helping Students Feel Capable, Connect, and Contribute

The only way to end misbehavior permanently is to raise students' self-esteem. In Cooperative Discipline the three C's are the building blocks of self-esteem. Students feel that they belong when they believe they are *capable* and know they can *connect* and *contribute* successfully (Alpert, 1989).

One of the most accurate predictions of success in school is a student's "I can" level. Students who believe that they can master the required learning tasks usually succeed. In teaching positive self-talk, classroom signs are helpful. Some possible messages are the following:

"You can if you think you can!"
"I can do it."
"With a little effort, I'll succeed."
"I'm smart enough to do good work."
"I can when I tell myself I can."
"I can change how I think and feel."
"I'm smart enough to find all the answers."

The strategies for helping a student feel *capable* are the following (Alpert, 1989):

1. *Make mistakes okay.* Make mistakes tolerable in the classroom. When students begin to talk about mistakes, they learn that making mistakes is a natural part of the learning process.

2. *Build confidence.* Teachers should focus on improvement. Emphasize trying new things by using an example such as, "I'd never have kissed anyone if I'd had to do it well the first time." Show faith in students by saying, "You can handle it" and "I know you can do it." Acknowledge that the task is difficult.

3. *Focus on past success.* Analyze students' past successes and plan to repeat past successes.

4. *Make learning tangible.* Use "I Can" cans. These are large, empty juice cans that students can decorate. Then they deposit strips of paper on which they've written the skills they've mastered. As their cans fill up, students

can see all the new things they've learned; so can their parents. Checklists, accomplishment albums, and flowcharts can also be used to make students see their learning progress in an observable way.

5. *Recognize achievement.* Children and youth love recognition for their progress. Use applause, stars, awards, exhibits of good work, and school assemblies to recognize students for their achievements.

Alpert (1989) says that a teacher can help students *connect* by developing A⁺ relationships with them. These relationships require the five A's: acceptance, attention, appreciation, affirmation, and affection.

Acceptance   The idea that the whole child comes to school means that the teacher accepts students as they are in the present. This acceptance must be sincere and unconditional. To say to a misbehaving student, "I'm not sure why but I'm glad you're in this class," means that the teacher accepts the doer not the deed. When a teacher says, "you're okay," the student is hearing, "I'm okay. I am accepted."

Attention   Teachers give attention to their students by making themselves available to them. They structure their classrooms so that they can greet or say good-bye to each student individually. They take time to listen to their students. They schedule "getting to know you" conferences early in the year and have a sign-up sheet for students who need special attention. When a teacher says in some way, "I see you," the student responds to this attention by thinking, "I am important."

Appreciation   Students crave appreciation. To show students that they are appreciated, teachers should thank them for something they've done to benefit the class, the school, or the teacher. Alpert (1989) encourages teachers to use three-part appreciation statements that describe (1) the student's action, (2) how the teacher feels about the action, and (3) the positive effect of the action. For example, "Eve, when you complete your math assignment on time like you did today, I feel great because the whole class can stay on schedule." When a teacher says "thank you" for an action, students know that their efforts were noticed and appreciated. Written notes are also effective ways to show students that they are appreciated.

Affirmation   To acknowledge a student's positive personality traits (i.e., curiosity, fairness, wit), teachers can make verbal or written affirmation statements: "You are creative." "You are dependable." "It's neat to have such a considerate student in class." These statements have very positive effects on students. When the teacher says, "I know something wonderful about you," the student hears "I am worthwhile."

Affection   Good teachers are not only those who can present content well but also those who can develop mutually affectionate and rewarding relationships with their students (Alpert, 1989). A teacher's affection should be given with no strings attached. It is not, "I like you when . . .". It is simply, "I like you because I like you." This teacher behavior causes a student to think, "My teacher likes me no matter what. If I make a mistake or get into trouble, she will still like me for being me." Affection can be shown by a smile, a hug, a handshake, or a kind word.

Using the five A's, acceptance, attention, appreciation, affirmation, and affection, are excellent ways to raise students' self-esteem so they can connect with others.

Teachers must help students contribute. In their thoughtful book, *Raising Children for Success,* Glenn and Nelson (1987) state that for children the need to be needed is often more powerful than the need to survive. What this means in the restructured school is that classrooms are organized so that each student feels needed and is needed. Students are encouraged to care about and contribute to their class and classmates.

How can teachers satisfy a student's need to be needed? There are two major strategies: (1) encourage students' contributions to the class and (2) encourage students to help other students (Alpert, 1989). When students are empowered to take classroom responsibilities, to have some voice in decisions, to make some curriculum choices, and to help others, their need to be needed is satisfied. The neat result is that the cooperative classroom emerges.

How do teachers encourage students' contributions to the class?

1. *Invite students' help with daily tasks.* Students can inventory books, take attendance, collect lunch money, operate audiovisual equipment, make bulletin boards, and so on.
2. *Request students' curriculum choices.* Teachers can present students with choices about when, how, and even where a certain subject or lesson should be conducted. They can choose to write and publish a book or to write a series of short stories. Younger students may choose procedures such as reading on the rug or at the table.
3. *Ask for students' input for rules.* Have the students convert the rules into a structure similar to the preamble of the U.S. Constitution. They can even develop a class constitution to organize rules and procedures.

The second strategy is to encourage students to help other students. When students help one another, their self-esteem rises because not only do they make a contribution they also have a chance to connect with their classmates. Students can help each other through peer tutoring, team projects, and peer recognition. (Applause, appreciation and affirmation statements, and happygrams are ways students can recognize peers.)

Teacher efforts to encourage students to contribute may especially help avoidance-of-failure students. School staffs who want to implement Cooperative Learning should study the written materials and films developed by Alpert (1989).

The Life Skills Program

A few years ago Crawford School in Aurora, Colorado, had severe discipline problems. In Chapter 4 we described how an Assertive Discipline workshop was an initial step in the restructuring of this school. Today Crawford has an orderly learning environment so that the school goal — "All students at Crawford will achieve at their full potential" — can become a reality. With this classroom management program in place, the school staff is now focusing on teaching their students critical social skills. The goal of the life skills program is that students would leave Crawford able to listen, to use self-control strategies, to send "I" messages, and to solve problems.

Each year parents receive a packet of materials including the forms used in the discipline program at Crawford School. A letter explains that the entire staff is committed to making the school a productive place to work and learn. Forms included in the packet are (1) a sample classroom discipline plan with rules, rewards, and consequences; (2) a set of written rules for behavior on the playground, in hallways, in restrooms, in the cafeteria, and in the office; (3) a notification of excessive absences letter; (4) an in-school suspension placement form; and (5) an achievement award for outstanding behavior. The materials included in the packet are presented in the appendix.

In the discipline letter parents are asked to help the school staff to achieve a consistent discipline plan by reviewing the classroom and school rules, by reading the consequences for serious discipline problems, and by supporting their child's teacher and school.

The Crawford School staff is serious about rewarding good student behavior. Each classroom and the school have rewards for good behavior. Parents of students who receive certificates are invited to an awards assembly. The students are also invited to a special lunch with the principal. Their photographs are displayed on the hall bulletin board. The awards include Citizen of the Month (those students whose good behavior consistently goes beyond following the school rules), Special Person of the Month (those students who are making a special effort to do a good job), and Cool Cats (those students who received no discipline slips during the month). A copy of the parents' letters and these award certificates are included in the appendix.

The classroom management/discipline program at Crawford was in place. There was a safe and orderly learning environment for learning in the school. This was an accomplishment for a school in a high crime rate section of the city with a mobile low socioeconomic (90 percent on free lunch; 70 percent minority) student body. Now the school staff was set to restructure the instructional program to help students learn the important social skills that are critical for their lives.

The Life Skills curriculum was designed to fit the Crawford campus. Teachers were surveyed as to what critical skills their students needed. Four skills were selected. They are Listening, Using Self-Control, I-Messages, and Problem Solving.

Life Skills core lessons are team taught by the counselor and the classroom teacher. The team teaching and posters describing each skill (see Figure 8-5) provide a common language about the Life Skills Program that is used by students and staff. Lessons integrating Life Skills concepts with content from health and children's literature support this program.

In the Listening lessons students are taught that good listeners look at the speaker, think about what is being said, keep their body quiet, say "Yes" or nod, and ask questions. Curriculum materials are available to teach listening skills to different age levels. For younger children, lessons with the I-Care-Cat, Barney Bear, and Pay Attention Owl are appropriate and motivating. For older children, listening triads and role playing is used (Starker & Bencomo, 1990).

We observed a fourth-grade class on a lesson about paraphrasing. The counselor asked the classroom teacher what she liked to do after school. Then the counselor paraphrased what the teacher had said. The pair demonstrated the same activity; however, this time the counselor did not listen well and could not paraphrase with accuracy. They discussed the process with the students. Then they demonstrated again. The counselor explained what she liked to do after school and the classroom teacher paraphrased carefully what the counselor had said. Then the classroom teacher demonstrated with a boy. She paraphrased what he liked to do after school. Then he paraphrased her. The teacher explained that paraphrasing is like riding a two wheel bike. The more you practice, the better you get. The class paired off, and all students practiced paraphrasing.

A positive note form showing a dog barking and saying, "ATTENTION! _____ has been a great listener today." is available for teachers to reinforce students' listening skills.

In the Using Self-Control lessons, students are taught to stop and count to ten when they are angry or out of control. Then the students are to think: how do I feel? Next they choose to walk, talk, write, or relax. They then evaluate: did it work? If no, they choose again. Children are taught to accept anger as a natural emotion and to deal with it in constructive ways. Appropriate curriculum materials are available to teach students to use self-control. Activities include pantomimes, songs, role plays, and situation charts.

Life Skills

Unique Features Include:

- MADE TO FIT FOR CRAWFORD WITH STAFF INPUT
- TAUGHT BUILDING WIDE
- FOCUS ON SOCIAL SKILLS AS CRITICAL LIFE SKILLS
- ADAPTED FROM A VARIETY OF SOURCES
- LESSON PLANS GRADE LEVEL APPROPRIATE
- "EXPANDABLE" CURRICULUM

Specific Social Skills Taught:

- LISTENING
- USING SELF-CONTROL
- I-MESSAGES
- PROBLEM SOLVING

(INCLUDING SUB-SKILLS FOR EACH)

Ways In Which They are Taught:

- PRIMARY: 6 CORE LESSON PLANS
- INTERMEDIATE: 4 CORE LESSON PLANS
- COUNSELOR
- TEACHER
- INSTRUCTIONAL RESOURCE TEACHER OR TEAM TEACH

Ways In Which They are Reinforced:

- COMMON LANGUAGE USED BY STUDENTS AND STAFF
- POSTERS THROUGHOUT SCHOOL
- EXPANDABLE LESSON PLAN MANUAL
- CONFLICT MANAGER PROGRAM
- HEALTH CURRICULUM
- D.A.R.E.
- BUILDING BRIDGES PROGRAM
- CHILDREN'S LITERATURE
- COUNSELING SERVICES

Source: Used with permission of Vern Martin.

We especially liked the song, "When you're angry and you know it, stamp your feet" (Starker & Bencomo, 1990).

In the I-Message lessons, students are taught to communicate by using the name of the person that they are talking to, to tell how they feel ("I feel _____"), to tell why ("when you _____"), and to tell what they want ("Please _____" or "I want _____"). For example, a first-grader is bouncing a ball. Nancy runs by and grabs the ball. The first-grader says, "Nancy, I feel bad when you grab my ball. Please don't grab it." The lessons contain many situations so that children can practice in role plays, with scrips, or with puppets using I-Messages (Starker & Bencomo, 1990).

In the Problem-Solving lessons, students are taught five basic steps: (1) identifying the problem, (2) identifying and affirming the feelings of each person involved, (3) searching for solutions, (4) evaluating the consequences of each solution, and (5) choosing the solution that works best and carrying it out. The chart for problem solving (Figure 8-5) recommends that students stop and ask, "What is my problem?" Then, "What are my choices?" Choose one and do it. Then evaluate: "How did I do?" If the action was not effective, choose again. The lessons included brainstorming, role playing, stories, and problem situations (Starker & Bencomo, 1990).

A brochure titled *Problem Solving: A Guide for Parents and Children* (Starker & Johnson, 1990) was distributed to Crawford parents. Parents are encouraged to use the guide and to take an active role in teaching their children to solve problems peacefully. The guide reviews listening, dealing with feelings, sending I-messages, and problem solving. A worksheet is included to be used as a guide when parents help children solve problems.

One way that the Life Skills concepts are supported is with the Conflict Management program. Forty fourth- and fifth-graders are selected to be Conflict Managers on the playground at Crawford School.

The selection process is quite democratic. Five children are chosen in each fourth- and fifth-grade classroom. The teachers recommend that students who are selected should be good listeners, caring, understanding, and trustworthy. However, the voting is done on a blank, secret ballot. Students receive a ballot numbered 1, 2, 3, and 4. Students may vote for any four students, including voting for themselves, in rank order. The five students receiving the most points are selected.

Conflict Managers receive six hours of training. They learn to help students to deal with conflicts and to solve problems.

The Conflict Managers are scheduled to work approximately one day per week on the playground. They eat lunch early on the days they work. On the playground, Conflict Managers wear orange belts and badges, and work in pairs. Students who break a school rule or have conflicts may have the Conflict Managers help them solve their problem rather than being sent directly to the office. If the Conflict Managers can help students solve their problems, they present the students FRESH awards. FRESH is an acronym that stands for Friends Resolving Every Situation Harmlessly.

Does the Conflict Management system work? The Crawford staff thinks so. Last year there was a 35 percent reduction in discipline slips. This year the program seems more effective.

Posters throughout the building emphasize the Life Skills concepts of Listening, Using Self-Control, Sending I-Messages, and Solving Problems. We believe it's a reasonable strategy for staffs in restructured schools to use to help students become more self-disciplined and be better problem solvers.

Summary

In restructuring schools, teachers and principals must establish effective classroom management and discipline first. Then other changes can be implemented. In this chapter the importance of teacher expectations and school expectations was emphasized. Different kinds of motivation strategies were presented. A careful set of preventive discipline techniques was explained. Then cooperative discipline strategies were explained. Finally, the Life Skills program at Crawford School was described. This new program was implemented after an effective classroom management program had been established.

References

A class by itself. (1985). *Nation's Buisiness,* 73(11): 20.

Allen, R. (1986). *Common sense discipline.* Workshop manual. Phi Delta Kappa Professional Development Institute.

Alpert, L. (1989). *A teacher's guide to cooperative discipline.* Circle Pines, MN: American Guidance Service.

Baker, K. (1985). Research evidence of a school discipline program. *Phi Delta Kappan* 66: 482–488.

Canter, L. (1976). *Assertive discipline: A take-charge approach for today's educator.* Seal Beach, CA: Canter and Associates.

Cooper, H. (1989a). *Homework.* White Plains, NY: Longman.

Cooper, H. (1989b). Synthesis of research on homework. *Educational Leadership,* 47(3): 85–91.

Dreikurs, R. (1968). *Psychology in the classroom,* 2nd ed. New York: Harper & Row.

Dreikurs, R., & Cassel, P. (1972). *Discipline without tears.* New York: Hawthorn.

Dreikurs, R., Grunwald, B., & Pepper, F. (1982). *Maintaining sanity in the classroom.* New York: Harper and Row.

Elam, S. (1990). The 22nd annual Gallup poll of the public's attitudes toward the public schools. *Phi Delta Kappan* 72(1): 41–55.

Emmer, E., Evertson, C., Sanford, J., Clements, B., & Worsham, M. (1989). *Classroom management for secondary teachers,* 2nd ed. Englewood Cliffs, NJ: Prentice Hall.

Evertson, C., Emmer, E., Clements, B., Sanford, J., & Worsham, M. (1989). *Classroom management for elementary teachers.* 2nd ed. Englewood Cliffs, NJ: Prentice Hall.

Gall, M., Gall, J., Jacobsen, D., & Bullock, T. (1990). *Tools for learning: A guide to teaching study skills.* Alexandria, VA: Association for Supervision and Curriculum Development.

Giddings, S. (1991). Read me, please! *The Prufrock Journal,* 2(3): 10–15.

Ginott, C. (1972). *Teacher and child: A book for parents and teachers.* New York: Avon.

Glasser, W. (1969). *Schools without failure.* New York: Harper & Row.

Glenn, S., & Nelson, J. (1987). *Raising children for success.* Fair Oaks, CA: Sunrise Press.

Glickman, C. (1991). Pretending not to know what we know. *Educational Leadership,* 48(8): 4–10.

Hunter, M. (1982). *Mastery teaching.* El Segundo, CA: TIP Publications.

Kounin, J. (1977). *Discipline and group management in the classroom.* New York: Holt, Rinehart, and Winston.

O'Neil, J. (1991). Working harder on schoolwork. *ASCD Update,* 33(1): 8–10.

Rutter, M., Maughan, B., Montimore, P., Austen, J., & Smith, A. (1979). *Fifteen thousand hours.* Cambridge, MA: Harvard University Press.

Ryan, M. (1991). To be young, gifted, and encouraged. *Parade.* June 9: 12–15.

Soloman, L.J., & Rothblum, E.D. (1984). Academic procrastination: Frequency and cognitive–behavior correlates. *Journal of Counseling Psychology,* 31(4): 503–509.

Starker, M., & Bencomo, J. (1990). *Life skills.* Aurora, CO: Crawford Elementary School.

Starker, M., & Johnson, S. (1990). *Problem solving: A guide for parents and children.* Aurora, CO: Aurora Public Schools.

Vasquez, B., Slavin, R., & D'Arcangelo, M. (1990). *Cooperative learning.* A videotape series. Alexandria, VA: Association for Supervision and Curriculum Development.

Wolfe, P. (1988). *Classroom management.* A videotape. Alexandria, VA: Association for Supervision and Curriculum Development.

Wong, H. (1983). *How you can be a successful teacher.* Audiocassette set. Reno, NV: Worldwide Communications.

CHAPTER NINE

Parent–School– Community Partnerships

Effective restructuring results in parent, school, and community partner- ships that are rewarding and productive for student learning and family stability.

*Rock-a-bye baby in the tree top
When the wind blows, the cradle will rock.
When the bough breaks, the cradle will fall.
And down will come baby, cradle, and all.*

This nursery rhyme has been passed down by parents to their children since the middle ages. Mothers and fathers have played the "rocking and catching" games with their babies for generations. They rock their babies and sing, "When the bough breaks, the cradle will fall." And they drop the baby. But it is just pretend. Mothers and fathers grab the falling babies and hug them. Babies love the game. For them, it represents security, love, and joyfulness.

As we think of the family that we grew up in, there was a right way to do everything. "Eat your vegetables before you eat dessert." "Do your chores and homework, then you can play." This kind of child rearing worked for our parents, our grandparents, and our great-grandparents.

Times have changed. Families do not have time to rock their babies and catch them. When the bough breaks, the baby *will* fall. There is no one in the home to catch the baby or to give the baby security, love, and joy.

Child rearing has changed for all parents—rich, middle income, and poor. Dad calls mother to explain that he has to work late. Mother picks up the kids after school or at day care. She stops at McDonald's and buys food. When they get home, she turns on the television to distract the kids as they eat their fast food supper while she starts a load of wash.

This is the good scenario. All day-care workers can describe bad scenarios. The mother or father who was so intoxicated that the day-care worker had to call a cab for the parent and the children. The divorced mother on Monday morning who says, "I hope you've got some diapers. My ex wouldn't buy any. Allyson has been wearing the same diaper since Saturday."

Our society is filled with families who do not take time to care for their children, to help them be secure, to make them feel loved, and to catch them when they fall (Bergin, 1991).

School faculties have to deal with the repercussions caused by families who have changed drastically. Many school programs are out of sync with the high number of at-risk students in their classrooms. Schools are restructuring to meet the needs of these students. This chapter presents strategies to build partnerships between parents, community members, and school staffs. Effective partnerships are required in today's society to help students to learn more and also to become responsible community members.

Home, school, and community relations has long been a part of the U.S. educational scene. Traditionally, these relationships took the form of parent-teacher organizations. They were probably poorly named from the beginning since the name left out the principal and district administrators who are vital links in the system as well as omitting meaningful contact with the nonparent community. Nonetheless, the parent-teacher organization either as a part of the PTA with its local, state, and national divisions or as an independent organization for the building or buildings in the district, along with one-to-one contacts with principals and others, seemed to be sufficient until the 1960s.

With changes in societal values and the meaning of parent and family structures, this traditional parent-teacher relationship failed to meet the needs of any of the parties — parents, students, school, or community. As student academic scores and employment skills failed to meet the demands of a changing world, each group tended to criticize and blame the other for the failures. By the 1980s, several organizations, such as the Educational Commission of the States, the Holmes Group, and the National Association for Educational Progress, began to investigate and report on the "failure of the school." These reports also made suggestions for improvement in a variety of areas: stronger academic standards and preparation for all students; using a wider variety of learning and teaching styles and strategies; greater use of technology in the learning process; and involving parents, community and students in the decision-making processes of the school, particularly at the building and district levels.

Parent, community, and student involvement today varies widely. In the Chicago Plan, some 6,000 parents and smaller numbers of community members and students cooperatively make major decisions with school staff at the building level. Nationwide, many schools have strong parent advisory councils, and some retain the traditional parent-teacher organizations with major roles of fundraising and minor roles in decision making. "Parent choice," where parents select the school their children attend, has also been a controversial outcome of these changes.

During the 1980s, the word *partnership* became the term most used to describe parent–school–community relationships. Schools and districts who have tried partnerships have found them to be rewarding and productive for all parties involved. Many authors on parent-school-community partnerships think they are what the United States is looking for and that the time has come to make partnerships a major part of the U.S. educational enterprise. Some qualities of partnerships are the following (Seeley, 1986, pp. 85–86):

- Partnership is essential and central to school reform.
- Partnership is not just for parents but must include community members, businesses, teachers, students, and administrators.
- Partnership needs to include collaboration as well as participation and involvement.
- Partnership is a new approach to public education, not just a quick fix with some niceties and add-ons to some programs.

The time has come to form a new view of the education our children receive, K–12, and perhaps in higher education, too. All Americans need to encourage and be a part of improvement in education appropriate to changes in technology and our way of life. The discussion in this chapter begins with a foundation for the partnership in terms of principles and interrelationships among parents, school, community, and students and the concepts and competencies of the school staff. Then, school-parent and school-community roles, responsibilities, and interactions are examined particularly in relation to communications and involvement. Student roles and responsibilities in the partnership are also emphasized. While examples are used to illustrate ideas throughout the discussion, the final section highlights successful partnerships for three types of districts — urban, suburban/small city/outer city, and rural. Strong parent-school-community relations are essential for successful restructuring. The ideas presented in this chapter give many choices to school staffs, parents, and communities who are working to restructure their programs.

Principles of Parent–School–Community Relationships

Several principles of effective parent-school-community relationships have been identified (Lipham & Fruth, 1976, pp. 165–168; Sorenson,

Poole, & Joyal, 1976, pp. 211–215). These principles with adaptations are as follows:

- School staffs must work closely with parents. This is a two-way operation where parents visit school, work as volunteers in the school, and participate in decision making and policy-making with the school staff; the staff members make home visits and get involved in the community with their constituents.
- Resources of the community should be used in planning and carrying out the instructional program. This not only expands learning for students but helps the staff know more about their community and involves community members in the school. It is important, too, to include nonparent adults, senior citizens, and others along with parents and staff to make decisions for the school.
- Staff should focus on the students—the most important group in any parent–school–community relations program. Students are probably the main communicators of their perceptions of what goes on in the school—to parents, other students, and nonparent adults in the community.
- Staff should avoid "crisis management." The notion of calling on outside groups for support when a crisis occurs weakens the relationship. The best method is to establish a parent–school–community program in peaceful times and maintain involvement of parents and community on a continuous and systematic basis.
- Staff should involve all parents and community representatives not just a handful of interested, usually professional people in school policies and practices.
- Educators should remember that they do not hold a monopoly on expertise about educational philosophy and practices. Today's public is well-informed and knows how to ask the right questions. Educators need to respect their constituency.
- Communications from personal contact through a variety of media are necessary to reach parents and community members.
- A more diverse parent and community population today requires a more flexible and inclusive program of parent–school–community relations. All groups in the constituency need to be interested, informed, involved and supportive to help allocate scarce resources; resolve conflicts; make changes in policies, operations and curriculum; choose values; and distribute power.

These principles form the foundation for the major interaction patterns among the four groups in parent–school–community relations: parents, school staff, community, and students.

Interrelationships among Parent–School–Community and Students

Major interaction patterns among the four groups are shown in two different diagrams. The interrelationships of parents–school–community, with the student placed at the tip of the pyramid, is shown in Figure 9-1. Here five routes — parent-student, school-student, community-student, parent-school, and community-school — form the basis of communication and involvement among the four groups (Schuster in Sorenson, Engelsgjerd, Francis, Miller, & Schuster, 1988, pp. 120–127). Since each group is a corner stone of the pyramid and each corner can be reached from any other corner, communication and involvement lines run in both directions between the groups.

A second model (Figure 9-2) is a bit more complicated (Lipham & Fruth, 1976). Here, the instructional program is at the center of the action with the teachers and child in constant interaction in relation to the cognitive and affective aspects of instruction. They are supported in their efforts by three

FIGURE 9-1 · *Interrelationships among Parent, School, Community, and Student Role Groups*

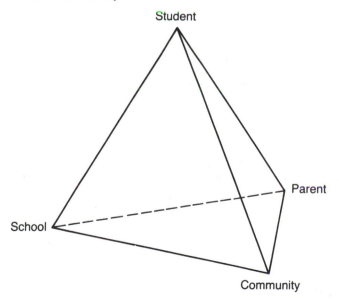

Source: Nancy Schuster in J. Sorenson, J. Engelsgjerd, M. Francis, M. Miller, and N. Schuster, *The Gifted Program Handbook* (Palo Alto, CA: Dale Seymour Publications, 1988), p. 120. Reprinted with permission.

FIGURE 9-2 • *A Model for Home–School–Community Relations*

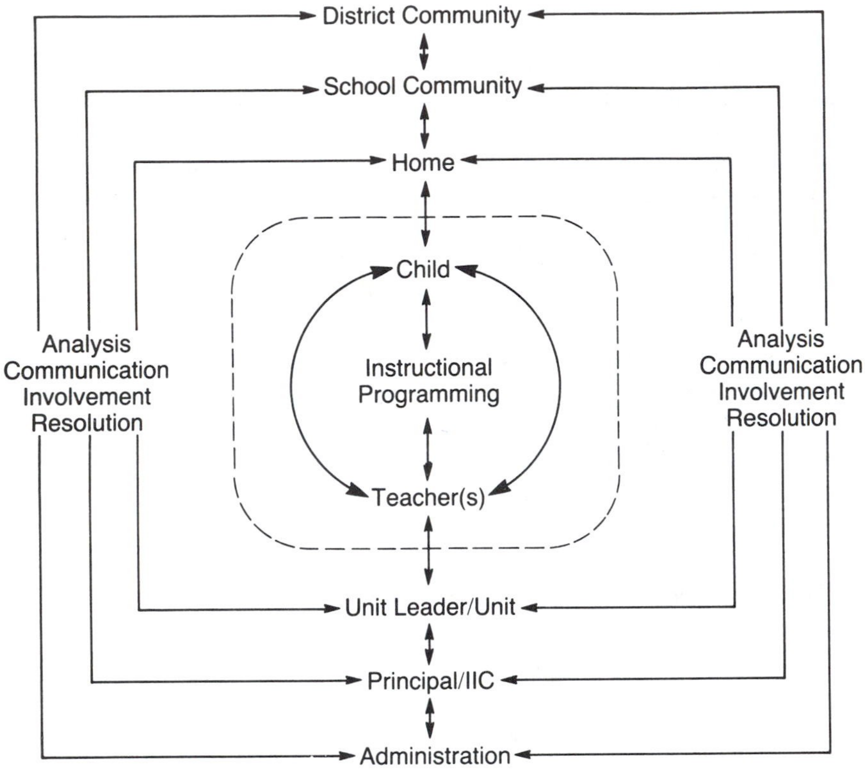

Source: Modified from J. M. Lipham and M. Fruth, *The Principal and Individually Guided Education* (Reading, MA: Addison-Wesley Publishing Company, 1976), p. 170. Reprinted with permission.

groups: the team leader and team teachers, who interact with parents and home; the principal and team leaders as the IIC who, with others, make decisions for the building, and interact with the school community; and the administration that interacts with the local district and state, national and global communities. Interaction among all groups is shown by vertical two-way arrows as well as input and output arrows for each group involved.

Concepts and Staff Competencies

Four concepts — analysis, communication, involvement, and resolution — to develop and maintain a successful parent–school–community partnership are presented here. Competencies staff need to implement the concepts are also discussed (Lipham & Fruth, 1976, pp. 172–183).

Analysis

Analysis involves three major activities on the part of the principal: identification of issues; identification of which groups participate in solutions to the issues; and association of issues and solver groups to develop a plan for communication, involvement, and resolution of conflict.

Issues can be identified in several ways. One is "on the job sense" or intuition, which is not always reliable. A second is by systematic survey, which uses mailed forms or interviews and is formal or informal depending on the topic, desired percentage of response, and available personnel. This method is relatively objective and can be used on a periodic basis to sense changes in issues. A third way is to conduct in-depth, open-ended interviews with people in the school–community. These interviews provide detail to survey issues, often help clarify issues, and suggest plans of action to resolve the issues as well as who to involve in the resolution. A fourth method employs a planned group dynamic process. Processes where groups participate have the advantage not only of identifying issues but also usually of clarifying the issues and identifying priorities among them.

Groups who will solve the problems related to issues can be identified in several ways, too. One is by the "role position" a person holds in the community. This technique will identify leaders and influential people, but cannot guarantee they will have interest in participating or influence in controlling the issue in a school–community relationship. A second way is to identify participants by their reputation. For example, the principal could start with a list of one hundred persons who were nominated when people were asked to "identify persons whom you know are interested and influential in the affairs of our school community." The list could be shortened by selecting only people who receive multiple nominations. The chief advantage of this method is that it is quick and easy to identify people for in-depth interviews and "issue" analysis.

Groups and issues can be associated with each other through several approaches. One is called "stakes" where an issue such as discipline may be related to the physical arrangements of a building such as open space, individual classrooms, and student freedom. Elements of reporting students' progress, such as letter grades, descriptions of progress, and/or satisfactory/unsatisfactory are details with which certain people associate. It is important to get information on which group relates to what element(s) of an issue and to get their input if it is to be solved with representation from all groups in the community.

Communication

Both the way in which the message is conveyed and its content are important. Communications need to be open and clear, have form and direction, and may be verbal or nonverbal. Some elements of communication include one-way/two-way communication; style of communication; vehicles of communication, such as face-to-face, telephone, written messages, electronic mail, and mass media (radio and television). Selecting the best vehicles for a particular type of communication is important. Another element includes the conditions for effective communications. For example, if face-to-face is selected for an important message from the principal to parents, the schedules of both parties need to be considered and sufficient time for analysis, communication, and resolution of issues as well as a plan of action for the future needs to be allowed. The location where the communication takes place is also important. Depending on the issue, it can be in the school, at home, or at a community location such as a library or center. The quality of the message, verbal or written, should be high level and well thought out.

Involvement

Four kinds of activities to provide effective communication among home, school, and community have been identified.

1. Home visits by staff are important. These visits need to be carried out according to usual access patterns of staff, parent, nurse, liaison or coordinator, or social worker. Visitation can be initiated by student, parent, or staff member.
2. Parent visits to the school are usually very effective. Besides showing parental interest, their expectations for the child, input, teacher expectations for the child, the role of the parents, and general responsibility of the school can be discussed. Regardless of who initiates the visit, a formal or informal plan for the meeting is necessary. Parent conferences are a special kind of parent visit — usually held in the school. An aide or the student may also attend to act as cultural or language liaison. Again, plans and preparation on the part of the teacher and other staff are necessary for successful conferences.
3. Parent and community members work as volunteers in the school. Volunteers can perform a variety of functions, but, regardless of the tasks, they are participating on the school's terms and are bound by school policies and objectives. Some schools have in-service programs for volunteers to acquaint them with the school to help them feel at home in the school and, of course, to be sure they know what is expected of them.

4. In many schools, parents and/or community members serve on school and district committees.

All of these areas of involvement are discussed with specific examples in later sections of this chapter.

Resolution

Four strategies to resolve issues are suggested: the rational decision process; persuasion; bargaining; and power play. The rational decision process assumes that the goals of the various groups are the same or mutually shared. Then, participants can work together to achieve common goals. This strategy usually works best for committees and problem-solving groups. Persuasion is often used when the goals of different groups in the parent–school–community relationship are different, but the differences are "changeable." Here, leaders use both reason and emotion to help change peoples' minds. Bargaining is used when goals of the participant groups are different, probably unchangeable, but probably negotiable. Each party usually loses some goals and retains others. Power play can be used when the goals are not only different but also not changeable or negotiable. Since one participant group will prevail due to its power position, there is little involvement. Sometimes this winner–loser mode leaves resentment that surfaces later. The nature of the issue, the attitudes of the participant groups, and the effectiveness of leadership to select the best mode to resolve the issue are all involved in effective resolution of parent–school–community issues.

The discussion that follows focuses on roles, responsibilities, and interaction patterns in partnerships — school and parents, school and community, and students with the three groups. Communication and involvement form the basis of each partnership.

School–Parent Roles, Responsibilities, and Interactions

"Studies show that schools with higher levels of achievement have considerably greater parent involvement." "While parent involvement has been on the decline, our children have been falling behind and dropping out." Schools can become more effective if they do involve parents, as long as they also do the rest of their job" (Henderson, 1988, pp. 147–153). Such statements which are supported by research studies, sustain the belief of the teachers, principals, administrators, researchers, and politicians as well as parents in the importance of school–parent partnerships. Yet, developing and maintaining a strong school–parent relationship is not easy. Nor is parent participation in U.S. schools new, unique, or novel. Parents have served on school committees as volunteers, resources, and consultants and organized together with staff in parent-teacher organizations with various goals, functions, and titles for nearly one hundred years.

Demographic and other changes in society have tended to weaken the ties between parents and school in recent decades. "Sixty percent of today's students live in families where a lone parent or both parents work outside the home" (Gough, 1991, p. 339). Also, differences in cultural background between parents and staff and the move from local to more state control of education brought about by funding changes have weakened the relationship.

Yet in the past years, as media have publicized the weak stature of U.S. students compared to those in other developed countries and U.S. student scores have shown decline or no growth, parental pressure for renewed involvement in the school has increased (Johnston & Slotnik, 1985).

There is considerable evidence to indicate that the school cares about the home conditions of its students (Boyer, 1989); parents of all races and social classes want their children to succeed in school and many parents are willing to help if they can (Brandt, 1989; Smith & Andrews, 1989). Also, there is good news that parent involvement in the schools pays off in terms of student achievement although there is no single best way to go about it (Lueder, 1989; Epstein in Brandt, 1989). A summary of thirty-five research studies indicated that parent involvement with the school in almost any form appears to produce measurable gain in student achievement regardless of aptitude and family background. A follow-up review of eighteen more studies verified these findings (Henderson, 1988).

It is the purpose of this section to explore how successful schools and districts with different kinds of racial and socioeconomic mixes have restructured and carried out successful parent–school programs. While the headings here consider communication and involvement for purposes of organization, these two activities are always interacting in an ongoing program.

Communication

Important intangibles in school–parent relationships are trust and respect. A lack of trust and respect on the part of school staff and parents have weakened or destroyed many successful programs. Staff members often believe parents are invading their territory or trying to tell them how to teach when they get involved in decision making for the school. Many parents are intimidated by school staffs and the school setting. Parents have indicated that a personal touch, such as a staff member who takes a personal interest in their children by calling to alert them about both academic and social problems meets their needs. Parents are "put off" by staffs who were "too business-like" or "patronizing" or who "talk down to them" (Lindle, 1989, pp. 12–13).

Most parents prefer a combination of personal and consistent two-way communications to keep them informed about what is going on in the school and to provide them with ways to share their attitudes, preferences, talents, and concerns with school staff. Communications discussed here including surveys, letters, local media contacts, newsletters, a parent handbook, home and school visitations, recognitions, and ways to keep parents well-informed.

Surveys

One principal used parent surveys in two different schools to help gauge how parents viewed the school program (Hoerr in Hunter, 1989, p. 38). Initially, he sent home a one-page sheet with open-ended questions such as, "I'm happy (or unhappy) about _____," and I'd like to know about _____." Parents could respond anonymously but were asked to indicate the child's grade level. About one-fourth of the parents responded. Over the years, he refined the survey and now uses a Likert-type "strongly agree" to "strongly disagree" response format along with open-ended questions. If parents are separated or divorced, each household receives a questionnaire. There is always an "other thoughts" item for parent input.

The principal mails the surveys to parents at regular times during the school year, such as after the first parent–teacher conference, to get their responses to statements such as:

- My parent–teacher conference was a good use of my time.
- During the conference, information shared gave me a good understanding of my child's current strengths and weaknesses.
- I feel that the school is providing learning experiences that are geared to my child's capabilities.

In the fall, the principal polls parents for their child's initial reactions to school: Is the school meeting their expectations? Was the open house successful? In May, he conducts a general survey about the values of the school, school quality in academics, environment, student diversity, as well as perceptions of special programs and the principal's role function.

Crawford Elementary School in Aurora, Colorado (one of our model schools), also used a survey as part of a year-long review to find out how well the school was meeting the needs of Crawford's students, parents, and school neighborhood community. The survey was sent out in October along with an explanatory cover letter with a tear-off response form, shown in

Figure 9-3. The Crawford Parent Questionnaire, which accompanied the letter, included questions and preferences about the following: background information on the children and adults in the family; school performance to indicate how they felt about the school and their child's performance there, along with how many events and activities they were involved in last year; what factors they thought should be added or improved at the school; activities they would like their child or children to participate in after school; hobbies or talents they were willing to share with Crawford students; questions on contacts and problems in their neighborhood; health services; and, finally, other services they might like the school to offer, such as classes in computers, English, GED, literacy, leadership, and communication skills. Parents were also asked about their interest in receiving information on life-coping skills such as how to deal with stress, drug and alcohol use, weight control, pregnancy, talking to teens, and disciplining children.

Ideas on surveys from two different kinds of schools have been discussed here. Each school that develops a survey would need to gear its questions and concerns to the needs and characteristics of its students, parents, and community.

Letters

Letters are probably the most widely used form of communication between school and parents. They might be of an individual nature concerning accomplishments of a parent's child in events such as Invent America; Odyssey of the Mind; Science Olympiad; or participation in art, music, sports, or other activities. Letters might also inform the parents about selection of their child for a special program such as gifted education or for various extracurricular or extended-day activities. Whatever the message, the letter is viewed mainly as one-way communication, but by asking for parent response with a tear off at the bottom, as shown in Figure 9-3, some parent participation is possible. A letter might take the form of an invitation asking a parent to serve on an advisory committee or a building or district committee to make decisions for the educational program. And, of course, letters are traditionally used to thank parents for help they have given the school as volunteers, aides, committee members, field trip chaperones, and so on. Whatever the topic of the letter, its content should be clearly stated and its language should convey the idea of partnership between school and parents.

Local Media Contacts

Photographs and descriptions of all kinds of events and programs should be available to the local media. Traditionally, media has covered sports and special events such as plays, musical productions, and speech competitions. The media today are more attuned to educational reporting and will cover school activities of all kinds. These activities include subject-oriented

FIGURE 9-3 • *Cover Letter to Accompany the Crawford Parent Questionnaire*

Crawford Elementary School　　　　　　　*October 1990*
1600 Florence Street
Aurora, Colorado 80010
340-3290

Dear Crawford Parent:

The faculty and staff at Crawford Elementary School are undertaking a year-long effort to review how our school is meeting the needs of Crawford families and our neighborhood. Could we do a better job? Are there services we (or someone else) could provide that would enrich your life and that of your children? Can we, at Crawford, help make your job as a parent easier? Think big! Don't limit yourself to what a traditional school does or should do. Imagine the very best—what can we do together.

Cyndi Kahn, a Denver lawyer and Crawford volunteer, is spearheading this project. Some of our goals include raising the ITBS scores at 4th grade by 50% in each of the next 3 years; narrowing the testing gap between minorities and Anglos by 5%, reducing transiency by 50%; creating after-school and off-track programs for as many students as want them; reducing poverty by helping families find jobs. These are ambitious goals, but you may have other dreams for your child, your school, and your neighborhood.

Together, we can build a vision for our Crawford community and make it happen. In January we intend to form a parent/community task force to look at various options, like an after-school day-care program, a family resource center, and off-track enrichment classes. We may ask you to serve on this committee. If you want to volunteer—even better. Sign up at the bottom of this letter.

The attached questionnaire is our first attempt, as part of this project, to survey your views and interests. Please take a few minutes to complete this form and have your child bring it back to school this week. Just do the best you can. If you prefer to be interviewed by phone or in person, please indicate that below. Thanks for your interest and support.

Sincerely,

Mr. Martin

Vern Martin
Principal

- -

Name _____　Phone _____

Address _____

I prefer to complete this questionnaire:

[ ] *by phone interview*　　　[ ] *by personal interview, please call to arrange*

[ ] *I want to work on the Crawford Community Task Force, which will start in January 1991.*

[ ] *I am interested in attending free parenting/leadership classes at Crawford. Please send more information.*

special activities such as dramatizations and the young author's fair in language arts; math fairs and competitions; science special classes, fairs, and competitions; social studies displays and simulations; or a variety of inter-disciplinary activities and uses of all kinds of technology.

The principal and staff might want to include the work of parents in the school as a particular focus of their publicity to strength their partner-ship. And, of course, announcements on meetings for parents and community members should be sent to the appropriate departments of newspapers, radio, and television stations on a routine basis.

Some steps one school used to get the staff more involved in media coverage included the following (Lipham & Fruth, 1976, p. 93):

- Principal encouraged team leaders and teachers to report tangible, visi-ble, and successful events and activities from their age/grade levels to the appropriate media. Teachers responsible for special programs in art, music, and physical education reported on their projects and the principal and administration reported schoolwide and districtwide activities.
- Principal encouraged staff members, in groups of four or five, to visit newspaper, radio, and television offices to meet people responsible for education reporting. Here they got involved in give and take sessions on the capabilities of each type of media. Getting to know each other encouraged future telephone contacts from teachers when something media worthy was going to happen at the school; it also encouraged media people to check on "what's up" occasionally.
- Pictures were taken at the school to accompany all media releases. These pictures could also be used in the school newspaper and parent newslet-ter as well.
- Media education personnel were placed on the invitation list to all school activities. Often letters were followed up by personal telephone invitations.
- Students in the intermediate grades, middle school, and high school published their own newspapers to learn the basic production process. Some older students also produced videotapes about the school and broadcast them over the local cable access channel.
- The staff and, in middle and high school, staff and students aggressively provided articles and pictures to the newspaper and other media and asked the media to contact them for more information. Staff, students, and parents also volunteered for television and radio interviews.

Once established, these kinds of contacts with the media will pay off for both school and media units. The media knows that staff and students have a wide variety of interesting activities going on and often call the school asking, "Isn't it about the time you have your Heritage Fair," or "What special programs could we tell our readers [or listeners] about this time?" Two-way communication with local media provides an ongoing partnership between school with parents and community as well as providing a history of school events and activities.

Newsletters

Most schools have a newsletter that is monthly or quarterly and goes to parents, school board members, and often to members of the school community. Copies might also be sent to media contacts and leaders in the wider district community. It can be edited by school personnel, parents, community members, or a combination of these. Contributions of articles should come from all parties — staff, parents, community members, and, on occasion, students. Some of the goals of the newsletter include the following:

- A chronicle of school meetings, events, and programs
- A place to invite parents and community to future meetings, events, and programs
- A vehicle for the principal to communicate with parents about what's happening in the school at various age/grade levels
- A vehicle to let parents know about what is happening in the larger state and national communities that might affect their schools
- Special columns such as reviews of new books, television programs or events related to school that might be of interest to parents

Today it is relatively easy and inexpensive to produce an attractive newsletter using computer software designed for that purpose. A variety of typefaces and sizes in most computer programs, along with graphic capabilities help whoever develops the newsletter to produce an interesting product. Reproducing photographs with the articles requires a little more sophisticated printing process. Looking back on several years of a school's regularly published newsletter probably provides its best history of accomplishments. At one of our model schools, parents produce *The Bowman Banner* each month.

Parent Handbook

The parent handbook covers general information about policy and goals of the school that might be of interest to parents and community. Some specific items include the following:

- A schedule of parent–school events, such as a meeting of the parent-staff organization and parent-teacher conference days
- A schedule of dates for special school events and vacations

- A listing of the goals of the school, including what they expect their students to accomplish
- A listing of names, titles, and phone numbers of offices, principals, team leaders, district superintendent, and perhaps school board members
- A list of special awards, accomplishments, and milestones of the school currently and during previous years

A special section of the handbook might deal with the ways parents could get involved with the school such as the following (Lipham & Fruth, 1976, p. 194):

- Join us for lunch any day—just let us know in the morning that you plan to come.
- Visit classes—make your date through the school office; visits can be arranged from mid-semester through mid-May.
- Informal parent-staff coffees offer a chance for parents and staff to interact and to share what they're doing and thinking. Coffees are scheduled for the third Thursday of every month from 4–6 P.M.
- Want to get involved in the school? Our students need your talents and skills to help us offer a richer program. We'd love to have you work with us. Let us know if you can help!
- The statement of goals and objectives of the school's parent-staff organization and the name, address, and phone numbers of a person to contact if persons want more information on joining the organization and getting involved in its work.

Descriptions of the content of two parent handbooks are given in the last section of this chapter.

Recognitions

"The human desire for recognition is eternal" as most teachers and other staff know. Recognition can be as simple as a verbal, "You did a great job" and as elaborate as a scholarship. Recognitions can be abstract and concrete, but, regardless of the form, it is a good idea to be sure that parents know that the student has been recognized and why the student received the recognition. Letters, which were discussed above, often accompany or are a follow up to student recognition, but some schools find telephone calls are more effective.

Emerson, an urban elementary school in Rosemead, California, found combining concrete recognitions with a phone call to parents in their native language to explain why the student received the recognition to be its most effective means of communication (Davis, 1989). Each week every teacher in the school selected two students from his or her classroom to honor. One as "student of the week" who was awarded a blue ribbon and a second as "super reader of the week" who received a red ribbon. Ribbons were awarded by the local PTA and were presented at Friday assemblies. Forty-two ribbons were awarded each week, or 1,470 per year, and over the nine years of the program, 13,230 ribbons were given.

Each teacher completed a simple "reason" slip for each award. Then, in evenings or on the weekends, people who spoke the native language of the parents (Emerson had parents with nineteen different languages or dialects) would call the parents and explain why the student won the ribbon. This was also an opportunity to tell parents how proud the school and teacher were of the child's efforts and to find out some of their concerns. Callers included the principal, his wife, home/school coordinators, and community members with foreign language capabilities. The principal estimated that parents of a child who attended Emerson for seven years received seven to fourteen positive calls. He suggested that parents who had received so much positive information about their child's education found it hard to resist when they were asked to become involved in any phase of the school's activities.

Many suburban, small city, and rural schools send home "positive notes" and follow up with a phone call as they deem necessary. Any kind of award and follow-up parent involvement is inexpensive and seems to reap rewards for the school as well as motivating the student to keep working.

Visitations

Visits are a form of two-way communication—parents visit schools and staff visit homes. Parent visits to school should be encouraged on a regular basis, and all parents, not just those "interested" few, should be encouraged to come. A conference in relation to the visit is usually necessary to make the effort worthwhile for both staff and parents. An underlying philosophy of parent visits might be, "All kids can get more out of school." Objectives related only to how the student is doing but focusing on how the school and parents, working together, can enhance the student's education need to be considered. For students who are having difficulties, academic or behavioral, some objectives and activities include the following:

- Parent observes some of the student actions that seem to be causing the problem.
- Parent is informed about special services—counseling, psychological, learning programs such as for the emotionally disturbed and learning disabled, Chapter 1, and so on—that are available, to help the student overcome the problem.
- Ways the parents can help the child at home—practice math facts, practice handwriting, reading to the child, and so on—are proposed.

- Parent observes child's strengths, such as leadership, verbal skills, art ability, and ways to promote them are discussed.

For the child who is "getting along just fine" but probably could get more out of school, parents might want to do the following:

- Observe child's strengths and weaknesses.
- Get more information about programs to strengthen the child's weaknesses such as peer tutoring; computer interaction programs in math and reading; and available extracurricular activities, clubs, and competitions to enhance the child's strength.
- Find out how parents can help the child at home by such activities as taking the child to museums, parks, and community events related to the child's interests in the environment and the outdoors.

For the excellent students, objectives might include looking at weaknesses as well as strengths and could include the following objectives:

- Parents observe weaknesses such as unsteady social skills, failure to accept more than one point of view, producing unreadable and messy reports.
- Inform parents of activities, clubs, special programs, advanced placement courses, career information, and opportunities such as taking courses at the local college or university that the school has available for the child.
- Devise a plan for school and parents to help child strengthen weaknesses and enrich or accelerate strengths.

Home visits by staff members—teachers, parent liaison or coordinator, and others—are becoming increasingly popular and effective, particularly in urban areas and rural areas where parents of children tend to have little contact with the school. At Lozano, one of our model schools, home visits resulted in increased parent participation and many parent volunteers. At Ellis School, an urban school in Roxbury, Massachusetts, seventy-five families were visited in the home in one year (Davies, 1991).

At Ellis, four women from the community who had experience in community work in counseling, adult education, or social services were recruited and trained and paid $10 per hour. Each visited four to five families per week. On their visits, they provided information to families about school expectations, curriculum, and rules and regulations. They also made suggestions and distributed material on how family members could help the children with their schoolwork—such as reading to their children and having the children read to a family member. Visitors also provided information and references to family concerns, needs, and interests. Information from the visit was fed back to the school staff to help them better meet the child's needs. Some of the requirements for the Ellis home visitor program were (Davies, 1991, pp. 377–378):

- A new definition of parent involvement is needed that is not limited to traditional parent activities in the school building; and families must be viewed as sources of strength, not as a burden.
- Funds are needed to pay the home visitors; funds from Chapter 1 or bilingual education can be used for this purpose.
- Training must be provided to the family members so they have a clear idea of their responsibilities and gain the skill to help their children.
- A modest amount of support and supervision is needed; a principal or Chapter 1 or bilingual teachers can provide this support.
- Administration and teachers need to be willing to communicate with the home visitors so the work in the classroom can be closely linked to the help the students receive at home.

Modifications of the program at Ellis can be made according to the socioeconomic characteristics of the parents and the needs of the children. Perhaps the most important value of visitation is the way it links school and home so both groups are "pulling in the same direction" to improve education for the students.

Information
Letting parents know about what the school has to offer their children and helping them do a better job of parenting can be included in a newsletter or can be sent home with children at opportune times or can be available when parents have questions or concerns about particular parts of the program. Many kinds of information can be handled in a pamphlet or brochure format while others can be better provided through telephone contacts or on videotape. Information can be prepared by staff, administrators, students, community members, commercial organizations, or a combination of several groups.

Some topics that the information pamphlets or tapes might cover are the curriculum in our school, special services available at our school, why and how we're restructuring our school, keeping students reading over the summer, clubs and organizations at our school, or a series of material on how parents can help students at home.

For example, at one of the model schools, Conrad Elvehjem School in McFarland, the curriculum booklet included reference to the districts' K–12 curriculum goals, the K–4 elementary philosophy statement, an explanation of their instructional management system, "We Agree" goals on the school's basic responsibilities and functions, and the school's commitment to three major goals of education — getting along with others, skills in decision making, and learning-unlearning-relearning. These are followed by descriptions of topics and implementation procedures for the basic curriculum: social studies, language arts, reading, math, and science. Parents who are interested in or have questions about the school's curriculum can gain an excellent view of it from this booklet.

Some districts prepare pamphlets on special program offerings. For example, a description of the K–12 gifted program for the district might include program philosophy and program goals; definitions of giftedness; identification procedures to select participants and percentage of student body involved in program; relationship of program to state standards and requirements; program options available — enrichment, compacting, acceleration; mentoring; and a program evaluation plan.

Some schools focus on ways to help parents work with their children at home. Research on homework indicates that this is an appropriate emphasis. A series of home learning programs were prepared for parents under the following headings: helping children develop self-esteem, how parents can encourage creativity, motivating your children to succeed in school, voluntary home reading, and homework tips for parents (Jones, 1991). Several activities that parents can do or look for are listed under each of the headings following an introductory paragraph. For example, some "homework tips for parents" are the following (Jones, 1991, p. 29):

- Set aside a family time daily when each family member is engaged in quiet activities while the children do their homework.
- Establish a time and place where homework is to be done.
- Make sure your children understand the assignment; if necessary, work through the first question or problem with them. If you can't help them, have them call a friend or the teacher for help.
- For elementary children, check over the completed assignment; sign and date it.

Four information packages using the telephone as the contact instrument between parent and school are described here (Warner, 1991, p. 374; Bauch, 1989). The "dial-a-teacher" program assists parents and student callers with homework. It is staffed by two teams of specialists, paid by Chapter 2 funds, from 5 to 8 P.M. Monday through Thursday. They "lead" students to the right answer rather than giving them solutions.

The "homework hot line" is a live call-in television program and is aired one night each week, 5 to 6 P.M. Two paid teacher specialists help callers with math problems, grades 1 through 6. Callers can talk with the teachers and simultaneously see the problem worked out on the television chalkboard.

American Cablevision and Comcast Cablevision carry the program on their public television channels.

The "parent line/communicator" is a computerized telephone hookup that provides callers access to about 140, three-to-four minute, tape-recorded messages on a variety of school-related subjects. Sample topics are parenting skills, adult education programs, and school policies, along with more than fifty messages on drug and alcohol abuse. The messages are prepared by the Institute for Drug and Alcohol Abuse and the line is open twenty-four hours a day.

The "TransParent School Model" is a more complicated program where parents can find answers to three questions over the phone each day. Two systems are used. In one, the school provides each teacher with an answering machine or electronic mailbox. The teacher enters a one-to-three minute message that describes homework, learning activities, and how parents can help the child's study at home. Parents can call anytime and hear what they need to know. In another district, teachers use a computer-based system to store messages in a computer and direct the autodialer to place calls to all parents or specific groups of parents. The following morning, they can get a printout record of calls completed. The potential for expansion of this system is great, too. Initial evaluations of the pilot program indicated that more homework was completed by students and there was better student achievement; better attendance; and greater shared partnership among school, students, and parents.

While print and telephone contacts each used one "sense" for communication, videotape encompasses sight in color and sound as well as action. Videotapes are effective to convey information on the school's music, art, or physical education offerings. They also show the spontaneity of extracurricular competitions in speech, science, social studies, and other areas. Students can write scripts and operate taping equipment as well as edit the products.

A little effort to keep parents and community members informed can make a big difference in school support. And, of course, parents and community members as well as staff and students can be involved in producing the materials. This information also provides a record of parent—school—community programs.

Involvement

Most teachers, principals, and administrators believe that parent involvement is the key to parent partnerships with the school and community. Many schools and research groups have identified different ways in which parents can become involved. Researchers at the Southwest Educational

Development Laboratory (SEDL) in Austin, Texas, who studied parent involvement in a five-state region found that "promising programs included many roles for parents: audience, home tutor, program supporter, co-learner, advocate, and decision maker" (Williams & Chavkin, 1989, p. 18). They also found seven elements common to these successful programs: written policies, administrative support, training for staff and parents, a partnership approach of "doing things jointly," two-way communication, networking, and evaluation.

Five major types of parent involvement have been identified by Joyce Epstein (in Brandt, 1989, p. 25) from her work on parent involvement in several geographical areas of the United States over the past decade. These are:

1. Basic obligations of parents. These relate to responsibility of family for children's health and safety; parenting and child-rearing skills; preparing children for school; and supervising, disciplining, and guiding children at each age level.
2. Basic obligations of school. These include communications from school to home about the school program and children's progress in various formats — memos, report cards, and conferences — all in a way parents can understand.
3. Parent involvement at school. This can include volunteers to assist teachers and students in the classroom or in other school sites, support by attending school activities; or attendance at workshops for the parents' own education or training.
4. Parent involvement in learning activities at home. Here, the parent assists the child with ideas or instructions from the teacher that are coordinated with the child's work at school.
5. Parent involvement in governance and advocacy. Parents take roles in groups such as the PTA or PTO, advisory councils, and committees at various levels. Parents are also involved in groups that monitor the school for improvement.

Some guidelines and philosophy for parent involvement include (Henderson, 1988, p. 153):

- The family, not the school, provides the primary educational environment for children.
- Involving parents in children's education improves the children's achievement.
- Effective parent involvement is well-planned, comprehensive, and continuous.
- Effects of parent involvement seem to be particularly strong for young children, but may also be effective with middle and high school students.

- Parent involvement at school is not enough; parents need to be involved at home to accomplish significant improvement in achievement.
- Children from low-income and minority families benefit most from parent involvement; parents do not have to be well-educated to make a difference.
- Student attitudes about themselves and their control over their environment are formed primarily at home, but can be influenced by school experiences.

Parent involvement is not a panacea to improve the schools, nor is it just a luxury. It is a function of democracy to participate in a public institution. And, who has a greater stake in the education of their children than the parents? It is the purpose of this section to share ideas and programs that have been implemented successfully with different kinds of student bodies in different-sized districts with diverse populations in different parts of the country. The discussion includes traditional parent involvement activities such as parent-teacher organizations, parent advisory councils, and parent-teacher conferences as well as more recent innovations such as parent centers, parents as volunteers and parent school seminars, workshops, and support groups. The term *parent* as used here also refers to the broader term *family,* which may include grandparents, uncles and aunts, brothers and sisters, and even neighbors who are involved with the informal education of the child (Davies, 1991). In one of our model schools, the extended family (mother, father, grandparents, uncles, and aunts) of an Asian-American student attended conferences and open houses. This may be one reason this ethnic group has been so successful in schools.

Parent–Teacher Organizations

Parent–teacher organizations are the traditional groups that link school and parents. They may be connected with the PTA, which has links to state and national level, or it may be a parent–teacher organization, often called the PTO, that operates at the local building or district level. While it is dangerous to categorize groups in school as diverse as those in the United States, most parent–teacher groups tend to function primarily as fund-raising organizations. Their secondary functions vary widely and their decision-making roles are often heavily influenced by the motivation, creativity, dedication, priorities, and skills of the principal and other members of the school staff. Smoothly functioning PTOs have strong representation through membership of school staff as well as parents. And some groups have added older students and community people as members and representatives on their executive committees. Some are now known as PTSOs (Parent-Teacher-Student Organizations).

Over the past two decades, school populations became more diverse, the number of single parents and two working-parent families increased, and values affected by changes in our way of life and that of the schools changed. Today, many PTOs no longer meet the needs of parents, school, or community and "have died a slow death." Some were replaced by one or more parent advisory councils. Some were replaced by comprehensive programs such as those described under Urban Parent–School–Community Partnerships later in this chapter. Others changed their focus a bit and renewed their efforts to meet the needs of the groups involved, particularly those of the students in the building or district. For example, the PTA at the Manz Elementary School in Eau Claire, Wisconsin, retains a fairly traditional organization. The group sponsors fund raising each year through a magazine subscription renewal program, which seems to be compatible with the school student population, their parents, and school community members. These funds purchase computers, special materials, and playground equipment for the school. The PTA also sponsors an end-of-year event day and picnic for students and their parents and staff. The Manz PTA developed and funded the book cart and staffed the mini-courses described in the Parent Center section of this chapter. They also recruit volunteers for various tasks in the schools according to current and changing needs.

The Manz staff believes the PTA is a vital and vibrant group and shows their support by 100 percent membership in the organization. The Manz School community is basically middle class. The Eau Claire district has limited cultural diversity, is the home of a state university, and is surrounded by a rural agricultural area.

Parent Advisory Committees

These committees or councils offer an opportunity for shared decision making in which parents are full participants with school staff. Committees carry out varied functions such as helping to form school policy on an advisory basis, playing an advocacy role with the community and board of education, forming task forces to deal with specific issues facing the school, and forming and sustaining a vital parent–staff organization.

Committees can be formed in different ways. Some boards of education mandate them and their areas of membership to act as mini boards of education, some are avenues of educational communication between staff and parents and community, and some act as buffers between schools and central offices. Sometimes, principals or superintendents are the driving force behind forming committees. Or, initiatives may come from teachers, parents, community members, or as part of a state research or other institutional group program.

Regardless of how committees start, they need guidelines to function successfully. Some tips for enduring, workable committees include the following (Jennings, 1989, pp. 42–45):

- Parent members should represent the academic, ethnic, and other diversity of the school or district population.
- Members should include parents, teachers, support staff, community members, the principal, and students (starting at age 12).
- A good size is 9 to 18 members: a typical committee might have 4 parents, 4 staff, 4 students, 1 or 2 nonparent community people, and the principal as ex officio. Fewer than 9 members restricts representation and more than 18 is unwieldy.
- Committees need a constitution that states their purpose, membership makeup (elected, appointed, combination; number and distribution), officers and terms, and so on.
- An orientation or training session is essential. Besides promoting interaction among members, it provides information for success. Topics might include roles, authority, purpose, decision-making techniques such as simulations, team building skills, ways to express varying views positively, resources, and so on.
- Committee meetings should be open to all school and community members.

Committee memberships can vary with the tasks they take on according to the needs, resources, and makeup of the community they represent. Regardless of where they operate, they bring together members with varied agendas. Parents want a good education for their children, the principal and teachers want a good education for all of the students in their school, students who are the recipients of the program want a motivating and exciting environment to learn in, and community members who do not have children in school want a good educational program within a budget that people can continue to afford. In a committee, representatives from all of these groups work together to share problems and seek acceptable solutions to them.

Parent–Teacher Conferences

For many schools, conferences have been the mainstay of their parent–school relations during the past two decades. Conference scheduling has become more flexible, many schools have dismissed students for the conference days, and some teachers take the "day shift" from 8 A.M. to 3 P.M. while others take the "night shift" and come in at 2 P.M. and stay until 9 P.M. At some schools, students attend the conference with the parents and teacher and, in schools with teams, the team leaders may also attend. In schools where parents understand only a foreign language, an aide or other community member may attend to make people feel more comfortable and to translate between the groups. Most schools have coffee and goodies available during conference time to increase informality and help everyone feel more at home in the conference situation.

Regardless of the conference structure, parents and teacher(s) are seeking a common ground to evaluate, understand, and improve the child's education. Some tips to help the staff prepare for the parent–teacher conference are the following (Wolf & Stephens, 1989, pp. 28–29):

- Select a comfortable place for the conference.
- Begin the conference with positive information.
- Have dated examples of the student's work available.
- Cite specific examples to support both positive and negative incidents.
- Explain how instruction is individualized to meet the student's needs.
- Encourage parents to discuss and clarify situations as needed.

Some things teachers should *not* do during the conferences are overwhelm parents with too much detail, use educational jargon, be evasive — if a teacher doesn't know the answer, the teacher should say so — or describe their personal problems to the parents.

In conducting the conference, the teacher should start by building rapport. In addition to perhaps offering a beverage, he or she might discuss a safe subject such as the weather or a recent school or civic event. Then move along to obtain information about the child from the parents. Here the teacher becomes a good listener and asks good questions; the teacher must not be negative. When providing information, the teacher has to decide whether there is sufficient time left in the conference to cooperatively design a solution to a problem or whether another conference needs to be scheduled.

Follow-up may be the most important part of the conference. Here, teachers and parents are sharing actions to solve a problem, encourage a child to excel, provide the child with a stronger challenge, or use special services of the school or community. A teacher may want to call the parents after two weeks or so to find out how things are going at home and to report the effect of their actions that have been observed at school. Some schools schedule longer amounts of time for conferences with parents of students who are having "serious problems." Common serious problems are frequent absences, repeated behavior problems, coming to school hungry or in poor physical or emotional condition, or lack of progress in learning areas. A greater amount of conference time allows both parties to be more relaxed as they approach the problem. One of the most common complaints of parents about conferences is that "teachers can't possibly discuss my child's progress and help us solve problems in fifteen minutes."

Many schools and districts like to schedule all conferences, K–12, at the end of the first six weeks' grading period. This helps them establish communication with the parents and talk about any serious situations early in the school year. The "Parents in Touch" program provides a variety of materials for teachers to share with parents at these conferences. These materials include activity calendars, contracts where parents, teachers, and students agree to fulfill certain commitments, and folders that explain school policies on homework, attendance, grading procedures, and important dates of the school year (Warner, 1991, pp. 372–373). "Parents in Touch" believes that parent–teacher conferences for K–12, is an excellent vehicle for two-way communication on matters that relate to student success.

Parent Centers

A fairly recent addition to parent–school relations is a "parent space" in the school building. It may be a room with staff and an elaborate program; a small, former storage or conference room; or a corner or cart somewhere in the building. Whatever provisions are made, staffs from school — elementary through high school — sing the praises of "spaces" where parents can come to make them feel they are truly a part of the culture of the school. In the model schools, Lozano and Diamond, parents were always present in the parent rooms, and they were positive about being in the school.

The parent center at Ellis School in Boston, Massachusetts, transformed the school and made possible a substantial, continuing and positive physical presence of parents in the school (Davies, 1991). This center consisted of a room staffed with two paid coordinators who were school parents and several volunteers. Parents stopped by to chat, plan, work, and get involved in a variety of the school's activities and programs, such as:

- English as a Second Language (ESL) and General Educational Development (GED) classes
- Grade-level breakfasts to bring together teachers, administrators, and parents so they may talk informally in a nonthreatening environment
- Breakfast for fathers to bring male family members into the school family
- Organization of a small library of books and toys for children
- Recruitment of parent volunteers as requested by teachers

Staff and administrators used the center as a resource. They could reach parents easily when children had a problem, make arrangements for events such as open house, order teaching materials there, and so on. About 43 percent of the school's families were reached through the center during the year.

Based on their experiences, the Ellis staff suggests the following requirements for a successful parent center (Davies, 1991, pp. 378–379):

- Some kind of physical space allocated entirely to the parents
- Adult-sized tables and chairs
- A paid staff of parents

- A telephone and, if possible, a computer or typewriter
- A coffee pot and, occasionally, snacks

Many schools in smaller towns, cities, and suburbs have developed more informal parent spaces. For example, Manz School, one of fifteen elementary schools in Eau Claire, Wisconsin, has a very effective parent cart, which is located in the hallway leading to the school media center. The cart contains some one hundred up-to-date books on all aspects of parenting. An annotated bibliography of the books is available for parents and others to review, check out at the school library, and take home. Some of the titles and authors include the following (Manz School PTA, 1991):

Between Parent and Child by Halm G. Ginott
Children at Risk by James Dobson
Encouragement Book by Don Dinkmeyer
Fatherhood by Bill Cosby
Helping Children Cope with Separation and Loss by Claudia Jewett
How Does it Feel When Your Parents Get Divorced? by Terry Berger
How to Keep the Children You Love Off Drugs by Ken Barun
How to Teach Children Responsibility by Harris Clemes and Reynold Bean
I Can't Talk About It: A Child's Book about Sexual Abuse by Doris Sanford
Learning Disabled Child: Ways that Parents Can Help by Suzanne Stevens
Parenting Isn't for Cowards by James Dobson
Parent's Guide to Raising a Gifted Child by James Alvino
Teach Your Child Decision Making by John Clabby

The books were purchased by the schools' active PTA and the bibliography was organized, annotated, and prepared for printing by parents. While this cart is not an elaborate arrangement, it is appropriate in this school and receives praise from both school staff and parents.

Parent Volunteers
One of the common ways for parents to get involved in the school is to volunteer — during the school day, after school, in the evenings, in special events or programs on nonschool days, or in summer programs. Volunteers can take the roles of aide, resource or expert, tutor, "teacher" or planner, manager, or coordinator.

Thousands of parents, along with grandparents, aunts and uncles, and community members act as aides in our schools. They help the school staff in a wide range of work from housekeeping and clerical tasks to direct assistance to student learning (Hunter, 1989). At the University of California at Los Angeles Laboratory School, researchers identified categories of parent competency such as skills in hobbies or crafts, direct knowledge and occupation experience, appropriate knowledge or skills in different cultures, and "willing to help out." Regardless of the school's needs, parents need to be invited to participate with staff when they are working in the school.

A "Dear Parent" letter that indicates that their skills and talents are needed in certain areas such as "knowing and valuing cultural differences," "arts and crafts," "the world of work," or "just helping out" gets parents interested. A tear-off portion on the bottom indicating a request for more information in the areas checked with a space for their child's name as well as their own gets things started (Hunter, 1989). While parent aides do not replace school staff, their knowledge, devotion, and enthusiasm enrich a curriculum beyond the possibilities of most staffs. And these programs are not dependent on school budgets, materials, or pupil–teacher ratios.

Many schools use volunteers as tutors in various subjects or other areas for students who are having learning difficulties or who have had an extensive absence for illness or other reasons. Often tutors have students read to them and tutors help them with words and expressions they are not doing correctly. The tutor can make note of repeated stumbling blocks for the student and report back to the teacher. Tutors can also frequently help students with basic math, spelling, and writing.

Many schools use parent aides in the media center when they check materials in and out, help prepare new materials for circulation, and arrange materials for special purposes. These routine tasks provide contact between the parents and students. Some aides listen to student book reports and others assist children who are working with computers and other equipment in the media center.

Schools with part-time media center directors use volunteers to keep the facility open to check materials in or out when they are not there. Often older students, from grades 4 to 6 also help. Whether the director is full or part-time, aides allow staff to use more of their time for instruction on computers and library skills, teaching special group activities, preparation of "interest tables," and grouping materials for teachers for units of study. Many parents who have not taught but have much to contribute feel more at home in the media center setting than in the classroom.

Parents can be volunteer mini-course instructors in their areas of interest and expertise. Manz School offered a series of ten mini courses called "Manz-U-Cation" from 3:40 to 4:40 P.M., once a week for four weeks, in February—a dark and dreary time of year in Wisconsin. Courses included origami, woodworking and electronics, fishing, Chinese cuisine, "Want to Be on TV?" and Norwegian. All instructors were parents, but, of course, other community members could also be included. Parents were notified of the offerings with a one-page cover letter explaining the arrangements and a brief listing of course title, content, target grade levels, number of students in the course, instructor, and dates. All courses were held at the school. This idea can be varied in many ways, such as:

- A one-day event on Saturday where students can take one, two-hour mini course in the morning and another in the afternoon with parents, staff, and students eating lunch together in the school cafeteria
- A series of ten to twenty summer enrichment courses of eight to twenty hours over a one- to two-week period
- Courses where both students and parents can participate together, such as computer programming, astronomy, archeology, photography, abuses, and so on

Whatever the schedule, mini courses need to be carried out cooperatively by parents and the school for organization, topic selection, instructor selection, space, and publicity. They must meet the needs of students and expertise of parent–community instructors.

Parents often plan and implement special events that are held on an annual or biennial basis. Some of these events are for all the children in the school and others are for special groups, such as special education or gifted students, music or art, science or math, social studies, or language arts groups. Some examples are described below.

"Family Day: An Investment in Our Future" strengthened ties between elementary students and their parents and promoted school pride as well (Smith, 1988). This day was the brain child of a Gary, Indiana, principal whose image of a celebration was families spending a day with their children watching films or videos, hearing speakers, singing together, and learning together. The school staff pitched in and set the date for the event at the end of the first grading period. They formed committees to locate videos and speakers, select activities, make lunch plans, and publicize the day. Students wrote "raps" to celebrate the family and sent out invitations.

Parents, staff, and students started the day by holding hands and encircling the school building. Then, they moved through the varied program, which closed with first grading period awards. Parents and children shared likes and dislikes, discovered each other's uniqueness, and learned to get along with each other. Parents learned about parenting, children learned they could say "no" to drugs, and parents and children danced in each other's styles. The evaluation indicated the 200 parents who were involved found the day "very rewarding," and shared many ideas for the next Family Day.

Parents in many schools plan events for special groups. One event that is sponsored by the community as well as parents is the "Special Olympics" for children with disabilities. Here, children get a chance to experience success and failure among their own group. Television, radio, and newspapers often give excellent coverage to these activities. Sometimes "local celebrities" help with the event. Some districts sponsor a "Special Marching Band" and "Special Art Exhibits" as well as the sports events for these children. The expressions of joy on the faces of both children and parents attest to their success.

Parents of gifted students have special responsibilities in addition to those of regular parents, which include learner, helper, school supporter, source of information, resource person sharing expertise, teacher, and agent for change (Alvino, 1985). Some tasks parents can do to help with the gifted program include the following (Schuster in Sorenson et al., 1988, pp. 123–124):

- Act as aides in classes or the media center.
- Arrange, chaperone, and provide transportation for some trips.
- Share expertise as instructor, mentor, or organizer.
- Coordinate fund-raisers for special opportunities for students.

These parents are particularly important because in most districts local funds are the main source of gifted program funding. Within the framework of the school, these parents and community members can provide opportunities for gifted and other students to participate in a variety of competitions and clubs such as "Math Counts" and "Great Books," as well as local fairs and productions in a variety of subject areas.

Some schools keep a computerized list or card file of volunteers and resource persons and their areas of expertise. New people including parents of new students in the school are added each year. Parent and community volunteer involvement and contributions are limited only by the combined creativity and resourcefulness of parents and others who are willing to contribute along with the initiative, cooperation, and encouragement of the staff and administration. Continued success of volunteer programs depends on the cooperation and mutual respect of all parties involved.

Workshops, Seminars, and Support Groups

These activities need to vary according to the needs and characteristics of the school and district. Regardless of differences, these activities give parents the opportunity for education, guidance, and sharing. They help them learn more about their child's academic, mental, and physical development; gain self-confidence in parenting skills; and often motivate them to continue their own education. These activities should be informal and focus on interaction and feedback by using processes such as role playing, simulations, brainstorming, and problem-solving techniques. Parents do not want to be told what to do. (Jones, 1991). The basic ideas behind these kinds of activities is to promote an exchange among parents, teachers and other staff, and community members — all people who influence the education of the children.

Topics, methods to assess interest of parents, and ways to convey information to parents and others have been addressed in various sections throughout this chapter. Sessions can be arranged using school staff, local resource people, and outside consultants. Commercial programs have also been developed to promote school–parent partnerships. Several of these are summarized below.

The Parent Focus Series is a parent education program offering ninety workshops that schools may obtain from the Parents In Touch organization (Warner, 1991). Some schools offer a series of five to six workshops from the program, others only one or two. Each workshop includes discussion, information, and videos on a variety of topics such as building children's self-esteem, helping with homework, early adolescent development, and teaching responsibilities. Schools offer the sessions during the day and during evening hours and child care is sometimes provided. Sessions are not designated as support groups but often serve that function. People affiliated with local agencies such as the Salvation Army, juvenile court, and family services often come to the sessions to share their expertise with parents when it is appropriate to the topic of the session.

In Indianapolis, Indiana, monthly parent education seminars are held at major work sites in the city to serve parents who cannot come to sessions at the school. Sessions are often held during lunch hours to which employees may bring a brown-bag lunch or the employers may provide lunch. Seminar topics are selected from the ninety offerings of the Parent Focus Series after the interest and needs of the employee parents have been surveyed. This school district believes that these meetings help strengthen partnerships not only between school and home but also between school and community when they are held at work sites. They also help students improve their academic success and reduce parent concerns about child-rearing problems as well as promote a supportive atmosphere among employees. The seminars are cosponsored by the Education Council of Indianapolis Chamber of Commerce and local businesses (Warner, 1991).

Other widely used commercial programs include the following (Jones, 1991, pp. 31–33):

- Systematic Training for Effective Parenting (S.T.E.P.), which runs for eighteen hours. Sessions are usually scheduled weekly for one to two hours. Topics include providing encouragement, developing mutual respect, disciplining consistently and according to child behavior, setting firm limits, exploring choices, and joint decision making. The program also helps parents learn how to reinforce their child's positive behavior. (Contact: Systematic Training for Effective Parenting, American Guidance Service, P.O. Box 190, Circle Pines, MN 55014-1796)

- Parent Effectiveness is a twenty-four-hour updated version of Parent Effectiveness Training (P.E.T.). Developers suggest a series of eight, three-hour sessions, one per week. It gives parents insights and skills for developing responsibility in children and improving family relationships. Specific topics include how to listen and talk to children; changing unacceptable behavior by changing the environment; and dealing with conflicts. (Contact: Effectiveness Training, Inc., 331 Stevens Avenue, Solana Beach, CA 92075.)
- Family Math is a workshop program of six to eight, one- to two-hour sessions. It helps parents and children, K–8, by providing activities to develop problem-solving skills and building an understanding of math using hands-on materials. (Contact: The Family Math Program, Lawrence Hall of Science, University of California, Berkeley, CA 94720)
- Active Parenting is a video-based program partially based on S.T.E.P. It has forty videotaped segments for use in two-hour sessions over a six- to eight-week period. It helps parents with parenting skills, particularly to raise cooperative and responsible children. (Contact: Active Parenting, 4669 Roswell Road, N.E., Atlanta, GA 30342)

School–Community Roles, Responsibilities, and Interactions

Since 80 percent of the taxpayers in some suburban areas and more than 50 percent of the taxpayers in most communities do not have children in school, it is essential to keep the community informed and involved in the schools. It is important, too, to consider an expanded definition of community as school funds come from local, county, state, and national sources. While the community of the school or district may be the most important one and will be the focus of our discussion here, these county, regional — several counties or a cluster of districts around a regional education center — state, and national communities will also be considered. And today our students are also in worldwide comparisons, so we need to also consider the global community. Since parents are also community members, many references to communication with and involvement of community were made in the school–parent section. School–community relations again focus around communication and involvement.

Communication

Information about the school needs to be available to all members of the school and district communities. One way to do this is through the media—not just at budget time, but on a regular basis. Television, radio, and newspaper feature stories; reports; and interviews with staff, parents, students, and community members as well as school-generated releases, which were discussed in detail under parent–school relations earlier in this chapter, provide these kinds of communications to the community. Some general topics for these communications include the following:

- Ways parents and community volunteers are involved in schools—during the day, in the evenings, and on weekends
- Ways parents and community members are involved in programs to improve parenting, help students at home, and use community self-help programs
- Special programs such as those for at-risk students, the world of work, abuse prevention, and gifted
- Field trips to community sites such as business and industry, museums, medical facilities, financial institutions, police and fire stations, and so on
- Community members as resource persons or "teachers" to the school to share their expertise
- Community–school partnerships involving technology, special equipment, and specialized facilities not available in the schools
- Showcasing the curriculum in different subjects so everyone knows what's being taught in the schools
- Preparation of television segments by students, staff, and community members for public access television; these may be assignments or projects for some courses in middle, junior, and senior high schools
- Community sites and personnel related to mentorships, work programs, and students as volunteers
- Student, staff, school, and district awards in all areas

Some schools and districts do not rely entirely on free publicity. They purchase pages in the newspaper and radio and television time on a regular basis to "advertise" what's going on in the schools and include many of the items listed above.

Other ways to communicate with community members include open invitations and encouragement to attend district school board meetings, meetings of all kinds at the school, and attendance at the annual or more frequent school open houses. Too often, only parents feel welcome at these events. Community members need to read more about what's going on in the schools than the hot lunch menus in the newspapers. They need to "step" inside a school building occasionally to realize that today's schools are truly providing an education for students — if the students are ready to accept it.

Involvement

The discussion here focuses on the community as a support group and as a resource for the school. The emphasis is on getting as many community members as possible involved with students and staff members.

Community as a Support Group for the School

While financial support is usually delegated to the school through representatives on school boards, city councils, state legislatures, and special funds and grants from the federal level, personnel support is less rigidly provided. It requires a sense of partnership and cooperation to plan, implement, and evaluate involvement and relationships.

Political support for the school must come from the community. Parents, school staff, and students can be advocates for the school, but nonparent community members must be supporters, too, in any successful program. This support can be solicited from all of the following groups:

- Individual citizens through information in media and involvement in local schools
- Service groups such as Rotary, Lions, Optimists
- Business and industry organizations
- Professional organizations such as those for engineers, educators, computer scientists, business people, other professionals
- Employee unions for all groups — industry, government, professions
- Religious groups
- Social clubs
- Senior citizen and community associations
- Cultural/ethnic groups (e.g., Mexican Americans, Hmong, Indo-Chinese)

Representatives from several of the groups listed above along with school personnel and students can provide encouragement and ways for community members to be informed and involved in what goes on in local and district schools. Better informed voters make better decisions about the schools.

Financial support can be requested from several of the groups listed above along with local and regional foundations and philanthropic groups. It is usually easier to get support for special events and programs than for general support since people are already taxed for the general school budget. Some activities for funding requests include the following:

- Trips to museums, state capitals, courts, other sites beyond local areas
- Trips for special groups such as special education students, gifted students, at-risk students, honor students, and so on, to special sites such as research or medical facilities, abuse centers, and events such as plays and symphony concerts
- Trips not usually included in the school budget by groups such as for academic competitions and school club activities
- Scholarships for students for special opportunities to attend academic camps such as those in science, space, math, drama, writing, environment, music, art, and so on
- Scholarships to attend nonacademic camps, postsecondary colleges, universities, technical schools
- Special equipment not sufficiently funded in budgets such as computers, special laboratory equipment, telescopes, simulations, media, and materials

Community as a Resource for the School

When teachers and administrators say, "We can't afford that" or "We can't do this," they are not considering the community resources as a part of the workings of the school. The local and district community as well as more distant communities are not only rich sources of special sites but are also ready and willing sources of specialized personnel with specialized expertise. Some of these groups from which the people can be recruited include individuals, clubs and organizations, business, industry, medical units, cultural units, educational institutions, and governmental agencies. The physical sites where the resource people work can also become locations for mentors and student volunteer programs.

Individuals in the community provide a source of lessons for students in music, sports—both individual, such as golf and tennis, and group, such as baseball and basketball—and foreign language training. Individuals can also act as instructors at libraries, museums, and other sites that offer classes after school, in the evening, and during the summer.

Local clubs and organizations range from scouting, church, and 4-H groups to academic and hobby/interest groups such as chess, model trains and airplanes, and coins and other collections. Not only are students welcome to join many of these groups, but adult members are willing to come to school to present and bring materials to illustrate their topics.

Business, industry, and medical and cultural organizations are sites for visitation for individual students or as part of a school group. They are also locations for mentorships, volunteers, and work locations for older students.

Personnel from these organizations are a gold mine for classes in all subjects of the curriculum. Who can better explain "how the heart works" or "how diseases are communicated" than a doctor who specializes in the field? Interaction with these people provides the students with first-hand information from the real world and an incentive to investigate career possibilities. It also provides the resource person a chance to interact with the students and staff in the schools. Meridith's Super Science Spree is an example of this type of community involvement.

All communities provide an array of public and private educational units, including colleges, universities, technical schools, libraries, and cultural units such as zoos, museums, historical buildings, and perhaps a planetarium, aquarium, or other special feature. Most of these institutions have an educational division and personnel to coordinate visits by students and staff and to schedule personnel to come to the schools to work with students there. Some encourage students to work at their sites as volunteers—to actually work on objects as "amateur archeologists"—and to prepare exhibit materials as well as for mentorships and other roles with their staff. Faculty and others with special expertise from colleges or universities are often willing to guide student visits to specialized laboratories and equipment as well as monitor student productions and displays. College/university students often work with school staff to coordinate academic and social clubs and extracurricular activities as well as act as resource people for classes. And, of course, many college/university students come to the schools for teaching practicums, internships as counselors or psychologists, assistant coaches, and so on.

Governmental agencies such as town, city, county, state, and federal headquarters and legislative and judicial units offer a myriad of sites and personnel to interact with students and staff. Too often, we fail to interest and involve our students in the "machinery" of our government. These sites are also good spots for volunteers and mentors.

Events and activities that require specialized space, equipment and facilities such as theaters for drama productions and musical events, computer facilities for advanced work and analyses from surveys and projects are often available in the community. Space for displays and interactions such as fairs for science, math, books, computer, or heritage events are better held in the community than in a gym where the space is already regularly scheduled for classes and shortens the display of the event. Science and engineering and advanced computer projects also often need special facilities and equipment.

Outreach services such as county, state, and federal extension service offices provide information and personnel on a wide variety of subjects from lawns and gardens, foods and nutrition, to environment and space. Local services such as public health, family services, and other tax-supported agencies are ready and willing to provide materials and personnel to the schools.

Most communities traditionally sponsor celebrations for Memorial Day, the Fourth of July, and Labor Day. Ethnic festivals featuring music, food, dress, and other special events are sponsored according to the interests of the community. Some such events include Circus Day parades and events in Milwaukee, Wisconsin; intergenerational celebrations in Westwood, Massachusetts, where paired fourth-grade students and senior citizens are pen pals during the year to "learn from each other," culminating in a lunch and musical performance (Friedman, 1988); and Read Aloud Week in Milton, Massachusetts, where one hundred community leaders visited the Collicot School so every classroom would have at least one visiting reader every hour during every day of the week (Griffin, 1988).

Community resources are readily available everywhere for those who wish to seek them out. Yet, they are used too seldom by the schools. Some administrators and staff say they "can't adjust the schedule" or "we're short on time in the school day as it is—we can't add that." Others are concerned that private businesses will tell the school what to teach or that students will be brainwashed when schools and businesses forge partnerships that involve money, gifts of equipment to the school, time of business personnel to work in the schools, and incentives to get involved. Such concerns prompted establishment of "guidelines for business involvement in the schools" by a national committee of educators. They suggested four ground rules to ensure positive results and to be sure the program (Association for Supervision and Development Task Force on Business Involvement in the Schools, 1989/1990, pp. 84–86):

- Is consistent with the values, goals, and objectives of the educational program
- Responds to a clearly understood educational need
- Supports and does not undermine either implicitly or explicitly an existing curriculum and instruction message
- Has been considered and assessed by groups with different views

In addition, this Task Force suggests that all school–business relationships be subject to an ongoing review.

Student Roles and Responsibilities in the Parent–School–Community Partnership

Students are, of course, the recipients of the efforts of any parent–school–community relationship. But they should not be passive bystanders. While their primary role is learner, they can also take active roles as tutors, mentors, experts, resource persons, volunteers, partners, and evaluators. Many Diamond Middle School students were active in both school and community programs like these.

As learners in the subject matter areas, students without learning problems have the responsibility to become independent, to do their assigned work, and to complete it to the best of their ability. Since grades are a major type of communication from the school to the parents, community, and colleges and universities, students who have the ability but are not doing well in school, need to review their study habits and try to improve them (Schuster in Sorenson et al., 1988). Schools need to help students re-evaluate their work and grades. Underachievement is one of the greatest weaknesses of U.S. students. The academic work may be too difficult, too easy, presented in a manner in which the student has difficulty learning, or have other blocks to learning.

Schools, parents, and community need to work cooperatively to be sure students are placed in learning programs that meet their needs. Is the regular curriculum challenging for most of the students? Are students with various types of learning problems placed in the appropriate programs? Are there provisions to serve able and highly able learners? Besides opportunities to meet their academic potentials, students also need opportunities to develop leadership and artistic and creative talents.

Students need to develop affective characteristics such as self-esteem, a moral value system consistent with a democratic society, concern for others, personal self-discipline, and the ability to work within the system to make changes when any aspect of their learning does not meet their needs. Many affective characteristics develop as the students mature through positive reinforcement from parents, teachers, and community members with whom the students interact.

Strategies such as the Dalton Plan, which was developed in the 1920s, were based on student cooperation and self-control. The main points of the Dalton Plan were the following (Edwards, 1991, pp. 400–401):

- Students learn responsibility and self-discipline by making daily choices about subject matter, level of difficulty, and scheduling time.
- Students can work slowly and learn thoroughly; today research indicates that at-risk students often fail because they don't have time to complete their work.
- Students can take risks and fail without penalty; they can redo unsatisfactory work.
- Students can work rapidly and advance quickly; able students are not held up.
- Students are actively involved at all times; contracts are not "busy work" or "fill in the blank" activities, they are interesting and challenging.

- Students work in a nonthreatening and noncompetitive environment — in pairs and small groups and are encouraged to help each other.
- Students can request individual help when needed.
- Students enjoy long-term relationships with teachers and peers; they do not change teachers and rooms each year.
- Students can miss school for days without falling behind; they pick up where they left off if they are ill, go on vacation, take field trips, and so on.
- Students can vary their school hours.

Obviously the Dalton Plan is not for everyone or every school or community, but many of its tenets and strategies are worthwhile and are entering our schools again through reform and restructuring movements. These include nongrading, team teaching and planning, cooperative learning, attention to learning and teaching styles, and a "learning how to learn" curriculum. These strategies were observed in many of our model schools and were discussed in detail in earlier chapters of this book.

Students can act as tutors to younger students and peers. They can tutor for remedial work or by reading to other students or listening to them read. They can tutor as "helpers" in computer labs, or in science and math classes when students are working in pairs, small groups, or alone. And they can tutor each other in coopertive learning groups and turn that extra energy into meaningful learning.

Students with special areas of expertise or talent can act as mentors for younger students or students their own age. They can mentor an individual student, a pair, or a small group of students who are working on a project in their "expert area" in science, art, music, computers, or any other subject area. Students can act as experts in an academic subject, hobby or craft, or sport. The possibilities here are endless. Students, teacher, parents, and community people need to help prepare students to be mentors and experts by offering training courses for leadership, content preparation, and methods.

Students can be volunteers in a wide variety of roles in their own schools and nearby libraries, or in media centers, computer labs, clubs for younger children, special topics, and so on; and in the community — museums, hospitals, businesses, industry, and other sites. Many opportunities were also discussed in the school–community section of this chapter.

Students can be part of a community-based model of curriculum evaluation. The design for evaluating the K–12 science program in Elliot City, Maryland, invited local scientists, administrators, science teachers, parents, students, and graduates to act as evaluators (Utterback & Kalin, 1989). This plan was so successful that other content areas were evaluated using the same design. Since students are the recipients of the learning program, who are more qualified to help in the evaluation?

Students participate in some or all parent–teacher conferences in many schools. The name of the conference excludes the primary constituent – the student – even though their academic performance, attitude, work habits, and social interactions are the topic and purpose of the conference (Hubert in Wolf & Stephens, 1989). Some in-service training for students, teachers, and parents before the conference ensures a successful outcome.

Students, particularly those age 8 and above, are more and more becoming actors in as well as receivers of the efforts of the parent–school–community partnership. This is particularly true in reform movements. "Community-wide partnerships turn over responsibility for school reform to those who stand to benefit most – to teachers and parents and to students and their future employers" (Seeley, 1986, p. 82).

Examples of Successful Partnerships

Many examples of successful activities, policies, and programs in three categories of districts – urban, suburban/outer city/small city, and rural – have been cited to illustrate the parent–school–community partnerships described throughout this chapter. Here, details of how one or several districts in each of these categories have carried out meaningful plans to form and continue partnerships will be examined. Some descriptions focus on one school, some on a district, and some include state and other agency guidelines in their plans.

Urban Parent–School–Community Partnerships

The San Diego City Schools (SDCS) plan is rooted in state policy and county support along with district action (Chrispeels, 1991). In January 1989, the California State Board of Education adopted a policy to guide the work of the state and its local districts to strengthen family–school partnerships. The policy recognized the multiple roles of parents and calls for programs and action to develop parenting skills, information on how parents can help their children learn, how to use community resources to support family and students, ways to promote two-way home–school communications, ways to involve parents as volunteers in both instruction and support activities, and ways to involve parents in school governance and advocacy roles.

The state has promoted parent involvement policy in three ways.

- It has sponsored a series of regional conferences to explain the policy, results of parent involvement research, and shared strategies other districts have used in their parent–school programs. Some 200 to 500 parents, teachers, principals, and district administrators attended each conference.

- It has disseminated information on research and parent involvement to support local districts.
- It has joined with the University of California schools to establish a joint committee on parent involvement. This body has cosponsored parent involvement with local districts in six counties and has published two booklets for parents in English and Spanish. It has also sponsored two symposia in which representatives from the education departments of the nine University of California campuses explore ways to relate preservice and in-service so teachers could work effectively with families from all socioeconomic levels.

County offices are the intermediate level agency in California and carry out many functions typical to districts or other intermediate agencies. San Diego County is a good example of how this intermediate agency can support parent involvement. The county office plays three main roles: (1) acts as an information clearinghouse; (2) acts as a source of direct services to parents; and (3) acts as a source of direct service to districts and schools for staff development and help in planning.

At the information level, the county office held annual county-wide conferences to share information. School teams made up of teachers, parents, community representatives, and others learn about exemplary programs and cooperatively plan a program for their own schools. The County office also developed a publication, "Communicating with Parents," that contained 300 pages of ideas and strategies to help administrators and teachers develop parent involvement for both the school and classroom.

Direct services to parents from the county office included the following:

- EdInfo, a telephone information system especially for parents: It has seventy-five pre-recorded messages in English and Spanish and is available twenty-four hours a day. Topics include parents as teachers, tests and testing, college and careers, drug and alcohol abuse, and home–school partnerships.
- Using county television facilities to communicate: "The Parent Hour" was a monthly feature with experts on discipline, self-esteem, help with reading, parent–teacher conferences, and so on. SDCS also used the station to host a call-in show that featured parents, the superintendent, and a panel of teachers who discussed critical issues in the city's schools.

Direct services from the county office to districts and schools included workshops to help them implement parent outreach programs such as the following:

- Family Math where parents and children come to school to enjoy math games and activities together
- Workshops on specific parent–school relationships
- Workshops for administrators and prospective administrators, held cooperatively with the California School Leadership Academy

Nine of the SDCS with support from the state and county offices, joined the Schools Reaching Out League, which has national support. In early 1988, SDCS established a thirty-three member task force of school and community representatives to explore parent involvement in the community. They decided they needed a policy on parent involvement. After much debate, they adopted a policy similar to the state one that presents a multifaceted definition of parent involvement. The board commits itself to the following policy (Chrispeels, 1991, p. 369):

- Involve parents as partners in school governance including shared decision making and advisory functions.
- Establish effective two-way communication with all parents, respecting the diversity and differing needs of families.
- Develop strategies and program structure at schools to help parents take an active part in their children's education.
- Provide support and coordination for school staff and parents to implement and sustain appropriate parent involvement, K–12.
- Use schools to connect students and families with community resources that provide education enrichment and support.

This policy gives shape and direction to district action as well as working in individual schools. The implementation plan that followed the policy focused on three main efforts: building the capabilities of staff members, creating partnerships, and providing follow-up and support services.

Some of the specifics of this policy include the following:

- Recognize that building capabilities of a teacher, administrator, or other staff is a prerequisite to working effectively in a family–school partnership. A quarterly informational newsletter and a manual that focused on the importance of staff attitudes and behaviors toward parents were developed.
- Create partnerships. The SCDS allocated $100,000 for parent involvement incentive grants and awarded sixteen grants from fifty-eight applications. One school, Oak Park Elementary, found that an effective way to involve parents was to train representative parent and teacher facilitators to meet with ethnic and racial groups separately to discuss issues and concerns and solve problems. After the separate meeting,

they met jointly to develop a parent involvement plan. A second school, Torrey Pines Elementary, used part of its grant money to implement a hands-on science program, developed and conducted by parent volunteers. In each primary class, six to eight parents came once each week to spend one and a half hours leading small groups of students in science activities. Groups covered a single topic such as ecology, space, and earth science, every six weeks. Teachers who observed learned two things: parents with well-designed lesson plans could be teachers, too; and Hispanic and Anglo students can work together actively and successfully in cooperative learning groups.

- Follow-up and support services provided by the district took four routes: clarify roles and responsibilities of parties involved; establish parent involvement as a part of improvement plans all schools are required to develop; parent involvement task forces continue to meet monthly to discuss issues to implement and serve as a sounding board for parent, community, and staff concerns; and forming interdivisional staff groups that bring together representatives from special education, curriculum and instruction, staff development, Chapter 1, and other categorical programs of the district to explore ways to coordinate and improve services.

The comprehensive SDCS plan is only one of many that focuses on urban areas. A "family support" movement that includes many scholars and projects with connections to major foundations and universities focuses on strengthening all aspects of the child's development, stresses parent education at home, and helps parents connect with other support systems (Davies, 1991). Many of these programs gained ideas from Missouri's statewide "Parents as Teachers" program. Each of these projects and scholars has its own philosophy and name, but collectively gives new definition to parent involvement. Three themes are common to all of them:

- *Parent success for all children.* All children can learn and be successful in school and none should be labeled as a failures because of family or community social, economic, or racial characteristics.
- *Serve the whole child.* In order to promote academic development and success, there must be links to social, emotional, and physical development.
- *Share responsibility.* School, family, and community agencies' and institutions' efforts must be shared and overlapped and all efforts must be coordinated.

The Institute for Responsive Education (IRE) used the three themes above as a basis to refine and expand parent involvement as a part of urban school reform. This group has support from five foundations. The League of Schools it has formed includes nineteen urban school districts in thirteen states and Puerto Rico. The districts have no single philosophy — except a commitment to the three themes. As a group, they are starting to develop some interesting new definitions of parent involvement which includes the following (Davies, 1991, pp. 377–378):

- The current definition of *parent* is too narrow to define today's reality. *Family* is more realistic and includes parents, grandparents, aunts and uncles, brothers and sisters, and neighbors or others who provide child care.
- New definitions go beyond parents to include all community agencies and institutions that serve children.
- Definitions go beyond having family members go to school; activities and services that occur in the home and community should be included.
- Definitions go beyond school staff agenda to include priorities of families and beyond academic activities to include all ways families educate their children.
- New definitions replace the old "deficit" view that urban families were beset with traumas and troubles with a new view that emphasizes the strengths contained within a family.

Suburban/Outer City/Small City Parent–School–Community Partnerships

In 1987, Van Hise Middle School received a presidential award of excellence for a middle school. Principal Marvin Meissen believes one of the most important factors in the school's success is the high expectations the school, parents, and community have for their students. This outer city school is located on the west side of Madison, Wisconsin, a city with a population of 180,000 in Dane County (which has a 250,000 population). Madison is the state capital, home of the University of Wisconsin–Madison, a large research and teaching university, and site of several insurance and technology businesses and industries. Yet, this school of 780 students, grades 6–8, has a 25 percent minority population whose parents' jobs include laborers, business people, and professionals. The minority population is about 35 percent black, 35 percent Hispanic and 30 percent Asian — mostly Indo-Chinese students whose parents are studying at the university. The socioeconomic characteristics of the majority of the students' parents are varied, but they tend to be well-educated, many of whom work for the university or the state.

Generally, parents at Van Hise expect to be involved. They want to know about the curriculum their children study and they are willing to share their experiences and expertise with the school. Parent sponsorship has included the following:

- Annual science fair
- Writer's workshop where published authors (many of them parents and school community members) interact with the students
- Tutors for students who need remedial help or need to catch up due to absence
- Mentors for gifted and talented students or those with special interests
- Mentors for students to "shadow" for career awareness in a wide variety of fields
- Coaches for the Science Olympiad and Future Problem Solving groups
- Intergenerational activities where students are paired with senior citizens for storytelling, mime, and dramatics
- Volunteers for clerical work in the school, media center, and so on
- Directors for students who are "service work volunteers" for groups such as the West Side Coalition that packages food for the elderly
- "Clearinghouse" for community member involvement for at-risk tutoring, contacts with social services, and work with minority and culturally different children

The PTO is an umbrella organization for Van Hise parent–school–community communications. It does some fund-raising, but mainly supports projects such as music and computers that are raising money for specific purposes. The PTO sponsors "go to school night" which 80 to 90 percent of the parents attend. This night is held after students complete first quarter work.

"Parent Networking" is an ongoing PTO project that started several years ago. Its purpose is to "solve problems before they start or go too far." Parents develop a directory of names and phone numbers for every student in the school. Then, as students develop new friends that their parents are not acquainted with and want to go to their home and "out" with them, parents can call and get acquainted before the students get together. The Network has also developed a "telephone tree" to help squelch unfounded rumors at the school, to seek volunteers for the school, or to inform parents quickly.

The PTO helps sponsor a "parent education program." A committee surveys the parents for topics of concern and interest. They usually choose subjects dealing with: the nature of the middle school aged student, sex education, alcohol and drug abuse, and topics to reassure parents that their middle schooler's actions and activities are "normal." Parents also get involved with breakfast meetings twice each year. The program begins at 7:10 and includes an awards presentation for "catching students being good." Breakfast meetings often bring parents, especially fathers, to schools who don't attend other activities.

A newsletter and handbook for students and parents are Van Hise's major written communications. The monthly newsletter is planned and written by parents with a liaison to the principal and staff. One issue, for example, included articles about past and future student events, "congratulations" to students who have won competitions and awards, notices for parents—PTO meetings, single parents' meeting, parent support group meeting, school policy matters such as how to deal with an increasing middle school population on the west side of Madison, responses to a survey of family meals and food preparation, the column titled "Principally Speaking," and a monthly calendar of school events.

The handbook for parents and students deals with a wide range of topics such as the following:

- Expectations for student achievement, school citizenship, dress, and appearance
- Rules and regulations on school schedules, attendance, visitors to school, permission for vacations and other absences, bus conduct, bicycles at school, lockers, study hall, lunch costs, and school schedule
- Safety provisions for fire and tornado drills, physical education, accidents, nurse, supervision of lunch and recreation areas, and medication policies
- Special services and opportunities such as the library and media center, progress reports and conferences, and tutoring
- Policy for assertive discipline, alcohol and other drugs, and student withdrawal

The handbook concludes with three general categories of information: a comprehensive list of activities and clubs such as sports and recreation, academics, forensics, and yearbook as well as a list of awards and recognitions given to students annually; special and support services such as Title IX, special education, instruction, and student groups; the middle school philosophy and goals, and a calendar of the year's events.

Van Hise Middle School is one of nine middle schools in Madison. It has high expectations for its students—academically and intellectually, for leadership, the arts, creativity, and sports—and it meets these expectations. The overall grade point average of Van Hise students is B+, or about 3.32 on a 4-point scale. Student success locally and at state and national levels is recorded in the local media as well as at school. Their motto might be "we turn potential into reality and success begets success." Low teacher and administrator turnover and high parent–school–community involvement creates a partnership that guides a challenging education for Van Hise students.

Rural Parent–School–Community Partnerships

"We couldn't have passed the referendum for a new middle–senior high school, opened 1991, in our district without our long-time, comprehensive school–parent–community partnership." These are the words of Marlene Hanson, Superintendent of the Whitehall, Wisconsin, School District. Whitehall's partnership has been developed over the past eleven years under the guidance of the superintendent and school staff with leadership from parents and community members. The vehicle for partnership had been a series of forty-six committees whose titles are listed in Figure 9-4. These committees — all with representation of staff, parents, and community — carry out serious business. Each one has goals, agendas, and minutes for meetings. These are shared with the superintendent and other administrators as well as committee members and are open records to the community. Students from grades 9 through 12 also serve on committees as appropriate to the goals. A typical committee of 8 members might have 2 to 3 staff, 2 to 3 parents, 2 to 3 non-parent community members, and varying numbers of students.

The eight Board committees (Figure 9-4) deal with policy, finance, health, and safety and responsibility. The other thirty-eight committees advise, plan, help implement, and evaluate nearly every curriculum program, testing in the district, technology, and special programs (e.g., special education, gifted and talented, and at-risk). They also work on in-service arrangements for staff, parents, and community members who steer the course of education for Whitehall's students.

This comprehensive committee system was started more than a decade ago when a dying and ineffective PTO did not respond to new efforts and ideas to make it effective. The superintendent chairs several committees; others are chaired by a representative from a variety of role groups. When a vacancy occurs, remaining committee members suggest one or more candidates to the Board of Education for final selection and approval. Superintendent Hanson suggests: "Committees bring issues closer to the people than any larger organization could and everybody serving on a committee gets involved. We have also been successful at getting people that appear to be negative on a particular issue, but are community leaders and interested in the school, to serve on committees to get them involved and to let them know what is really going on inside the schools."

The Whitehall district is located in west central Wisconsin. It includes a town of 2,000 people and its surrounding agricultural area. Its K–12 population of 700 students comes from area farms (about 20 percent), from rural residences (40 percent), and the town (40 percent). Like most rural areas, the Whitehall district has witnessed a declining student population from 900 in 1980 to 700 in 1992 as well as almost constant economic recession. This era has also brought consolidation in its farms and farm-related businesses.

FIGURE 9-4 · *Whitehall School District Committees*

Board Committees

1. Education Committee
2. Finance Committee
3. Needs Assessment Committee
4. Negotiations Committee
5. Policy Committee
6. Property Committee
7. Safe and Healthful Facilities Committee
8. Transportation Committee

Other District Committees

9. Agriculture Advisory Committee
10. Book Selection and Review Committee
11. Chapter I Advisory Committee
12. Chapter II Advisory Committe
13. Competency Based Testing (CBT) Advisory Committee
14. Exceptional Education Needs Students/CBT Committee
15. Grade Promotion/Retention Committee
16. Graduation Status/CBT Committee
17. Language Arts/CBT Committee
18. Limited English Proficiency (LEF)/CBT Committee
19. Math/CBT Committee
20. Policy and Goal Committee
21. Reading/CBT Committee
22. Record Keeping Committee
23. Standards Committee
24. Test Result Reporting Committee
25. Transfer Student/CBT Committee
26. Instructional Technology Committee
27. Exceptional Educational Needs (EEN) Committee
28. Gifted and Talented Committee
29. Guidance Advisory Committee
30. Home Economics Advisory Committee
31. Health Advisory Committee
32. Library Media Center (LMC) Committee
33. In-service Evaluation/Application Committee
34. In-service Planning Committee
35. Instructional Improvement Commitrtee
36. Long-Range Planning Committee
37. Planning Committee
38. Reading Advisory Committee
39. Reading Is Fundamental (RIF) Committee
40. Basal Selection Committee
41. Reconsideration Committee
42. Student Assistance Program (Alcohol and Other Drug Abuse—AODA)
43. Student At Risk Committee
44. Restructuring Committee
45. SIC (School Improvement Committee)
46. Youth Activity Council (Food Service)

When the committee system began, the district had just built new administrative offices, along with vocational and music instructional facilities, and an auditorium on one end of town several blocks from the old junior/senior high school. Buses ran every hour to transport students from one place to the other. The district had intended to add general instructional and athletic space to the new campus, but the farm depression of the 1980s dashed their dream of one campus—except for the determination and dedication of the leadership in the school, among parents, and in the community. Superintendent Hanson believes the committee system kept people close to school needs and problems. "Within the community, involvement of some gets more and more people involved so they feel they are an integral part of the school."

Community members participate in a wide variety of activities in the district. They are welcome to attend workshops or take university courses. The district funds their participation at the same level as they do for the school staff—course tuition and workshop fees. Committees sponsor activities such as gifted and talented night where parents and community members can interact with students. In fact, this program was so popular that a school fair night for all students was added where they could show their work. Two half days from 5 to 9 P.M. were allotted—one half day to set up exhibits in the school and another for display. Performances by choirs, forensics groups, bands, and others also became part of this event. Some 700 to 800 parents and community members attend each fair.

Parent-teacher conferences, which are held twice each year, also have an extended role. In addition to the usual conference, displays, and surveys, information and district plans for the future are featured in booths in the gym. Videos produced by students and staff are also known. Before the referendum for the new high school, these conferences were an opportunity for the students and staff to let parents and others know about needs, designs, plans, and so on. And, during the building period, it was an opportunity to keep everyone posted on its progress.

Publications from the district provide a chronicle of its actions and a statement of its goals and progress. The Whitehall District Newsletter is published monthly during the school year. It is eight to twelve pages long, set on computer with an attractive heading, and clearly and interestingly written. Most importantly, it is chock-full of news. For example, the eight-page February issue dealt with topics such as:

- A survey to parents to determine their interest in enrichment and remedial summer school classes for students
- A progress report on the new high school building
- A summary of minutes of the last Board of Education meeting
- Activities and accomplishments of student groups—Academic Decathlon, band, expansion of the RIF reading programs, and so on

- Names of junior and senior high school students with high and perfect attendance records during the first semester
- Informational articles on alcohol and drug abuse, "killer fads," and latch-key children
- Listing of school events and lunch menus for the coming month

The May issue contained many of the same types of articles with an emphasis on graduation activities, end of year competition participants, summer opportunities for teachers at colleges and universities, and district summer programs and workshops for students. The newsletter is bulk mailed to everyone in the district.

Another publication is the Annual Report, which summarizes the state of the district. The quote from Hodding Carter at the top of the first page gives flavor to the publication: "There are only two lasting bequests we can hope to give our children. One of these is roots; the other, wings." Below the quote is a picture of the new school and a listing of Board of Education members and administrators along with their phone numbers. These are followed by:

- A district administrator message
- District goals with objectives and the progress that had been made toward them
- Elementary school goals and progress
- Middle and senior high school goals and progress
- Activities of students — field trips, special events such as Earth Day, and names of students from each school who were involved in competitions
- A report on the "standards" audit by the Wisconsin Department of Public Instruction indicating that Whitehall receives an "exemplary" (the highest) rating in curriculum planning, achievement testing, library and media, in-service, gifted and talented programming, annual public disclosure, and health
- Results of testing in terms of achievement and educational ability along with data for major subject areas for grades K, 1, 2, 4, 6, 8, and 10; comparisons to state and national data were also included
- District, elementary, and middle and senior high school goals for the coming year.

Another quote, by Robert Maynard Hutchins, had been carefully selected for the last page of the Annual Report: "The object of education is to prepare the young to educate themselves throughout their lives."

Many Whitehall parents and community members act as volunteers in the schools, K–12, each year. They are major "teachers" for the Great Books and Odyssey of the Mind programs as well as for mini courses in their areas of expertise. They are recruited by word of mouth, suggestions of others, and through written requests in the district newsletter. Volunteers include parents, senior citizens who act as reading tutors or as listeners for students who need someone to talk to, and other community members. Some work as helpers in the instructional media center. Various committees sponsor a program and luncheon each spring to thank the volunteers for their contributions. When materials needed to be moved from the old IMC to the "Knowledge Center" or IMC in the new building, volunteers, along with students, got the job done.

With all this involvement, the referendum for a new middle/senior high school in the district passed by a 4 to 1 margin even though Whitehall is in the heart of dairy farming country where recession has been a problem for over a decade. But so many people knew so much about the school and the needs of its students, they were willing to sacrifice to provide their children with an education for the twenty-first century. The new high school is state of the art in design, automation, and technology. But its most unique feature may be that it is a labor of love to this community from the school's administrators and staff, parents, and community members. Their children who were educated in the old building have been successful in colleges and universities and the world of work. Now, Whitehall students are going to have even greater opportunities to meet the challenges of the world in the years ahead.

Summary

Roles, responsibilities, and interaction among the members of the parent, school, community, and student partnership during the restructuring of school programs have been the focus of this chapter. The discussion began with the principles, interrelationships, concepts, and staff competencies that underlie the partnership. Then, school–parent and school–community roles, responsibilities, and interactions were explored. Student roles and responsibilities in the partnerships were also a part of the discussion. Examples of successful activities and practices were used throughout the discussion. The final section elaborated on successful restructured partnerships for urban, suburban/small city/outer city, and rural schools and districts. Support from the state and federal level was also discussed.

References

Alvino, J. (1985). *Parents' guide to raising a gifted child.* New York: Ballantine.
Association for Supervision and Curriculum Development (ASCD) Task Force on Business Involvement in the School. (1989/1990). Guidelines for business involvement in the schools. *Educational Leadership, 47*(2): 84–86.

Bauch, J. (1989). The TransParent school model: New techniques for parent involvement. *Educational Leadership,* 47(2): 32–34.

Bergin V. (1991). Addressing a generation at risk. Keynote Address at Contemporary Youth Issues Annual Conference. Austin, TX: Southwest Texas State University.

Boyer, E. (1989). What teachers say about children in America. *Educational Leadership,* 46(8): 73–75.

Brandt, R. (1989). On parents and school: A conversation with Joyce Epstein. *Educational Leadership,* 47(2): 24–27.

Chrispeels, J. (1991). District leadership in parent involvement. *Phi Delta Kappan,* 72(5): 367–371.

Davies, D. (1991). Schools reaching out. *Phi Delta Kappan,* 72(5): 376–382.

Davis, B. (1989). A successful parent involvement program. *Educational Leadership,* 47(2): 21–23.

Edwards, J. (1991). To teach responsibility, bring back the Dalton plan. *Phi Delta Kappan,* 72(5): 398–401.

Friedman, B. (1988). Intergenerational celebrations. *Educational Leadership,* 45(8): 52–55.

Gough, P. (1991). Tapping parent power. *Phi Delta Kappan,* 72(5): 339.

Griffin, W. (1988). Read aloud week at Collicut School. *Educational Leadership,* 45(8): 57.

Henderson, A. (1988). Parents are a school's best friend. *Phi Delta Kappan,* 70(2): 147–153.

Hunter, M. (1989). Join the "par-aide" in education. *Educational Leadership,* 47(2): 36–41.

Jennings, W. (1989). How to organize successful parent advisory committees. *Educational Leadership,* 47(2): 42–45.

Johnston, M., & Slotnik, J. (1985). Parent participation in the schools: Are the benefits worth the bother? *Phi Delta Kappan,* 66(6): 430–433.

Jones, L. (1991). *Strategies for involving parents in their children's education.* Bloomington, IN: Phi Delta Kappa Educational Foundation.

Lindle, J. (1989). What do parents want from principals and teachers? *Educational Leadership,* 47(2): 12–13.

Lipham, J., & Fruth, M. (1976). *The principal and individually guided education.* Reading, MA: Addison-Wesley.

Lueder, D. (1989). Tennessee parents were invited to participate and they did. *Educational Leadership,* 47(2): 15–17.

Manz School PTA. (1991). *Books on parenting.* Eau Claire, WI: Manz PTA Parenting Book Cart Bibliography.

Seeley, D. (1986). Partnerships time has come. *Educational Leadership,* 44(1): 82–85.

Smith, V. (1988). Family day: An investment in our future. *Educational Leadership,* 45(8): 56.

Smith, W., & Andrews, R. (1989). *Instructional leadership.* Arlington, VA: Association for Supervision and Curriculum Development.

Sorenson, J., Engelsgjerd, J., Francis, M., Miller, M., & Schuster, N. (1988). *The gifted program handbook.* Palo Alto, CA: Dale Seymour.

Sorenson, J., Poole, M., & Joyal, L. (1976). *The unit leader and individually guided education.* Reading, MA: Addison-Wesley.

Utterback, P., & Kalin, M. (1989). A community-based model of curriculum evaluation. *Educational Leadership,* 47(2): 49–50.

Warner, I. (1991). Parents in touch. *Phi Delta Kappan,* 72(5): 372–374.

Williams, D., & Chavkin, N. (1989). Essential elements of strong parent involvement programs. *Educational Leadership,* 47(2): 18–20.

Wolf, J., & Stephens, T. (1989). Parent/teacher conferences: Finding common ground. *Educational Leadership,* 47(2): 28–31.

CHAPTER TEN

Staff Development in Restructured Schools

Management is doing things right; leadership is doing the right things.

Staff development is a frustrating term for many teachers. One teacher explained: "Each August I'm required to attend in-service training. This staff development strikes me as something that someone does to someone else. A central office administrator or an outside consultant comes to our school with TYNT (this year's new thing). He explains how it works and how it fits in with LYNT (last year's new thing). My teaching doesn't change but I've got more paperwork to document that I'm doing TYNT and LYNT. I hate August in-service workshops!"

The changes that have occurred in schools in the past ten to fifteen years have mainly come from mandates outside the schools. Principals and teachers have accepted legislated changes, district directives, or textbook driven curriculum with few challenges. They accepted these mandated changes even though they believed that the change would do more harm than good. Mandating educational change is the opposite of empowerment. It sends a message to teachers and principals that they are inadequate and unappreciated for their efforts and that people outside the schools, often people who are rarely in the classrooms, are the experts with the answers. It leads teachers to feel bad about themselves (Weissglass, 1990) and their working conditions. Those working conditions have included more red tape and bureaucracy, more political interference, more state regulations, more tests, and more paperwork. The reform movement has left teachers and principals with less power and more responsibilities. It's no wonder that some have chosen to retire early and others to do just the minimum.

The majority of the teaching force in the United States is now composed of people who are middle-aged and immobile. Their average age is approaching fifty. Few of these veteran teachers or principals seem to be displaying or enjoying the benefits of their age and experience. Disenchantment is rampant among them. Many who were once the key members and top contributors to their schools' instructional programs have become stable or stagnant educators (Evans, 1989).

It's hard to conceive that these veteran teachers that Evans (1989) described as teaching without spirit or enthusiasm are the same age as the sparkling, energetic, excited teachers and principals that we observed in the model schools we described in Chapter 4.

What made those teachers and principals so positive, confident, and effective? What happens in outstanding schools that causes ordinary teachers to choose to give their best efforts to teach students who are hard to teach? And, in this process, what causes these ordinary teachers to become extraordinary teachers?

What we will describe in this chapter are the leadership and change processes that help school staffs to restructure their instructional programs so that they can deliver effective services to their students. A sequence for staff development and a sample program are included.

Effective Staff Development Strategies

A veteran teacher said, "I'm in favor of change as long as it doesn't change anything." Change isn't easy. We all want change; everyone likes to have more excitement, better health, more money, more fun, more friends. At the same time, everyone wants things to stay the same: Aunt Bonnie's burnt sugar cake, your parents' home, the order of a church service, the aisles of grocery stores, and old-time values. Change isn't easy because some of the things changed are those we wanted to keep the same.

What does it mean to restructure a school? It means change. And that to many teachers, administrators, and parents is scary. In a school, everything important touches everything else of importance. Change one consequential part of a school, and all other parts will be affected. This natural synergy becomes virtually inescapable in times when school budgets are very tight. Adding something means dropping something; emphasizing one program means de-emphasizing another. Restructuring affects all. Everyone must change if anything is to change. This means reexamining assumptions, renegotiating compromises, and being decisive with priorities. To pretend that restructuring can be done without honest confrontation is an illusion. Avoiding the pains of changing means avoiding restructuring (Sizer, 1991).

How did the eight schools described in Chapter 4 change and become the effective model programs they are today? There was no standard pattern. *Successful schools don't work because they followed a prescriptive staff development program: they work because they followed the professional judgments of their teachers and principals* (Glickman, 1991). These professional decisions that were made by eight different faculties have resulted in quality programs for their students.

The restructured programs in the model schools such as the family-like classrooms at Montview, the content-rich programs at Meridith, or year-round education at Crawford were viewed as effective because they got results. The restructured school has to stand or fall on whether it gets results.

David (1991) says that restructuring is different from previous reform efforts. One, it is driven by a focus on student performance, based on the premise that all students can and must learn at higher levels. The "All students CAN learn" program at Lozano fits this concept. Two, it is a long-term commitment to fundamental systematic change.

In the past, reforms have tried to change one piece at a time. Restructuring tackles all the pieces (David, 1991). Guskey (1990a) suggests integrating innovations such as mastery learning, cooperative learning, learning styles, and critical thinking and implementing them all together. Since many of these innovative strategies seem to complement each other, this seems like a sound recommendation. A well-conceived combination of innovative strategies should attain greater results in student learning than any single strategy.

Changing instructional practices, school organization, curriculum, and assessment is the content of restructuring. Restructuring also means changing school governance and administration so that decisions are made collaboratively by the people who are closest to the point of impact of those decisions and are most affected by the decisions. This will create a school in which teachers, administrators, students, and parents work together to achieve common goals. This is what shared decision making and teacher empowerment is all about (Hollifield, 1991). These changes in the model schools have had a direct impact on student outcomes such as motivation, achievement, learning, and citizenship.

For restructuring to succeed, district support from the outset is essential. Neither top down nor grass-roots efforts alone is sufficient. A collaborative effort by district administrators and the school-based leadership is the most successful approach for lasting change (Ray, 1989).

Why will restructuring succeed in improving student outcomes when our track record on school change and school reform is not a good one? Our study of eight model schools and Hollifield's (1991) analysis identifies two major differences from past change efforts.

1. Restructuring that results in site-based management gives each school staff not only the responsibility but also the authority and capability to bring about change—a situation that has not existed before.
2. There is a body of solid research evidence of those changes in instructional practices, school organization, and curriculum that improve student motivation, achievement, learning, and citizenship.

Changes through restructuring can be quite different from past reforms: These reforms were decreed as top-down mandates to be implemented by teachers and administrators who had no part in determining the value of the reform for their schools. In addition, most previous reforms have not been based on solid research evidence. Many were quite inappropriate for today's at-risk students (Hollifield, 1991).

We have been involved in mandated reforms that we knew would not work because no research evidence or sound professional judgment had been used to select the reform. An example is the basic skills reform. One teacher explained, "It doesn't make any sense. I've taken all the thoughtful, fun activities out of my classroom to make certain I've covered thoroughly a set of minimal skills. Who makes decisions like this? I'm turned off and so are my students."

The scenario for reform in the restructured school is simple and straight-forward. Site-based participatory decision-making processes enable school staffs to implement real change. Education research provides guidelines, practices, and programs for effective change. Faculty and administrators at the model schools were empowered to restructure their schools; they selected research-based programs that resulted in positive student outcomes. With tongue in cheek, Hollifield (1991) says that the marriage of site-based management and education research will last and, like the children of Lake Wobegon, the children in restructured schools will all be above average.

However, major changes do not occur easily. Guskey (1990b) says that there is a stage in restructuring called fear and rumor. Westerberg and Brickley (1991) reported that as time for implementation of the restructured program draws near, students, parents, and teachers are prone to doubt, even panic, as they are bombarded with rumors and speculations about the future. "What if our students can't meet our new standards?" "Will I be sued if one of my advisees does not do well in high school?" "My chorus won't be able to compete in the interscholastic contest with this year-round calendar." "I'm a second-grade teacher. Nesting! I can't teach three different ages of students." "What will restructuring mean to my courses?"

Reality tells us that school staffs considering restructuring should be prepared to handle the inevitable fears and rumors that accompany change.

The leadership teams for restructuring must be aware that this fear is normal. Principal Tim Westerberg and Teacher Dan Brickley (1991) believe that a good sense of humor helps when a letter to the editor suggests the new program is a "plot to keep students from learning."

Usually a small event causes this stage to end. Westerberg and Brickley (1991) explained: "We were so worried that there were not enough details in our implementation document. We were concerned that the faculty would be critical of it. Then one team member asked, 'Why does it have to be perfect? Let's submit our flawed document to the faculty and ask for their help.' It worked. Since that meeting there has been faculty support for the project."

A study of the Mastery in Learning Project illustrates the change processes schools go through as they restructure their programs.

The Mastery in Learning Project

The structure of schools causes isolation. Teachers are isolated in classrooms and administrators in their offices. The nature of collective bargaining contributes to this isolation. Teachers work independently; so do principals. The National Education Association (NEA) asked what would happen if all staff members—teachers, principals, counselors, and others—engaged in true professional collaboration (McClure, 1988).

The Mastery in Learning Project is a school-based improvement effort that allows teachers and administrtors to explore the benefits of collegiality. The Project is NEA's response to school improvement by restructuring and site-based management. The twenty-six schools initially selected represented the demographic and organizational diversity of schools throughout the nation. One of our models, Diamond Middle School, was a member of the initial network of schools. Now over sixty schools participate in this project.

The following four essential assumptions guide the Mastery in Learning Project's approach to school renewal (The Mastery in Learning Project, 1987):

1. A school's curriculum must have content, integrity, and social significance.
2. A school community must hold high expectations for students.
3. The central priorities of schools—learning, teaching, and curriculum—must guide all other educational decisions.
4. Every decision about learning and instruction that can be made by a local school faculty must be made by that faculty.

Principal Joanne Hennessay (1990) reported that the restructuring at Diamond Middle School had been guided by the above principles. She also emphasized that decisions must be based on research. One service that the Mastery of Learning Project provides network schools is instant (within twenty-four hours) research findings. The use of research improved the new instructional program as Diamond changed from a junior high school to a middle school.

To participate in the Mastery in Learning Project, 75 percent or more of the faculty must agree to change and improve their school (McClure, 1988). Once Diamond was accepted as a network school, the project staff developed a school profile. What is Diamond like now? A description of the school was created by information from teachers, site administrators, central office staff, students, and parents.

Hennessay (1990) said the next stop—producing a faculty inventory also produced fireworks. DIADs (two-person teams), then TRIADs (three teams combined), and finally the entire faculty in two groups discussed three questions (The Mastery in Learning Project, 1987).

1. What is so wonderful about this school that you would never want to change?
2. What is so bad that we should change it tomorrow?
3. What problems need resolution but have no easy solutions and will require time for study?

When the two groups shared, the fireworks began. Problems were identified—and feelings were hurt.

Principal Hennessay explained: "The idea was for us to find five problem areas and develop plans to improve them. This was hard to do. We were a good school before the project. We didn't have low reading, writing, or math scores. We searched for problems. There was no consensus as to what the problems were."

Team leader Ron Godfrey said, "The school profile gave an accurate picture of what Diamond was like. Then we started opening closets looking for problems. We spent almost a year trying to correct weaknesses. It was awful. the Site-Based Management committee had a crisis meeting at the Assistant Principal's home. That meeting was the turning point. We knew what we were doing wasn't working. That night we decided instead of looking in closets, we should open windows and let in fresh air."

"What do you mean?"

Ron continued, "What it meant was that we should stop searching for problems. We looked at the research to see what we could bring in to improve our school. We brought in cooperative learning, learning styles, thinking skills, the adviser-advisee program, and interdisciplinary teaming. Our entire approach to teaching has changed."

Principal Hennessay (1990) explained, "It was negative for a good staff to keep looking at problems. We were letting a few 'Snakes in the Swamp' stop us from moving forward. Once we looked at the research, we found ways we could work better with middle school students. The project has been successful."

McClure (1988) reports that similar change processes, like those at Diamond Middle School, happened at other project schools. He describes a series of steps that staffs go through as they restructure and move toward site-based management. The steps include the following:

Commitment. The faculty commit their energies to solving the schoolwide problems that they have identified. Often new leaders emerge during this step.

Dispiritedness. When the faculty discovers that no one from outside can provide solutions, they become dispirited. McClure (1988) calls this the "Halloween Syndrome" because it often occurs at the end of the second month of the school year.

Regeneration. At this point, only 20 to 50 percent of the staff remain active workers. These faculty members almost begin again. They review the original findings, talk at length about rekindling commitment and what commitment means, and assess how other faculty members could be brought into active work. This is a critical phase in the reform. Recommitment and adaptation leads to ownership of the project and internalization of its goals.

Seeking small successes. The faculty acts on a few simple, straightforward ideas; for example, using cooperative learning at Diamond. Activities with immediate visible results recapture the interest of faculty members in the restructuring project and create a sense of accomplishment.

Using research. This stage empowers the school faculty. As they begin to use current research on teaching, learning, and curriculum to analyze problems and to identify available options, their decision-making power is expanded.

Experimentation. Together a staff selects and introduces pilot efforts, assesses their outcomes, and modifies them to achieve more desirable outcomes.

Comprehensiveness. The faculty moves from fragmented efforts to comprehensive school restructuring. This comprehensive plan is based on current education research and is focused on high, relevant standards for students.

The faculty at Diamond Middle School has progressed through these steps and has implemented a sound, research-based program. That's why the school has received national attention and was selected as one of the model schools in this book.

Ron Godfrey described what has happened to him. "I'm a better teacher now, and I was a good one before restructuring. I get less annoyed. I'm much more patient. I'm able to provide for the individual differences of my students. Teachers need to be switch hitters — able to use different strategies for different learning styles. Our learning objectives don't change — how kids achieve the objectives does. I teach my kids that it's OK not to be sequential. I give them choices in homework assignments. I've even led staff development programs in learning styles and cooperative learning."

Ron's answer reaffirmed our convictions of the great promise restructuring has for both students and teachers.

Staff Development in the Model Schools

What stimulates a school faculty to change? Lots of things. At the model schools that we visited, change was stimulated by many activities, which included the following:

Leadership by dynamic principals
On-site committees
Visitations to innovative schools
Coaching
Consultants who worked in the school a week or longer
Simulations of whole language classrooms
Able teachers who conducted staff training and presented at professional meetings

There was no standard process that the school followed. However, there are a number of parts that must be in place if restructuring is to occur.

1. There must be a commitment to the school mission. This requires time and much teacher involvement in the development and refinement in the school goals and the mission statement. At the model schools, we found teachers and principals who understood and believed in their school goals and mission. Their collective ownership of these shared values helped them to envision a program to accomplish remarkable school improvement.

2. The faculty must have knowledge of the effective practices that education research has identified. More is now known than ever before about the qualities of superior teaching, the ways people learn, the elements of a curriculum that serve students best, and the kinds of environments that facilitate student learning. Access to these research findings is needed by teachers and administrators as they improve school programs.

3. Teaming skills are required. In good schools, good teachers have always worked together. In site-based management where teachers are empowered to make decisions closer to the learning problem, teaming is critical. Teachers and administrators must become those "good" teachers who can communicate, make decisions, and support each other. Later in this chapter a sequence of team-building skills will be presented.

4. The learning community concept exists in the school. This means

that there is a lifelong commitment by the teachers and administrators to professional growth and renewal. One of the strengths of each of the faculties of the model schools was their ability and inclination to learn and to inquire more deeply into the nature of good teaching and learning. Each of the schools had regularly scheduled team, faculty, and instructional improvement committee meetings to study and to act collectively on this study.

The changes at Crawford Elementary School are good examples of restructuring in action. When Principal Vern Martin arrived, Crawford's test scores were the lowest in the district. Martin's first task was to survey the faculty to determine their opinion of the school's main problems. Discipline, a lack of security and stability in students' lives, and parent apathy were identified as the main problems. Martin decided to address the first two. Funds were acquired for a discipline workshop. An outcome of this workshop was a set of rules, consequences, and rewards. To provide a more structured environment the staff used the research findings to change from a departmentalized program to self-contained classrooms. An outgrowth of this planning was a mission statement and a set of school goals. As the faculty studied and worked together, many research-based changes — diagnostic-prescriptive teaching, high achievement expectations including opportunities for acceleration, process education, problem solving, and, recently, year-round schooling — were implemented.

Research-Supported Staff Development Strategies

As we stated earlier in this chapter, staff development is a frustrating term for teachers. Every techer in U.S. schools has taken in-service courses, workshops, and other staff development training programs. Most teachers and administrators have been disappointed with the usefulness of these experiences. Yet two key facts exist:

1. Staff development and school improvement are intimately related.
2. Classroom management and school improvement overlap.

Staff development in the restructured school must not disappoint teachers and administrators.

In recent years, teaching has emerged as a profession with an identified core of research-based knowledge. Even though teachers cannot control external factors that affect students (socioeconomic status, family or neighborhood situations, or previous learning history), they do have a set of effective strategies that works with students. Teachers are decision makers. All principles of learning and methodologies are subject to teacher judgment.

The effective teacher must think, use research-validated principles, and intuition to make appropriate decisions for students (Hunter, 1990).

Research on staff development has shown that what the teacher *thinks* about teaching determines what the teacher *does* when teaching (Showers, Joyce, & Bennett, 1987). The question is, "How can we affect teachers' thinking so that they make decisions that are based on education research?" We cannot directly affect teachers' attitudes and psychological make-up. However, quality staff development can powerfully influence and increase teachers' professional skills, which will have a profound effect on their self-esteem and the quality of decisions they make (Hunter, 1990). The results will be a partnership between education research and teaching practices.

At no other time in the history of education have there been more new strategies available to educators. As they restructure, school staffs can choose from a wide variety of research-based models and strategies. Innovative ideas such as cooperative learning, mastery learning, the effective school model, nongraded–continuous-progress curricula, critical thinking, and learning styles are proven strategies; all have been presented in previous chapters.

Guskey (1990a) has suggested that integrating these innovative strategies and implementing a combination of them will be much more effective than implementing any single strategy. He believes that the most common practice of implementing one strategy this year, another next year, and so on, has not worked. Practitioners often need more than one year to grow comfortable with any change. For most teachers, the first year is a time of trial and experimentation. The new strategy must be adjusted to fit the conditions of the classrooms in the restructured school. It takes time for teachers to become comfortable with the new and unfamiliar practices — and hard work. If support and follow-up activities are withdrawn after a year in order to devote the school's resources to another innovative strategy, the first strategies' effects are not likely to reach many students. What causes teachers to continue to use a new strategy is *results* with their students (Guskey, 1990b). If the new strategy has not been in place long enough to see its true effects with students, few teachers will persevere to refine their use of the strategy. Many teachers will view the new strategy as a fad since the school leaders are busy introducing another idea. They will abandon the practice and return to their old, familiar ways of teaching (Guskey, 1990a). They will not be willing to give the same amount of time and effort to this year's new program.

Most of the model schools that we visited followed the change practices suggested by Guskey (1990a). They selected a number of innovative strategies that they believed would help them achieve their school goals. They integrated those strategies that complemented each other and implemented them over a period of time longer than a year.

A Sequence for Staff Development

A sequence for an effective staff development program follows:

1. *Plan: Think big, start small.* The site-based management team should choose appropriate strategies and encourage teachers to begin using them. The key to change sequence is "Think Big" and implement slowly (Guskey, 1990b). No school staff can restructure to have mastery learning, critical thinking, and cooperative learning in all subjects in the same year. Mae West once said, "Anything worth doing is worth doing slowly." Restructuring takes time.

2. *Work in teams.* Teaming makes changing easier. Two or more teachers working together can cut the work of implementing new strategies by 75 percent (Guskey, 1990b). Organizational structures should be designed so that teachers can work together daily as they are studying and implementing new strategies.

3. *Use available resources.* Guskey (1990b) recommends that the site-based management team beg, borrow, and steal resources from all available sources. This includes relating the school improvement processes to resources available for special education, gifted/talented, and Chapter 1. Leaders in the model schools were quite effective in combining resources and also in attaining additional funding to achieve their goals.

4. *Involve all personnel in the selection of time and place for training.* It doesn't seem to matter where or when the training is held as long as all personnel are involved with selection of time and place. It doesn't seem to matter what the role of the trainer is. Teachers, administrators, and professors can all be effective trainers. What does matter is the training design. Almost all teachers can take useful information back to the classroom when the training includes (1) presentation of theory, (2) demonstration of the new strategy, (3) opportunity for practice of the strategy during the training session, and (4) prompt feedback about their initial practice (Showers et al., 1987).

5. *Follow-up staff development training.* Guskey (1990b) believes that follow-up may be more important than the initial training. Teachers are more likely to keep and use the new strategy if they receive coaching (either expert or peer) while they are trying the new idea in their classrooms. Teacher commitment to use a new strategy comes after they feel confident that they can use it. Once teachers develop the skill to use a new strategy well, they choose to use this method whenever it is appropriate for their students (Showers et al., 1987).

6. *Support teachers as they implement new strategies.* Teachers have many concerns about using a new strategy. The first concern is personal:

"What does this mean for me? Must I stop using my current teaching method to use this new strategy?" The next concern is management: "How will using this new strategy affect my classroom organization? Will it affect my grading?" For example, many teachers who took pride in themselves for having quiet, orderly classrooms have had many concerns about implementing cooperative learning. A third concern is the impact of the innovation on students: "How will this new strategy affect my kids positively?" Knowing these concerns, effective principals and unit leaders become supporters (almost cheerleaders) for teachers as they try out the new strategy (Guskey, 1990b). They enthusiastically support teachers' early attempts to use the new idea. They visit again to observe engagement and confer to make suggestions. On the next visit, they support the improved teaching. This careful support helps teachers implement the new strategy effectively.

7. *Provide feedback on student learning.* The bottom line is "Are students learning?" Does the new strategy make a difference? Are students learning more? The model school staffs did an excellent job of collecting data and using these data to make instructional decisions. Teachers were aware of how their students were doing.

8. *Continue support and provide follow-up training.* The principal and IIC must continue to support teachers as the new strategy becomes a regular part of the restructured school's instructional program. This can be done in many ways. One model school scheduled review training sessions each year so that teachers would maintain and refine their skills. Another helped teachers increase their expertise so that they could be trainers for other schools. One model school encouraged their teachers to describe their programs as a presentation at state and national professional meetings. Support like this helps the restructured school to continue to improve.

Earlier in this section we reported the research finding: what the teacher *thinks* about teaching determines what the teacher *does* when teaching. When teachers change their teaching to try a new strategy and this change results in increased student learning, their thinking about teaching also changes. As a result of this successful implementation of a new strategy, their attitudes and beliefs about teaching will also change. Success is the most powerful motivational device for teachers. Quality staff development programs will introduce teachers carefully to research-based strategies so that they can be successful in helping their students to learn.

Stages of Professional Growth

One issue that is seldom addressed as schools restructure is the process of becoming a professional teacher. We observed teachers in the model schools performing at a high level of competence. This takes time. Competent teachers need experience and opportunities for professional growth. In a study of sixty-two teachers in effective elementary schools, Bechtol (1984) found that most teachers had been teaching three or four years before they considered themselves performing at a truly professional level.

In restructured schools, teachers are expected to perform at higher levels of competence. They are expected to expand their instructional repertoires. They are expected to respond more flexibly to the individual needs of their students. They are expected to take responsibility for the welfare and growth, not only of students but also for their professional colleagues. Finally, they are expected to exercise leadership for school improvement and the accomplishment of school goals.

Are these unreasonable expectations? Of course not. We observed teachers meeting these expectations in all the model schools. What it does mean is that the development of professional expertise is an individual process that takes time, opportunity, and support.

Leithwood (1990) has identified the following six stages in the development of professional expertise.

1. *Developing survival skills.* The beginning teacher has partially developed classroom management skills, limited knowledge and skill in use of several teaching models, and assesses students primarily to meet external demands.

2. *Becoming competent in the basic skills of instruction.* At this level, teachers have well-developed classroom management skills. They have the skills to use several teaching models. They can assess students for formative purposes and for achievement of easy to meassure instructional goals.

3. *Expanding one's instructional flexibility.* At this level, teachers' classroom management skills are automatic. They are capable of using a variety of teaching models to maintain student interest. They can assess students for both formative and summative purposes.

4. *Acquiring instructional expertise.* At this level, teachers have integrated their classroom management with their instructional program. There is little attention given to classroom management as a separate issue. Teachers are skilled in using a broad repertoire of teaching models to achieve a wide variety of instructional goals and to provide for their students' learning styles. They use a wide array of assessment techniques, both formative and summative, to make instructional decisions.

5. *Contributing to the growth of colleagues' instructional expertise.* At this stage, teachers have high levels of expertise in classroom instruction. They are able to reflect about their own competence and to explain their instructional choices in relation to education research, beliefs, and values. They can assist other teachers in acquiring instructional expertise by working with

student teachers, mentoring beginning teachers, coaching colleagues, and presenting staff development programs.

6. *Participating in a broad array of educational decisions at all levels of the education system.* At this stage, teachers are committed to school improvement and are able to accept responsibility for achieving school goals. These teachers are able to exercise leadership, both formal and informal, with groups of adults both inside and outside of the school. They have a good understanding of the ways schools work and of the effects of decisions at many levels of the education system.

In looking at these six stages of the development of professional expertise (Leithwood, 1990), one can see that Stages 1 through 4 are concerned with teachers' classroom expertise. Stages 5 and 6 address the out-of-classroom roles of the mature, professional teacher.

While the roles of teachers as described in Stages 5 and 6 are not new, they have received greater attention recently. Peer coaching and mentoring assume that teachers at Stage 5 have instructional expertise. The view of teachers as formal and informal leaders in Stage 6 is consistent with the responsibilities teachers are given in restructuring school programs. At this stage, teachers are empowered to make site-based decisions.

Teacher leaders in the model schools were functioning at Stages 5 and 6. The roles of Instructional Resource Teacher and PAS (Program Assessment and Support) teacher are examples of instructional expertise. Unit leaders or members of the IIC are examples of formal school leadership roles.

The Principal's Role in Staff Development

How do the stages of development of profesional expertise relate to staff development in the restructured school? How do they affect the planning of the principal and the teachers in leadership roles in this change process? It seems sensible that those planning staff development should be sensitive to each individual teacher's stage of professional expertise and seek to help the teacher improve to the next level. The stages provide a framework for principals to formulate their own approach to teacher development (Leithwood, 1990).

In most schools, there are teachers functioning at different levels. Beginning teachers are working to survive. Other teachers are working to develop professional expertise. A few teachers seem to be plateaued at Stage 4. Teachers at Stages 5 and 6 are the formal and informal leaders of the school. What is the principal's role in working with teachers at these different stages?

1. *Principals should prevent new teachers from having a painful beginning.* New teachers can be given realistic classroom assignments, assistance

in the development of classroom management skills, provision of a supportive mentor, and the avoidance of heavy-handed supervision (Leithwood, 1990). Another helpful strategy is to pair the new teacher with a teacher/buddy who will help the beginner to adapt socially to the new school and community. This teacher/buddy system is useful for the young beginning teachers who are embarrassed to ask their mentors and principals some questions. It is also useful for the older-than-average beginning teacher who needs help with child care and other community agencies.

2. *Principals should establish a school culture that is based on norms of collaboration and professional inquiry.* The reason teachers often appear to stabilize in the middle stages is inadequate stimulation, not an innate shortcoming (Sprinthall & Theis-Sprinthall, 1983). The structures of many schools may stifle teacher development. These schools are characterized by informal norms of autonomy and isolation for teachers, as well as entrenched routines and regularities (Leithwood, 1990). In such schools, there was little evidence of collegiality, collaboration, or professional dialogue.

Principals' teacher development strategies are most likely to be successful in a school in which teachers are encouraged to consciously reflect on their own practices, to share ideas about their instruction, and to try out new techniques in the classroom (Leithwood, 1990). Good principals model these practices. They are willing to collaborate with teachers to experiment with new strategies, and then to reflect about their own teaching.

In the model schools we observed an on-going professional dialogue about student learning and effective practice. There was an excitement about faculty meetings because these were times when teaching practices were discussed and plans were made to use research findings to solve school problems. One principal explained: "We stimulate each other to try new ideas and to work together." At these schools we observed teachers who developed both professional competence and confidence.

3. *Principals should carefully diagnose the starting points for teacher development.* Teachers are not passive persons who are waiting for their principals "to develop them." Instead, teachers are persons who are actively striving to accomplish goals that they believe are important in their work (Leithwood, 1990). As principals work to help teachers develop professional expertise, the key to success is careful diagnosis. When a work area identified by the principal matches a goal the teacher is trying to achieve, opportunity for teacher development is positive.

The most obvious method available to principals for carrying out diagnosis is teacher evaluation. All principals spend a considerable amount of time evaluating teachers. Unfortunately, the systems of teacher evaluation used in most schools have had little influence on teacher development (Leithwood, 1990). Glickman (1991) says teacher evaluation does not relate to schoolwide instructional improvement. He calls it a myth and a boondoggle that has been the greatest robber of educational resources in our times. The evaluation system only improves a school when the majority of teachers border on incompetence.

A more open-ended evaluation system may be useful. A system that has a "needs assessment front end" so that both principals and teachers can select goals that both agree are relevant to teacher development. This plan allows both the principal and the teacher to diagnose and to select improvement strategies that relate to the teacher's knowledge, skills, and attitudes.

4. *Principals should recast routine administrative activities into powerful teacher development strategies.* A principal's day is demanding. A principal's activities are typically characterized by brevity, fragmentation, and variety. Rarely it seems that principals spend more than ten minutes at a time on a single task. They make 150 different decisions in an average day. Communication of one sort or another is the primary goal of most principals' activities. About three quarters of such activities are interpersonal; over half involve face-to-face contact. Principals' work requires high levels of spontaneity; the largest single expenditure of a principal's time is reported to be unanticipated meetings (Leithwood, 1990). One principal reported that he'd spent his whole afternoon in "got a minute?" conferences.

Another principal described his complex, fragmented job to a service club (Bechtol, 1991):

> *Elementary principals have complex, demanding jobs. I work with 4-year-olds who are still not toilet trained, to 12-year-olds who know far too much about sex, drugs, and R-rated movies, to gifted children with eleventh- or twelfth-grade reading levels.*
>
> *I work with parents who are still children themselves in many ways to grandmothers raising their grandchildren; parents who are very supportive to those who are openly antagonistic.*
>
> *I work with truly master teachers who have very effective instructional, evaluative, and motivational skills and strategies to beginning teachers who need a great deal of guidance and support.*
>
> *The organization I manage has over 1,000 people. The average age is 8. Half of them forget their lunch money and a lot of them need their noses wiped.*
>
> *Essentially I work with people to solve problems. I spend most of my day in verbal interaction dealing with unplanned and often poorly understood problems, crises, and dilemmas. Problems must be handled quickly and decisively. Reaching a solution that helps an individual or group without affecting others is often difficult.*
>
> *Being an elementary principal is often a pressure-packed, highly stressful job. I have full responsibility for a school of children. I must help assess their learning abilities, make sure they are safe, provide*

learning materials for them, take care of a wide variety of problems they bring from home, and so on.

I am also responsible for the entire school staff. I must make time for each teacher who needs to talk, evaluate all professional and paraprofessional staff, plan and conduct staff development, attend conferences and ARD meetings, etc.

At the same time, I must meet the demands of the "system"; paperwork, too many meetings, and a variety of supervisors, and handle parent concerns and demands. Is there any other profession where a person encounters so many different people, situations, and problems, that has such a diversity of demands and responsibilities?

How in such a fragmented day can a principal provide leadership so that teachers improve their professional expertise and the school program is restructured for student growth? Almost all principals face the demands of the day described above. Leithwood (1990) reports that highly effective principals are different from "typical" principals even in brief meetings. The difference is the consistency that effective principals are able to bring to their activities and decisions. Less effective principals seem to make decisions in relatively piecemeal fashion; their decisions about budgets, instruction, discipline, and staffing seem to be based on different criteria. As a consequence, the overall effects of these decisions seem to be at cross purposes to each other.

Highly effective principals base their decisions and actions on a relatively consistent set of criteria. Their actions relate directly to the goals of the school and link to the instructional system. The effects of what looks like a series of many trivial, unrelated, and often unanticipated decisions made by these highly effective principals eventually add up to something that causes school improvement. The glue that holds together the decisions of effective principals is the goals that they and their staffs have developed for their schools (Leithwood, 1990).

The principals in the model schools had a vision of what their schools needed to look like in order for the goals to be accomplished. This clear, often quite detailed vision guided their daily decisions.

What principals pay attention to—and what they don't—is the most powerful communication of what they value. DuFour (1990) recommends that principals ask themselves the following questions about their leadership behavior:

1. What do I plan for?
2. What do I monitor?
3. What do I model?

4. What do I reinforce by recognition and celebration?
5. What behaviors am I willing to confront?

What these questions imply is that effective principals have such a clear vision of what their restructured schools will look like that they can monitor, model, reinforce, and celebrate appropriate behaviors. They can confront. They can look a misbehaving student in the eye and say, "I know you can learn and behave, and I expect you to do that."

In summary, effective principals use the energy and momentum that is naturally created by the demands of their work for teacher development and instructional improvement. Their decisions are purposive and intelligent.

A Sample Staff Development Program:
Team-Building Skills

All the model schools described in Chapter 4 used some form of team-teaching strategies. Working together as an effective team is not a natural skill that most teachers have. The unit teams at McFarland and Lake George and the interdisciplinary teams ast Diamond Middle School worked hard to develop into functional teams. The team-building skills sequence helped the teams to work together quicker and more efficiently. It is an example of a staff development program that has been used to restructure schooling to provide for individual students. The sequence helps a group of three, four, or five independent teachers change into an effective team that can restructure their instructional program to meet the needs of their students.

What makes an effective team? How does the effective team function? The effective team has open communication, a living philosophy of education, problem-solving skills, and a helping relationship. In a truly helping relationship, team members build trust, and the more trust they build, the more they share and develop their potential. Trust is the key word in achieving this supportive, helping relationship, and in developing the effective team.

The Johari Window, which is presented in Figure 10-1, illustrates in a simple way what should be accomplished in the team-building sequence.

The top, left box is the "common knowledge" box, which includes knowledge of things that you and I know about me: I am five foot eight, have blue eyes, like to teach social studies, and so on. In the bottom, left box are the things I know about myself, but you don't know about me. Some of these things are my secrets, things I'm not going to let you know. Some are things that I haven't had time to tell you; give me time and I will. One caution: team building is not open, freewheeling sensitivity training; team members cannot handle intimate personal details and work together daily.

FIGURE 10-1 • *The Johari Window*

Things about myself that I—

Things about myself the other person—	know	don't know
knows	common knowledge	*my blind spots* such as bad breath, that my best friends haven't told me about yet
does not know	my secrets and things I haven't had a chance to tell yet	my hidden potential of things I never dreamed I could do or be

Source: Adapted from Luft (1963).

The top, right box is the "blind spot box" or the "bad breath box." These are the things you can see or have discovered about me, but of which I am unaware. The lower, right box, the "hidden potential box," includes the things I don't know about myself and you don't know about me either. This box contains the skills that I have the potential to develop.

In a good team, the "common knowledge box" grows larger and larger. As it expands, it dips into the "hidden potential box," and gradually each team member develops more skills and expertise. The team becomes effective and functional.

To speed up this process, a series of team-building activities has been developed (Bechtol, 1973). They include the following:

1. Getting acquainted (warm-up activities)
2. Listening
3. Developing trust
4. Clarifying values
5. Helping each other
6. Identifying strengths
7. Arriving at agreement ("We agree")

These team-building activities can be accomplished in a number of ways. One way is to have the principal or a consultant lead the teams through the activities in a workshop or at a retreat. Another way is for the ICC or the

Site-Based Management Committee to go through the activities and then have each unit leader lead his or her team through the activities. No matter which plan is selected, the sequence indicated below should be followed.

Teams must be organized prior to the team-building skills sessions. All activities are designed to be completed within the unit or interdisciplinary team, and adequate time (six to ten hours) must be set aside to complete the activities.

Getting Acquainted (Warm-Up Activities)

Three types of whips are described here. *Whips* are quick verbal exercises that help team members get to know each other.

1. Proud whip: Each team member shares with the team something that he or she has done the past year and tells why he or she is particularly proud of it.
2. What my name means to me: Each team member states his or her full name to the team and tells what it means to him or her.
3. Hero/heroine whip: Each team member selects a person from history, movies, novels, and so on, who he or she would recommend as a hero or heroine for the students in the team and explains why.

Another kind of warm-up activity is *unfoldment.* Unfoldment activities provide opportunities for team members to personally disclose events from their lives that have affected them as teachers and as individuals. Completing these activities increases the team members' awareness and acceptance of each other. Two types of unfoldment activities are described below (McHolland & Pestrue, 1968). The team-building skills leader first models a personal unfoldment for the entire group. He or she will then direct each team member to do a personal unfoldment or a paired interview. These are equivalent activities; the leader will select the one that is better for the team(s) being trained.

1. *Personal unfoldment:* The following narrative is used to introduce this exercise: "We are now going to do depth unfoldment. I will model the unfoldment process for you. I will have six minutes, as will each person here, in which to unfold myself in a personal way so that you will all become better acquainted with who I am as a professional educator and who I am as a person. During the unfoldment, each of us should share those experiences from early in life to the present moment that we feel contributed to our being the persons we are now. These need not necessarily or even primarily be traumatic experiences, but you may include them. Sometime during the unfoldment, perhaps in the last minute, share the peak experience in your life."

Each team should appoint a timer. If a person is unable to use the full six minutes, the team should use the remaining time to ask questions. The leader should enforce the time limit in order to accomplish the goals of the session and in order to protect a team member from taking an undue share of time, which could create group hostility or personal anxiety. Because a positive feeling usually exists following the unfoldment, a break is not recommended unless the group is very tired.

2. *Paired interviews:* This activity is done as follows: Choose a member of your team whom you do not know well. It is your task to find out in an interview as much about your partner as possible. Take notes and ask any questions you wish. The person being interviewed has the right to refuse to answer any questions. After an eight- to ten-minute interview, return to the team and tell about the person your interviewed. Stand behind the person as you tell about him or her, place your hand on his or her shoulder, and report in the first person. Then change roles and repeat the procedure. As in unfoldment, one of the final statements should be a peak experience.

Listening

One of the skills effective teams must have is the ability to listen to each other. In this exercise, all team members should feed back to the first person who shared in an unfoldment or interview report just how much they remember. The feedback should continue around the group in the order that they shared.

This exercise focuses on both listening skills and empathy. Group members may discover how well they listened or should listen. In addition, the persons who are being talked about will discover that the group already knows a lot about them.

Developing Trust (Blind Walk)

The leader directs the team to pair off in twos and asks one member of each pair to close his or her eyes and allow himself or herself to be led by the partner. The pair may go out of the room or even out of the building. We recommend a "blind tour" of the building. They should return to the room in eight to ten minutes. When they return, the partners switch roles and repeat the exercise. This is a nonverbal exercise. The partners should not talk, but rely on nonverbal communication to accomplish the guidance during the blind walk.

At the end of the exercise (after both partners have completed their walks), it is important to allow time to debrief or talk about the activity.

The team members will be anxious to talk because they have been silent for almost twenty minutes.

A feeling of cooperation and trust is the desired outcome of this exercise.

Clarifying Values

By completing the form on Preferred Qualities of Students (Figure 10-2), team members become aware of their different values (Hurley & Randolph, 1971). Considering these qualities helps unit members look at teaching strategies and discipline.

FIGURE 10-2 · *Preferred Qualities of Elementary or Middle School Students*

Instructions: After reading completely through the qualities or chacteristics of children, as listed below, assign number "1" to the quality that you believe would be the most desirable quality in this list for a _____-year-old child. Then assign "2" to the attribute that you regard as second most important, "3" to the third most important, and so on until you have assigned a number to all ten of those listed qualities. You may, of course, change your mind or correct any assigned numbers as you go along. Please assign a number to each of these ten attributes, even if you find it quite difficult to make some choices. No tie scores, please.

Characteristics	*Rank*	
Responsible and trustworthy	_____	A
Neat and clean	_____	B
Curious	_____	C
Interacts well with others	_____	D
Considerate and cooperative	_____	E
Assertive and self-reliant	_____	F
Able to make friends	_____	G
Respectful toward adults	_____	H
Fun-loving and carefree	_____	I
Imaginative and creative	_____	J

Source: Adapted from J. Hurley and C. Randolph, "Behavioral Attributes Preferred in Eight-Year-Olds," *JSAS Catalog of Selected Documents in Psychology*, Fall 1971.

When each member of the team has completed the form, team members should compare their answers freely. When all teams have completed their answers, the leader of the team-building session should instruct each participant to add his or her scores for B, E, and H and compare the total with the total for C, F, and J. A higher score on B, E, and H indicates a preference for a more structured school environment. A higher score on C, F, and G indicates a preference for an unstructured school environment.

There are no right answers, but different values of team members may become apparent. Teams with both structured and unstructured teachers are more able to provide for students' learning styles.

Helping Each Other (Helper–Helpee)

This exercise demonstrates how an effective team functions. Each team member takes a turn at being the helpee, while the other team members serve as helpers. The helpee shares a real problem with the team, such as, "I have trouble structuring cooperative groups in mathematics," "I'm not successful reteaching skills," or "I can't manage kids with smart mouths like Betty and Cliff." Then the helpers try to help the helpee solve the problem.

The following process is used:

1. *Clarification:* The helpers ask the helpee questions to clarify the problem.
2. *Alternatives:* The helpers present alternative solutions to the problem while the helpee listens quietly.
3. *Application:* The helpee selects the best of the alternative solutions and describes how he or she may use this plan.

Adequate time must be provided for the completion of this activity.

Identifying Strengths (Strength Bombardment)

By this time in the sequence of team-building activities, the unit members should be getting to know a lot about each other. It is now appropriate to ask them to identify the personal strengths of the other team members (McHolland & Pestrue, 1968).

For this exercise, each team member will need a sheet of newsprint. The sheets are taped to the wall, and each one is divided into two columns (the column on the right should be only four to six inches wide. At the top of the left column is written "Strengths Others See in Me" and at the top of the right column, "Strengths I See in Myself." The name of the person whose strengths are to be identified is written at the top of the newsprint.

The leader should model the writing process by making a newsprint and listing the strengths of someone that all the participants know (for example, the principal or superintendent). The leaders will list strengths in many areas, such as effective teacher, good mother, good listener, creative, attractive, and so on. Then the leader would role play this person affirming or negating these strengths.

Next, the chairs should be arranged so that each person can easily walk up to the newsprint and write. The first segment of the exercise is nonverbal; no talking is allowed. The team members take turns writing the strengths of the team member on the newsprint with a felt pen. When the newsprint is filled or no one else wants to record a strength, the verbal phase begins. Each person who listed a strength will look at the person and explain why he or she wrote the strength or will clarify what the strength means. Finally, the person whose strengths have been listed stands and validates (or negates) the strengths by checking them in the column titled "Strengths I See in Myself." That person also verbalizes why these are seen as strengths. He or she may also add a strength that was not listed. When he or she finishes, one of the team members should remove the newsprint from the wall and present it to him or her. The process continues until every member of the unit team has a record of his or her personal strengths.

Arriving at Agreement ("We Agree")

Arriving at agreement is the most important of the team-building skills. In this situation, each team must be given adequate time to complete this activity fully. The purpose of the "We agree" activity is to build a living team philosophy. The words "We agree" should be written on the chalkboard or newsprint. Then the team should generate as many statements as possible that all can agree on, such as "Children learn . . . ," "The role of the teacher is . . . ," "The school should . . . ," "The team will . . . ," "Our student outcomes this year are . . . ." The "We agree" activity helps each team member build and internalize the team philosophy.

It cannot be overemphasized how crucial this activity is. Every statement suggested for the "We agree" philosophy must become a statement that is acceptable to each member of the unit team. Much discussion within an open atmosphere is necessary to allow team members to explain their feelings toward a statement. Also, each teacher should thoroughly understand the meaning of a statement before agreeing to it. Many changes and compromises may have to be made before a statement is acceptable to all members of the team. The statements that are agreed upon are combined to form the unit team's philosophy. Those statements that do not receive complete agreement are not included in the team's philosophy (though they may be kept for future discussion).

In the long run, the "We agree" statements are edited or converted into objectives and made public to the other teams, the students, the parents, and the community.

If all the teachers in the schools are participating in the team-building sequence, school goals and a school mission statement can be developed from the "We agree" statements. Each team's statements should be edited and reproduced in print and on a transparency. The statements can be presented and discussed at a faculty meeting. A committee including the principal can combine these statements so that they become the nucleus for the development of school goals and a mission statement.

Process meetings may be required so that all teachers have an opportunity to discuss and suggest improvements for the school goals so that they internalize these goals the same way that they internalize the "We agree" statements.

Restructuring's Costs: Commitment and Sacrifice

Today's teachers and principals are the best trained and most capable in U.S. history. However, they have been assigned to teach the hardest to educate group of students in the country's history. And in many schools it looks as if we are losing the battle to improve young lives through education. Students continue to give up, drop out, and self-destruct because teachers are unable to meet their individual needs (White, 1989). What we need to consider is a thought of Winston Churchill: "It's not good enough to do our best; sometimes we have to do what is required."

The teachers and principals in the model schools were successful because they gave their students what was required: *commitment* and *personal sacrifice*. How did they do this? By giving their students more time, by using their own money when other funds were not available, and by demonstrating courage by standing up for their students.

Time

Good teachers must find more time to help their students achieve in school. Good teachers stay an extra thirty or sixty minutes each night, tutor one extra child, decorate their room to motivate their students, make that extra parent phone call, create that brilliant lesson, take some students on a Saturday trip, and dig deeper into their personal lives and share more of their time with their students (White, 1989).

Money

Good teachers use their own money to give to their students greater chances for success. They may help send a special student to camp; buy something for the classroom that will stimulate learning; or hire students to do a nonessential job that gives them pride and pocket money to buy shampoo, deodorant, and so on. These teachers know how to use their seed money to reap great dividends with their students (White, 1989).

Courage

Good teachers demonstrate it more. If a student is getting a bum deal, they stand up for him or her. If parents are indifferent, they visit the home and challenge them to help. If their students are in the grip of drugs or gangs, they lead the charge against these practices. They have the courage to take risks for their students (White, 1989).

We are suggesting that restructuring schooling to provide for individual students requires more than good organizational and teaching strategies and appropriate staff development. It requires commitment and personal sacrifice by teachers and principals. The cost may be a few fights with your spouse about "always working on school things" or "spending our money on your students." It may be putting jobs or personal safety on the line for students. The reward is the satisfaction of making a difference in someone's life.

Restructuring is a time for educators to show the depth of their commitment and their willingness to sacrifice for a worthy cause. We should never doubt that a small group of thoughtful, committed educators can restructure a school to provide for individual students. Margaret Mead reminds us that small groups of determined people are the only thing that have ever caused institutions to change. Her words are reassuring.

Once the restructured program has been implemented, we believe that when a visitor asks an upper elementary or middle school student this question, "When you are much older, in high school or college, and someone asks you what was the most important thing you learned at this school, what will you say?" the student will answer without hesitation, "To believe in myself."

Summary

In this chapter the leadership and change processes that school staffs can use to restructure instructional programs were described. These strategies included descriptions from both the model schools and those in the Mastery in Learning Project. A sequence for staff development to implement a restructured program was presented. The relationship of the stages of a teacher's professional development and restructuring was described. The role of the principal in staff development and restructuring was explained. Finally, the requirements for successful restructuring — personal commitment and sacrifice — were presented.

References

Bechtol, W. (1973). *Individualizing instruction and keeping your sanity.* Chicago: Follett.

Bechtol, W. (1976). Guiding the I & R unit. In J. Jorenson, M. Poole, & L. Joyal (Eds.), *The unit leader and individually guided education* (pp. 91–124). Reading, MA: Addison-Wesley.

Bechtol, W. (1984). *Effective Practices in the Multicultural Elementary Classroom.* San Marcos: Southwest Texas State University.

Bechtol, W., Jr. (1991). Responsibilities of the principal. Presentation to the Oak Hills Rotary Club, San Antonio, TX.

David, J. (1991). What it takes to restructure education. *Educational Leadership,* 48(8): 11–15.

DuFour, R. (1990). How effective principals get results. Presentation at the Annual Conference of the Association for Supervision and Curriculum Development, San Antonio, TX.

Evans, R. (1989). The faculty in midcareer: Implications for school improvement. *Educational Leadership,* 46(8): 10–15.

Glickman, C. (1991). Pretending not to know what we know. *Educational Leadership,* 48(8): 4–10.

Guskey, T. (1991a). Integrating innovations. *Educational Leadership,* 47(5): 11–15.

Guskey, T. (1990b). Integrating staff development. Presentation. Educational Service Center Region XIII, Austin, TX.

Hennesay, J. (1990). Mastery in learning project. Presentation at the International Conference of the Association for Individually Guided Education, Cambridge, MA.

Hollifield, J. (1991). Restructuring's great promise: Improved student outcomes. *Doubts and Certainties,* 5(6): 1–5.

Hunter, M. (1990). Preface: Thoughts on staff development. In B. Joyce, ed. *Changing school culture through staff development* (pp. xi–xiv). Alexandria, VA: Association for Supervision and Curriculum Development.

Hurley, J., & Randolph, C. (1971). Behavioral attributes preferred in eight-year-olds. *JSAS Catalog of Selected Documents in Psychology,* Fall.

Leithwood, K. (1990). The principal's role in teacher development. In B. Joyce (Ed.), *Changing school culture through staff development* (pp. 71–90). Alexandria, VA: Association for Supervision and Curriculum Development.

Luft, J. (1963). *Group processes: An introduction to group dynamics.* Palo Alto, CA: National Press.

The mastery in learning project. (1987). Information packet. Washington, DC: National Education Association.

McClure, R. (1988). The evolution of shared leadership. *Educational Leadership,* 46(3): 60–62.

McHolland, J., & Pestrue, J. (1968). *Human potential seminars.* Mimeographed. Evanston, IL: Kendall College.

Ray, P. (1989). The journey toward becoming a staff developer. *Journal of Staff Development,* 10(3): 28–32.

Showers, B., Joyce, B., & Bennett, B. (1987). Synthesis of research on staff development: A framework for future study and a state-of-the-art analysis. *Educational Leadership,* 45(3): 77–87.

Sizer, T. (1991). No pain, no gain. *Educational Leadership,* 48(8): 32–34.

Springhill, N., & Theis-Springhill, L. (1983). The teacher as an adult learner. In Gary Griffin (Ed.), *Staff Development.* Chicago: University of Chicago Press.

Weissglass, J. (1990). Constructivist listening for empowerment and change. *The Educational Forum,* 54(4): 351–370.

Westerberg, T., & Brickley, D. (1991). Restructuring a comprehensive high school. *Educational Leadership,* 48(8): 23–26.

White, P. (1989). Personal sacrifice. *Instructor,* 99(2): 94.

APPENDIX

The Appendix contains a set of instructional activities for teachers to use to help elementary and middle school students to develop higher level thinking skills. It also contains sample administrative forms and management strategies to help principals implement restructured school programs.

One management strategy, "Starting the School Year," describes how teachers can obtain student cooperation in following classroom rules and procedures and in completing assignments. This description is especially useful for beginning teachers and for teachers in different settings.

Instructional Activities: Higher Level Thinking

Forms and Strategies for Classroom Management

DING-A-LING DEFINITIONS IN MATH AND SCIENCE

1. _____ What gentlemen go to the beach to become

2. _____ Advice to a young man when he takes his girlfriend home

3. _____ A couple who goes bowling

4. _____ How may I make a sweater?

5. _____ What little acorns say when they grow up

6. _____ What to call a dead parrot

7. _____ Where people go for committing crimes

8. _____ What to do when it rains

9. _____ Primitive drum music

10. _____ What happens when someone bumps your arm during a geometry construction

11. _____ How to dig a ditch

12. _____ What you hope to do when you go zoid hunting

13. _____ A huge purple spring flower

14. _____ Only medium tall

15. _____ The day after a sunsoon

16. _____ What does a barber do?

17. _____ Condition my shoelaces are in

18. _____ What gram hunters hope to do

19. _____

20. _____

Some words to choose from:

kilogram	geometry	rectangle
moonsoon	polygon	tangent
Fahrenheit	coincide	lever
eclipse	unit	logarithm
ultraviolet	digit	meter
tide	atmosphere	trapezoid
aquifer	geyser	water table
parabolas	prism	

Source: Unknown

NUMBER AND WORD JUMBLE

Instructions: Each item contains the first letter of words that make up a fact, saying, title, phrase, etc. **Example: 26 L of the A** would be *26 letters of the alphabet.*

1. 26 L of the A _____

2. 7 W of the A W _____

3. 12 S of the Z _____

4. 16 O in a P _____

5. 54 C in a D (with J) _____

6. 1001 A N _____

7. 9 P on a B T _____

8. 12 I in a F _____

9. 9 P in the S S _____

10. 88 K on a P _____

11. 13 S on the A F _____

12. 3 C in a F _____

13. 32 D F at which W F _____

14. 18 H on a G C _____

15. 100 P in a D _____

16. 4 and 20 B B in a P _____

17. 90 D in a R A _____

18. 8 S on a S S _____

19. 4 Q in a G _____

20. 24 H in a D _____

21. 11 P on a F T _____

22. 64 S on a C _____

23. 40 D and N of the G F _____

24. 5 D in a Z C _____

Source: Unknown

SWEET LOVER'S DELIGHT

Directions: Find the name of the candy bar or candy product for the phrase on the left.

1. Five Greasy Ones   _____

2. Three Jolly Ones   _____

3. Baseball Giant   _____

4. What Bees Make   _____

5. Some Small Hills   _____

6. A Planet   _____

7. A Nut and Happiness   _____

8. Heavenly Body   _____

9. American Story Writer   _____

10. Pleasingly Plump   _____

11. Type of Laughter   _____

12. Famous Street in New York   _____

13. Mutinous Ship   _____

14. Feline Pet   _____

15. Open to Everybody   _____

16. Can't Think of the Name   _____

17. Final Result of a Game   _____

18. Sound When Eating Raw Carrots   _____

19. Opposite of Jump High   _____

20. Respected Gentleman of Bar Family   _____

21. Noise when Green Wood Burns   _____

22. A Lonely English Field   _____

23. Fast Racer   _____

24. Crowd Close Together   _____

25. Teacher's Delight   _____

FOOTBALL FUN

First: List all of the professional football teams you know.

Then: Be a bit *flexible* in your thinking. What team is . . . ?

1. I.O.U.'s _____
2. Six shooter _____
3. Toy baby with fins _____
4. Boeing 747 _____
5. Sun-tanned bodies _____
6. Iron workers _____
7. Used to be gals _____
8. Lubricators _____
9. Opposite of ewes _____
10. Rodeo horses _____
11. Ocean-going birds _____
12. Indian leaders _____
13. Credit card users _____
14. American gauchos _____

15. Hot epidermis _____
16. Army ants _____
17. Rank in Boy Scouts _____
18. Fundamental rules _____
19. Six rulers _____
20. Helpers to relocate _____
21. King of beasts _____
22. Streakers are these _____
23. A dollar for corn _____
24. Seven squared _____
25. Trained to kill _____
26. Hostile attackers _____
27. Louis Armstrong's theme song __
28. Loyal Americans _____

Answers to Professional Football Teams

1. Bills
2. Colts
3. Dolphins
4. Jets
5. Browns
6. Steelers
7. Bengals
8. Oilers
9. Rams
10. Broncos
11. Seahawks
12. Chiefs
13. Chargers
14. Cowboys

15. Redskins
16. Giants
17. Eagles
18. Cardinals
19. Vikings
20. Packers
21. Lions
22. Bears
23. Buccaneers
24. Forty Niners
25. Falcons
26. Raiders
27. Saints
28. Patriots

Source: Unknown

SPORTS-O-WHATS

1. Identify the city and state where each of the professional football teams play (e.g., Vikings in Minneapolis, Minnesota).

2. Search out the derivation of the name of each team (e.g., Bears) and explain how it relates to the geographical setting in which the team plays.

3. Search out the colors and designs of the uniform for each team. How do the design and colors relate to the team's name and geographical location? Are there exceptions? If so, explain them.

4. Make your own list of Sports-o-Whats (like Football Fun) for the following:

   - Major league baseball teams
   - National Basketball Association teams
   - National Hockey League teams
   - Big Ten, Big Eight, and other college/university teams
   - Other sport teams and leagues

5. Carry out 1, 2, and 3 above for other kinds of teams—baseball, basketball, hockey, and so on.

6. Pretend you are an athlete in your favorite sport and create your own baseball-type card. Exchange cards with others in your class. How are the cards alike and different? Collect a set for the class bulletin board and write a story about them for a newspaper.

7. Become philosophical and search for information and try to explain the fascination people have with sports in the United States and in the world. Where did it start, and why? Look at both historical and present-day reasons for the popularity of sports. In your investigation, include sociological and psychological as well as physical aspects of sports. Also, consider the economic impact of sports in terms of employment in professional and school personnel, radio, newspaper, and television coverage and other relevant areas. When you have gathered considerable information, write one or a series of newspaper articles or television or radio scripts for broadcast. Also, you might want to make an audio or videotape of your program.

8. Research the history of the Olympic Games from their beginnings to the present. Make a timeline to illustrate the history—including dates, verbal explanations, and, if possible, drawings or copies of drawings you found in books. Develop a television or radio script on the basis of your information and emphasize how the early games were alike and different from the current ones. Add any special information you wish, including visuals.

9. Using previous team and individual player performance records, make inferences and predictions on scores of games (football, baseball, basketball, etc.). Then compare your predictions and the actual scores when the games are played. Chart your predictions and actual scores on the same graph and, if you wish, calculate your total percentage of error for the season. Create another product of your own design using the information you have gathered.

10. Injuries are a big part of sports. How is protective equipment designed in relation to body parts in football, baseball, hockey, basketball, and other sports? Relate the design to the force and velocity of the person playing a particular sport. Use diagrams along with dialogue to explain the design of equipment for one sport and give a report to the class or write an article for the sports section of the school newspaper.

11. Create a new sport—individual or team. Write a set of rules for the game, design a site ideal for playing your sport along with necessary equipment to play it as safely as possible. Design a brochure to give to coaches and fellow students to interest them in your sport. (Tip: Research the history of sports for some ideas to help you generate a new one; include sports that native people play or played.)

12. Investigate the economic impact of professional and college sports in terms of geographical location of the game site, television and radio revenues, and employment. Develop this information to present to the city council.

INSIDE THE RAINBOW

Pretend that you are in a space vehicle that is flying through a rainbow. Find the answers to the following questions and activities!

1. What causes a rainbow? When do you usually see them? Why?

2. What is the order of the colors in a rainbow as you observe it from the horizon upward? Explain the relationship of the order of the colors to the wavelengths of light. How does refraction enter in?

3. Obtain a prism or several of them from a science teacher. Hold the prism in bright light. What happens? How is this related to a rainbow?

4. What is a spectroscope? What is it used for and how does it relate to a rainbow and the wavelengths of light? Make a diagram to help explain how wavelengths and rainbow colors are related? Be creative!

5. Integrate the information you obtained in the questions and activities above into a story, magazine article, or television script about a trip you could take "inside the rainbow." Add characters, vehicles, environments, and other things or situations as needed to make your work interesting and exciting.

Key words: rainbow, color, wavelength, spectroscope, refraction, light

RAISE A RUCKUS
Onomatopoeia—Sound Words

1. Make a list of sounds that have a steady rhythm (clock, dripping water faucet). Choose one idea to write a poem about. Match the rhythm of the poem to the rhythm of the sound. Tape yourself reciting the poem with the sound as your background.

2. Using "Old MacDonald Had a Farm" as a model, write the lyrics to a song about another noisy place. Teach your song to the class.

3. Write the alphabet vertically on your paper. Write a word describing a sound beginning with each letter of the alphabet. Make up a color code system to classify the sounds in your list. Try some easy categories like loud and soft and in-between sounds. How about some harder ones like summer and winter sounds? Now a few to really make us think, like yellow sounds, shiny sounds. What else? Were any sounds hard to classify? Why?

4. Radio shows used sound effects to make their stories more realistic. With a group of three to four others, choose a familiar story from your reading book. Practice reading your selection with accuracy and expression. Next, add sound effects to your reading. Tape the final product. Share the tape with another class.

5. Working in a group of six to eight, create a people machine. Each person becomes a moving part of the machine. Determine what job your machine is to perform and what parts will be needed to accomplish the task. When you have your machine working well in a silent fashion, add sound to it with each person making a sound appropriate to the part.

   **Key words:** rhythm, onomatopoeia, poetry, lyrics, expression

Used with permission of Mary Kay Francis.

I'VE GOT YOUR NUMBER!

There will be 7 billion people in the world in 2000. They are located in millions of households and offices in over 200 countries. How can these people communicate with each other? The secret is to organize the world into areas and give each area a different logical code. The telephone system is a good example.

Today, almost every person in the world can call another person almost anywhere at any time. In the 1920s, you told a live operator a simple number such as 52J and most calls were local. By the 1940s, you could dial a local number and some regional numbers for an automatic connection. By the 1960s, telephones were used in most parts of the world, and long-distance calling for business and personal use became part of everyday life.

Now, each telephone in the world needs its own individual number. First the United States and then other countries of the world were divided into regions and given an "area code" in addition to the individual residence or business number. Within the United States you could dial directly using a "1" (for long distance), plus a 3-digit area code, plus the 7-digit number. An example would be 1-800-555-1212. For international calling, you use an access number plus a country cluster code, plus the individual number. To call someone in Paris, France, today you might use a number or code such as this: 011 (international access code) + 33 (France) + 1 (Paris) + 234-5678 (individual number).

The postal delivery system is another good example of coding. As mail became heavier and went greater distances, the United States in 1963 was organized into areas which were coded into a 5-digit system called the Zone Improvement Plan (ZIP), the familiar "zip codes." For example, the ZIP 53705 is broken down as follows: "5" indicates a part of the midwest; "3" indicates southern and southeastern Wisconsin; "7" indicates the city of Madison; and "05" an area or zone of the city of Madison. Part of the ZIP is the 2-letter code of the state such as "WI" for Wisconsin, "CA" for California, etc.

Countries around the world are adopting postal codes to make world mail delivery more efficient. Some countries have a 2-letter code followed by four or five numbers (DK-4500 is Denmark) or a combination of letters and numbers (TOL1RO is Canada).

Number and letter codes can form millions of combinations to reach every individual in the world through modern communications technology such as telephones, mail, fax machines, satellite transmissions, and yet undiscovered ways. Using communications technology efficiently and effectively is a challenge for the twenty-first century.

Objectives

01. To integrate three types of codes—ZIP, telephone, and state—that were established in the United States in the 1960s in terms of (1) need for development, (2) rationale, and system behind the codes, (3) how they are updated, and (4) how they have spread to other countries in the world.

02. To develop *consistent* alternative or modified versions of the present ZIP, telephone, country, and state codes for the 170 countries of the world.

Exploring Activities

01. Study the rationale and system underlying the development of the zip codes in the United States in the 1960s and write a story or make a tape explaining it to someone from another country.

02. There are currently 42,396 zip codes in the United States. You cannot possibly put these on a map, but you can show the sequence of zip code numbers by plotting the *first two digits* of the zip codes on an outline map of the United States.

03. Investigate the history of the development of the original forty telephone area codes in the United States in the 1960s. Find these codes in a city telephone directory or an encyclopedia. Duplicate the list and map or plot the codes on

a map of the United States. Then, make a game for your classmates in which they would estimate which area code goes with each state or group of states. Give points for correct answers. Are the area code numbers logical? Do they have any relation to geographical areas? Investigate to find out and prepare a talk, tape, or news article about the rationale and development of telephone area codes in the United States. Include addition of recent area codes.

Problem-Solving Activities

01.   World-wide Country Codes. In 1963, as a part of the development of zip codes, the U.S. Postal Service designed an official set of two-letter abbreviations or codes for the states of the country. Find this set of codes in an almanac, dictionary, or encyclopedia. These codes supersede any previous codes that had been used. Note that both letters are capitalized and there is *not* a period after the second letter unless it is the end of a sentence.

Some countries in Europe, such as Denmark, have also developed country codes; for example, Denmark is DK. The people use DK as a part of their international address and also on their auto license plates. Luxembourg uses a single L in the same manner. Investigate to find out more country letter codes. Then, develop a set of two-letter codes like those we use for our states for all countries in the world. Be sure to make a country code for the United States, too. Make the codes as meaningful as possible, such as DK for Denmark. Remember, no two abbreviations can be alike. You will want to first find an alphabetized list of the 170 countries in an almanac or dictionary, then develop your codes. Also, you do not want to duplicate a state code with a country code. You might want to use a computer to help you in this project.

02.   Codes for the Twenty-First Century. After considering all the different kinds of codes and abbreviations in the telephone and postal codes, think ahead to codes we need for fax machine and satellite transmissions and consider how they could be simplified to eliminate overlapping and overwhelming different sets of numbers. After you have thought about this and investigated plans for fax and satellite access and transmission from your local area, design a whole new system for the 170 countries of the world to integrate all codes. These new codes could be used for telephone, mail, fax, satellite, and any other form of communication.

Put your codes next to an alphabetized list of countries and also plot them on a map of the world. Present your products to a session of the Rotary or other organization that has an interest in world developments. Try to interest others in your project and take it to the telephone company or post office in your area. GOOD LUCK! (A computer would be very helpful for this project.)

Copyright EDCRAFT, 1989, Juanita Sorenson, Madison, Wisconsin.

YOU'RE IN THE MONEY!

When people first started to trade with each other, they paid "in kind." For example, a horse bought four sheep or a bushel of wheat bought two bushels of potatoes. This system, called "bartering," was cumbersome, and later a system of coins or money was developed to pay for goods and services. Coins had to be convenient in size, long wearing, and of some value. They needed to have a distinctive appearance so they could be readily identified but not easily duplicated. Gold or silver usually made the highest value coins, and copper and zinc were used for coins of lower value. A country or kingdom stamped its identification on its coins and gave them names and values. Thus, a metal currency system developed around the world. You may have read about old Roman coins of 2,000 years ago or crude gold "pieces of eight" coins of Spain about 800 years ago.

Each country created a basic coin, such as the French franc, German mark, English pound, Spanish peseta, or American dollar. For convenience in daily trading, they named smaller divisions of their coins (100 centimes to a franc, 20 shillings to a pound, or 100 cents to a dollar). Currencies have changed over the centuries, and many people today have made a hobby of collecting old coins. In modern times, most countries have also developed paper in varying values but with the same names as their basic coin. For example, the United States has paper currency in denominations of $1, $5, $10, and so on.

Trading between countries with different currencies can become complicated, and exchange values need to be set. Also, currency values change over a period of time for a number of reasons, such as wars, amount of foreign trade, droughts, earthquakes, changes in leadership in government, and the economic well-being of the country.

Since trade and communication have become international, conferences of several nations, which are held every few decades, have attempted to make the values of different currencies more stable. This kind of meeting was held in 1985 and involved several European countries, the United States, and Japan. In recent years the major European trading partners of the United States have used the term "Eurodollar" for a combination of currencies. This is not a coin or paper money, but perhaps some day in the future the world will use a single currency for easier trading among nations.

Objectives

01. To investigate the money system of the United States and of other foreign countries, recognize the basic money units of major countries; recognize that the currency of one country can be exchanged for that of another; recognize that the value of the dollar compared to the currency of other countries can vary depending on political, economic, and social factors.
02. To evaluate and present both sides of an argument on a statement related to money in the United States and the world and create up-to-date and practical currency for the United States and the world.

Exploring Activities

01. In a dictionary or encyclopedia, find the names of the basic money units (for example, the dollar for the United States) for fifteen countries besides the

United States: Great Britain, Germany, Japan, France, The Netherlands, Egypt, Australia, China, Russia, Israel, Argentina, India, Mexico, Canada, and Thailand. Make a chart with columns for *country, name of basic money unit,* and three vacant columns to add more information later.

02. Since currencies or money are traded on an international market, their values may vary in relation to each other each day. Find a foreign exchange chart or table in a local Sunday newspaper or the daily *Wall Street Journal* in the "money" or "financial" section. Then, mark one of your columns in the chart from exploring activity 01 as "foreign exchange rate in relation to dollar" and add the date. Complete the column on the chart for as many countries as you can find on the newspaper list. Remember, in a U.S. newspaper, the other currencies are compared to the dollar; for example, one U.S. dollar will buy about 1.7 German marks.

Problem-Solving Activities

01. The cent or penny is probably the most discussed coin we have in the United States because you can't buy anything with just one of them. Yet we all have several pennies in our pocket or purse. Many items cost $2.99 or a similar uneven price, and sales taxes nearly always make the amount due come out with pennies left over, such as 53 cents, $1.03, or $4.49. Support or reject this statement: *The United States should stop making one-cent coins.* Provide reasons for your response.

02. Review the relationships between the dollar and currency values for the fifteen countries in your chart in exploring activity 01. For example, for one U.S. dollar (October 15, 1991) you would receive:

    1.70 Deutschmarks (Germany); 129.95 Japanese yen
    5.79 French francs; 0.58 British pound (England)

Wide variations of values make currency exchange confusing and cumbersome for international business and individual travelers. To carry out these exchanges, each country has official exchange agencies and banks. Each time an individual or business exchanges money, it pays a *commission* for the service. The commission varies from a few hundredths of a percent per unit for large amounts of money to 2 to 3 percent for a $20 traveler's check.

    While changing currency makes jobs for people who work in exchange departments, it also costs businesses and individuals millions of dollars. In a world where we can communicate instantly via satellite and fax machines, it seems that we need an international currency that could be used in every country of the world. Learn all you can about international currency, and then design a new set of currency to use throughout the world. Keep the system simple so people can use it in everyday life. Explain your system and include illustrations of your set of currency. Include a rationale for your system along with its advantages and disadvantages over the ones we use now. Plan to take your idea to the United Nations.

Copyright EDCRAFT, 1989, Juanita Sorenson, Madison, Wisconsin.

STATES OF THE UNITED STATES

1. Name the capital cities of each state and locate them on a U.S. map. Explain why each capital has its particular location and name.
2. Search out the nickname of each state (e.g., Badgers for Wisconsin), and try to find and explain the reason for the nickname. (Tip: Consider the date of statehood in your explanation.)
3. Consider and develop new nicknames for the states if they were entering the union today.
4. Design new license plates and new slogans that would be appropriate for any ten states today.
5. Draw new state boundaries for all 50 states that will place approximately the same number of people in each state (without moving the people).
6. Draw a new map of the United States with the states having a geographical size in proportion to their populations (e.g., North Dakota would be a smaller state than Rhode Island).
7. Design a flag for each state that could represent that state in the 1990s. Provide a rationale for each part of the design.
8. Write a poem that would represent a state or a group of states (e.g., Midwestern states, West Coast states).
9. Write words and music for a new song that would represent the United States or a state in the 1990s.
10. Search out the "states with the mostest" for the following: highest population, highest elevation, most square miles, longest river, greatest number of lakes, highest income per person, most oil, most government-owned land, most miles of coastline, most representatives in Congress, etc. Make a Guiness-type "Book of Records" for the states.
11. On U.S. maps, show the population density of the country in 1900, 1950, and 1990. What shifts in population have occurred and what are the causes of these shifts? Summarize your answers in an article, poster, or other format.
12. Obtain a map of the United States that shows elevations and landforms. Compare the population density in 1990 or later with the types of landforms. What interesting relationships do you find? Why? Explain your findings in an article, chart, or news broadcast.
13. Research the types of climate in different parts of the United States. Select the "ten best sites" for a vacation according to a set of criteria you develop. Design a travel brochure to lure tourists to the ten sites. Use only real and authentic information in your brochure.
14. Visit five different travel bureaus or offices and ask them the ten most frequently visited areas in the United States according to their sales records. Compare these destinations to the ones you selected on the basis of climate. What other factors beside climate affect the popularity of tourist sites? Develop your findings into a travelogue, speech, or other format.

Copyright EDCRAFT, 1989, Juanita Sorenson, Madison, Wisconsin.

PROBLEM-SOLVING WORKSHEET

This worksheet is designed to accompany Figure 6-7, Practical Problem-Solving Model.

1. Explore the problem.
   Make several problem statements;
   include criteria.

   _____

   _____

2. State the problem.
   Select the best statement from
   step 1.

   _____

   _____

3. General optional solutions.
   Brainstorm alternative ways to
   solve the problem; relate to the
   criteria and problem statement.

   _____

   _____

   _____

4. Select the best solution.
   Select the best statement from
   step 3.

   _____

   _____

5. Generate optional designs to test
   solution.
   List several alternative designs;
   include tasks.

   _____

   _____

   _____

6. Select and implement the best design.
   Select the best design from step 5;
   implement it and gather data.

   _____

   _____

   _____

7. Organize and interpret results.
   Summarize the results from
   implementation in several formats.

   _____

   _____

8. Evaluate the results.
   Select the best interpretation from
   step 7 and decide whether or not
   it solves the problem as stated in
   step 2.

   YES—the results solve the problem;
   go to 10.

   NO—the results do *not* solve the
   problem; go to 9.

9. NO: Start over, review, revise.

   Return to step 1 to review the action at each step; revise as necessary
   to solve the problem.

10. YES: Communicate the results.

    Share the results with others so they
    can repeat, verify, and accept them.
    The problem is solved, at least
    temporarily.

A SAMPLE HOMEWORK ASSIGNMENT LETTER

To the parents of

Today, for whatever reason, your child did not turn in a homework assignment. I have noticed in the past a definite correlation between a student not turning in homework and getting low grades.

There may be, of course, a valid reason for your child not having a homework paper. Should your child complete his homework paper and return it with this letter signed by you I will accept it with no grade penalty.

I will not accept the homework late without this letter.

Should your child return this letter signed but without attaching homework, a 0 will be assigned but no further discipline will be taken.

Should your child not return this letter signed by you I will refer him/her to the office.

If you think an extension of time is appropriate please note that below (no reason required) and return the letter with your child tomorrow.

Sincerely,

John Hayslip

_____

Parent's Signature

Used with permission of John Hayslip.

STARTING THE SCHOOL YEAR

This is a sample of a classroom management plan that is written for the first days of school.

The plan includes:

1. A list of rules
2. A short description of the school assignment, including a diagram of the classroom
3. A list of procedures
4. A description of Day One, including the teaching of rules and procedures and assigning students academic work
5. A description of Day Two, including the reteaching of rules and procedures and evaluating students' academic work
6. A list of motivation strategies

The plan is written before the teacher meets with the class.

RULES

1. Listen quietly while others are speaking.
2. Follow directions the first time.
3. Treat others as you would like to be treated.
4. Be responsible.
5. Obey all school rules.

EXPLANATION OF RULES

1. There should be absolutely no talking when a teacher or classmate is talking. Hands should be raised for permission to talk.
2. Students should listen carefully to the teacher and follow her instructions.
3. The students should work on getting along with each other. They should be polite and courteous to each other. They should not bother each other in any way. This includes touching, hitting, name calling, and talking with foul language.
4. Students should clean up after themselves. They should keep the room, class library, and student cubicles orderly and neat. They should ask permission to borrow supplies and return them when finished. The students are responsible for their own work and behavior.
5. This rule reminds students that they are representatives of our classroom in other parts of the school. They should obey and respect rules in the cafeteria, playground, and hallways. Other teachers have the authority to enforce these rules upon them.

Source: Adapted from K. Miori, *Classroom Management Plan* (San Marcos, TX: Southwest Texas State University, 1990).

An Example of a Good Room Arrangement

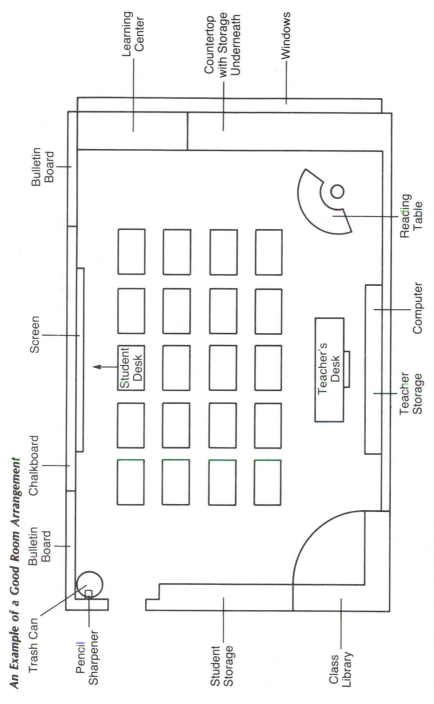

Trash Can

Pencil Sharpener

Bulletin Board

Chalkboard

Screen

Bulletin Board

Learning Center

Countertop with Storage Underneath

Windows

Student Desk

Reading Table

Computer

Teacher's Desk

Teacher Storage

Student Storage

Class Library

Source: Adapted from K. Miori, *Classroom Management Plan* (San Marcos, TX: Southwest Texas State University, 1990).

DESCRIPTION OF SCHOOL ASSIGNMENT
AND CLASSROOM ARRANGEMENT

I have accepted a teaching position at Brown Independent School District. There are two elementary schools in Brown reaching a total of 1,280 elementary age students. I will be teaching third grade at Mica Elementary. There are approximately 835 students at Mica Elementary in grades K–5. Thirty-five percent of the students in the district come from low socioeconomic households and are on the state-supported meal plan.

I have twenty students in my class. There are eleven girls and nine boys. Eighteen of my students are part of the extensive busing program due to the 451 square miles the district covers. Many of my students also come from low socioeconomic households. My class is a self-contained room, and I am responsible for teaching all subjects except P.E. and music.

The classroom will have twenty desks facing the front chalkboard and overhead screen. A language arts and math learning center will be in the front corner of the classroom. A computer will be available for the students' use. A class library/reading center will be in the back corner of the classroom. It will have a large rug, a rocking chair, and pillows. The children's coats and lunches will be stored in the cubicles located by the door. Plants will be placed on the cabinet underneath the windows. I plan to add a science learning center with an aquarium later in the year.

I want to offer my students a cheerful yet comfortable environment. I want them to feel proud of their room.

PROCEDURES

Teacher's Desk or Storage Areas

Students are not allowed to remove or touch anything on the teacher's desk or in the storage area without her permission. If the teacher is at her desk, only *one* student will be allowed to approach her at a time.

Students' Desks and Cubicles

Each child is responsible for his/her desk. Students will not bother or touch any other student's desk or supplies without permission from that student. The cubicles are marked with each of the children's names. Coats, lunches, and art supplies are to be stored in this area as soon as the child comes to class in the morning.

Storage for Games and Activities

Each student will be allowed to work games, puzzles, etc., when his/her seatwork is completed. Each student will be given a 3" × 12" piece of oaktag with his/her name written on it. This is his or her marker.

When the student removes an item from the shelf, he/she will place the marker in its place. The marker will remind the student where the activity belongs, and I can monitor who is using the games.

Bathroom and Water Fountain

Students may use the restroom without permission only when the teacher is not presenting a lesson or at designated times. Students will go the restroom one at a time. Each student's name will be listed on a small chart. When the child leaves to go to the restroom or water fountain, he or she will clip the large plastic clothespin beside his or her name. When the child returns, he or she will place the clothespin at the top of the chart. The water fountain will be used by one child at a time. Other children must stand at least one person away from the student who is drinking.

Pencil Sharpener

Students should sharpen their pencils as soon as they get to school. During class, students may sharpen their pencils without permission *only* when the teacher is not presenting a lesson. Only one student is allowed at the pencil sharpener at a time.

Trash Can

Students may walk to the trash can to throw away trash at any time as long as the teacher is not presenting a lesson. Students must always walk up to the trash can and not "shoot baskets" from their seats.

Leaving the Classroom

The students will be called by rows. The quietest row will proceed first. Students should not talk or misbehave in any way while lining up or walking to the designated area. The helping hand for the day will be the leader each time. The last one out should turn out the lights.

Computers

Every student must have permission from the teacher to use the computer. A student cannot use the computer until he or she passes the initial test on handling and using the computer. The student will be issued a disk to use. He or she will sign his or her name on a tablet stating the time he or she signed on and signed off. He or she must write down the name of the program he or she used. The student may only print material when given permission. The student will return the disk to the teacher when completed. The computer area must be cleaned after each use.

Entering the Classroom

The students will sit down quietly. They will get prepared for their next assignment. There should be no talking unless permission is given to whisper.

Discipline Procedure

> First offense: Name on board as a warning
> Second offense: Check mark by name and loss of five minutes at recess
> Third offense: Two checks by name and loss of entire recess. The student must sit by the teacher and watch the other children play.
>
> Fourth offense: Three checks by name, loss of entire recess, no classroom privileges, isolation at lunch, and call parents
> Fifth offense: Four checks by name and sent to principal's office

Collecting Assignments

Homework assignments will be passed forward to the front desk. The class helper will collect these from the students. The papers will be paperclipped and placed in a red basket on my desk labeled "Homework In." In-class worksheets are to be placed by the child in his/her personal folder as soon as they are completed. The folders are listed in alphabetical order and divided by boy–girl. Tests and other specified papers are to be placed in the blue basket on the teacher's desk when completed.

Center and Stations (when seatwork is completed)

The students may use these areas when all seatwork is completed. Talking will not be allowed. A flowchart stating directions for each center is posted in large letters on the center itself. Each center is to be self-checked by the student.

Student Attention and Participation

Each student will face the teacher as he or she talks and listen attentively. Students should raise their hands and wait to be called on before answering. The teacher will tell the students when she wants choral answers.

Talk Among Students

No talking will be allowed during lesson presentations unless permitted by the teacher. During cooperative learning, whispering will be allowed. A "Zip It Up" sign will signal the students to talk quietly.

Beginning the School Day

The students will meet in the hallway with the other third-grade classes to say the Pledge of Allegiance and to sing a song. Each class will be allowed to leave the hallway and enter the classroom when the teacher's name is called. As each child enters the room, he or she will remove his or her name card from the chart by the door and place it in the "I'm Here!" basket. Names left on the board will show the teacher who is absent. The students should hang up their backpacks and place their lunches in their cubicles. Students should sharpen their pencils and get supplies ready for the day. They should sit at their desks and begin writing in their journals. During this time, lunch count and money will be taken. A timer will ring when the students should quit writing in their journals and put them away. Every Friday several students will be given a chance to share a story from their journal. After the journals are stored, the students should focus on the teacher and wait for her instructions or announcements. This will be completed by 8:20.

Ending the School Day

Ten minutes before class is over, the teacher will summarize the important topics the students studied. She will repeat what homework is due the following day to remind the students of the books they need. All supplies will be stored and desk areas cleaned. The teacher will call each group by row to pick up their belongings and to get in line. The rows will be called in the order according to their behavior that day. The helping hand will get to be first in line. If anyone in the group forgets to push in his chair or pick up trash around his desk, that row must sit back down. The teacher will escort the students to the buses.

Completion of Seatwork

Each student who has completed seatwork may read a library book, magazine from the class library, or work at the learning stations. Students should be quiet so they don't interrupt others who are still working.

Small-Group Activities

The students will be divided into three reading groups. Each group will have a captain for the week. The teacher will call the group's name aloud when she is ready for that group. The students will gather their materials and go to the reading table quietly. The other students will work independently at their desks on material previously demonstrated to them. If students working individually need help, they may ask their group captain. If the group captain is unable to answer the question, he or she may request help from the teacher. He or she may only interrupt the teacher once and it must be absolutely necessary. (The captain may ask the other group captain for help.) The teacher will answer questions from the students between reading groups.

Class Library

This area is used for special privileges. Students may use the pillows and relax while they are reading. The rocking chair is reserved strictly for the teacher when reading to students. No talking is allowed in this area. It is an area of tranquility. No books may be taken home from this area. They are strictly for classroom use. Students must take care of the class library or privileges may be taken away. No checkout procedure is required. Books will be returned to the shelf when completed.

Classroom Helpers

Each child will have traced his or her hand on tagboard, cut it out, and written his or her name on the hand. The hands will be mixed up and hung from a hook. The hands will remain in that order for the entire year. Every week a new hand will be placed in front. This child is the helper for the teacher each day until a new week starts. The helper's responsibilities will include class leader, watering the plants, running errands, erasing chalkboards, and distributing and collecting papers.

Cafeteria

Cafeteria money will have been collected and count taken during the morning procedure. The students will line up by rows and tickets will be issued by rows. The students will get their lunches at this time. The next row will not be called until the previous row is situated in line. Students will walk to the cafeteria quietly. The teacher will escort them. If talking occurs in the line, the student must go to the end of the line. The students will sit in the third-grade area. The teacher will not be in the cafeteria with the children. The cafeteria aides will monitor their behavior. All discipline problems will be reported to the teacher. Children are responsible for cleaning their eating area and returning their trays. When the children are finished eating, they will remain seated until the teacher returns. The children will line up boy–girl–boy–girl, etc., when told to line up. They will be escorted back to the classroom.

Playground

The children may play in the area designated for third-grade classes. Playground rules will be followed. Any violators will have to sit out the remainder of the recess beside the teacher. The teacher will blow a whistle one minute before the bell rings. The students must get in line (boy–girl) with the class leader in front by the ringing of the recess bell. The students will walk back to the building with a minimum of talking. Once inside the building, there should be no talking because others are in class.

Fire and Disaster Drills

When the bell rings, the students will automatically stop what they are doing. They will stand up and push in their chairs without talking. The students will get in line by rows. They will exit through the double doors at the end of the hallway. The class will stand by the slide on the playground in a straight line without talking until the bell rings to return.

Description of Day One

Time	Description	Activity
8:00–8:05	I will personally welcome each student who enters the classroom. "Good Morning. Welcome to the third grade. Please find your nametag on the bulletin board and select a desk. There are activity sheets on your desk to work until I begin class."	Greet Students
8:05–8:20	The students will be told to put away their activity sheets for now. After the sheets are stored, I will introduce myself. I will tell the students that I am proud and honored to teach at B.I.S.D. and that they should be proud to be students at this school. I will tell them that this is my first year at this school, and I have many exciting activities in store for them. Each of the students will then be given an opportunity to stand out and introduce himself or herself. I will take roll during this time.	Introductions (Teacher & Class)
8:30–8:40	I will point out the various features of our room. I will place special emphasis on having our own classroom computer and classroom library. I'll tell the students how we need to take pride in our room and keep it clean and tidy. I will point out where the pencil sharpener and trash can are located. Next, I will talk about the student storage area. Each cubicle will have the child's name marked on it. I will let the children proceed by rows to find their supplies. I will praise them on how well they followed directions. I will explain the Morning Procedure that they should follow every day.	Room Introduction

Time	Description	Activity
8:40–9:00	The children will focus their attention on the front bulletin board. We will discuss in depth the first three rules listed. The children will state reasons why each of these rules are important. I will ring the bell and demonstrate how they need to place their finger against their lips to indicate that they are quiet and listening. They will also focus their eyes on me at this time. I will reinforce them positively by smiling and saying, "I like the way that Mary and Sam are looking at me and paying attention."	Discussion of Rules and Procedures
9:00–9:10	I will explain the directions for a get-acquainted game. Each child will receive a tagboard cutout of a geometric figure (triangle, square, circle, etc.). They will only receive half of the cutout. The students must find the person that has the other half of their object. Once all the children have found their other half, they must ask each other to name at least one thing that they like to do; for example, "I like bicycle riding." I will call on various pairs at random to say their partners' names and what activity they like to do. Each child will repeat the same procedure.	Get-Acquainted Game
9:10–9:20	Following the game, I will have each child return to his or her seat and praise him or her for following directions and treating others as he or she would like to be treated. The children will be issued a piece of tagboard. They will trace their hands, cut them out, and place their names on the hands. These hands will be laminated and used to indicate who is the helping hand of the day.	Class Activity
9:20–9:30	After the children have completed the activity, I will discuss the rule of being responsible. The students will be able to prove that they are responsible by cleaning up their area, returning their supplies to the cubicle, and turning in their hands. The procedure for handing in materials will be discussed. I will refocus the students' attention by raising my hand and placing my finger to my lips for silence. The children will follow the same procedure. I will tell the students, "You follow directions so well. Let's give ourselves a pat on the back." Each child will pat himself or herself on the back.	Discussion of Rules and Procedures

Time	*Description*	*Activity*
9:30–10:00	I will issue three textbooks to the students and record the numbers. A step-by-step demonstration will be given on how to cover books properly. The children will write their names in the books. We will talk about how the books are school property and how we should be responsible for them by keeping them covered, clean, and free of marks on the inside.	Book Checkout
10:00–10:15	School procedures for leaving the room, returning from recess, and going to the bathroom will be discussed. Students will be selected at random to role play the correct procedures after they have been discussed. The fifth rule of obeying all school rules will be elaborated upon. The children will not be allowed to run in the halls and they should listen to all other adults. "The playground monitors are representatives of me, the teacher. You will follow their rules just like you follow our classroom rules. Look at the bottom of our bulletin board underneath our rules. It states, 'I know you can do it!' This sign will always be posted somewhere in our room. I have faith in you. Let's line up, as we practiced, for recess."	School Procedures and Rules
10:15–10:30	Students have recess.	
10:30–10:35	Bathroom and water break.	
10:35–10:55	The children will enter the room as practiced. I will reinforce their behavior by saying, "Amanda and Tommy are doing a wonderful job of sitting quietly at their desks. You all are doing very well." I will have the children gather around the rocking chair in the classroom library. I will read a short story to them. We will discuss the characters in the book and their actions. The students will practice raising their hands to answer questions.	Reading
10:55–11:05	The children will focus their attention on the small poster clipped to the chalkboard. This Assessment poster is a model of a paper heading. Each child will be given a piece of lined paper and will copy the heading on the paper. I will stress how this heading must be on every paper. I will walk around and monitor	Handwriting Assessment

Time	Description	Activity
	the children's progress. A short, funny poem will be read and then issued to the students. They will copy this poem in their best handwriting. The process for handing in papers will be recalled before the students turn in their work.	
11:05–11:55	The procedure for lining up will be reviewed. I will reinforce the correct behavior. The students will go to Music–P.E. They will return to my room before going to lunch.	Music–P.E.
11:55–12:05	I will discuss the lunchroom procedure. Each child will be allowed to use the restroom and wash his or her hands. The students will line up according to the procedure. I will compliment those who do it well.	Procedures and Restroom Break
12:05–12:25	Lunch	Lunch
12:25–12:55	The children will be instructed to open their math textbooks. A short review on adding and subtracting double digit numbers will be given. The procedure for raising a hand will be reinforced during this review. A pre-assessment test will be given on adding and subtracting. The first two problems will be worked together as a class. The papers will be turned in to the teacher using the correct procedure. I will lower the students' level of concern by telling them that I will not be recording this grade. "I want you to do your very best so that I can determine what area you need help in."	Math
12:55–1:25	The students will open their social studies textbooks. We will have a short lesson about the compass rose and cardinal directions. All the children should be successful on the map activity I give them. The classroom procedure for exchanging papers will be discussed. The children will exchange papers to grade. If the children answered at least three out of the five questions correctly, the grader will draw a happy face on the paper. The papers will be returned. The children will file them in their personal folders after the procedure for in-class worksheets is discussed.	Social Studies and Procedures

Time	*Description*	*Activity*
1:25–1:45	I will state, "You have worked very hard for the past hour. Let's stand up, wiggle, turn around, and sit down without talking." The teacher will demonstrate the relaxation technique to the students. The children will follow. "Roy did a good job of not talking and so did Ellen." I will then introduce journal writing. The students are reminded that this will be a part of their daily morning procedure. Samples of previous writing will be read to the class. The students will prepare a notebook to be used strictly for this activity. I will reinforce how well certain individuals are following directions. The children will be told how journal activities work. A topic will be assigned at this time to get the students started. In the future, they will write about their own feelings, fears, experiences, and so on.	Language Arts/Creative Writing
1:45–2:15	The students will be issued brown, black, red, and orange construction paper. A bell will be rung to gain the students' attention. The students will focus on the teacher as directions are being given. The children are going to make trees in the Fall to decorate the windows. When each student finishes, he/she will bring his/her tree to the teacher, and it will be taped to the window. I will say, "Richard is being responsible by cleaning his desk area and storing his supplies. Amy is also doing a good job." After all of the trees are in place, I will comment how pretty and bright our room looks now.	Art
2:15–2:30	The students will remove their spelling books from their desks. The format for the spelling book will be discussed. The students will be given a short pre-test, which will be turned in. I will reinforce their performance on handing in their papers.	Spelling
2:30–2:35	Restroom break. The students will be reminded of procedures for leaving and returning to the room.	Restroom Break
2:35–2:45	I will present bus procedures. Each student will be handed a card with his/her number, name, and bus on it. The card will be pinned to the shirt of each student.	Bus Procedures

Time	Description	Activity
2:45–2:55	Procedures for ending the school day will be discussed and followed through. Papers and forms to be completed by the parents will be issued. I will review the five rules learned and tell each student to have a safe trip home.	Ending the School Day

Description of Day Two

Time	Description	Activity
8:00–8:05	I will smile and welcome each student at the door. I will remind them to place their name cards in the "I'm Here" basket.	Greeting
8:05–8:15	The morning procedure will be followed. The students will be reminded to start writing in their journals and keep writing until the timer rings. I will reinforce the students who don't talk and who follow the procedure correctly.	Morning Procedure
8:15–8:40	Students will be asked to recall rules that were discussed yesterday and to tell why they are important. The computer procedure will be introduced. A short lesson on the proper handling of the disks will be given. Students will be given the opportunity to handle the disks. An old disk will be taken apart to show the students how the device works and how fragile it is. I will reinforce students who are listening to my directions and raising their hands when they have a question. The students will be gathered around the computer during this demonstration.	Review of rules/ Computer procedure/ Computer lesson
8:40–9:05	The students will open their basal readers to the first story. Each child will be given an opportunity to read part of the story aloud. I will begin writing comments to myself noting missed words by individual students. The class will be asked questions concerning the story. This will give the students an opportunity to practice	Reading

Time	*Description*	*Activity*
	raising their hands. I will not call on students whose hands are not raised. I will reinforce those performing the correct behavior.	
9:05–9:40	A grammar lesson will be given. The concept of a noun will be discussed. Students will practice showing thumbs up or thumbs down when the teacher names various words indicating whether or not the word is a noun. This activity will help me assess how many children know what a noun is. Eyes focusing on the teacher and no talking will be reinforced.	Grammar
9:40–10:00	Spelling tests will be returned. The first helping hand of the day will be introduced and allowed to pass the papers out. The children will begin on Chapter 2 of the book because mastery was reached on the Chapter 1 words given during the pre-test. I will have the children pat themselves on the back for a job well done. A spelling assignment will be given to be completed in class.	Spelling
10:00–10:15	Procedures for fire drills, completed seatwork, and discipline will be discussed. The children will walk through the entire fire drill sequence several times until it is done correctly. The children will be told that the discipline plan will be followed. "I hope we won't have to enforce this plan, but I will if I have to. I know that you are going to be a good group of students."	Procedures
10:15–10:30	Recess break. I will commend those who followed the procedure correctly.	Recess
10:35–11:00	The students will line up according to the procedure behind the helping hand of the day. We will walk to the library without talking. I will reinforce the students doing a good job. The librarian will discuss her rules and procedures with the students. The children will be allowed to check out a book to take home. The students will line up boy–girl–boy–girl behind the helping hand to leave the library.	Library

Time	Description	Activity
11:00–11:05	The students will be responsible and return to the room to place their library books in their cubicles before going to Music–P.E.	Drop Books
11:05–11:55	The students will go to Music–P.E.	Music–P.E.
11:55–12:05	Restroom break.	Restroom Break
12:05–12:25	Lunch	Lunch

Motivation Strategies

Level of Concern

When introducing a new and difficult concept, I will lower the level of concern so the children will feel less anxious about the topic. I will not take a grade on a paper if the children had difficulty with the concept. I will wait until the children have a better understanding of the topic. If the children are off-task, I will raise their level of concern by monitoring their work, maintaining eye contact, giving tests, and setting time limits on work.

Feeling Tone

The atmosphere of the classroom will be positive. My students will know that I expect results. There will be a sign with large letters stating, "I know you can do it" underneath the rules. I expect my class to be proud of themselves and of their room. I will reinforce the children's actions by stating how well they are performing a task and by smiling at them. The children will "pat themselves on the back" when a job has been done as a class.

Interest

One of my goals as a teacher is to make every school day a new and exciting experience. I want to offer my students a variety of interesting topics and methods for exploring new ideas. The computer will help motivate children concerning the writing process and math word problems. Ditto sheets will be kept to a minimum. Hands-on science activities will eliminate the boredom of memorizing terms. Children will be able to define terms in their own words because they will understand the concept. Learning center activities will be bright, colorful, and enjoyable while providing the child with useful information.

Success

Children will be observed individually in order to determine their level of success. Assignments will be given to reinforce this success. I will try to tell every student at least one thing that they did well each day. Whenever possible, cooperative learning groups will be used so the student feels like part of a group and feels successful.

Knowledge of Results

Knowledge of results will be a key motivational strategy. Children, as well as their parents, will be kept up to date on their progress. I will write personal comments on papers as often as possible. Some papers will be graded in class by the child or by another student. Problems missed on these papers will be discussed in order to give immediate feedback.

Rewards

The students will receive a variety of rewards. These rewards will include one free homework assignment, choosing a story for the teacher to read, ten minutes of free time, listening to a story on the headphones, or relaxing for a specified time in the class library. The traditional rewards will also be given. These include stickers, stars, and positive notes to the parents. Happy faces will be drawn on papers well done. The class as a whole will also receive party awards during exceptional times of the year. There will also be rewards for those students who follow the rules and do not get warned for misbehaving.

PARENT LETTER: CONSISTENT DISCIPLINE

Aurora Public Schools

Crawford Elementary School
1600 Florence Street
Aurora, Colorado 80010
(340-3290)

Dear Parents:

We welcome you to Crawford School. We are committed to making our school a productive place to work and learn. The entire staff at Crawford has established a CONSISTENT discipline plan. This plan will use a system of consequences for inappropriate behavior as well as rewards for positive actions.

Each teacher has written a set of rules and consequences to be used in the classroom. Additionally, as a staff, we have written rules and consequences for the playground, hallways, restrooms, and the cafeteria.

We ask your help in reaching this important goal.

1. Please read and review your child's classroom rules.
2. Read and review the enclosed list of consequences for serious discipline problems.
3. Support your child's teacher and the school in its effort to provide a safe and orderly environment for learning.

Enclosed you will find a sample of the most frequently used forms of communication between school and home. Included are samples of class rules and consequences, pink slip (notice of broken rules), notice of excessive absences, in-school suspension placement and positive reinforcers.

We are equally serious about rewarding good behavior. Each classroom and the school has rewards for good behavior.

Thank you for your support.

The Crawford Staff
        Teachers
        Aides
        Administrators

Used with permission of Vern Martin.

PINK SLIP

Name	Date	Rule Broken

Home Room #/Location of Infraction	Signed

RULES

Playground

1. Follow adult directions the first time given.
2. Keep hands, feet, and objects to yourself.
3. Stay in assigned areas.
4. No teasing or cussing.
5. Nothing on playground except school equipment.

Cafeteria

1. Follow adult directions the first time given.
2. Keep hands, feet, and objects to yourself.
3. Food is to be *eaten* ONLY in the Cafeteria.
4. Sit in assigned areas.
5. Speak in soft voices. Do not yell.

Hallways

1. Walk quietly.
2. Keep hands, feet, and objects to yourself.
3. Have a completed Hall Pass.
4. Go directly to your destination.

Restrooms

1. Climbing on the stalls is forbidden.
2. Speak in soft voices. Do not yell.
3. Use equipment properly.
4. Throwing of toilet paper on walls and ceiling is forbidden.

Office

1. Stop at the Office first!
2. Bring the Proper Pass to the Office with you.
3. Follow adult directions the first time they are given.
4. Hands, feet, and objects are to be kept to yourself.

Used with permission of Vern Martin.

PARENT NOTIFICATION LETTER OF EXCESSIVE ABSENCES

Aurora Public Schools

Crawford Elementary School
1600 Florence Street
Aurora, Colorado 80010
(340-3290)

Dear _____,

We need your help! Your child _____ has been absent from school on a frequent basis:

Dates: _____

_____

_____

Please help your child understand the importance of being in school, as children miss out on very essential information that sets the stage for future learning.

Thank you very much for your assistance.

Note: Excessive absences may interfere with adequate progress and result in a recommendation for retention.

Sincerely,

_____

Classroom Teacher

_____

Principal

_____ First Contact—Letter expressing concern after five (5) absences per quarter.

_____ Second Contact—We will notify the *Department of Social Services* after ten (10) absences.

Used with permission of Vern Martin.

IN-SCHOOL SUSPENSION LETTER

Aurora Public Schools

Crawford Elementary School
1600 Florence Street
Aurora, Colorado 81101
(340-3290)

Dear _____,

    I regret to inform you that _____ was placed

in our In-School Suspension Room for _____

_____ on _____,

_____.

    We tried to call, but couldn't reach you. Please discuss this situation with your child.

    Thank you for your support.

                         Sincerely,

Used with permission of Vern Martin.

PRINCIPAL'S AWARD FOR OUTSTANDING BEHAVIOR

Achievement Award

presented to

_____

for outstanding behavior.

_____

Date

_____

Principal

CITIZEN OF THE MONTH LETTER

Aurora Public Schools

Crawford Elementary School
1600 Florence Street
Aurora, Colorado 80010
340-3290

Dear Parents or Guardians of _____ ,

Your child has been selected as a Citizen of the Month by his/her teacher. This is a special award to recognize those individuals whose good behavior consistently goes beyond following the school rules. In our efforts to honor such outstanding behavior, we would like to extend this invitation for you to join us at the Awards Assembly in Crawford's Little Theater on

_____, _____ at _____ a.m./p.m.

Your child will receive a certificate, lunch with the principal, and have his/her picture taken for a hall bulletin board. Please make plans to be here if at all possible.

Thank you for your support, we look forward to seeing you.

Sincerely,

Vern Martin, Principal

Marcia Damrell, Assistant Principal

Used with permission of Vern Martin.

CRAWFORD COOL CATS

Crawford Cool Cats

In Recognition Of Good Behavior

Assistant Principal

Principal

Used with permission of Vern Martin.

SUPER CITIZEN OF THE MONTH

Crawford Super Citizen of the Month

_____   _____
Student   Room

_____
Assistant Principal

_____
Principal

Used with permission of Vern Martin.

MIDDLE SCHOOL PHILOSOPHY

 **CANYON VISTA MIDDLE SCHOOL**

8455 Spicewood Springs Road
Austin, Texas 78759-6049
512/331–1666

It is our belief that middle school students are unique individuals undergoing a myriad of physiological, psychological, and sociological changes. We strive to meet the varied needs of our students by focusing on the individual needs of each student. We believe that all students deserve the opportunities to acquire knowledge, skills, and attitudes, which will enable them to be productive and responsible members of our school, their family, and our community.

Canyon Vista Middle School provides educational opportunities that allow students to achieve to their fullest potential, while developing basic skills necessary to function effectively in an ever-changing society.

In order to guide our students, policies, and practices, we have developed the following core beliefs:

We believe in . . .

- providing a curriculum that challenges each student at his or her level of ability, one that does not frustrate the less able learner or bore the most able learner.
- providing a program of instruction that matches the unique developmental characteristics of young adolescents.
- providing frequent homework that is carefully evaluated by the teacher. Homework requires thought, reasonable intellectual effort, the competent demonstration of learned skills, and the acquisition of new knowledge.
- utilizing a rotating schedule, which better meets the needs of the varying attention spans of young adolescent students.
- maintaining an orderly, well-structured atmosphere for learning.

Used with permission of Don Dalton.

MISSION STATEMENT

CANYON VISTA MIDDLE SCHOOL

8455 Spicewood Springs Road
Austin, Texas 78759-6049
512/331–1666

Canyon Vista Middle School's commitment is to "make learning happen" for all students in a challenging and caring environment.

SCHOOL MOTTO: We challenge the future.

DISTRICT GOALS

Accountability for Instruction: All students shall be expected to meet or exceed educational performance standards.

Curriculum and Instruction: The administrative and teaching staffs shall ensure a well-balanced curriculum and a quality instructional program so that students may realize their learning potential and prepare for productive lives.

Staff: The District shall attract and retain a qualified and effective staff.

Organization and Management: The organization and management of all levels of the educational system shall be productive, efficient, and accountable.

Finance: The Board shall exercise local control by setting policy and obtaining the revenue necessary to maintain excellence and equity in education for all learners.

Parent and Community Involvement: Parents and other members of the community shall be partners in the improvement of schools.

Research and Evaluation: The instructional program shall be monitored, evaluated, and improved by the development and use of effective methods.

Communications: Communications among all public education interests shall be consistent, timely, and effective in building and maintaining confidence in the quality of education and financial management.

Citizenship: Competence in personal and social relations shall be developed.

Used with permission of Don Dalton.

Author Index

Subject Index